Kaplan Publishing are constantl[y]
ways to make a difference to you[r]
exciting online resources really [are]
different to students looking for

G000127204

This book comes with free MyKaplan online resources so that you can study anytime, anywhere. This free online resource is not sold separately and is included in the price of the book.

Having purchased this book, you have access to the following online study materials:

CONTENT	ACCA (including FFA,FAB,FMA)		FIA (excluding FFA,FAB,FMA)	
	Text	Kit	Text	Kit
iPaper version of the book	✓	✓	✓	✓
Interactive electronic version of the book	✓			
Check Your Understanding Test with instant answers	✓			
Material updates	✓	✓	✓	✓
Latest official ACCA exam questions*		✓		
Extra question assistance using the signpost icon*		✓		
Timed questions with an online tutor debrief using the clock icon*		✓		
Interim assessment including questions and answers	✓		✓	
Technical articles	✓	✓	✓	✓

* Excludes F1, F2, F3, FFA, FAB, FMA

How to access your online resources

Kaplan Financial students will already have a MyKaplan account and these extra resources will be available to you online. You do not need to register again, as this process was completed when you enrolled. If you are having problems accessing online materials, please ask your course administrator.

If you are already a registered MyKaplan user go to www.MyKaplan.co.uk and log in. Select the 'add a book' feature and enter the ISBN number of this book and the unique pass key at the bottom of this card. Then click 'finished' or 'add another book'. You may add as many books as you have purchased from this screen.

If you purchased through Kaplan Flexible Learning or via the Kaplan Publishing website you will automatically receive an e-mail invitation to MyKaplan. Please register your details using this email to gain access to your content. If you do not receive the e-mail or book content, please contact Kaplan Flexible Learning.

If you are a new MyKaplan user register at www.MyKaplan.co.uk and click on the link contained in the email we sent you to activate your account. Then select the 'add a book' feature, enter the ISBN number of this book and the unique pass key at the bottom of this card. Then click 'finished' or 'add another book'.

Your Code and Information

This code can only be used once for the registration of one book online. This registration and your online content will expire when the final sittings for the examinations covered by this book have taken place. Please allow one hour from the time you submit your book details for us to process your request.

Please scratch the film to access your MyKaplan code.

Please be aware that this code is case-sensitive and you will need to include the dashes within the passcode, but not when entering the ISBN. For further technical support, please visit www.MyKaplan.co.uk

KAPLAN

PUBLISHING

Paper F5

Performance Management

EXAM KIT

British Library Cataloguing-in-Publication Data

A catalogue record for this book is available from the British Library.

Published by:

Kaplan Publishing UK

Unit 2 The Business Centre

Molly Millar's Lane

Wokingham

Berkshire

RG41 2QZ

ISBN: 978-1-78415-227-7

© Kaplan Financial Limited, 2015

Printed and bound in Great Britain

Acknowledgements

The past ACCA examination questions are the copyright of the Association of Chartered Certified Accountants. The original answers to the questions from June 1994 onwards were produced by the examiners themselves and have been adapted by Kaplan Publishing.

We are grateful to the Chartered Institute of Management Accountants and the Institute of Chartered Accountants in England and Wales for permission to reproduce past examination questions. The answers have been prepared by Kaplan Publishing.

CONTENTS

Section

Key features in this edition

In addition to providing a wide ranging bank of real past exam questions, we have also included in this edition:

- An analysis of all of the recent new syllabus examination papers.

- Paper specific information and advice on exam technique.

- Our recommended approach to make your revision for this particular subject as effective as possible.

  This includes step by step guidance on how best to use our Kaplan material (Complete text, pocket notes and exam kit) at this stage in your studies.

- Enhanced tutorial answers packed with specific key answer tips, technical tutorial notes and exam technique tips from our experienced tutors.

- Complementary online resources including full tutor debriefs and question assistance to point you in the right direction when you get stuck.

You will find a wealth of other resources to help you with your studies on the following sites:

www.MyKaplan.co.uk

www.**acca**global.com/students/

Quality and accuracy are of the utmost importance to us so if you spot an error in any of our products, please send an email to mykaplanreporting@kaplan.com with full details, or follow the link to the feedback form in MyKaplan.

Our Quality Co-ordinator will work with our technical team to verify the error and take action to ensure it is corrected in future editions.

INDEX TO QUESTIONS AND ANSWERS

INTRODUCTION

The style of current Paper F5 exam questions are different to old syllabus questions. In addition, the structure of the F5 exam was changed for exams from December 2014 onwards.

Before December 2014, the exam contained five compulsory questions worth 20 marks each. The exam now contains 20 multiple-choice questions worth 2 marks each, three questions worth 10 marks each and 2 questions worth 15 marks each.

Accordingly, the old ACCA questions within this kit have been adapted to reflect the new style and structure.

Note that the majority of the questions within this kit are past ACCA exam questions.

The specimen paper is included at the end of this kit.

KEY TO THE INDEX

PAPER ENHANCEMENTS

We have added the following enhancements to the answers in this exam kit:

Key answer tips

Most answers include key answer tips to help your understanding of each question.

Tutorial note

Most answers include more tutorial notes to explain some of the technical points in detail.

Top tutor tips

For selected questions, we "walk through the answer" giving guidance on how to approach the questions with helpful 'tips from a top tutor', together with technical tutor notes.

These answers are indicated with the "footsteps" icon in the index.

ONLINE ENHANCEMENTS

 Timed question with Online tutor debrief

For selected questions, we recommend that they are to be completed in full exam conditions (i.e. properly timed in a closed book environment).

In addition to the examiner's technical answer, enhanced with key answer tips and tutorial notes in this exam kit, online you can find an answer debrief by a top tutor that:

- works through the question in full
- points out how to approach the question
- how to ensure that the easy marks are obtained as quickly as possible, and
- emphasises how to tackle exam questions and exam technique.

These questions are indicated with the "clock" icon in the index.

 Online question assistance

Have you ever looked at a question and not know where to start, or got stuck part way through?

For selected questions, we have produced "Online question assistance" offering different levels of guidance, such as:

- ensuring that you understand the question requirements fully, highlighting key terms and the meaning of the verbs used
- how to read the question proactively, with knowledge of the requirements, to identify the topic areas covered
- assessing the detail content of the question body, pointing out key information and explaining why it is important
- help in devising a plan of attack

With this assistance, you should then be able to attempt your answer confident that you know what is expected of you.

These questions are indicated with the "signpost" icon in the index.

Online question enhancements and answer debriefs are available on MyKaplan at:

www.MyKaplan.co.uk

OBJECTIVE TEST QUESTIONS

PRACTICE QUESTIONS

SPECIALIST COST AND MANAGEMENT ACCOUNTING TECHNIQUES

BUDGETING AND CONTROL

PERFORMANCE MEASUREMENT AND CONTROL

ANALYSIS OF PAST PAPERS

The table below summarises the key topics that have been tested in the new syllabus examinations to date.

Note that the references are to the number of the question in this edition of the exam kit, but the Specimen Paper is produced in its original form at the end of the kit and therefore these questions have retained their original numbering in the paper itself.

	D09	J10	D10	J11	D11	J12	D12	J13	D13	J14	D14
Specialist cost and management accounting techniques											
ABC		Q1	Q4				Q5		Q5	Q1	
Target costing						Q2					
Lifecycle costing					Q4			Q3			
Throughput accounting				Q5					Q2		Q2
Decision making techniques							Q1	Q1			
Key factor analysis											
Linear programming		Q3	Q3							Q2	
Pricing	Q5			Q2						Q1	
Relevant costing	Q5				Q1	Q1					Q3
Uncertainty and risk				Q1				Q1		Q4	
Budgeting											
Budgeting			Q5	Q3	Q3	Q3	Q4	Q5	Q3		
Forecasting	Q3					Q3					
Learning curves	Q2							Q3	Q3		Q1
Standard costing and variance analysis											
Standard costing						Q4					
Variances		Q1, 2	Q1		Q5	Q4	Q2	Q4	Q5		
Labour idle time											
Mix	Q1				Q5			Q4		Q5	Q5
Planning and operational			Q1				Q2	Q4	Q5		
Performance measurement and control											
Performance measurement	Q1,4	Q2, 5	Q2				Q3	Q2,4	Q4		Q4
ROI/RI				Q4		Q5				Q3	
Transfer pricing		Q4			Q2			Q1	Q3		
Not for profit organisations						Q2		Q5			

EXAM TECHNIQUE

Section A Questions (objective testing)

- **Do not skip any of the material** in the syllabus.
- **Read each question** *very* carefully.
- **Double-check your answer** before committing yourself to it.
- Answer **every** question – if you do not know an answer, you don't lose anything by guessing. Think carefully before you **guess**. The examiner has indicated that many candidates are still leaving blank answers in the real exam.
- If you are answering a multiple-choice question, **eliminate first those answers that you know are wrong**. Then choose the most appropriate answer from those that are left.
- Remember that **only one answer to a multiple-choice question can be right**. After you have eliminated the ones that you know to be wrong, if you are still unsure, guess. Only guess after you have double-checked that you have only eliminated answers that are *definitely* wrong.
- **Don't panic** if you realise you've answered a question incorrectly. Getting one question wrong will not mean the difference between passing and failing.
- Read the ACCA FAQs article on the website published at the end of 2014: http://www.accaglobal.com/uk/en/student/acca-qual-student-journey/qual-resource/acca-qualification/f4/technical-articles/mcq-dec14.html

Section B Questions

- Use the allocated **15 minutes reading and planning time** at the beginning of the exam:
    - read the questions and examination requirements carefully, and
    - begin planning your answers.
- **Divide the time** you spend on questions in proportion to the marks on offer:
    - there are 1.8 minutes available per mark in the examination
    - within that, try to allow time at the end of each question to review your answer and address any obvious issues

    Whatever happens, always keep your eye on the clock and **do not over run on any part of any question!**
- Spend the last **five minutes** of the examination:
    - reading through your answers, and
    - **making any additions or corrections.**
- If you **get completely stuck** with a question:
    - leave space in your answer book, and
    - **return to it later.**
- Stick to the question and **tailor your answer** to what you are asked.
    - pay particular attention to the verbs in the question.

- If you do not understand what a question is asking, **state your assumptions**.

  Even if you do not answer in precisely the way the examiner hoped, you should be given some credit, if your assumptions are reasonable.

- You should do everything you can to make things easy for the marker.

  The marker will find it easier to identify the points you have made if your **answers are legible**.

- **Written questions**:

  Your answer should have:

  – a clear structure

  – a brief introduction, a main section and a conclusion.

  Be concise. It is better to write a little about a lot of different points than a great deal about one or two points.

- **Computations**:

  It is essential to include all your workings in your answers. Many computational questions can be answered using a standard step by step approach.

  e.g. ABC computations, linear programming and variance calculations.

  Be sure you know these steps before the exam and practice answering a range of questions using the same step by step approach.

- **Reports, memos and other documents**:

  Some questions ask you to present your answer in the form of a report, a memo, a letter or other document.

  Make sure that you use the correct format – there could be easy marks to gain here.

PAPER SPECIFIC INFORMATION

THE EXAM

FORMAT OF THE EXAM

		Number of marks
Section A comprises	20 multiple choice questions of 2 marks each	40
Section B comprises	3 × 10 mark questions	30
	2 × 15 mark questions	30

There will be an even mixture of written requirements and computational requirements. The two 15 mark questions will come from decision making techniques, budgeting and control or performance measurement and control areas of the syllabus.

Total time allowed: 3 hours plus 15 minutes reading and planning time.

Note that:

- All syllabus areas will be examined.

- The exam may contain one question from each syllabus area. However, some exam questions have examined more than one syllabus area in the same question.

- Questions will be based around a short scenario. It is important to refer back to this scenario when answering the question.

PASS MARK

The pass mark for all ACCA Qualification examination papers is 50%.

READING AND PLANNING TIME

Remember that all three hour paper based examinations have an additional 15 minutes reading and planning time.

ACCA GUIDANCE

ACCA guidance on the use of this time is as follows:

This additional time is allowed at the beginning of the examination to allow candidates to read the questions and to begin planning their answers before they start to write in their answer books.

This time should be used to ensure that all the information and, in particular, the exam requirements are properly read and understood.

During this time, candidates may only annotate their question paper. They may not write anything in their answer booklets until told to do so by the invigilator.

KAPLAN GUIDANCE

As all questions are compulsory, and 40% of the exam is in MCQ format. There are no decisions to be made about choice of questions, other than in which order you would like to tackle them.

Therefore, in relation to F5, we recommend that you take the following approach with your reading and planning time:

- **Answer the MCQs in Section A, and make sure no question is left unanswered.** If you don't know, have a guess!

- **Skim through the Section B questions**, assessing the level of difficulty of each question.

- **For each section B question, write down** on the question paper next to the mark allocation **the amount of time you should spend on each part.** Do this for each part of every question.

- **Decide the order** in which you think you will attempt each Section B question:

  This is a personal choice and you have time on the revision phase to try out different approaches, for example, if you sit mock exams.

  A common approach is to tackle the question you think is the easiest and you are most comfortable with first.

  Psychologists believe that you usually perform at your best on the second and third question you attempt, once you have settled into the exam, so not tackling the most difficult question first may be advisable.

  It is usual however that students tackle their least favourite topic and/or the most difficult question in their opinion last.

  Whatever you approach, you must make sure that you leave enough time to attempt all questions fully and be very strict with yourself in timing each question.

- **For each Section B question** in turn, read the requirements and then the detail of the question carefully.

  Always read the requirement first as this enables you to **focus on the detail of the question with the specific task in mind**.

  For computational questions:

  Highlight key numbers/information and key words in the question, scribble notes to yourself on the question paper to remember key points in your answer.

  Jot down proformas required if applicable.

  For written questions:

  Take notice of the format required (e.g. letter, memo, notes) and identify the recipient of the answer. You need to do this to judge the level of financial sophistication required in your answer and whether the use of a formal reply or informal bullet points would be satisfactory.

  Plan your beginning, middle and end and the key areas to be addressed and your use of titles and sub-titles to enhance your answer.

For all questions:

Spot the easy marks to be gained in a question and parts which can be performed independently of the rest of the question. For example, a definition of a variance or an explanation of the steps carried out in target costing.

Make sure that you do these parts first when you tackle the question.

Don't go overboard in terms of planning time on any one question – you need a good measure of the whole paper and a plan for all of the questions at the end of the 15 minutes.

By covering all questions you can often help yourself as you may find that facts in one question may remind you of things you should put into your answer relating to a different question.

- With your plan of attack in mind, **start answering your chosen Section B question** with your plan to hand, as soon as you are allowed to start.

 Always keep your eye on the clock and do not over run on any part of any question!

DETAILED SYLLABUS

The detailed syllabus and study guide written by the ACCA can be found at:

www.**acca**global.com/students/

KAPLAN'S RECOMMENDED REVISION APPROACH

QUESTION PRACTICE IS THE KEY TO SUCCESS

Success in professional examinations relies upon you acquiring a firm grasp of the required knowledge at the tuition phase. In order to be able to do the questions, knowledge is essential.

However, the difference between success and failure often hinges on your exam technique on the day and making the most of the revision phase of your studies.

The **Kaplan complete text** is the starting point, designed to provide the underpinning knowledge to tackle all questions. However, in the revision phase, pouring over text books is not the answer.

Kaplan Online fixed tests help you consolidate your knowledge and understanding and are a useful tool to check whether you can remember key topic areas.

Kaplan pocket notes are designed to help you quickly revise a topic area, however you then need to practice questions. There is a need to progress to full exam standard questions as soon as possible, and to tie your exam technique and technical knowledge together.

The importance of question practice cannot be over-emphasised.

The recommended approach below is designed by expert tutors in the field, in conjunction with their knowledge of the examiner and their recent real exams.

The approach taken for the fundamental papers is to revise by topic area. However, with the professional stage papers, a multi topic approach is required to answer the scenario based questions.

You need to practice as many questions as possible in the time you have left.

OUR AIM

Our aim is to get you to the stage where you can attempt exam standard questions confidently, to time, in a closed book environment, with no supplementary help (i.e. to simulate the real examination experience).

Practising your exam technique on real past examination questions, in timed conditions, is also vitally important for you to assess your progress and identify areas of weakness that may need more attention in the final run up to the examination.

In order to achieve this we recognise that initially you may feel the need to practice some questions with open book help and exceed the required time.

The approach below shows you which questions you should use to build up to coping with exam standard question practice, and references to the sources of information available should you need to revisit a topic area in more detail.

Remember that in the real examination, all you have to do is:

- attempt all questions required by the exam
- only spend the allotted time on each question, and
- get them at least 50% right!

Try and practice this approach on every question you attempt from now to the real exam.

EXAMINER COMMENTS

We have included the examiners comments to the specific new syllabus examination questions in this kit for you to see the main pitfalls that students fall into with regard to technical content.

However, too many times in the general section of the report, the examiner comments that students had failed due to:

- "not answering the question"

- "a poor understanding of why something is done, not just how it is done"

- "simply writing out numbers from the question. Candidates must understand what the numbers tell them about business performance"

- "a lack of common business sense" and

- "ignoring clues in the question".

Good exam technique is vital.

THE KAPLAN PAPER F5 REVISION PLAN

Stage 1: Assess areas of strengths and weaknesses

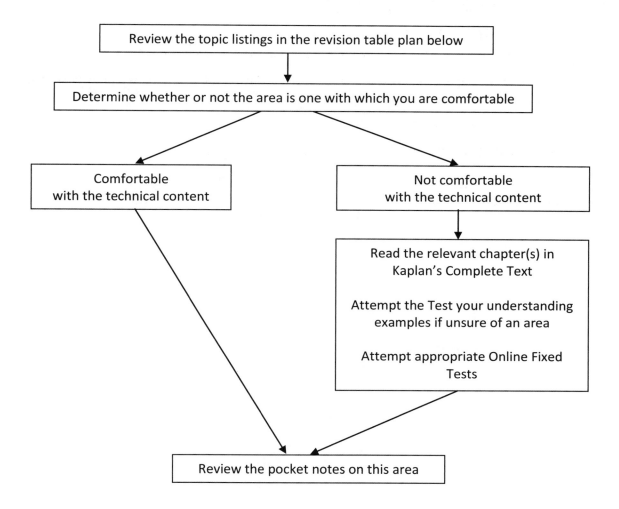

Stage 2: Practice questions

Follow the order of revision of topics as recommended in the revision table plan below and attempt the questions in the order suggested.

Try to avoid referring to text books and notes and the model answer until you have completed your attempt.

Try to answer the question in the allotted time.

Review your attempt with the model answer and assess how much of the answer you achieved in the allocated exam time.

Fill in the self-assessment box below and decide on your best course of action.

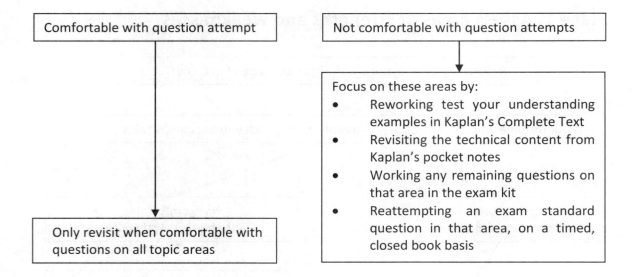

| Comfortable with question attempt | Not comfortable with question attempts |

Focus on these areas by:
- Reworking test your understanding examples in Kaplan's Complete Text
- Revisiting the technical content from Kaplan's pocket notes
- Working any remaining questions on that area in the exam kit
- Reattempting an exam standard question in that area, on a timed, closed book basis

Only revisit when comfortable with questions on all topic areas

Note that :

 The "footsteps questions" give guidance on exam techniques and how you should have approached the question.

 The "clock questions" have an online debrief where a tutor talks you through the exam technique and approach to that question and works the question in full.

Stage 3: Final pre-exam revision

We recommend that you **attempt at least one three hour mock examination** containing a set of previously unseen exam standard questions.

It is important that you get a feel for the breadth of coverage of a real exam without advanced knowledge of the topic areas covered – just as you will expect to see on the real exam day.

Ideally this mock should be sat in timed, closed book, real exam conditions and could be:

- a mock examination offered by your tuition provider, and/or

- the Specimen paper in the back of this exam kit, and/or

- the last real examination paper (available shortly afterwards on MyKaplan with "enhanced walk through answers" and a full "tutor debrief").

KAPLAN'S DETAILED REVISION PLAN

Specialist cost and management accounting techniques

Topic	Complete Text Chapter	Pocket note Chapter	Questions to attempt	Tutor guidance	Date attempted	Self assessment
– ABC	2	2	1 to 13 inclusive in Section A. Question 200 in Section B.	This is a key costing technique. In Question 200, 'Gadget Co', make sure that you can calculate the cost per unit using both full absorption costing, and an ABC approach. As well as the calculations in this question, be ready to explain the reasons for the development of ABC, the pros and cons of ABC and the implications of ABC. Successful completion of the recommended questions should reassure you that you would be able to tackle an ABC question in the exam.		
– Target costing	2	2	14 to 20 inclusive in Section A. Question 202 in Section B.	This is an excellent question on target costing in the not-for-profit –ector. It is important that you can calculate the total cost and the cost gap and that you are able to discuss the process of target costing as well as recommending methods for closing the cost gap. Exam questions may also ask for a discussion of the implications of target costing or of the use of target costing in the service industry.		

– Lifecycle costing	2	2	21 to 27 inclusive in Section A. Question 205 in Section B.	This is a relatively straightforward technique but it is still important to practice at least one question to ensure you have the required knowledge.
– Environmental management accounting	2	2	36 to 40 in Section A. Question 273 b) in Section B.	This is a good written question on EMA. It is important that you can explain what is meant by EMA and that you understand how it should be used. Make sure that you reference your points back to the scenario.
– Throughput accounting	2	2	28 to 35 inclusive in Section A. Question 203 in Section B.	Two good questions covering the different calculations and written areas that could be examined on throughput accounting. This is a more difficult costing technique and it is therefore important to complete these questions before the exam.
Decision making techniques				
– Cost volume profit analysis	3	3	53 to 62 inclusive in Section A. Question 224 in Section B.	A good question covering the very examinable topic of multi-products breakeven charts. A complete question with well-split requirements that also refer to an article on the ACCA website - an absolute must.

– Linear programming	4	4	63 to 69 inclusive in Section A. Question 229 in Section B.	Excellent questions on linear programming. In addition to the six step approach, the examiner is likely to examine some peripheral areas such as shadow prices, slack or linear programming assumptions.		
– Pricing	5	5	70 to 81 inclusive in Section A. Question 231 in Section B.	An old exam question that has been split to fit the new format. It mixes calculations with written parts.		
– Relevant costing	6	6	41 to 52 inclusive in Section A. Question 223 in Section B.	This is a tricky area but a methodical approach to answering questions should help. If you are not sure about a particular number, take a guess and move on. The aim is not to get the question 100% correct but to get through the question in time and to score a pass in the question.		
– Uncertainty and risk	7	7	87 to 94 inclusive in Section A. Question 239 in Section B.	The calculations are important and the decision trees techniques must be well rehearsed. Look for other questions to practice in this area as you must also be prepared to discuss the various methods of managing risk. Some of the terms, e.g. minimax regret, make this area appear difficult but the underlying concepts are relatively straightforward.		

Budgeting and control

– Budgeting	8	8	95 to 108 inclusive in Section A. Question 242 in Section B.	Do not overlook this area. Knowledge of the written areas of budgeting can help you to score relatively easy marks in the exam, like most well-prepared candidates did when this question was set.
– Learning curves	9	9	113 to 117 inclusive in Section A. Question 245 in Section B.	An excellent question on learning curves and representative of what you should expect in the exam. Be prepared to discuss the reservations with the learning curve.
– Mix and yield variances	10	10	125 to 135 inclusive in Section A. Question 257 in Section B.	This requires a calculation of mix and yield variances and is good preparation for the exam. It is also a very recent exam question.
– Planning and operational variances	10	10	136 to 142 inclusive in Section A. Question 260 in Section B.	This is representative of the type of question that may come up on this area.

Performance measurement and control

– ROI/RI	12	12	172 to 180 inclusive in Section A. 280 Section B	It is important that you can calculate the ROI and RI but you must also be able to discuss the pros and cons of each of these methods.

KAPLAN PUBLISHING

– Transfer pricing	12	12	173, 174 inclusive in Section A. Question 272 in Section B.	A difficult but recent question on transfer pricing requiring an in depth understanding of the information contained in the scenario.
– Not for profit organisations	13	13	184 to 189 inclusive in Section A. Question 290 in Section B.	In-depth questions on not for profit organisations but these will serve as excellent preparation for any exam question on this area.
– Information systems	14	14	140 to 150 Section A. Question 275 in Section B.	Two questions on systems and information but these will serve as excellent preparation for any exam question on this area.

Note that not all of the questions are referred to in the programme above. We have recommended a large number of exam standard questions and successful completion of these should reassure you that you have a good grounding of all of the key topics and are well prepared for the exam.

The remaining questions are available in the kit for extra practice for those who require more questions and focus on some areas

FORMULAE

Learning curve

$Y = ax^b$

Where
y = cumulative average time per unit to produce x units
a = the time taken for the first unit of output
x = the cumulative number of units produced
b = the index of learning (log LR/log 2)
LR = the learning rate as a decimal

Demand curve

$P = a - bQ$

$$b = \frac{\text{Change in price}}{\text{Change in quantity}}$$

a = price when Q = 0

MR = a − 2bQ

Section 1

OBJECTIVE TEST QUESTIONS

SPECIALIST COST AND MANAGEMENT ACCOUNTING TECHNIQUES

ACTIVITY BASED COSTING

1   VPS is a large manufacturing business that is introducing an activity based costing system into its business. VPS ships components via its own logistics operation to its central manufacturing centre in Glasgow from a wide variety of locations. It is attempting to identify the correct cost driver for the cost pool called 'component handling'.

   Which of the following would be the correct figure to use?

   A   Average components per unit

   B   Total number of components shipped

   C   Average distance travelled by a component

   D   Total components-distance travelled

2   Weaver Ltd prints two weekly newspapers: the Crystal Courier (40,000 copies in one weekly production run) and the Palace Bugle (25,000 copies in total, split over two production runs every week.) Production run set-up costs amount to $2,150 every week. Weaver uses Activity Based Costing and the number of production runs as a cost driver.

   What is the set-up cost for each copy of the Palace Bugle?

   A $0.018 per copy

   B $0.033 per copy

   C $0.043 per copy

   D $0.057 per copy

3   The following statements have been made about ABC and cost drivers.

   (1)   A cost driver is any factor that causes a change in the cost of an activity.

   (2)   For long-term variable overhead costs, the cost driver will be the volume of activity.

   (3)   Traditional absorption costing tends to under-allocate overhead costs to low-volume products.

   Which of the above statements is/are true?

   A   (1) and (3) only

   B   (2) and (3) only

   C   (1) and (2) only

   D   (1), (2) and (3)

4   The following statements have been made in relation to activity-based costing:

(1)   A cost driver is a factor which causes a change in the cost of an activity.

(2)   Traditional absorption costing tends to under-estimate overhead costs for high-volume products.

Which of the above statements is/are true?

A   (1) only

B   (2) only

C   Neither (1) nor (2)

D   Both (1) and (2)

5   The ABC Company manufactures two products, Product Alpha and Product Beta. Both are produced in a very labour-intensive environment and use similar processes. Alpha and Beta differ by volume. Beta is a high-volume product, while Alpha is a low-volume product. Details of product inputs, outputs and the costs of activities are as follows:

	Direct labour hours/unit	Annual output (units)	Number of purchase orders	Number of set-ups
Alpha	5	1,200	75	40
Beta	5	12,000	85	60
			160	**100**

Fixed overhead costs amount to a total of $420,000 and have been analysed as follows:

	$
Volume-related	100,000
Purchasing related	145,000
Set-up related	175,000

Using a traditional method of overhead absorption based on labour hours, what is the overhead cost per unit for each unit of product Alpha?

A $6.36

B $22.75

C $31.82

D $122.55

6 The ABC Company manufactures two products, Product Alpha and Product Beta. Both are produced in a very labour-intensive environment and use similar processes. Alpha and Beta differ by volume. Beta is a high-volume product, while Alpha is a low-volume product. Details of product inputs, outputs and the costs of activities are as follows:

	Direct labour hours/unit	Annual output (units)	Number of purchase orders	Number of set-ups
Alpha	5	1,200	75	40
Beta	5	12,000	85	60
			160	**100**

Fixed overhead costs amount to a total of $420,000 and have been analysed as follows:

	$
Volume-related	100,000
Purchasing related	145,000
Set-up related	175,000

Using a traditional method of overhead absorption based on labour hours, what is the overhead cost per unit for each unit of product Beta?

A $6.36

B $22.75

C $31.82

D $122.55

7 The ABC Company manufactures two products, Product Alpha and Product Beta. Both are produced in a very labour-intensive environment and use similar processes. Alpha and Beta differ by volume. Beta is a high-volume product, while Alpha is a low-volume product. Details of product inputs, outputs and the costs of activities are as follows:

	Direct labour hours/unit	Annual output (units)	Number of purchase orders	Number of set-ups
Alpha	5	1,200	75	40
Beta	5	12,000	85	60
			160	**100**

Fixed overhead costs amount to a total of $420,000 and have been analysed as follows:

	$
Volume-related	100,000
Purchasing related	145,000
Set-up related	175,000

Using Activity Based Costing as method of overhead absorption, what is the overhead cost per unit for each unit of product Alpha?

A $6.36

B $22.75

C $122.55

D Cannot be determined without more information

8   The ABC Company manufactures two products, Product Alpha and Product Beta. Both are produced in a very labour-intensive environment and use similar processes. Alpha and Beta differ by volume. Beta is a high-volume product, while Alpha is a low-volume product. Details of product inputs, outputs and the costs of activities are as follows:

	Direct labour hours/unit	Annual output (units)	Number of purchase orders	Number of set-ups
Alpha	5	1,200	75	40
Beta	5	12,000	85	60
			160	100

Fixed overhead costs amount to a total of $420,000 and have been analysed as follows:

	$
Volume-related	100,000
Purchasing related	145,000
Set-up related	175,000

Using Activity Based Costing as method of overhead absorption, what is the overhead cost per unit for each unit of product Beta?

A $6.36

B $22.75

C $122.55

D   Cannot be determined without more information

9   A company manufactures two products, C and D, for which the following information is available:

	Product C	Product D	Total
Budgeted production (units)	1,000	4,000	5,000
Labour hours per unit/in total	8	10	48,000
Number of production runs required	13	15	28
Number of inspections during production	5	3	8

Total production set up costs $140,000

Total inspection costs $80,000

Other overhead costs $96,000

Other overhead costs are absorbed on the basis of labour hours per unit.

Using activity-based costing, what is the budgeted overhead cost per unit of product D?

A $43.84

B $46.25

C $131.00

D $140.64

10 A company is changing its costing system from traditional absorption costing based on labour hours to Activity Based Costing. It has overheads of $156,000 which are related to taking material deliveries.

The delivery information about each product is below.

Product:	X	Y	Z
Total units required	1,000	2,000	3,000
Delivery size	200	400	1,000

Total labour costs are $360,000 for 45,000 hours. Each unit of each product takes the same number of direct hours.

Assuming that the company uses the number of deliveries as its cost driver, what is the increase or decrease in unit costs for Z arising from the change from Absorption Costing to Activity Based Costing?

A   Decrease of $14 per unit

B   Increase of $14 per unit

C   Decrease of $30 per unit

D   Increase of $30 per unit

11 A company uses activity-based costing to calculate the unit cost of its products. The figures for Period 3 are as follows: production set-up costs are $84,000. Total production is 40,000 units of each of products A and B, and each run is 2,000 units of A or 5,000 units of B.

What is the set-up cost per unit of B?

A $0.10

B $0.08

C $0.60

D $0.29

12 DRP Ltd has recently introduced an ABC system. It manufactures three products, details of which are set out below:

Product:	D	R	P
Budgeted annual production (units)	100,000	100,000	50,000
Batch size (units)	100	50	25
Machine set-ups per batch	3	4	6
Purchase orders per batch	2	1	1
Processing time per unit (minutes)	2	3	3

Three cost pools have been identified. Their budgeted costs for the year ending 30 June 2003 are as follows:

Machine set-up costs	$150,000
Purchasing of materials	$70,000
Processing	$80,000

What is the budgeted machine set-up cost per unit of product R?

A $6.52

B $0.52

C $18.75

D $1.82

13   A company makes products A and B. It is experimenting with Activity Based Costing. Production set-up costs are $12,000; total production will be 20,000 units of each of products A and B. Each run is 1,000 units of A or 5,000 units of B.

What is the set-up cost per unit of A, using ABC?

A $0.50

B $0.10

C $2.00

D $10.00

TARGET COSTING

14   The following are all steps in the implementation of the target costing process for a product:

(1)   Calculate the target cost

(2)   Calculate the estimated current cost based on the existing product specification

(3)   Set the required profit

(4)   Set the selling price

(5)   Calculate the target cost gap

Which of the following represents the correct sequence if target costing were to be used?

A   (1), (2), (3), (4), (5)

B   (2), (3), (4), (1), (5)

C   (4), (3), (1), (2), (5)

D   (4), (5), (3), (1), (2)

15   **In target costing, which of the following would be a legitimate strategy to reduce a cost gap for a product that existed in a competitive industry with demanding shareholders?**

A   Increase the selling price

B   Reduce the expectation gap by reducing the selling price

C   Reducing the desired margin on the product

D   Mechanising production in order to reduce average production cost

16   **Which of the following strategies would be immediately acceptable methods to reduce an identified cost gap?**

A   Reduce the desired margin without discussion with business owners

B   Reduce the predicted selling price

C   Source similar quality materials from another supplier at reduced cost

D   Increase the predicted selling price

17 The predicted selling price for a product has been set at $56 per unit. The desired mark-up on cost is 25% and the material cost for the product is estimated to be $16 before allowing for additional materials to allow for shrinkage of 20% (for every 10 kg of material going in, only 8 kg comes out). Labour is the only other cost and 2 hours are needed.

What is the most the business can pay per labour hour, if a cost gap is to be avoided?

A $12.40

B $14.40

C $24.80

D   Cannot be determined without any more information

18 The target cost for a product has been calculated to be $38.00, which is 5% less than the actual cost currently achievable. The business is considering providing some internal training to improve efficiency of labour and hence reduce the cost gap. The current material cost is $10 per unit and this will not change as efficiency changes. Labour rates are $8 per hour.

How much of an efficiency improvement (measured by the % reduction in labour time per unit will be necessary to remove the cost gap completely). *Accurate to 2 decimal places*

A   5.00%

B   6.67%

C   7.10%

D   7.28%

19 The selling price of product Zigma is set to be $250 for each unit and sales for the coming year are expected to be 500 units. If the company requires a return of 15% in the coming year on its investment of $250,000 in product Zigma, the target cost for each unit for the coming year is

A $145

B $155

C $165

D $175

20 The following statements have been made about target costing in service industries:

(1)   Consistent methods of cost attribution are needed for target costing, and this is not straightforward in service industries because of the intangibility of products.

(2)   Direct charging is needed for target costing, and this is not straightforward in service industries because of the intangibility of products.

Which of the above statements is/are true?

A   (1) only

B   (2) only

C   (Neither (1) nor (2)

D   Both (1) and (2)

LIFECYCLE COSTING

21 The following costs have arisen in relation to the production of a product:

(i) Planning and concept design costs

(ii) Testing costs

(iii) Production costs

(iv) Distribution and customer service costs

In calculating the life cycle costs of a product, which of the above items would be included?

A (iii) only

B (i), (ii) and (iii) only

C (i), (ii) and (iv) only

D All of the above

22 SNT is a Japanese electronics giant specialising in the production of game consoles. SNT is planning to introduce the latest 'next-generation' console and range of games in the summer of 2015. Development of the new console is due to commence on January 1, 2015 and SNT is currently working out at what price the new console should be sold then.

The new console is expected to incur the following costs in the four years it will be developed and commercialised:

	2015	2016	2017	2018
Consoles manufactured and sold	10,000	12,000	11,100	3,000
R&D costs	$950,000	$0	$0	$0
Marketing costs	$230,000	$120,000	$20,000	$5,000
Production cost per console	$450	$430	$290	$290
Warranty costs per console	$30	$30	$40	$45
End of life costs	$0	$0	$0	$125,000

Using lifecycle costing, what is the cost per console?

A $410.21

B $417.56

C $455.35

D $496.62

23 SNT is a Japanese electronics giant specialising in the production of game consoles. SNT is planning to introduce the latest 'next-generation' console and range of games in the summer of 2015. Development of the new console is due to commence on January 1, 2015 and SNT is currently working out at what price the new console should be sold then.

The new console is expected to incur the following costs in the four years it will be developed and commercialised:

	2015	2016	2017	2018
Consoles manufactured and sold	10,000	12,000	11,100	3,000
R&D costs	$950,000	$0	$0	$0
Marketing costs	$230,000	$120,000	$20,000	$5,000
Production cost per console	$450	$430	$290	$290
Warranty costs per console	$30	$30	$40	$45
End of life costs	$0	$0	$0	$125,000

Market research has indicated that customers will be prepared to pay an average price of $420 per console, but SNT's Chief Executive believes this will not be sufficient to make production worthwhile.

The Chief Executive has made the following statements:

(1) The cost per console, calculated using lifecycle costing principles, is higher than the price customers are prepared to pay.

(2) More attention to R&D costs in 2015 could reduce warranty costs in later years.

Which of the above statements is/are true?

A (1) only

B (2) only

C Neither (1) nor (2)

D Both (1) and (2)

24 A colleague has claimed the following to be benefits of lifecycle costing:

(i) It provides the true financial cost of a product

(ii) The length of the lifecycle can be shortened

(iii) Expensive errors can be avoided in that potentially failing products can be avoided

(iv) Lower costs can be achieved earlier by designing out costs

(v) Better selling prices can be set

(vi) Decline stages of the lifecycle can be avoided

Which of the above statements is/are correct?

A (i), (iii), (iv) and (v)

B (i) and (iii) only

C (iii) and (iv) only

D All of them

25 The following statements relate to the justification of the use of life cycle costing:

(i) Product life cycles are becoming increasingly short. This means that the initial costs are an increasingly important component in the product's overall costs.

(ii) Product costs are increasingly weighted to the start of a product's life cycle, and to properly understand the profitability of a product these costs must be matched to the ultimate revenues.

(iii) The high costs of (for example) research, design and marketing in the early stages in a product's life cycle necessitate a high initial selling price.

(iv) Traditional capital budgeting techniques do not attempt to minimise the costs or maximise the revenues over the product life cycle.

Which of these statements are substantially true?

A (i), (ii) and (iv)

B (ii), and (iii) only

C ((i) and (iv) only

D All of them

26 The following statements relate to life cycle costing:

(i) Life cycle costing takes into account all costs incurred in a product life cycle with exception of sunk costs incurred on research and development.

(ii) Life cycle costing ensures a profit is generated over the life of the product.

(iii) Life cycle costing is most useful for products with an even weighting of costs over their life.

Which of the above statements is/are true?

A (i) and (ii)

B (ii) only

C (ii) and (iii)

D All of them

27 Company B is about to being developing a new product for launch in its existing market. They have forecast sales of 20,000 units and the marketing department suggest a selling price of $43/unit. The company seeks to make a mark-up of 40% product cost. It is estimated that the lifetime costs of the product will be as follows:

1 Design and development costs $43,000

2 Manufacturing costs $15/unit

3 Plant decommissioning costs $30,000

The company estimates that if it were to spend an additional $15,000 on design, manufacturing costs/unit could be reduced.

What is the life cycle cost?

A $18.65

B $22

C $22.87

D $24

THROUGHPUT ACCOUNTING

28 **Which ONE of the following would serve to increase the Throughput Accounting Ratio?**

  A An increase in the speed of the fastest machine in the production process

  B An unexpected increase in the factory rent

  C A 5% wage increase linked to an 8% improvement in productivity

  D A 10% sales discount to stimulate demand by 20%

29 Huron Ltd manufactures a product called the GL1. The GL1 requires five hours of machine time. Machine time is a bottleneck resource, as there are only four machines which are available eight hours a day, five days a week. Each GL1 sells for $210 and has direct material costs of $26 per unit, labour costs of $19 per unit and factory overhead costs of $15 per unit. These costs are based on weekly production and sales of 150 units.

  What is the throughput accounting ratio (to 2 decimal places)?

  A 0.87

  B 1.15

  C 1.31

  D 2.62

30 Skye Limited has a two process and details of these processes are as follows:

  Process P: Each machine produces 6 units an hour and Skye has 8 machines working at 90% capacity.

  Process Q: Each machine produces 9 units per hour and Skye has 6 machines working at 85% capacity.

  One of Skye products is Cloud. Cloud is not particularly popular but does sell at a selling price of $20 although discounts of 15% are usual. Material costs are $5 and direct labour costs are double the material cost. Cloud spends 2 hours in process P but 3 hours in process Q.

  What is Cloud's TP per hour in its bottleneck process?

  A $5.50

  B $6.00

  C $12.00

  D $17.00

31 Ontario Ltd makes three products, GL1, GL2 and GL3. Details for the three products are shown below:

	GL1	GL2	GL3
	$	$	$
Selling price	40	50	60
Direct material	12	8	6
Direct labour	6	12	10
Variable overhead	3	6	5
Fixed overhead	9	18	15

The three products use the same machine, which is the bottleneck in the process. The total number of hours available in the period on the machine is 200 and the times required per unit on the machine for each product are shown below:

GL1	GL2	GL3
2 min	4 min	5 min

The total factory cost is $120,000.

The maximum demand for each product in the period is:

GL1	GL2	GL3
Units	Units	Units
3,000	5,000	2,000

What is the throughput accounting ratio for each product?

A   Cannot be calculated without more information

B   They all share the same TPAR of 1.4

C   1.4 for GL1, 1.05 for GL2 and 1.08 for GL3

D   1.4 for GL1, 1.08 for GL2 and 1.05 for GL3

32 The following statements have been made about throughput accounting:

A   Throughput accounting considers that the only variable costs in the short run are materials and components.

B   Throughput accounting considers that time at a bottleneck resource has value, not elsewhere.

C   Throughput accounting views stock building as a non-value-adding activity, and therefore discourages it.

D   Throughput accounting was designed as a decision-making tool for situations where there is a bottleneck in the production process.

Which ONE of the above statements is not true of throughput accounting?

A   A

B   B

C   C

D   D

33   Which of the following is a definition of the throughput accounting ratio?

   A   Throughput contribution/hours on bottleneck

   B   Conversion costs per hour/throughput per hour

   C   Throughput per hour/conversion costs per hour

   D   Total conversion costs/total throughput

34   The following information is available for a single product:

Units produced		500
Time taken		200 hours
Maximum time available		200 hours
Materials purchased	1,000 kg costing	$3,000
Materials used		800 kg
Labour costs		$2,000
Overheads		$1,500
Sales		$9,000

   What is the throughput accounting ratio for this product?

   A   0

   B   1.00

   C   1.50

   D   1.70

35   A company has recently adopted throughput accounting as a performance measuring tool. Its results for the last month are shown below.

Units produced		1,150
Units sold		800
Materials purchased	900 kg costing	$13,000
Opening material inventory used	450 kg costing	$7,250
Labour costs		$6,900
Overheads		$4,650
Sales price		$35

   There was no opening inventory of finished goods or closing inventory of materials.

   What is the throughput accounting ratio for this product?

   A   0

   B   0.80

   C   1.30

   D   1.50

ENVIRONMENTAL ACCOUNTING

36   The following statements have been made about environmental cost accounting:

(1)   The majority of environmental costs are already captured within a typical organisation's accounting system. The difficulty lies in identifying them.

(2)   Input/output analysis divides material flows within an organisation into three categories: material flows; system flows; and delivery and disposal flows.

Which of the above statements is/are true?

A   (1) only

B   (2) only

C   Neither (1) nor (2)

D   Both (1) and (2)

37   The following statements have been made about the issues faced by businesses in the management of their environmental costs:

(1)   The costs involved are difficult to define.

(2)   Environmental costs can be categorised as quality related costs.

(3)   Cost control can be an issue, in particular if costs have been identified incorrectly in the first place.

Which of the above statements is/are true?

A   (1) only

B   (2) and (3) only

C   None of them

D   All of them

38   **Which of the following are advantages of using Activity Based Costing for Environmental Management Accounting?**

(i)   Higher environmental costs can be reflected in higher prices.

(ii)   cost savings achieved through environmental policies can be measured.

(iii)   it is simple to determine the environmental costs and cost drivers.

(iv)   It considers all environmental effects of the company's actions.

A   (i) and (ii) only

B   (ii) only

C   (ii) and (iii)

D   (ii) and (iv)

39 The following are types of environmental prevention costs:

(i) Monitoring, testing and inspection costs.

(ii) Site decontamination.

Which of the above statements is/are true?

A (i) only

B (ii) only

C Both (i) and (ii)

D Neither (i) nor (ii)

40 **Environmental costs are difficult to deal with for an accountant. Which of the following is not a reason for this?**

A Costs are often hidden

B Costs are mostly minor

C Costs are often very long term

D Accounting systems rarely split off these costs automatically

DECISION-MAKING TECHNIQUES

RELEVANT COST ANALYSIS

41 UU Company has been asked to quote for a special contract. The following information about the material needed has been given:

Material X:

Book value	Scrap value	Replacement cost
$5.00 per kg	$0.50 per kg	$5.50 per kg

The contract requires 10 kgs of Material X. There are 250 kgs of this material in inventory which was purchased in error over two years ago. If Material X is modified, at a cost of $2 per kg, it could then be used as a substitute for material Y which is in regular use and currently costs $6 per kg.

What is the relevant cost of the materials for the special contract?

A $5

B $40

C $50

D $55

42   VV Company has been asked to quote for a special contract. The contract requires 100 hours of labour. However, the labourers, who are each paid $15 per hour, are working at full capacity.

There is a shortage of labour in the market. The labour required to undertake this special contract would have to be taken from another contract, Z, which currently utilises 500 hours of labour and generates $5,000 worth of contribution.

If the labour was taken from contract Z, then the whole of contract Z would have to be delayed, and such delay would invoke a penalty fee of $1,000.

What is the relevant cost of the labour for the special contract?

A $1,000

B $1,500

C $2,500

D $7,500

43   An organisation is considering the costs to be incurred in respect of a special order opportunity. The order would require 1,250 kgs of material D, that is readily available and regularly used by the organisation on its normal products.

There are 265 kgs of material D in inventory which cost $795 last week. The current market price is $3.24 per kg. Material D is normally used to make product X. Each unit of X requires 3 kgs of material D, and if material D is costed at $3 per kg, each unit of X yields a contribution of $15.

What is the relevant cost of material D to be included in the costing of the special order?

A $3,990

B $4,050

C $10,000

D $10,300

44   H has in inventory 15,000 kg of M, a raw material which it bought for $3/kg five years ago, for a product line which was discontinued four years ago. M has no use in its existing state but could be sold as scrap for $1.00 per kg. One of the company's current products (HN) requires 4 kg of a raw material, available for $5.00 per kg. M can be modified at a cost of $0.75 per kg so that it may be used as a substitute for this material. However, after modification, 5 kg of M is required for every unit of HN to be produced.

H has now received an invitation to tender for a product which could use M in its present state.

What is the relevant cost per kg of M to be included in the cost estimate for the tender?

A $0.75

B $1.00

C $3.00

D $3.25

45 In order to utilise some spare capacity, K is preparing a quotation for a special order which requires 2,000 kgs of material J.

K has 800 kgs of material J in inventory (original cost $7.00 per kg). Material J is used in the company's main product L. Each unit of L uses 5 kgs of material J and, based on an input value of $7.00 per kg of J, each unit of L yields a contribution of $10.00.

The resale value of material J is $5.50 per kg. The present replacement price of material J is $8.00 per kg. Material J is readily available in the market.

What is the relevant cost of the 2,000 kgs of material J to be included in the quotation?

A $11,000

B $14,000

C $16,000

D $18,000

46 A company is calculating the relevant cost of the material to be used on a particular contract. The contract requires 4,200 kgs of material H and this can be bought for $6.30 per kg. The company bought 10,000 kgs of material H some time ago when it paid $4.50 per kg. Currently 3,700 kgs of this remains in inventory. The inventory of material H could be sold for $3.20 per kg.

The company has no other use for material H other than on this contract, but it could modify it at a cost of $3.70 per kg and use it as a substitute for material J. Material J is regularly used by the company and can be bought for $7.50 per kg.

What is the relevant cost of the material for the contract?

A $17,210

B $19,800

C $26,460

D $30,900

47 Ace Limited is considering a new project that will require the use of a currently idle machine. The machine has a current book value of $12,000 and a potential disposal value of $10,500 (before $200 disposal costs) and hence has been under depreciated by $1,500 over its life to date. If the machine is to be fit for purpose on the new project it will have to be relocated at a cost of $500 and refitted at a further cost of $800.

What is the relevant cost of using the machine on the new project?

A $9,000

B $10,300

C $11,600

D $13,300

48 Blunt is considering a new project but is unsure how much overhead to include in the calculations to help him decide whether or not to proceed. Existing fixed overheads are absorbed at the rate of $8 per hour worked. Blunt is certain that the project will involve an incremental 500 labour hours.

The project will involve extra machine running costs and these variable overheads cost him $4 per hour. The number of extra machine hours is expected to be 450 hours. The difference between this figure and the 500 labour hours above is expected idle time.

The project will require a little more temporary space that can be rented at a fixed cost of $1,200 for the period of hire. This overhead is not included in the fixed overhead absorption rate above.

What is the overhead to be charged against the project decision?

A $3,000

B $3,200

C $7,000

D $7,200

49 Cleverclogs is short of labour for a new one-off project needing 600 hours of labour and has choices as to where to source this. He could hire new people temporarily from an agency at a cost of $9 per hour. Alternatively he could recruit new temporary staff at a fixed cost of advertising of $1,200 but then only pay $6 per hour for the time. He could also redirect some staff from existing work who are currently paid $7 per hour and who make sandals that generate a contribution of $3 per hour after all variable costs. Sandals are a good selling product and Cleverclogs will lose the production and the related sales whilst staff are working on the new one-off project.

What is the relevant cash flow?

A $1,800

B $3,600

C $4,200

D $4,800

50 Drippy is producing a list of relevant cash flows regarding a decision she has to make. She is considering launching a new type of USB memory stick that guarantees better protection to the host computer.

Drippy manages many existing products and has a standing arrangement with a technology magazine for advertising space entitling her to advertise each month. The contract has just been signed and covers the next twelve months. Payment is made in the month following an advert appearing. Drippy is going to use the magazine to advertise her exciting new USB stick.

Is the cost of the advertising space best described as a:

A   Sunk cost

B   Historic cost

C   Relevant cost

D   Committed cost

51   Which of the following terms would not normally be used to describe a relevant cost for a decision?

   A   Incremental

   B   Future

   C   Material

   D   Cash

52   X plc intends to use relevant costs as the basis of the selling price for a special order: the printing of a brochure. The brochure requires a particular type of paper that is not regularly used by X plc although a limited amount is in X plc's inventory which was left over from a previous job. The cost when X plc bought this paper last year was $15 per ream and there are 100 reams in inventory. The brochure requires 250 reams. The current market price of the paper is $26 per ream, and the resale value of the paper in inventory is $10 per ream.

   What is the relevant cost of the paper to be used in printing the brochure?

   A $2,500

   B $4,900

   C $5,400

   D $6,500

COST VOLUME PROFIT ANALYSIS

53   Betis Limited is considering changing the way it is structured by asking its employed staff to become freelance. Employees are currently paid a fixed salary of $240,000 per annum, but would instead be paid $200 per working day. On a typical working day, staff can produce 40 units. Other fixed costs are $400,000 pa.

   The selling price of a unit is $60 and material costs are $20 per unit.

   What will be the effect of the change on the breakeven point of the business and the level of operating risk?

   A   The breakeven point reduces by 6,000 units and the operating risk goes down

   B   The breakeven point reduces by 4,571 units and the operating risk goes down

   C   The breakeven point reduces by 4,571 units and the operating risk goes up

   D   The breakeven point reduces by 6,000 units and the operating risk goes up

54 P CO makes two products – P1 and P2 – budgeted details of which are as follows:

	P1	P2
	$	$
Selling price	10.00	8.00
Cost per unit:		
Direct materials	3.50	4.00
Direct labour	1.50	1.00
Variable overhead	0.60	0.40
Fixed overhead	1.20	1.00
Profit per unit	**3.20**	**1.60**

Budgeted production and sales for the year ended 30 November 2015 are:

Product P1	10,000 units
Product P2	12,500 units

The fixed overhead costs included in P1 relate to apportionment of general overhead costs only. However P2 also includes specific fixed overheads totalling $2,500.

If only product P1 were to be made, how many units (to the nearest unit) would need to be sold in order to achieve a profit of $60,000 each year?

A 25,625 units

B 19,205 units

C 18,636 units

D 26,406 units

55 The CS ratio for a business is 0.4 and its fixed costs are $1,600,000. Budget revenue has been set at 6 times the amount of the fixed costs.

What is the margin of safety % measured in revenue?

A 58.3%

B 58.7%

C 59.1%

D Cannot be determined without more information

56 An organisation manufactures and sells a single product, the G. It has produced the following budget for the coming year:

	$000	$000
Sales revenue (20,000 units)		5,000
Manufacturing costs		
Fixed	1,600	
Variable	1,400	
Selling costs		
Fixed	1,200	
Variable	400	
Cost of sales		(4,600)
Profit		400

If inventory levels are negligible, what is the breakeven point in units?

A   13,634

B   13,750

C   17,500

D   28,000

57 A company manufactures and sells a single product with a variable cost per unit of $36. It has a contribution ratio of 25%. The company has weekly fixed costs of $18,000.

What is the weekly breakeven point, in units?

A   1,500

B   1,600

C   1,800

D   2,000

58 The management accountant of a company has calculated his firm's breakeven point from the following data:

Selling price per unit	$20
Variable costs per unit	$8
Fixed overheads for next year	$79,104

It is expected that next year, the firm will produce and sell 7,500 units.

What is the margin of safety?

A   12.1%

B   13.8%

C   47.3%

D   89.6%

59 The management accountant of Caroline plc has calculated the firm's breakeven point from the following data:

Selling price per unit	$20
Variable costs per unit	$8
Fixed overheads for next year	$79,104

It is now expected that the product's selling price and variable cost will increase by 8% and 5.2% respectively.

These changes will cause Caroline's breakeven point for next year to:

A   Rise by 9.0%

B   Rise by 2.8%

C   Fall by 2.8%

D   Fall by 9%

60 Edward sells two products with selling prices and contributions as follows:

	Product F	Product G
Selling price	$40	$20
Contribution	$10	$4
Budgeted sales units	150,000	100,000

Edwards's fixed costs are $1,400,000 per year.

What is Edwards's current breakeven revenue to the nearest $?

A $100,000

B $200,000

C $5,600,000

D $5,894,737

61 Edward sells two products with selling prices and contributions as follows:

	Product F	Product G
Selling price	$40	$20
Contribution	$10	$4
Budgeted sales units	150,000	100,000

Edwards's fixed costs are $1,400,000 per year.

Edward now anticipates that more customers will buy the cheaper product G and that budgeted sales will be 150,000 units for each product.

If this happens what would happen to the breakeven revenue?

A   Increase by the extra revenue from G of 50,000 × $20/u or $1,000,000

B   Decrease by the extra revenue from G of 50,000 × $20/u or $1,000,000

C   Increase by a different amount

D   Decrease by a different amount

62   The following breakeven chart has been drawn for a company's single product:

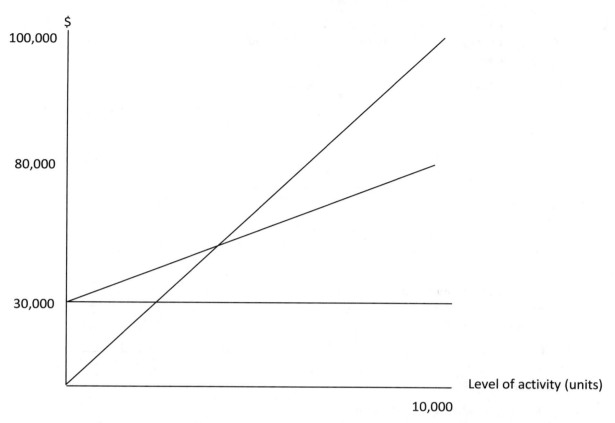

Which of the following statements about the product are correct?

(i)   The product's selling price is $10 per unit.

(ii)   The product's variable cost is $8 per unit.

(iii)   The product incurs fixed costs of $30,000 per period.

(iv)   The product earns a profit of $70,000 at a level of activity of 10,000 units.

A   (i), (ii) and (iii) only

B   (i) and (iii) only

C   (i), (iii) and (iv) only

D   (i), (ii) and (iv) only

LIMITING FACTORS

63 A company has the following production planned for the next four weeks. The figures reflect the full capacity level of operations. Planned output is equal to the maximum demand per product.

	Product A $/unit	Product B $/unit	Product C $/unit	Product D $/unit
Selling price	160	214	100	140
Raw material cost	24	56	22	40
Direct labour cost	66	88	33	22
Variable overhead cost	24	18	24	18
Fixed overhead cost	16	10	8	12
Profit	30	42	13	48
Planned output	300	125	240	400
Direct labour hours per unit	6	8	3	2

The direct labour force is threatening to go on strike for two weeks out of the coming four. This means that only 2,160 hours will be available for production, rather than the usual 4,320 hours.

If the strike goes ahead, which product or products should be produced if profits are to be maximised?

A   D and A

B   B and D

C   D only

D   B and C

64 E manufactures four products from different quantities of the same material which is in short supply. The following budgeted data relates to the products:

	Product E1 $/unit	Product E2 $/unit	Product E3 $/unit	Product E4 $/unit
Selling price	90	112	123	103
Materials ($6 per kg)	24	33	41	30
Conversion costs	40	65	65	55
	64	98	106	85
Profit	26	14	17	18
Machine time per unit **in hours**	0.5	0.5	0.6	0.6

The conversion costs include general fixed costs that have been absorbed using a rate of $30 per machine hour.

What is the product ranking for the most profitable use of the raw materials?

	1st	2nd	3rd	4th
A	E1	E4	E2	E3
B	E1	E4	E3	E2
C	E3	E2	E4	E1
D	E4	E2	E1	E3

65 Q plc makes two products – Quone and Qutwo – from the same raw material. The selling price and cost details of these products are as shown below:

	Quone $	Qutwo $
Selling price	20.00	18.00
Direct material ($2.00 per kg)	6.00	5.00
Direct labour	4.00	3.00
Variable overhead	2.00	1.50
	12.00	9.50
Contribution per unit	8.00	8.50

The maximum demand for these products is 500 units per week for Quone, and an unlimited number of units per week for Qutwo.

What would the shadow price of these materials be if material were limited to 2,000 kgs per week?

A $nil

B $2.00 per kg

C $2.66 per kg

D $3.40 per kg

66 P is considering whether to continue making a component or to buy it from an outside supplier. It uses 12,000 of the components each year.

The internal manufacturing cost comprises:

	$/unit
Direct materials	3.00
Direct labour	4.00
Variable overhead	1.00
Specific fixed cost	2.50
Other fixed costs	2.00
	12.50

If the direct labour were not used to manufacture the component, it would be used to increase the production of another item for which there is unlimited demand. This other item has a contribution of $10.00 per unit but requires $8.00 of labour per unit.

What is the maximum price per component, at which buying is preferable to internal manufacture?

A $8.00

B $10.50

C $12.50

D $15.50

67 The following details relate to three services provided by RST Company:

	Service R	Service S	Service T
	$	$	$
Fee charged to customers	100	150	160
Unit service costs:			
Direct materials	15	30	25
Direct labour	20	35	30
Variable overhead	15	20	22
Fixed overhead	25	50	50

All three services use the same type of direct labour which is paid $25 per hour.

The fixed overheads are general fixed overheads that have been absorbed on the basis of machine hours.

What are the most and least profitable uses of direct labour, a scarce resource?

	Most profitable	*Least profitable*
A	S	R
B	S	T
C	T	R
D	T	S

68 A linear programming model has been formulated for two products, X and Y. The objective function is depicted by the formula C = 5X + 6Y, where C = contribution, X = the number of product X to be produced and Y = the number of product Y to be produced.

Each unit of X uses 2 kg of material Z and each unit of Y uses 3 kg of material Z. The standard cost of material Z is $2 per kg.

The shadow price for material Z has been worked out and found to be $2.80 per kg.

If an extra 20 kg of material Z becomes available at $2 per kg, what will the maximum increase in contribution be?

A   Increase of $96

B   Increase of $56

C   Increase of $16

D   No change

69 The shadow price of skilled labour for CBV is currently $8 per hour.

What does this mean?

A   The cost of obtaining additional skilled labour resources is $8 per hour

B   There is a hidden cost of $8 for each hour of skilled labour actively worked

C   Contribution will be increased by $8 per hour for each extra hour of skilled labour that can be obtained

D   Total costs will be reduced by $8 for each additional hour of skilled labour that can be obtained

PRICING DECISIONS

70 **Which of the following statements is true of pricing?**

A   Discrimination is always illegal so everyone should pay the same amount

B   Early adopters get a discount for being first in the market

C   Pricing against a similar competitor is important in the Internet age

D   Price to make the most sales in that way you will always get the most profit

71 **Which of the following conditions would need to be true for a price skimming policy to be sensible?**

A   An existing product where the owners have decided to increase prices to move the product up market

B   Where the product has a long lifecycle

C   Where the product has a short lifecycle

D   Where only modest development costs had been incurred

72 The following circumstances may arise in relation to the launch of a new product:

(i) Demand is relatively inelastic

(ii) There are significant economies of scale

(iii) The firm wishes to discourage new entrants to the market

(iv) The product life cycle is particularly short

Which of the above circumstances favour a penetration pricing policy?

A (ii) and (iii) only

B (ii) and (iv)

C (i), (ii) and (iii)

D (ii), (iii) and (iv) only

73 **Which of the following conditions would have to be true for a price penetration policy to be sensible?**

A Where demand is highly inelastic

B Where there is a short lifecycle

C Where the normal margins gained are very low

D Where demand is highly elastic

74 **Which of the following conditions must be true for a price discrimination policy to be sensible?**

A Buying power of customers must be similar in both market segments

B Goods must not be able to move freely between market segments

C Goods must be able to move freely between market segments

D The demand curves in each market must be the same

75 **In a traditional pricing environment which of the following "C" words is not traditionally considered when setting a price?**

A Cost

B Cash flow

C Competition

D Customers

76   A product has a prime cost of $12, variable overheads of $3 per unit and fixed overheads of $6 per unit.

Which pricing policy gives the highest price?

A   Prime cost + 80%

B   Marginal cost + 60%

C   TAC + 20%

D   Net margin of 14% on selling price

77   If demand for a product is 5,000 units when the price is $400 and 6,000 units when the price is $380, what are the demand and MR equations?

	Demand	MR
A	P = 300 − 0.02Q	MR = 300 − 0.02Q
B	P = 500 + 0.02Q	MR = 500 + 0.04Q
C	P = 300 + 0.02Q	MR = 300 + 0.02Q
D	P = 500 − 0.02Q	MR = 500 − 0.04Q

78   If the demand for a product is 5,000 units when the price is $400 and 6,000 units when price is $380, what is the optimal price to be charged in order to maximise profit if the variable cost of the product is $200?

A $150

B $200

C $350

D $700

79   The following price and demand combinations have been given:

P1 = 400, Q1 = 5,000

P2 = 380, Q2 = 5,500

The variable cost is a constant $80 per unit and fixed costs are $600,000 pa.

What is the demand function?

A   P = 200 − 0.04Q

B   P = 600 − 0.04Q

C   P = 600 + 0.04Q

D   P = 200 − 20Q

80 The following price and demand combinations have been given:

P1 = 400, Q1 = 5,000

P2 = 380, Q2 = 5,500

The variable cost is a constant $80 per unit and fixed costs are $600,000 pa. The optimal price is:

A $80

B $340

C $6,500

D $13,000

81 A brand new game is about to be launched. The game is unique, has a short shelf life and can only be played on the Star2000 gaming console, another one of the businesses products. Students are entitled to a small discount but brand loyalty is rare in this market. Which of the following pricing strategies could not be sensibly be used to price the game?

A Price skimming

B Price discrimination

C Penetration pricing

D Complimentary product pricing

MAKE-OR-BUY AND OTHER SHORT TERM DECISIONS

82 **In a make or buy decision which FOUR of the following are to be correctly included in the considerations?**

Drag the correct items in to the box below:

(i) The amount of re-allocated rent costs caused by using the production space differently.

(ii) The variable costs of purchase from the new supplier.

(iii) The amount of the bribe from the potential new supplier.

(iv) The level of discount available from the new supplier.

(v) The redundancy payments to the supervisor of the product in question.

(vi) The saved labour costs of the production staff re-directed to other work.

(vii) The materials no longer bought to manufacture the product.

A Items (i), (iv), (v) and (vi)

B Items (ii), (iv), (v) and (vii)

C Items (iii), (iv), (v) and (vi)

D Items (iii), (iv), (v) and (vii)

83 Appler is considering the relevant cash flows involved in a short-term decision. An important client has asked for the minimum price for the processing of a compound. The compound involves the following:

Material A: Appler needs 500 kg of material for the compound but has 200 kg in stock present. The stock items were bought 3 months ago for $5/kg but have suffered 10% shrinkage since that date. Material A is not regularly used in the business and would have to be disposed of at a cost to Appler of $400 in total. The current purchase price of material A is $6.25/kg.

Material B: Appler needs 800 kg of material B and has this in stock as it is regularly needed. The stock was bought 2 months ago for $4/kg although it can be bought now at $3.75/kg due to its seasonal nature.

Processing energy costs would be $200 and the supervisor says he would allocate $150 of his weekly salary to the job in the company's job costing system.

Based upon the scenario information, what is the total cost of material A and B to be built in to the minimum price calculation?

A $6,125

B $5,875

C $4,475

D $4,875

84 Appler is considering the relevant cash flows involved in a short-term decision. An important client has asked for the minimum price for the processing of a compound. The compound involves the following:

Material A: Appler needs 500 kg of material for the compound but has 200 kg in stock present. The stock items were bought 3 months ago for $5/kg but have suffered 10% shrinkage since that date. Material A is not regularly used in the business and would have to be disposed of at a cost to Appler of $400 in total. The current purchase price of material A is $6.25/kg.

Material B: Appler needs 800 kg of material B and has this in stock as it is regularly needed. The stock was bought 2 months ago for $4/kg although it can be bought now at $3.75/kg due to its seasonal nature.

Processing energy costs would be $200 and the supervisor says he would allocate $150 of his weekly salary to the job in the company's job costing system.

Based upon the scenario information, what is the total cost for processing and supervision to be included in the minimum price calculation?

A $Nil

B $150

C $200

D $350

85 Ace Limited is considering whether or not to cease production of leather-bound diaries.

Which of the following THREE items are valid factors to consider in this decision?

(i) The diaries made a loss in the year just passed.

(ii) The diaries made a positive contribution in the year just passed.

(iii) The market outlook in the long term looks very poor.

(iv) The budget for next year shows a loss.

(v) The business also sells pens and many diary buyers will often also buy a pen.

(vi) The business was founded to produce and sell diaries.

(vii) The NPV of future cash flows over the next 5 years shows –$25m.

A Items (iii), (iv), and (v)

B Items (iii), (v) and (vii)

C Items (i), (iv) and (vii)

D Items (ii), (v), (v) and (vii)

86 Gloop is considering the further processing of its face foundation cream by adding an anti-aging compound. Existing sales are 25,000 tubs of cream but this is expected to increase by 25% if the anti-aging compound is added. The anti-ageing compound will cost $2.50 per tub and a royalty will be payable on sales revenue of 1.5% to the patent holder (Startled Limited). Gloop also thinks that the selling price of the cream will increase from $15 to $20 per tub. Other material costs will unaffected at $6 per tub.

Gloop operates a total absorption costing system and allocates fixed costs to products at the rate of $2 per $1 of sales revenue.

How much better off financially will Gloop be if it decides to proceed with this idea?

A $125,000

B $134,500

C $137,500

D $200,000

DEALING WITH RISK AND UNCERTAINTY IN DECISION-MAKING

87 Shuffles is attempting to decide which size of fork-lift truck to buy to use in its warehouses. There are three grades of truck, the A series, B series and the C series. The uncertainty faced is the expected growth in the on-line market it serves, which could grow at 15%, 30% or even 40% in the next period.

Shuffles has correctly produced the following decision table and has calculated the average daily contribution gained from each combination of truck and growth assumption.

Decision table		Type of truck		
		A series	B series	C series
Growth rate	15%	$2,400	$1,800	$3,600
	30%	$1,400	$1,900	$4,500
	40%	$4,900	$2,800	$3,900

Which truck would the pessimistic buyer purchase?

A   A series

B   B series

C   C series

D   Not possible to determine from the available information

88 Shuffles is attempting to decide which size of fork-lift truck to buy to use in its warehouses. There are three grades of truck, the A series, B series and the C series. The uncertainty faced is the expected growth in the on-line market it serves, which could grow at 15%, 30% or even 40% in the next period.

Shuffles has correctly produced the following decision table and has calculated the average daily contribution gained from each combination of truck and growth assumption.

Decision table		Type of truck		
		A series	B series	C series
Growth rate	15%	$2,400	$1,800	$3,600
	30%	$1,400	$1,900	$4,500
	40%	$4,900	$2,800	$3,900

Which truck would the optimistic buyer purchase?

A   A series

B   B series

C   C series

D   Not possible to determine from the available information

89 Shuffles is attempting to decide which size of fork-lift truck to buy to use in its warehouses. There are three grades of truck, the A series, B series and the C series. The uncertainty faced is the expected growth in the on-line market it serves, which could grow at 15%, 30% or even 40% in the next period.

Shuffles has correctly produced the following decision table and has calculated the average daily contribution gained from each combination of truck and growth assumption.

Decision table		Type of truck		
		A series	B series	C series
Growth rate	15%	$2,400	$1,800	$3,600
	30%	$1,400	$1,900	$4,500
	40%	$4,900	$2,800	$3,900

Based upon the scenario information, if the buyer was prone to regretting decisions that have been made which truck would the buyer purchase?

A   A series

B   B series

C   C series

D   Not possible to determine from the available information

90 Shuffles is attempting to decide which size of fork-lift truck to buy to use in its warehouses. There are three grades of truck, the A series, B series and the C series. The uncertainty faced is the expected growth in the on-line market it serves, which could grow at 15%, 30% or even 40% in the next period.

Shuffles has correctly produced the following decision table and has calculated the average daily contribution gained from each combination of truck and growth assumption.

Decision table		Type of truck		
		A series	B series	C series
Growth rate	15%	$2,400	$1,800	$3,600
	30%	$1,400	$1,900	$4,500
	40%	$4,900	$2,800	$3,900

Based upon the scenario information, if the probabilities of the given growth rates are 15%: 0.4, 30%: 0.25 and 40%: 0.35, which truck would the risk-neutral buyer purchase?

A   A series

B   B series

C   C series

D   Not possible to determine from the available information

91 The following statements have been made about the use of simulation:

(i) Simulation models the behaviour of a system.

(ii) Simulation models can be used to study alternative solutions to a problem.

(iii) The equations describing the operating characteristics of the system are known.

(iv) A simulation model cannot prescribe what should be done about a problem.

Which ONE of the above statements is NOT true?

A (i)

B (ii)

C (iii)

D (iv)

92 A company can make either of two new products, X and Y, but not both. The profitability of each product depends on the state of the market, as follows:

Market state	Profit from product		Probability of market state
	X $	Y $	
Good	20,000	17,000	0.2
Fair	15,000	16,000	0.5
Poor	6,000	7,000	0.3

What is the expected value of perfect information as to the state of the market?

A $0

B $600

C $800

D $1,000

93 Tree Co is considering employing a sales manager. Market research has shown that a good sales manager can increase profit by 30%, an average one by 20% and a poor one by 10%. Experience has shown that the company has attracted a good sales manager 35% of the time, an average one 45% of the time and a poor one 20% of the time. The company's normal profits are $180,000 per annum and the sales manager's salary would be $40,000 per annum.

Based on the expected value criterion, which of the following represents the correct advice which Tree Co should be given?

A Do not employ a sales manager as profits would be expected to fall by $1,300

B Employ a sales manager as profits will increase by $38,700

C Employ a sales manager as profits are expected to increase by $100

D Do not employ a sales manager as profits are expected to fall by $39,900

94 A company is considering the development and marketing of a new product. Development costs will be $2m. There is a 75% probability that the development effort will be successful, and a 25% probability that it will be unsuccessful. If development *is* successful and the product *is* marketed, it is estimated that:

	Expected profit	*Probability*
Product very successful	$6.0m	0.4
Product moderately successful	$1.8m	0.4
Product unsuccessful	($5.0m)	0.2

What is the expected value of the project?

A ($0.41m)

B $2.12m

C $1.59m

D $0.41m

BUDGETING AND CONTROL

BUDGETARY SYSTEMS

95 The following statements have been made about Activity-Based Budgeting (ABB):

(1) The costs determined using ABC are used as a basis for preparing budgets.

(2) The aim of ABB is to control the number of units output rather than the costs themselves.

Which of the above statement(s) is/are true?

A (1) only

B (2) only

C Neither (1) nor (2)

D Both (1) and (2)

96 The following statements have been made about budgetary systems in the performance hierarchy:

(1) Developing new products in response the changes in technology is a budgeting activity that would fall within operational planning and control.

(2) Budgetary systems at strategic planning levels look at the business as a whole and define resource requirements.

Which of the above statement(s) is/are true?

A (1) only

B (2) only

C Neither (1) nor (2)

D Both (1) and (2)

97   The purpose of a flexible budget is to:

A   Compare actual and budgeted results at virtually any level of production

B   Reduce the total time in preparing the annual budget

C   Allow management some latitude in meeting goals

D   Eliminate cyclical fluctuations in production reports by ignoring variable costs

TYPES OF BUDGET

98   What is the name given to a budget which has been prepared by building on a previous period's budgeted or actual figures?

A   Incremental budget

B   Flexible budget

C   Zero based budget

D   Functional budget

99   The following statements have been made about feed-forward control budgetary systems:

(1)   Feedforward control systems have an advantage over other types of control in that it establishes how effective planning was.

(2)   Feedforward control occurs while an activity is in progress.

Which of the above statement(s) is/are true?

A   (1) only

B   (2) only

C   Neither (1) nor (2)

D   Both (1) and (2)

100   An incremental budgeting system is:

A   a system which budgets only for the extra costs associated with a particular plan

B   a system which budgets for the variable manufacturing costs only

C   a system which prepares budgets only after the manager responsible has justified the continuation of the relevant activity

D   a system which prepares budgets by adjusting the previous year's values by expected changes in volumes of activity and price/inflation effects

101   Which of the following is an advantage of non-participative budgeting as compared to participative budgeting?

A   It increases motivation

B   It is less time consuming

C   It increases acceptance

D   The budgets produced are more attainable

102 EFG uses an Activity Based Budgeting system. It manufactures three products, budgeted details of which are set out below:

	Product E	Product F	Product G
Budgeted annual production (units)	75,000	120,000	60,000
Batch size (units)	200	60	30
Machine set-ups per batch	5	3	9
Purchase orders per batch	4	2	2
Processing time per unit (minutes)	3	4	4

Three cost pools have been identified. Their budgeted costs for the year ending 30 September 20X3 are as follows:

Machine set-up costs	$180,000
Purchasing of materials	$95,000
Processing	$110,000

What is the budgeted machine set-up cost per unit of product F?

A $0.1739

B $0.35

C $6.96

D Cannot be determined without any more information

103 A master budget comprises the:

A budgeted income statement and budgeted cash flow only

B budgeted income statement and budgeted balance sheet only

C budgeted income statement and budgeted capital expenditure only

D budgeted income statement, budgeted balance sheet and budgeted cash flow only

104 The following statements have been made regarding different types of budget:

(i) A flexible budget can be used to control operational efficiency.

(ii) Incremental budgeting can be defined as a system of budgetary planning and control that measures the additional costs that are incurred when there are unplanned extra units of activity.

(iii) Rolling budgets review and, if necessary, revise the budget for the next quarter to ensure that budgets remain relevant for the remainder of the accounting period.

Which of the above statement(s) are true?

A (i) and (ii) only

B (ii) and (iii) only

C (iii) only

D (i) only

105 X Co uses rolling budgeting, updating its budgets on a quarterly basis. After carrying out the last quarter's update to the cash budget, it projected a forecast cash deficit of $400,000 at the end of the year. Consequently, the planned purchase of new capital equipment has been postponed.

Which of the following types of control is the sales manager's actions an example of?

A   Feedforward control

B   Negative feedback control

C   Positive feedback control

D   Double loop feedback control

106 A definition of zero-based budgeting is set out below, with two blank sections.

"Zero-based budgeting: a method of budgeting which requires each cost element _____, as though the activities to which the budget relates _____."

Which combination of two phrases correctly completes the definition?

	Blank 1	Blank 2
A	to be specifically justified	could be out-sourced to an external supplier
B	to be set at zero	could be out-sourced to an external supplier
C	to be specifically justified	were being undertaken for the first time
D	to be set at zero	were being undertaken for the first time

107 The following statements have been made about the drawbacks of zero-based budgeting:

(1)   The number of activities could be so large that the amount of paperwork generated from zero-based budgeting will be unmanageable.

(2)   It is difficult to incorporate qualitative factors into a zero-based budgeting exercise.

Which of the above statement(s) is/are true?

A   (1) only

B   (2) only

C   Neither (1) nor (2)

D   Both (1) and (2)

108 The following statements have been made about the drawbacks of activity-based budgeting:

(1)   It is not always useful or applicable, as in the short term many overhead costs are not controllable and do not vary directly with changes in the volume of activity for the cost driver.

(2)   ABB will not be able to provide useful information for a total quality management programme (TQM).

Which of the above statement(s) is/are true?

A   (1) only

B   (2) only

C   Neither (1) nor (2)

D   Both (1) and (2)

QUANTITATIVE ANALYSIS IN BUDGETING

109 The following table shows the number of clients who attended a particular accountancy practice over the last four weeks and the total costs incurred during each of the weeks:

Week	Number of clients	Total cost
		$
1	400	36,880
2	440	39,840
3	420	36,800
4	460	40,000

Applying the high low method to the above information, which of the following could be used to forecast total cost ($) from the number of clients expected to attend (where x = the expected number of clients)?

A   7,280 + 74x

B   16,080 + 52x

C   3,200 + 80x

D   40,000/x

110 The management accountant of a business has identified the following information:

Activity level	800 units	1,200 units
Total cost	$16,400	$23,600

The fixed costs of the business step up by 40% at 900 units

What is the variable cost per unit?

A $8.00

B $18.00

C $19.67

D $20.00

111 The management accountant of a business has identified the following information:

Activity level	800 units	1,200 units
Total cost	$16,400	$23,600

The fixed costs of the business step up by 40% at 900 units

What is the fixed cost at 1,100 units?

A $6,400

B $7,600

C $10,000

D $14,000

112 The budgeted electricity cost for a business is $30,000 based upon production of 1,000 units. However if 1,400 units were to be produced the budgeted cost rises to $31,600.

Using the high/low approach what would be the budgeted electricity cost if 2,100 units were to be produced?

A $8,400

B $17,600

C $26,000

D $34,400

113 The time for the first unit produced was 100 hours. The time for the second unit was 90 hours.

What is the learning rate?

A   95%

B   90%

C   89.1%

D   100%

114 The time for the first batch of 50 units was 500 hours. The total time for the first 16 batches of 50 units was 5,731 hours.

What is the learning rate?

A   85%

B   90%

C   92%

D   94%

115 The time for the first batch of 50 units was 400 hours but the labour budget is the subject of a learning effect where the learning rate is 90%. The rate of pay for labour is $12 per hour.

The business had received and satisfied an order for 600 units but it has now received a second order for another 800 units.

The value of b is = –0.152

What will be the cost of this second order?

A $3,459

B $6,749

C $41,509

D $80, 990

116 The times taken to produce each of the first four batches of a new product were as follows:

Batch number	Time taken
1	100 minutes
2	70 minutes
3	59 minutes
4	55 minutes

What was the rate of learning closest to?

A   85.0%

B   84.3%

C   78.6%

D   70.0%

117 Caroline has recently developed a new product. The nature of Caroline's work is repetitive, and it is usual for there to be an 80% learning effect when a new product is developed. The time taken for the first unit was 22 minutes. An 80% learning effect applies.

What is the time to be taken for the fourth unit in minutes?

A   17.6 minutes

B   14.08 minutes

C   15.45 minutes

D   9.98 minutes

STANDARD COSTING

118   Which of the following best describes a 'basic standard' within the context of budgeting?

A   A standard which is kept unchanged over a period of time

B   A standard which is based on current price levels

C   A standard set at an ideal level, which makes no allowance for normal losses, waste and machine downtime

D   A standard which assumes an efficient level of operation, but which includes allowances for factors such as normal loss, waste and machine downtime

119 The following statements have been made about budgets and standards:

(i) Budgets can be used in situations where output cannot be measured, but standards cannot be used in such situations.

(ii) Budgets can include allowances for inefficiencies in operations, but standards use performance targets which are attainable under the most favourable conditions.

(iii) Budgets are used for planning purposes, standards are used only for control purposes.

Which of the above statements is/are true?

A (i) , (ii) and (iii)

B (i) and (ii) only

C (i) only

D (ii) and (iii) only

120 An accurate definition of standard costing is a system of budgeting where:

A all activities are examined without reference to history each year

B output level and costs are predetermined, actual results then compared with these predetermined costs and variances analysed

C actual costs are compared with predetermined costs for the level of activity

D costs are assigned to a manager in order that controllable and non-controllable costs are accounted for

121 Which of the following accounting procedures are used for controlling costs conditional on a given volume of production?

	Flexible budgeting	Standard costing
A	Yes	Yes
B	Yes	No
C	No	Yes
D	No	No

122 The following are management accounting techniques:

(i) Actual versus flexed budget calculations

(ii) Variance analysis

(iii) Trend of costs analysis

Which of the above techniques could be used by a company to control costs?

A (i) and (ii) only

B (i) and (iii) only

C (ii) and (iii) only

D (i), (ii) and (iii)

123   When considering setting standards for costing, which of the following would NOT be appropriate?

    A   The normal level of activity should always be used for absorbing overheads

    B   Average prices for materials should be used, encompassing any discounts that are regularly available

    C   The labour rate used will be the rate at which the labour is paid

    D   Average material usage should be established based on generally-accepted working practices

124   The following statements have been made about both standard costing and total quality management (TQM):

    (1)   They focus on assigning responsibility solely to senior managers

    (2)   They work well in rapidly changing environments

Which of the above statements is/are true?

    A   (1) only

    B   (2) only

    C   Neither (1) nor (2)

    D   Both (1) and (2)

MATERIALS MIX AND YIELD VARIANCES

125   The following statements relate to the materials mix variance:

    (i)   A favourable total mix variance would suggest that a higher proportion of a cheaper material is being used instead of a more expensive one.

    (ii)   A favourable total mix variance will usually result in a favourable material yield variance.

Which of the above statements are true?

    A   (i) only

    B   (i) and (ii)

    C   (ii) only

    D   (i) and (ii)

126 The following statements relate to the materials yield variance:

(i) An adverse total yield variance would suggest that less output has been achieved for a given input, i.e. that the total input in volume is more than expected for the output achieved.

(ii) A favourable total mix variance will usually result in an adverse material yield variance.

Which of the above statements are true?

A   (i) only

B   (i) and (ii)

C   (ii) only

D   (i) and (ii)

127 JC Ltd mixes three materials to produce a chemical SGR. The following extract from a standard cost card shows the materials to be used in producing 100 kg of chemical SGR:

	kg
Material A	50 @ $10 per kg
Material B	40 @ $5 per kg
Material C	20 @ $9 per kg
	110

During October 23,180 kg of SGR were produced using the following materials:

	kg
Material A	13,200
Material B	7,600
Material C	5,600
	26,400

What is the total material mix variance?

A $1,984 A

B $7,216 A

C $9,200 A

D $16,416 A

128 JC Ltd mixes three materials to produce a chemical SGR. The following extract from a standard cost card shows the materials to be used in producing 100 kg of chemical SGR:

	kg
Material A	50 @ $10 per kg
Material B	40 @ $5 per kg
Material C	20 @ $9 per kg
	___
	110

During October 23,180 kg of SGR were produced using the following materials:

	kg
Material A	13,200
Material B	7,600
Material C	5,600
	_____
	26,400

What is the total material yield variance?

A $1,984 A

B $7,216 A

C $9,200 A

D $16,416 A

129 Mr. Green makes salads. The standard plate of salad has 30 g of lettuce (L), 50 g of peppers (P) and 80 g of beetroot (B). The standard prices of the three ingredients are $0.2/kg, 0.4/kg and 0.8/kg respectively. The actual prices were $0.22/kg, $0.38/kg and $0.82/kg.

Mr. Green has been experimenting and so in July he changed the mix of vegetables on the plate thus: 1,500 plates contained 62,000 grams of lettuce, 81,000 grams of peppers and 102,000 grams of beetroot.

What is the cost difference between the actual mix and the standard mix to the nearest cent?

A $0

B $9.72

C $11.41

D $11.59

130 Mr. Green makes salads. The standard plate of salad has 30 g of lettuce (L), 50 g of peppers (P) and 80 g of beetroot (B). The standard prices of the three ingredients are $0.2/kg, 0.4/kg and 0.8/kg respectively.

Mr. Green has been experimenting and so in July he changed the mix of vegetables on the plate thus: 1,500 plates contained 62,000 grams of lettuce, 81,000 grams of peppers and 102,000 grams of beetroot.

What is the yield variance (do not round your answer)?

A $2.8125 Fav

B $2.8125 Adv

C $2,812.5 Fav

D $2,812.5 Adv

131 A company has a process in which the standard mix for producing 9 litres of output is as follows:

	$
4.0 litres of D at $9 per litre	36.00
3.5 litres of E at $5 per litre	17.50
2.5 litres of F at $2 per litre	5.00
Total	58.50

A standard loss of 10% of inputs is expected to occur. The actual inputs for the latest period were:

	$
4,300 litres of D at $9.00 per litre	38,700
3,600 litres of E at $5.50 per litre	19,800
2,100 litres of F at $2.20 per litre	4,620
Total	63,120

Actual output for this period was 9,100 litres.

What is the total materials mix variance?

A $2,400 (A)

B $2,400 (F)

C $3,970 (A)

D $3,970 (F)

SALES MIX AND QUANTITY VARIANCES

132 Yellow sells two types of squash ball, the type A and the type B. The standard contribution from these balls is $4 and $5 respectively and the standard profit per ball is $1.50 and $2.40 respectively. The budget was to sell 5 type A balls for every 3 type B balls.

Actual sales were up 20,000 at 240,000 balls with type A balls being 200,000 of that total. Yellow values its stock of balls at standard marginal cost.

What is the value of the sales mix variance?

A $45,000 Fav

B $45,000 Adv

C $50,000 Fav

D $50,000 Adv

133   **What is the value of the sales quantity variance?**

A $36,750 Fav

B $36,750 Adv

C $87,500 Fav

D $87,500 Adv

134   Jones' monthly absorption costing variance analysis report includes a sales mix variance, which indicates the effect on profit of actual sales mix differing from the budgeted sales mix. The following data are available.

		Product X		Product Y
	$	$	$	$
Selling price		12		11
Less Variable cost	6		2	
Fixed cost	2		3	
	—	(8)	—	(5)
Standard net profit per unit		4		6

July sales (units)		
Budget	3,000	6,000
Actual	2,000	8,000

What is the favourable sales mix variance for July?

A $8,000

B $5,333

C $4,000

D $2,667

135 You have been provided with the following information relating to three products:

	Product X	Product Y	Product Z
Demand (units)	1,000	2,000	3,000
Selling price	$15	$20	$30
Profit per unit	$2	$5	$2

Actual sales for the year showed the following results.

	Product X	Product Y	Product Z
Units sold	1,100	2,050	2,800
Sales value	$17,050	$38,950	$86,800
Profit	$3,080	$10,455	$6,160

What is the sales quantity variance?

A $150 adverse

B $50 favourable

C $1,208 adverse

D $1,695 favourable

PLANNING AND OPERATIONAL VARIANCES

136 The following statements have been made about material price planning variances:

(1)   The publication of material price planning variances should always lead to automatic updates of standard costs.

(2)   The causes of material price planning variances do not need to be investigated by managers at any level in the organisation.

Which of the above statement(s) is/are true?

A   (1) only

B   (2) only

C   Neither (1) nor (2)

D   Both (1) and (2)

137 Leaf limited has had a mixed year. Its market share has improved two percentage points to 20% but the overall market had contracted by 5% in the same period. The budgeted sales were 504,000 units and standard contribution was $12 per unit.

What is the level of actual sales?

A   Two percentage points up on budget at 510,080 units

B   Three percent down overall on budget at 488,880 units

C   Three percent up on budget at 519,120 units

D   Up by a little over five and a half percent to 532,000 units

138 Leaf Limited has had a mixed year. Its market share has improved two percentage points to 20% but the overall market had contracted by 5% in the same period. The budgeted sales were 504,000 units and standard contribution was $12 per unit.

The sales market size variance is:

A $1,680,000 Fav

B $1,680,000 Adv

C $302,400 Adv

D $302,400 Fav

139 Leaf Limited has had a mixed year. Its market share has improved two percentage points to 20% but the overall market had contracted by 5% in the same period. The budgeted sales were 504,000 units and standard contribution was $12 per unit.

The sales market share variance is:

A $638,400 Adv

B $638,400 Fav

C $336,000 Adv

D $336,000 Fav

140 The following statements have been made about planning and operational variances:

(1)   Operational managers are not usually held accountable for planning variances.

(2)   Planning variances can lead to managers revising some fundamental budgetary assumptions.

Which of the above statement(s) is/are true?

A   (1) only

B   (2) only

C   Neither (1) nor (2)

D   Both (1) and (2)

141 The following statements have been made about planning and operational variances:

(1)   Planning and operational variances are deemed to be within the control of the production manager.

(2)   The production manager is usually to be held responsible for the material usage operational variance.

Which of the above statement(s) is/are true?

A   (1) only

B   (2) only

C   Neither (1) nor (2)

D   Both (1) and (2)

142 The following statements have been made about planning and operational variances:

(1) Planning and operational variances are calculated when it is necessary to assess a manager on results that are within his/her control.

(2) Revised standards are required because variances may arise partly due to an unrealistic budget, and not solely due to operational factors.

Which of the above statement(s) is/are true?

A (1) only

B (2) only

C Neither (1) nor (2)

D Both (1) and (2)

PERFORMANCE ANALYSIS AND BEHAVIOURAL ASPECTS

143 The finance director of Paint Mixers Ltd has produced the table below showing the variance results for the first three months of the year:

	January	February	March
Material price variance	$3,000 A	$2,000 A	$1,000 A
Material mix variance	$2,000 A	$750 A	$100 F
Material yield variance	$4,000 A	$2,000 A	$50F

Which of the following interpretations of the variances analysis exercise above is NOT correct?

A The purchasing manager should be able to threaten to switch suppliers to get better deals and address the adverse material price variance

B The materials mix variance is entirely under the control of the production manager

C The favourable yield variance in March could be the result of operational efficiency

D The responsibility for the initial poor performance must be borne by both the purchasing manager and the production manager

144 The following statements have been made in relation to the use of standard costs in rapidly changing environments:

(1) Variance analysis results will take into account important criteria such as customer satisfaction or quality of production.

(2) Achieving standards is suitable in most modern manufacturing environments.

Which of the above statement(s) is/are true?

A (1) only

B (2) only

C Neither (1) nor (2)

D Both (1) and (2)

PERFORMANCE MEASUREMENT AND CONTROL

PERFORMANCE MANAGEMENT INFORMATION SYSTEMS

145   The following statements have been made about planning and control as described in the three tiers of Robert Anthony's decision-making hierarchy:

(1)   Strategic planning is concerned with making decisions about the efficient and effective use of existing resources.

(2)   Operational control is about ensuring that specific tasks are carried out efficiently and effectively.

Which of the above statements is/are true?

A   (1) only

B   (2) only

C   Neither (1) nor (2)

D   Both (1) and (2)

146   **Long-term sales forecasts are an example of accounting information used at which level of control in an organisation?**

A   Strategic planning

B   Management control

C   Tactical control

D   Operational control

147   The following are all types of information systems:

(i)   A Management Information System producing management accounts showing margins for individual customers.

(ii)   An Expert System holding specialist tax information.

(iii)   An Executive Information System giving access to internal and external information in summarised form, with the option to drill down to a greater level of activity.

Which of the above would NOT be suited to all levels of management in an organisation?

A   (i)

B   (ii)

C   (iii)

D   None of the above is suited to all levels.

148 The following statements have been made about Transaction Processing Systems (TPS):

(1) Data is processed rapidly, and on a regular basis, for example daily.

(2) TPS systems monitor and collect forecast data.

Which of the above statement is/are true?

A (1) only

B (2) only

C Neither (1) nor (2)

D Both (1) and (2)

149 **Electronic Executive Information Systems (EIS) and Expert Systems (ES) are examples of:**

A Customer relationship management software

B Database management systems

C Computer networking

D Decision based software

150 You have been presented with a summary report of sales in the last month, with a breakdown of totals per product, and with variances from the corresponding monthly sales plan.

This report is an output from:

A A transaction processing system

B A management information system

C An executive Information system

D None of the above

SOURCES OF MANAGEMENT INFORMATION

151 The following statements have been made about using external information:

(1) External information is usually more reliable than internal information.

(2) External information can be general and vague, and may not really help an organisation with decision making.

Which of the above statement is/are true?

A (1) only

B (2) only

C Neither (1) nor (2)

D Both (1) and (2)

152 Which of the following sources of information would be considered internal?

  A   Interviewing potential customers

  B   Reading business magazines

  C   Receiving updates from tax authorities

  D   Looking through sales records for the last year

153 Where would you most likely find information concerning the frequency of machine breakdowns causing lost production?

  A   The fixed asset register

  B   The machine maintenance schedule

  C   Production output reports

  D   The purchase ledger account for the supplier that provides replacement machine parts

154 Which of the following could be described as an expert system?

  A   An ATM dispensing cash provided there is enough money in the account

  B   A stock management system, which highlights stock-outs

  C   A marketing database holding records of past advertising campaigns and the sales generated by those campaigns

  D   A tax calculator which predicts the level of tax payable in different scenarios

155 Which of the following is the most reliable source of information on a country's inflation rate?

  A   Spending on groceries by a family from one point of time to the next

  B   Journalist reports concerning the difficulties local families are having making ends meet

  C   Average house prices measured across the country from one point of time to the next

  D   The government figures for RPI or CPI

156 The qualities of good information contained in reports are more easily remembered using the mnemonic ACCURATE. Which one of the following is not normally associated with a quality of good information?

  A   Adaptable to the needs of the user

  B   Acceptable to the user

  C   Accurate

  D   Understandable by the user

MANAGEMENT REPORTS

157 Strategic reports have many features, which of the following would be most likely true of a strategic report?

A   Prepared regularly

B   Normally considered accurate and reliable

C   Highly summarised showing overall trends

D   Demonstrates current position

158 Local managers within organisations often use operational reports. Which of the following features of reports would be most true of an operational report?

A   Summarised information

B   Mainly external information on local competition

C   Accurate information on current position

D   Infrequent

159 The following are all types of controls required when generating and distributing commercially sensitive business information.

(1)   Passwords.

(2)   Audit trails.

(3)   Distribution lists.

Which of the above are examples of processing controls?

A   (1) only

B   (2) only

C   (2) and (3)

D   Both (1) and (3)

160 The following statements have been made about a type of procedure that can be used to make sure confidential data is kept secure:

(1)   Logical access control is concerned with preventing those who do not have access to a computer from gaining access to data or software.

(2)   Physical access control is concerned with preventing those who already have access to a computer from gaining access to data or software.

Which of the above statement is/are true?

A   (1) only

B   (2) only

C   Neither (1) nor (2)

D   Both (1) and (2)

PERFORMANCE ANALYSIS IN PRIVATE SECTOR ORGANISATIONS

161 The following are types of Key Performance Indicators:

(i) Return on Capital Employed

(ii) Gross profit percentage

(iii) Acid Test ratio

(iv) Gearing ratio

Which of the above KPIs would be used to assess the liquidity of a company?

A (i) and (ii) only

B (iii) only

C (iv) only

D (iii) and (iv) only

162 Why would a company want to encourage the use of non-financial performance indicators?

A To encourage short-termism

B To look at the fuller picture of the business

C To enable results to be easily manipulated to the benefit of the manager

D To prevent goal congruence

163 Michigan is an insurance company. Recently, there has been concern that too many quotations have been sent to clients either late or containing errors. The department concerned has responded that it is understaffed, and a high proportion of current staff has recently joined the firm. The performance of this department is to be carefully monitored.

Which ONE of the following non-financial performance indicators would NOT be an appropriate measure to monitor and improve the department's performance?

A Percentage of quotations found to contain errors when checked.

B Percentage of quotations not issued within company policy of three working days

C Percentage of department's quota of staff actually employed

D Percentage of budgeted number of quotations actually issued

164 Which of the following items would best go into the Customer Perspective within a traditional balanced scorecard?

A Customer profitability analysis

B New product requests from customers

C Customer satisfaction ratings

D Customer ordering processing times

165 HH plc monitors the % of total sales that derives from products developed in the last year. Which part of the balanced scorecard would this measure be classified under?

    A   Financial perspective

    B   Customer perspective

    C   Internal perspective

    D   Learning perspective

166 Which of the following is the best measure of quality to be included within a building block model in a rapidly growing clothing business?

    A   Number of returns in the month

    B   Number of faulty goods returned as a percentage of number of orders received in the month

    C   Average customer satisfaction rating where customers were asked a range of questions including quality, delivery and customer service

    D   Number of faulty goods returned as a percentage of deliveries made in the month

167 Which of the following is not a dimension of performance contained within the Building Block model:

    A   Resource utilisation

    B   Quality

    C   Equity

    D   Flexibility

168 The following extracts relate to Company X and Company Y for 20X1:

	Co X	Co Y
	$000	$000
Revenue	20,000	26,000
Cost of sales	(15,400)	(21,050)
Gross profit	4,600	4,950
Expenses	(2,460)	(2,770)
Operating profit	2,140	2,180

What is the operating profit margin for both companies for 20X1?

	Co X	Co Y
A	10.7%	8.38%
B	8.38%	10.7%
C	23%	19%
D	12%	10%

169 Companies A and B are both involved in retailing. Relevant information for the year ended 30 September 20X1 was as follows:

	A	B
	$000	$000
Sales revenue	50,000	200,000
Profit	10,000	10,000
Capital employed	50,000	50,000

Which of the following statements is true?

A   The profit margin of both companies is the same

B   Company B is generating more profit from every $1 of asset employed than Company A

C   Company B is using its assets more efficiently

D   Company B is controlling its costs better than Company A

170 The following extracts relate to company W for 20X1 and 20X2:

	20X1	20X2
Statement of profit or loss extract:		
Revenue	20,000	26,000
Statement of financial position extract:		
Receivables	4,400	6,740
Cash	120	960

What is the receivables collection period for 20X1 and 20X2?

	20X1	20X2
A	80 days	95 days
B	82 days	108 days
C	75 days	111 days
D	95 days	80 days

171 The trading account of Calypso for the year ended 30 June 20X0 is set out below:

	$	$
Sales		430,000
Opening inventories	50,000	
Purchases	312,500	
	362,500	
Closing inventories	(38,000)	
Cost of sales		(324,500)
Gross profit		105,500

The following amounts have been extracted from the company's statement of financial position at 30 June 20X0.

	$
Trade receivables	60,000
Prepayments	4,000
Cash in hand	6,000
Bank overdraft	8,000
Trade payables	40,000
Accruals	3,000
Declared dividends	5,000

Calculate the inventories days (using average inventories) and the current ratio for Calypso Ltd for the period.

	Inventory days	*Current ratio*
A	33 days	1.25:1
B	49 days	1.25:1
C	49 days	1.93:1
D	33 days	1.93:1

DIVISIONAL PERFORMANCE AND TRANSFER PRICING

172 Dust Co has two divisions, A and B. Each division is currently considering the following separate projects:

	Division A	Division B
Capital required for the project	$32.6 million	$22.2 million
Sales generated by the project	$14.4 million	$8.8 million
Operating profit margin	30%	24%
Cost of capital	10%	10%
Current return on investment of division	15%	9%

If residual income is used as the basis for the investment decision, which division(s) would choose to invest in the project?

A   Division A only

B   Division B only

C   Both Division A and Division B

D   Neither Division A neither Division B

173 JB Ltd is a divisionalised organisation comprising a number of divisions, including divisions A and B. Division A makes a single product, which it sells on the external market at a price of $12 per unit. The variable cost of the product is $8 per unit and the fixed cost is $3 per unit. Market demand for the product considerably exceeds Division A's maximum production capacity of 10,000 units per month.

Division B would like to obtain 500 units of the product from Division A. If Division A does transfer some of its production internally rather than sell externally, then the saving in packaging costs would be $1.50 per unit. What transfer price per unit should Division A quote in order to maximise group profit?

A $8

B $10.50

C $11

D $13.50

174 Oxco has two divisions, A and B. Division A makes a component for air conditioning units which it can only sell to Division B. It has no other outlet for sales.

Current information relating to Division A is as follows:

Marginal cost per unit	$100
Transfer price of the component	$165
Total production and sales of the component each year	2,200 units
Specific fixed costs of Division A per year	$10,000

Cold Co has offered to sell the component to Division B for $140 per unit. If Division B accepts this offer, Division A will be shut.

If Division B accepts Cold Co's offer, what will be the impact on profits per year for the group as a whole?

A   Increase of $65,000

B   Decrease of $78,000

C   Decrease of $88,000

D   Increase of $55,000

175 Summary financial statements are given below for JE, the division of a large divisionalised company:

Balance sheet		*Income statement*	
	$000		$000
Non-current assets	2,400	Revenue	7,300
Current assets	1,000	Operating costs	(6,800)
Total assets	3,400	Operating profit	500
		Interest paid	(320)
Divisional equity	1,500	Profit before tax	180
Long-term borrowings	900		
Current liabilities	1,000		
Total equity and liabilities	3,400		

The cost of capital for the division is estimated at 11% each year. The annual rate of interest on the long-term loans is 9%. All decisions concerning the division's capital structure are taken by central management.

What is the divisional return on capital employed (ROCE) for the year ended 31 December?

A   5.3%

B   7.5%

C   14.7%

D   20.8%

176 Summary financial statements are given below for JE, the division of a large divisionalised company:

Balance sheet		Income statement	
	$000		$000
Non-current assets	2,400	Revenue	7,300
Current assets	1,000	Operating costs	(6,800)
	———		———
Total assets	3,400	Operating profit	500
	———	Interest paid	(320)
			———
Divisional equity	1,500	Profit before tax	180
Long-term borrowings	900		———
Current liabilities	1,000		
	———		
Total equity and liabilities	3,400		
	———		

The cost of capital for the division is estimated at 11% each year. The annual rate of interest on the long-term loans is 9%. All decisions concerning the division's capital structure are taken by central management.

What is the divisional residual income (RI) for the year ended 31 December?

A   −$84

B $180

C $236

D $284

177 Pro is a division of Mo and is an investment centre. The head office controls finance, HR and IT expenditure but all other decisions are devolved to the local centres.

The statement of financial position for Pro shows net value of all assets and liabilities to be $4,500m at the start of the year and $4,890m at the end. It carries no debt itself although the group has debt liabilities.

The management accounts for income read as follows:

	$m
Revenue	3,500
Cost of sales	1,800
Local administration	250
IT costs	50
Distribution	80
Central administration	30
Interest charges	90
Net profit	1,200

Ignore taxation.

If the cost of capital is 12%, what is the division's residual income?

A $660

B $830

C $1,110

D $1,280

178 What is the divisional ROI to the nearest % point?

    A   25%

    B   27%

    C   28%

    D   30%

179 Division D of Erie Ltd is considering a project which will increase annual profit by $15,000, but will require average receivables levels to increase by $100,000. The company's target return on investment is 10%, and the imputed interest cost of capital is 9%. Division D currently earns a return on investment of 13%.

Would the return on investment (ROI) and Residual Income (RI) performance measures motivate the manager of Division D to act in the interest of Erie Ltd as a whole?

    A   The ROI would motivate the manager to act in the interest of the company as a whole, but the RI would not

    B   The RI would motivate the manager to act in the interest of the company as a whole, but the ROI would not

    C   Both the ROI and the RI would motivate the manager to act in the interest of the company as a whole

    D   Neither the ROI nor the RI would motivate the manager to act in the interest of the company as a whole

180 Division A of a company makes units which are then transferred to other divisions. There is a competitive intermediate market for these units, with a price of $15 per unit. Division A then incurs a selling cost of $2. Variable production costs amount to $7 per unit and fixed costs to $3 per unit. The division has spare capacity. The following statements have been made regarding the minimum transfer price that will encourage the divisional manager of A to transfer units to other divisions:

    (1)   Any price above variable cost will generate a positive contribution, and will therefore be accepted.

    (2)   The division will need to give up a unit sold externally in order to make a transfer, this is only worthwhile if the income of a transfer is greater than the net income of an external sale.

Which of the above statement(s) is/are true?

    A   (1) only

    B   (2) only

    C   Neither (1) nor (2)

    D   Both (1) and (2)

181 Division B of a company makes units which are then transferred to other divisions. The division has no spare capacity. The following statements have been made regarding the minimum transfer price that will encourage the divisional manager of B to transfer units to other divisions:

(1) Any price above variable cost will generate a positive contribution, and will therefore be accepted.

(2) The division will need to give up a unit sold externally in order to make a transfer, this is only worthwhile if the income of a transfer is greater than the net income of an external sale.

Which of the above statement(s) is/are true?

A   (1) only

B   (2) only

C   Neither (1) nor (2)

D   Both (1) and (2)

182 TM plc makes components which it sells internally to its subsidiary RM Ltd, as well as to its own external market.

The external market price is $24.00 per unit, which yields a contribution of 40% of sales. For external sales, variable costs include $1.50 per unit for distribution costs, which are not incurred on internal sales.

TM plc has sufficient capacity to meet all of the internal and external sales. The objective is to maximise group profit.

At what unit price should the component be transferred to RM Ltd?

A $1.50

B $12.90

C $14.40

D $24.00

PERFORMANCE ANALYSIS IN NON-FOR-PROFIT ORGANISATIONS AND THE PUBLIC SECTOR

183   Def Co provides accounting services to government. On average, each staff member works six chargeable hours per day, with the rest of their working day being spent on non-chargeable administrative work. One of the company's main objectives is to produce a high level of quality and customer satisfaction.

Def Co has set its targets for the next year as follows:

(1)   Cutting departmental expenditure by 5%

(2)   Increasing the number of chargeable hours handled by advisers to 6.2 per day

(3)   Obtaining a score of 4.7 or above on customer satisfaction surveys

Which of the above targets assesses economy, efficiency and effectiveness at Def Co?

	Economy	Efficiency	Effectiveness
A	1	3	2
B	2	1	3
C	3	2	1
D	1	2	3

184   A government is looking at assessing hospitals by reference to a range of both financial and non-financial factors, one of which is survival rates for heart by-pass operations and another is 'cost per successfully treated patient'.

Which of the three E's in the 'Value For Money' framework is not measured here?

A   Economy

B   Effectiveness

C   Efficiency

D   Externality

185   **Which of the following describe difficulties in assessing performance in not-for-profit organisations?**

(i)   Benefits and costs are not always easy to quantify.

(ii)   These organisations often have multiple stakeholders and therefore multiple objectives.

(iii) These organisations often have unlimited funds and are therefore not motivated to measure performance.

A   (i) only

B   (i) and (ii)

C   (ii) only

D   (ii) and (iii)

186 A government is looking at assessing state schools by reference to a range of both financial and non-financial factors, one of which is average class sizes and another is exam success rates.

Which of the three E's in the 'Value For Money' framework is not covered by these measures?

A   Economy

B   Effectiveness

C   Efficiency

D   Externality

187 The following statements have been made about measuring performance in not-for-profit organisations:

(1)   Output does not usually have a market value, and it is therefore more difficult to measure effectiveness.

(2)   Control over the performance can only be satisfactorily achieved by assessments of 'value for money'.

Which of the above statements is/are true?

A   (1) only

B   (2) only

C   Neither (1) nor (2)

D   Both (1) and (2)

188 The following statements have been made about measuring effectiveness in not-for-profit organisations:

(1)   Effectiveness targets cannot usually be expressed financially, and therefore non-financial targets must be used.

(2)   The effective level of achievement could be measured by comparing actual performance against target.

Which of the above statement(s) is/are true?

A   (1) only

B   (2) only

C   Neither (1) nor (2)

D   Both (1) and (2)

EXTERNAL CONSIDERATIONS AND BEHAVIOURAL ASPECTS

189   The senior manager is suspicious of a local manager's accounts and thinks that the profit performance may have been overstated.

Which of the following would be a plausible explanation of an overstatement of profit?

A   Delaying payments to payables

B   Shortening the useful economic life of a non-current asset

C   Overstatement of a prepayment

D   Overstatement of an accrual

190   **Which of the following statements regarding standard setting is correct?**

A   Imposed standards are more likely to be achieved

B   Managers across the organisation should be targeted using the same standards

C   Standards should be set at an ideal level with no built in stretch

D   Participation in standard setting is more motivating than where standards are imposed

191   **When setting performance measures, external factors should be taken into account. Which of the following statements regarding external factors is FALSE?**

A   Stakeholders will have different objectives and companies may deal   with   this   by having a range of performance measures to assess the achievement of these objectives

B   A downturn in the industry or in the economy as a whole could have a negative impact on performance

C   It is only important for companies to take account of internal stakeholders when setting performance targets

D   Company performance could be affected if a competitor reduces its prices or launches a successful advertising campaign

192   When setting performance measurement targets it should be considered that there is the possibility that managers will take a short term view of the company and may even be tempted to manipulate results in order to achieve their targets.

Which of the following would assist in overcoming the problems of short-termism and manipulation of results?

A   Rewards should be linked to a wider variety of performance measures including some nonfinancial measures

B   Managers should only be rewarded for the results achieved in their own departments

C   Any capital investment decision should be judged using the payback method of investment appraisal

D   Setting targets involving the overall performance of the company will be more motivating for managers

193 Stakeholders will have different objectives and companies may deal with this by having a range of performance measures to assess the achievement of these objectives.

Which of the following statements is true in relation to stakeholders?

A   The aim of all performance measures should be to increase short term profit

B   The only interest of the government is that companies pay their taxes

C   Shareholders will be looking for increasing dividends and increased share price

D   Only internal stakeholders need to be considered by companies

Section 2

PRACTICE QUESTIONS

SPECIALIST COST AND MANAGEMENT ACCOUNTING TECHNIQUES

194   ABKABER PLC   *Online question assistance*

Abkaber plc assembles three types of motorcycle at the same factory: the 50cc Sunshine; the 250cc Roadster and the 1000cc Fireball. It sells the motorcycles throughout the world. In response to market pressures Abkaber plc has invested heavily in new manufacturing technology in recent years and, as a result, has significantly reduced the size of its workforce. Historically, the company has allocated all overhead costs using total direct labour hours, but is now considering introducing Activity Based Costing (ABC). Abkaber plc's accountant has produced the following analysis.

	Annual output (units)	Annual direct labour hours	Selling price ($ per unit)	Raw material cost ($ per unit)
Sunshine	2,000	200,000	4,000	400
Roadster	1,600	220,000	6,000	600
Fireball	400	80,000	8,000	900

The three cost drivers that generate overheads are:

- Deliveries to retailers – the number of deliveries of motorcycles to retail showrooms

- Set-ups – the number of times the assembly line process is re-set to accommodate a production run of a different type of motorcycle

- Purchase orders – the number of purchase orders.

The annual cost driver volumes relating to each activity and for each type of motorcycle are as follows:

	Number of deliveries to retailers	Number of set-ups	Number of purchase orders
Sunshine	100	35	400
Roadster	80	40	300
Fireball	70	25	100

The annual overhead costs relating to these activities are as follows:

	$
Deliveries to retailers	2,400,000
Set-up costs	6,000,000
Purchase orders	3,600,000

All direct labour is paid at $5 per hour. The company holds no inventories.

Required:

Calculate the total profit on each of Abkaber plc's three types of product using each of the following methods to attribute overheads:

(i)   the existing method based upon labour hours

(ii)   activity based costing.

(Total: 10 marks)

195   FIT CO LIFECYCLE (DEC 2011 EXAM)

Fit Co specialises in the manufacture of a small range of hi-tech products for the fitness market. They are currently considering the development of a new type of fitness monitor, which would be the first of its kind in the market. It would take one year to develop, with sales then commencing at the beginning of the second year. The product is expected to have a life cycle of two years, before it is replaced with a technologically superior product. The following cost estimates have been made.

	Year 1	Year 2	Year 3
Units manufactured and sold		100,000	200,000
Research and development costs	$160,000		
Product design costs	$800,000		
Marketing costs	$1,200,000	$1,000,000	$1,750,000
Manufacturing costs:			
Variable cost per unit		$40	$42
Fixed production costs		$650,000	$1,290,000
Distribution costs:			
Variable cost per unit		$4	$4.50
Fixed distribution costs		$120,000	$120,000
Selling costs:			
Variable cost per unit		$3	$3.20
Fixed selling costs		$180,000	$180,000
Administration costs	$200,000	$900,000	$1,500,000

Note: You should ignore the time value of money.

Required:

(a)   Calculate the life cycle cost per unit.   (6 marks)

(b)   Discuss the benefits of life cycle costing.   (4 marks)

(Total: 10 marks)

196 ABC IS NOT THE SOLUTION

Activity based costing (ABC) is not a new idea, indeed it has been around since the late 1980's and despite academics encouraging its use it really has not had the impact its creator (Robert S Kaplan) would have hoped.

Amongst the many reasons for the above are the following:

Property costs

Although often very significant in organisations (rent, rates, insurances, repairs and so on) identification of a single driver is difficult if not impossible. Consequently this major cost has to be dealt with using more traditional overhead treatments so reducing the impact that ABC can have on product costing calculations.

Controllability

Although in some cases the identification of a cost driver and the calculation of a cost per driver is relatively easy, for example delivery cost per delivery, the issue remains that the inherent internal cost is predominantly fixed and so controlling (or reducing) that cost using ABM is simply not possible.

Required:

Briefly discuss the two issues above in order to better explain why ABC is not the solution to poor management information it could have been.

(Total: 10 marks)

197 WEBCAMS (JUNE 2013 EXAM)

Cam Co manufactures webcams, devices which can provide live video and audio streams via personal computers. It has recently been suffering from liquidity problems and hopes that these will be eased by the launch of its new webcam, which has revolutionary audio sound and visual quality. The webcam is expected to have a product life cycle of two years. You are provided with the following relevant information for the webcam:

Projected lifetime sales volume	50,000 units
Target selling price per unit	$200
Target profit margin (35% selling price)	$70
Target cost per unit	$130
Estimated lifetime cost per unit (see note below for detailed breakdown)	$160

Note: Estimated lifetime cost per unit:

	$	$
Manufacturing costs		
Direct material (bought in parts)	40	
Direct labour	26	
Machine costs	21	
Quality control costs	10	
Rework costs	3	
	———	
		100
Non-manufacturing costs		
Product development costs	25	
Marketing costs	35	
	———	
		60
		———
Estimated lifetime cost per unit		160
		———

The average market price for a webcam is currently $150.

The following information has been identified as relevant:

(1) Direct material cost: all of the parts currently proposed for the webcam are bespoke parts. However, most of these can actually be replaced with standard parts costing 55% less. However, three of the bespoke parts, which currently account for 20% of the estimated direct material cost, cannot be replaced, although an alternative supplier charging 10% less has been sourced for these parts.

(2) Direct labour cost: the webcam uses 45 minutes of direct labour, which costs $34.67 per hour. The use of more standard parts, however, will mean that whilst the first unit would still be expected to take 45 minutes, there will now be an expected rate of learning of 90% (where 'b' = –0.152). This will end after the first 100 units have been completed.

(3) Rework cost: this is the average rework cost per webcam and is based on an estimate of 15% of webcams requiring rework at a cost of $20 per rework. With the use of more standard parts, the rate of reworks will fall to 10% and the cost of each rework will fall to $18.

Required:

Recalculate the estimated lifetime cost per unit for the webcam after taking into account points 1 to 3 above.

(Total: 10 marks)

198 ENVIRONMENTAL MANAGEMENT ACCOUNTING

FXT is a pharmaceutical company trying to decide whether to continue with the production of one of its drugs. On economic grounds, the decision to continue manufacture is marginal; However, in the light or recent high–profile corporate scandals linked to environmental disasters, FTX is particularly anxious to make an informed decision based mainly on the environmental effects of continued production.

Following up on a review of its operations and various reports from its Operations Director, FXT's management accountant has identified the company's main environmental costs as follows:

1   Waste disposal

2   Water consumption

3   Energy consumption

4   Transport and travel

Required:

Explain how the costs listed above arise and what control measures could be implemented by FXT in order to manage them.

(Total: 10 marks)

199 GADGET CO (DEC 10 EXAM)

The Gadget Co produces three products, A, B and C, all made from the same material. Until now, it has used traditional absorption costing to allocate overheads to its products. The company is now considering an activity based costing system in the hope that it will improve profitability. Information for the three products for the last year is as follows:

	A	B	C
Production and sales volumes (units)	15,000	12,000	18,000
Selling price per unit	$7.50	$12	$13
Raw material usage (kg) per unit	2	3	4
Direct labour hours per unit	0.1	0.15	0.2
Machine hours per unit	0.5	0.7	0.9
Number of production runs per annum	16	12	8
Number of purchase orders per annum	24	28	42
Number of deliveries to retailers per annum	48	30	62

The price for raw materials remained constant throughout the year at $1.20 per kg. Similarly, the direct labour cost for the whole workforce was $14.80 per hour. The annual overhead costs were as follows:

	$
Machine set up costs	26,550
Machine running costs	66,400
Procurement costs	48,000
Delivery costs	54,320

Required:

(a) Calculate the full cost per unit for products A, B and C under traditional absorption costing, using direct labour hours as the basis for apportionment. **(5 marks)**

(b) Calculate the full cost per unit of each product using activity based costing.

(10 marks)

(Total: 15 marks)

200   DUFF CO (JUNE 2014, ADAPTED)

Duff Co manufactures three products, X, Y and Z. Demand for products X and Y is relatively elastic whilst demand for product Z is relatively inelastic. Each product uses the same materials and the same type of direct labour but in different quantities. For many years, the company has been using full absorption costing and absorbing overheads on the basis of direct labour hours. Selling prices are then determined using cost plus pricing. This is common within this industry, with most competitors applying a standard mark-up.

Budgeted production and sales volumes for X, Y and Z for the next year are 20,000 units, 16,000 units and 22,000 units respectively.

The budgeted direct costs of the three products are shown below:

Product	X	Y	Z
	$ per unit	$ per unit	$ per unit
Direct materials	25	28	22
Direct labour ($12 per hour)	30	36	24

In the next year, Duff Co also expects to incur indirect production costs of $1,377,400, which are analysed as follows:

Cost pools	$	Cost drivers
Machine set up costs	280,000	Number of batches
Material ordering costs	316,000	Number of purchase orders
Machine running costs	420,000	Number of machine hours
General facility costs	361,400	Number of machine hours
	1,377,400	

The following additional data relate to each product:

Product	X	Y	Z
Batch size (units)	500	800	400
No of purchase orders per batch	4	5	4
Machine hours per unit	1.5	1.25	1.4

Duff Co wants to boost sales revenue in order to increase profits but its capacity to do this is limited because of its use of cost plus pricing and the application of the standard mark-up. The finance director has suggested using activity based costing (ABC) instead of full absorption costing, since this will alter the cost of the products and may therefore enable a different price to be charged.

Required:

(a) Calculate the budgeted full production cost per unit of each product using Duff Co's current method of absorption costing. All workings should be to two decimal places. **(4 marks)**

(b) Calculate the budgeted full production cost per unit of each product using activity based costing. All workings should be to two decimal places. **(11 marks)**

(Total: 15 marks)

201 THE UNIVERSAL HEALTH SYSTEM (JUNE 2012 EXAM)

The Universal Health System (UHS) provides the entire healthcare service to residents in Illopia. The UHS is funded centrally through revenues from taxpayers. However, the government is not involved in the day-to-day running of the UHS, which is largely managed regionally by a number of self-governing trusts, such as the Sickham UHS Trust.

The Sickham UHS Trust runs one hospital in Sickham and, like other trusts in Illopia, receives 70% of its income largely from the UHS' 'payments by results' scheme, which was established two years ago. Under this scheme, the trust receives a pre-set tariff (fee income) for each service it provides. If the Trust manages to provide any of its services at a lower cost than the pre-set tariff, it is allowed to use the surplus as it wishes. Similarly, it has to bear the cost of any deficits itself. Currently, the Trust knows that a number of its services simply cannot be provided at the tariff paid and accepts that these always lead to a deficit. Similarly, other services always seem to create a surplus. This is partly because different trusts define their services and account for overheads differently. Also, it is partly due to regional differences in costs, which are not taken into account by the scheme, which operates on the basis that 'one tariff fits all'.

The remaining 30% of the Trust's income comes from transplant and heart operations. Since these are not covered by the scheme, the payment the Trust receives is based on the actual costs it incurs in providing the operations. However, the Trust is not allowed to exceed the total budget provided for these operations in any one year.

Over recent years, the Trust's board of directors has become increasingly dissatisfied with the financial performance of the Trust and has blamed it on poor costing systems, leading to an inability to control costs. As a result, the finance director and his second in command – the financial controller – have now been replaced. The board of directors has taken this decision after complaining that 'the Trust simply cannot sustain the big deficit between income and spending'. The new financial controller comes from a manufacturing background and is a great advocate of target costing, believing that the introduction of a target costing system at the Sickham UHS Trust is the answer to all of its problems. The new financial director is unconvinced, believing target costing to be only really suitable in manufacturing companies.

Required:

(a) **Explain the main steps involved in developing a target price and target cost for a product in a typical manufacturing company.**   **(6 marks)**

(b) **Describe how the Sickham UHS Trust is likely, in the current circumstances, to try to derive:**

  (i)   **a target cost for the services that it provides under the 'payment by results' scheme; and**   **(2 marks)**

  (ii) **a target cost for transplants and heart operations.**   **(2 marks)**

(c) **Explain THREE of the particular difficulties that the Sickham UHS Trust may find in using target costing in its service provision.**   **(5 marks)**

                                                                          (Total: 15 marks)

202 THIN CO (JUNE 2011 EXAM)

Thin Co is a private hospital offering three types of surgical procedures known as A, B and C. Each of them uses a pre-operative injection given by a nurse before the surgery. Thin Co currently rent an operating theatre from a neighbouring government hospital. Thin Co does have an operating theatre on its premises, but it has never been put into use since it would cost $750,000 to equip. The Managing Director of Thin Co is keen to maximise profits and has heard of something called 'throughput accounting', which may help him to do this. The following information is available:

1   All patients go through a five step process, irrespective of which procedure they are having:

  •   step 1: consultation with the advisor

  •   step 2: pre-operative injection given by the nurse

  •   step 3: anaesthetic given by anaesthetist

  •   step 4: procedure performed in theatre by the surgeon

  •   step 5: recovery with the recovery specialist.

2   The price of each of procedures A, B and C is $2,700, $3,500 and $4,250 respectively.

3   The only materials' costs relating to the procedures are for the pre-operative injections given by the nurse, the anaesthetic and the dressings. These are as follows:

	Procedure A	Procedure B	Procedure C
	$ per procedure	$ per procedure	$ per procedure
Pre-operative nurse's injections	700	800	1,000
Anaesthetic	35	40	45
Dressings	5.60	5.60	5.60

4   There are five members of staff employed by Thin Co. Each works a standard 40-hour week for 47 weeks of the year, a total of 1,880 hours each per annum. Their salaries are as follows:

- Advisor: $45,000 per annum
- Nurse: $38,000 per annum
- Anaesthetist: $75,000 per annum
- Surgeon: $90,000 per annum
- Recovery specialist: $50,000 per annum.

The only other hospital costs (comparable to 'factory costs' in a traditional manufacturing environment) are general overheads, which include the theatre rental costs, and amount to $250,000 per annum.

5   Maximum annual demand for A, B and C is 600, 800 and 1,200 procedures respectively.

Time spent by each of the five different staff members on each procedure is as follows:

	Procedure A	Procedure B	Procedure C
	Hours per procedure	Hours per procedure	Hours per procedure
Advisor	0.24	0.24	0.24
Nurse	0.27	0.28	0.30
Anaesthetist	0.25	0.28	0.33
Surgeon	0.75	1	1.25
Recovery specialist	0.60	0.70	0.74

Part hours are shown as decimals e.g. 0.24 hours = 14.4 minutes (0.24 × 60). Surgeon's hours have been correctly identified as the bottleneck resource.

Required:

(a)   Calculate the throughput accounting ratio for procedure C.

Note: It is recommended that you work in hours as provided in the table rather than minutes.   **(6 marks)**

(b)   **The return per factory hour for products A, B and C has been calculated and is $2,612·53, $2,654·40 and $2559.52 respectively. The throughput accounting ratio for A, B and C has also been calculated and is 8.96, 9.11 and 8.78 respectively.**

Calculate the optimum product mix and the maximum profit per annum.   **(6 marks)**

(c)   **Briefly comment on how profit could be increased further.**   **(3 marks)**

(Total: 15 marks)

203 JOLA PUBLISHING CO (JUNE 08 EXAM)

Jola Publishing Co publishes two forms of book.: a children's book (CB), sold in large quantities to government controlled schools. The CB is produced in only four large production runs but goes through frequent government inspections and quality assurance checks. The paper used is strong, designed to resist the damage that can be caused by the young children it is produced for. The book has only a few words and relies on pictures to convey meaning.

The second book is a comprehensive technical journal (TJ), produced in monthly production runs, 12 times a year. The paper used is of relatively poor quality and is not subject to any governmental controls and consequently only a small number of inspections are carried out. The TJ uses far more machine hours than the CB in its production.

The directors are concerned about the performance of the two books and are wondering what the impact would be of a switch to an activity based costing (ABC) approach to accounting for overheads. They currently use absorption costing, based on machine hours for all overhead calculations. They have accurately produced an analysis for the accounting year just completed as follows:

	CB	TJ
	$ per unit	$ per unit
Direct production costs:		
Paper	0.75	0.08
Printing ink	1.45	4.47
Machine costs	1.15	1.95
Overheads	2.30	3.95
Total cost	5.65	10.45
Selling price	9.05	13.85
Margin	3.40	3.40

The main overheads involved are:

Overhead	% of total overhead	Activity driver
Property costs	75.0%	Machine hours
Quality control	23.0%	Number of inspections
Production set up costs	2.0%	Number of set ups

If the overheads above were re-allocated under ABC principles then the results would be that the overhead allocation to CB would be $0.05 higher and the overhead allocated to TJ would be $0.30 lower than previously.

The directors are keen to introduce ABC for the coming year and have provided the following cost and selling price data:

1 The paper used costs $2 per kg for a CB but the TJ paper costs only $1 per kg. The CB uses 400g of paper for each book, four times as much as the TJ uses.

2   Printing ink costs $30 per litre. The CB uses one third of the printing ink of the larger TJ. The TJ uses 150 ml of printing ink per book.

3   The CB needs six minutes of machine time to produce each book, whereas the TJ needs 10 minutes per book. The machines cost $12 per hour to run.

4   The sales prices are to be $9.30 for the CB and $14.00 for the TJ.

As mentioned above there are three main overheads, the data for these are:

Overhead	Annual cost for the coming year ($)
Property costs	2,160,000
Quality control	668,000
Production set up costs	52,000
Total	2,880,000

The CB will be inspected on 180 occasions next year, whereas the TJ will be inspected just 20 times. Jola Publishing will produce its annual output of 1,000,000 CBs in four production runs and approximately 10,000 TJs per month in each of 12 production runs.

Required:

(a)   Calculate the cost per unit and the margin for the CB and the TJ using machine hours to absorb the overheads.   (6 marks)

(b)   Calculate the cost per unit and the margin for the CB and the TJ using activity based costing principles to absorb the overheads.   (9 marks)

(Total: 15 marks)

204   LIFECYCLE COSTING

'Companies operating in an advanced manufacturing environment are finding that about 90% of a product's life cycle cost is determined by decisions made early in the cycle. Management accounting systems should therefore be developed that aid the planning and control of product life-cycle costs and monitor spending at the early stages of the life cycle.'

Required:

Having regard to the above statement:

(a)   Briefly explain the product life cycle concept   (2 marks)

(b)   Explain life cycle costing and state what distinguishes it from more traditional management accounting practices.   (8 marks)

(Total: 10 marks)

205 EDWARD CO (DEC 07 EXAM) *Walk in the footsteps of a top tutor*

Edward Limited assembles and sells many types of radio. It is considering extending its product range to include digital radios. These radios produce a better sound quality than traditional radios and have a large number of potential additional features not possible with the previous technologies (station scanning, more choice, one touch tuning, station identification text and song identification text etc).

A radio is produced by assembly workers assembling a variety of components. Production overheads are currently absorbed into product costs on an assembly labour hour basis.

Edward Limited is considering a target costing approach for its new digital radio product.

Required:

(a) **Briefly describe the target costing process that Edward Limited should undertake.**

(3 marks)

A selling price of $44 has been set in order to compete with a similar radio on the market that has comparable features to Edward Limited's intended product. The board have agreed that the acceptable margin (after allowing for all production costs) should be 20%.

Cost information for the new radio is as follows:

Component 1 (Circuit board) – these are bought in and cost $4.10 each. They are bought in batches of 4,000 and additional delivery costs are $2,400 per batch.

Component 2 (Wiring) – in an ideal situation 25 cm of wiring is needed for each completed radio. However, there is some waste involved in the process as wire is occasionally cut to the wrong length or is damaged in the assembly process. Edward Limited estimates that 2% of the purchased wire is lost in the assembly process. Wire costs $0.50 per metre to buy.

Other material – other materials cost $8.10 per radio.

Assembly labour – these are skilled people who are difficult to recruit and retain. Edward Limited has more staff of this type than needed but is prepared to carry this extra cost in return for the security it gives the business. It takes 30 minutes to assemble a radio and the assembly workers are paid $12.60 per hour. It is estimated that 10% of hours paid to the assembly workers is for idle time.

Production overheads – recent historic cost analysis has revealed the following production overhead data:

	Total production overhead ($)	Total assembly labour hours
Month 1	620,000	19,000
Month 2	700,000	23,000

Fixed production overheads are absorbed on an assembly hour basis based on normal annual activity levels. In a typical year 240,000 assembly hours will be worked by Edward Limited.

Required:

(b) **Calculate the expected cost per unit for the radio and identify any cost gap that might exist.**

(12 marks)

(Total: 15 marks)

Walk in the footsteps of a top tutor

For tips on approaching the question, work through the boxed notes in order.

Once each requirement has been completed review the answer detail. Use this approach to reading and answering the question when tackling other questions.

(2) New product

(1) Start by reading each requirement and allocating time (1.8 mins per mark). Now read back through the question. Make notes or annotate the question whilst reading.

Edward Limited assembles and sells many types of radio. It is considering extending its product range to include digital radios. These radios produce a better sound quality than traditional radios and have a large number of potential additional features not possible with the previous technologies (station scanning, more choice, one touch tuning, station identification text and song identification text etc).

A radio is produced by assembly workers assembling a variety of components. Production overheads are currently absorbed into product costs on an assembly labour hour basis.

(3) Traditional absorption costing

Edward Limited is considering a target costing approach for its new digital radio product.

(4) New costing approach being considered

Required:

(a) **Briefly describe the target costing process that Edward Limited should undertake.** **(3 marks)**

(5) Now answer part (a) – separate notes at end of question.

A selling price of $44 has been set in order to compete with a similar radio on the market that has comparable features to Edward Limited's intended product. The board have agreed that the acceptable margin (after allowing for all production costs) should be 20%.

(7) This is the target selling price and margin. Calculate target cost using this info.

Cost information for the new radio is as follows:

(8) Include this cost.

Component 1 (Circuit board) – these are bought in and cost $4.10 each. They bought in batches of 4,000 and additional delivery costs are $2,400 per batch.

(9) Spread this cost over the number of batches

Component 2 (Wiring) – in an ideal situation 25 cm of wiring is needed for completed radio. However, there is some waste involved in the process as w occasionally cut to the wrong length or is damaged in the assembly process. Edward Limited estimates that 2% of the purchased wire is lost in the assembly process. Wire costs $0.50 per metre to buy.

(10) Adjust usage for loss.

Other material – other materials cost $8.10 per radio.

(11) Include these costs.

Assembly labour – these are skilled people who are difficult to recruit and retain. Edward Limited has more staff of this type than needed but is prepared to carry this extra cost in return for the security it gives the business. It takes 30 minutes to assemble a radio and the assembly workers are paid $12.60 per hour. It is estimated that 10% of hours paid to the assembly workers is for idle time.

(12) Adjust hours for idle time.

Production overheads – recent historic cost analysis has revealed the following production overhead data:

(13) A mix of fixed and variable costs. Use hi-low to separate.

	Total production Overhead ($)	Total assembly labour hours
Month 1	620,000	19,000
Month 2	700,000	23,000

(6) Now read this requirement and allocate time. Read back through the remainder of the question, making notes or annotating the question in the same way as before.

Fixed production overheads are absorbed on an assembly hour basis based on normal annual activity levels. In a typical year 240,000 assembly hours will be worked by Edward Limited.

(14) Use to calculate the OAR.

(15) Now answer part (b). Set up a summary of costs with separate workings where required

Required:

(b) Calculate the expected cost per unit for the radio and identify any cost ga might exist.

(12 r

(Total: 15 r

Notes

- This is only a short scenario and so it should not take long to read and annota question. That should leave plenty of time to plan and write up the answer to requirements (a) and (b).

- Requirement (a) is worth 3 marks. Aim for 3–4 concise points. Brainstorm the key points first. Headings could be used for each key stage of the target costing process.

206 YAM CO (JUNE 09 EXAM)

 Timed question with Online tutor debrief

Yam Co is involved in the processing of sheet metal into products A, B and C using three processes, pressing, stretching and rolling. Like many businesses Yam faces tough price competition in what is a mature world market.

The factory has 50 production lines each of which contain the three processes: Raw material for the sheet metal is first pressed then stretched and finally rolled. The processing capacity varies for each process and the factory manager has provided the following data:

	Processing time per metre in hours		
	Product A	*Product B*	*Product C*
Pressing	0.50	0.50	0.40
Stretching	0.25	0.40	0.25
Rolling	0.40	0.25	0.25

The factory operates for 18 hours each day for five days per week. It is closed for only two weeks of the year for holidays when maintenance is carried out. On average one hour of labour is needed for each of the 225,000 hours of factory time. Labour is paid $10 per hour.

The raw materials cost per metre is $3.00 for product A, $2.50 for product B and $1.80 for product C. Other factory costs (excluding labour and raw materials) are $18,000,000 per year. Selling prices per metre are $70 for product A, $60 for product B and $27 for product C.

Yam carries very little inventory.

Required:

(a) Identify the bottleneck process and briefly explain why this process is described as a 'bottleneck'.
(3 marks)

(b) Calculate the throughput accounting ratio (TPAR) for each product assuming that the bottleneck process is fully utilised.
(8 marks)

(c) Assuming that the TPAR of product C is less than 1, explain how Yam could improve the TPAR of product C.
(4 marks)

(Total: 15 marks)

 Calculate your allowed time, allocate the time to the separate parts.

207 GLAM CO (DEC 2014)

Glam Co is a hairdressing salon which provides both 'cuts' and 'treatments' to clients. All cuts and treatments at the salon are carried out by one of the salon's three senior stylists. The salon also has two salon assistants and two junior stylists.

Every customer attending the salon is first seen by a salon assistant, who washes their hair; next, by a senior stylist, who cuts or treats the hair depending on which service the customer wants; then finally, a junior stylist who dries their hair. The average length of time spent with each member of staff is as follows:

	Cut	Treatment
	Hours	Hours
Assistant	0.1	0.3
Senior stylist	1	1.5
Junior stylist	0.5	0.5

The salon is open for eight hours each day for six days per week. It is only closed for two weeks each year. Staff salaries are $40,000 each year for senior stylists, $28,000 each year for junior stylists and $12,000 each year for the assistants. The cost of cleaning products applied when washing the hair is $0.60 per client. The cost of all additional products applied during a 'treatment' is $7.40 per client. Other salon costs (excluding labour and raw materials) amount to $106,400 each year.

Glam Co charges $60 for each cut and $110 for each treatment.

The senior stylists' time has been correctly identified as the bottleneck activity.

Required:

(a) Briefly explain why the senior stylists' time has been described as the 'bottleneck activity', supporting your answer with calculations. **(4 marks)**

(b) Calculate the throughput accounting ratio (TPAR) for 'cuts' and the TPAR for 'treatments' assuming the bottleneck activity is fully utilised. **(6 marks)**

(Total: 10 marks)

208 SOLAR SYSTEMS CO (DEC 2013 EXAM)

Solar Systems Co (S Co) makes two types of solar panels at its manufacturing plant: large panels for commercial customers and small panels for domestic customers. All panels are produced using the same materials, machinery and a skilled labour force. Production takes place for five days per week, from 7 am until 8 pm (13 hours), 50 weeks of the year. Each panel has to be cut, moulded and then assembled using a cutting machine (Machine C), a moulding machine (Machine M) and an assembly machine (Machine A).

As part of a government scheme to increase renewable energy sources, S Co has guaranteed not to increase the price of small or large panels for the next three years. It has also agreed to supply a minimum of 1,000 small panels each year to domestic customers for this three-year period.

Due to poor productivity levels, late orders and declining profits over recent years, the finance director has suggested the introduction of throughput accounting within the organisation, together with a 'Just in Time' system of production. Material costs and selling prices for each type of panel are shown below.

	Large panels	Small panels
	$	$
Selling price per unit	12,600	3,800
Material costs per unit	4,300	1,160

Total factory costs, which include the cost of labour and all factory overheads, are $12 million each year at the plant.

Out of the 13 hours available for production each day, workers take a one hour lunch break. For the remaining 12 hours, Machine C is utilised 85% of the time and Machines M and A are utilised 90% of the time. The unproductive time arises either as a result of routine maintenance or because of staff absenteeism, as each machine needs to be manned by skilled workers in order for the machine to run. The skilled workers are currently only trained to work on one type of machine each. Maintenance work is carried out by external contractors who provide a round the clock service (that is, they are available 24 hours a day, seven days a week), should it be required.

The following information is available for Machine M, which has been identified as the bottleneck resource:

	Large panels	Small panels
	Hours per unit	Hours per unit
Machine M	1.4	0.6

There is currently plenty of spare capacity on Machines C and A. Maximum annual demand for large panels and small panels is 1,800 units and 1,700 units respectively.

Required:

(a) Calculate the throughput accounting ratio for large panels and for small panels and explain what they indicate to S Co about production of large and small panels.

(9 marks)

(b) Suggest and discuss THREE ways in which S Co could try to increase its production capacity and hence increase throughput in the next year without making any additional investment in machinery.
(6 marks)

(Total: 15 marks)

DECISION MAKING TECHNIQUES

209 ACCESS INC

Access Inc makes electrically-driven disability scooters aimed at elderly and/or disabled customers. At present, wheels and tyres are bought from external suppliers but all other parts are manufactured in-house. The scooters have a strong reputation due mainly to innovative designs, special power units that can be recharged at home and seats that enable easy access for a wide range of disabilities. Access Inc also sells power units to other firms.

Current monthly costs are as follows:

	Seating department $	Power unit department $
Costs		
Direct materials	9,300	4,140
Direct labour	12,600	9,450
Apportioned overheads	26,700	17,200
	48,600	**30,790**
Production level	60 units	90 units

Note: The power unit department currently produces 90 units a month – 60 being used in Access' own scooters, and 30 being sold externally at $376 each. A new order has been won to supply an additional 10 scooters per month. However, the directors are considering how best to meet the additional demand:

- Sufficient capacity exists for the company to increase its monthly production to 70 scooters, except that making an extra 10 seating assemblies would require reallocation of labour and other resources from the power unit to the seating department. This would cut power unit output by 20 units per month.

- The alternative course would be to buy 10 seating assemblies from an outside supplier and fit the 10 power units from the present production of 90 units. The cheapest quote for seating assemblies is $610 per assembly.

Required:

(a) **Based on the figures given, show whether Access should make or buy the extra seats.** **(4 marks)**

(b) **Discuss what other factors should be considered before a final decision is taken to make or to buy the extra seats.** **(6 marks)**

(Total 10 marks)

210   ROBBER CO (JUNE 2012)

Robber Co manufactures control panels for burglar alarms, a very profitable product. Every product comes with a one year warranty offering free repairs if any faults arise in this period.

It currently produces and sells 80,000 units per annum, with production of them being restricted by the short supply of labour. Each control panel includes two main components – one key pad and one display screen. At present, Robber Co manufactures both of these components in-house. However, the company is currently considering outsourcing the production of keypads and/or display screens. A newly established company based in Burgistan is keen to secure a place in the market, and has offered to supply the keypads for the equivalent of $4·10 per unit and the display screens for the equivalent of $4·30 per unit. This price has been guaranteed for two years.

The current total annual costs of producing the keypads and the display screens are:

	Keypads	Display screens
Production	80,000 units	80,000 units
	$000	$000
Direct materials	160	116
Direct labour	40	60
Heat and power costs	64	88
Machine costs	26	30
Depreciation and insurance costs	84	96
Total annual production costs	374	390

Notes:

(1)   Materials costs for keypads are expected to increase by 5% in six months' time; materials costs for display screens are only expected to increase by 2%, but with immediate effect.

(2)   Direct labour costs are purely variable and not expected to change over the next year.

(3)   Heat and power costs include an apportionment of the general factory overhead for heat and power as well as the costs of heat and power directly used for the production of keypads and display screens. The general apportionment included is calculated using 50% of the direct labour cost for each component and would be incurred irrespective of whether the components are manufactured in-house or not.

(4)   Machine costs are semi-variable; the variable element relates to set up costs, which are based upon the number of batches made. The keypads' machine has fixed costs of $4,000 per annum and the display screens' machine has fixed costs of $6,000 per annum. Whilst both components are currently made in batches of 500, this would need to change, with immediate effect, to batches of 400.

(5)   60% of depreciation and insurance costs relate to an apportionment of the general factory depreciation and insurance costs; the remaining 40% is specific to the manufacture of keypads and display screens.

Required:

(a)   Advise Robber Co whether it should continue to manufacture the keypads and display screens in-house or whether it should outsource their manufacture to the supplier in Burgistan, assuming it continues to adopt a policy to limit manufacture and sales to 80,000 control panels in the coming year.   (8 marks)

(b)   Robber Co takes 0.5 labour hours to produce a keypad and 0.75 labour hours to produce a display screen. Labour hours are restricted to 100,000 hours and labour is paid at $1 per hour. Robber Co wishes to increase its supply to 100,000 control panels (i.e. 100,000 each of keypads and display screens).

Advise Robber Co as to how many units of keypads and display panels they should either manufacture and/or outsource in order to minimise their costs.   (7 marks)

(Total: 15 marks)

211   CUT AND STITCH (JUNE 10 EXAM)

Cut and Stitch (CS) make two types of suits using skilled tailors (labour) and a delicate and unique fabric (material). Both the tailors and the fabric are in short supply and so the accountant at CS has correctly produced a linear programming model to help decide the optimal production mix.

The model is as follows:

Variables:

Let W = the number of work suits produced and L = the number of lounge suits produced

Constraints

Tailors' time: $7W + 5L \leq 3,500$ (hours) – this is line T on the diagram

Fabric: $2W + 2L \leq 1,200$ (metres) – this is line F on the diagram

Production of work suits: $W \leq 400$ – this is line P on the diagram

Objective is to maximise contribution subject to:

$C = 48W + 40L$

On the diagram provided the accountant has correctly identified OABCD as the feasible region and point B as the optimal point.

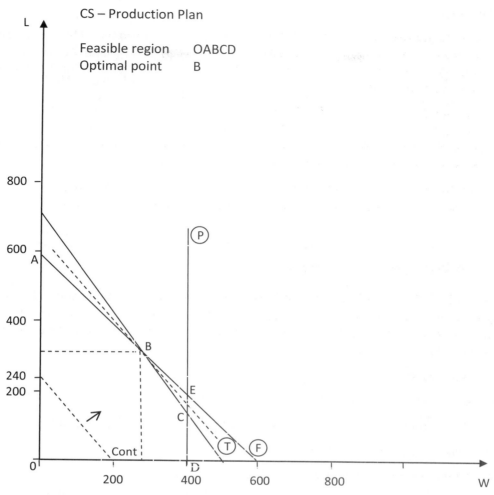

CS – Production Plan

Feasible region   OABCD
Optimal point   B

Required:

(a) **Find by appropriate calculation the optimal production mix and related maximum contribution that could be earned by CS.**
(4 marks)

(b) **Calculate the shadow prices of the fabric per metre and the tailor time per hour.**
(6 marks)

(Total: 10 marks)

212 HAMMER (JUNE 10 EXAM)

Hammer is a large garden equipment supplier with retail stores throughout Toolland. Many of the products it sells are bought in from outside suppliers but some are currently manufactured by Hammer's own manufacturing division 'Nail'.

The prices (a transfer price) that Hammer charges to the retail stores are set by head office and have been the subject of some discussion. The current policy is for Hammer to calculate the total variable cost of production and delivery and add 30% for profit. Hammer argues that all costs should be taken into consideration, offering to reduce the mark-up on costs to 10% in this case. The retail stores are unhappy with the current pricing policy arguing that it results in prices that are often higher than comparable products available on the market.

Hammer has provided the following information to enable a price comparison to be made of the two possible pricing policies for one of its products.

Garden shears

Steel: the shears have 0.4 kg of high quality steel in the final product. The manufacturing process loses 5% of all steel put in. Steel costs $4,000 per tonne (1 tonne = 1,000 kg)

Other materials are bought in and have a list price of $3 per kg although Hammer secures a 10% volume discount on all purchases. The shears require 0.1 kg of these materials.

The labour time to produce shears is 0.25 hours per unit and labour costs $10 per hour.

Variable overheads are absorbed at the rate of 150% of labour rates and fixed overheads are 80% of the variable overheads.

Delivery is made by an outsourced distributor that charges Nail $0.50 per garden shear.

Required:

(a) **Calculate the price that Hammer would charge for the garden shears under the existing policy of variable cost plus 30%.** **(6 marks)**

(b) **Calculate the change in price if the pricing policy switched to total cost plus 10%.**

(4 marks)

(Total: 10 marks)

213 CHAIR CO (DEC 2014)

Chair Co has developed a new type of luxury car seat. The estimated labour time for the first unit is 12 hours but a learning curve of 75% is expected to apply for the first eight units produced. The cost of labour is $15 per hour. The cost of materials and other variable overheads is expected to total $230 per unit.

Chair Co plans on pricing the seat by adding a 50% mark-up to the total variable cost per seat, with the labour cost being based on the incremental time taken to produce the 8th unit.

Required:

(a) **Calculate the price which Chair Co expects to charge for the new seat.**

   Note: The learning index for a 75% learning curve is –0.415. **(5 marks)**

(b) The first phase of production has now been completed for the new car seat. The first unit actually took 12.5 hours to make and the total time for the first eight units was 34.3 hours, at which point the learning effect came to an end. Chair Co are planning on adjusting the price to reflect the actual time it took to complete the 8th unit.

   Required:

   (i) **Calculate the actual rate of learning and state whether this means that the labour force actually learnt more quickly or less quickly than expected.**

   (3 marks)

   (ii) **Briefly explain whether the adjusted price charged by Chair Co will be higher or lower than the price you calculated in part (a) above. You are NOT required to calculate the adjusted price.** **(2 marks)**

(Total: 10 marks)

214 HEAT ONE CO (JUNE 2011 EXAM)

Heat Co specialises in the production of a range of air conditioning appliances for industrial premises. It is about to launch a new product, the 'Energy Buster', a unique air conditioning unit which is capable of providing unprecedented levels of air conditioning using a minimal amount of electricity. Heat Co is now trying to ascertain the best pricing policy that they should adopt for the Energy Buster's launch onto the market. Demand is very responsive to price changes and research has established that, for every $15 increase in price, demand would be expected to fall by 1,000 units. If the company set the price at $735, only 1,000 units would be demanded.

The costs of producing each air conditioning unit are as follows:

	$	
Direct materials	42	
Labour	12	(1.5 hours at $8 per hour. See note below)
Fixed overheads	6	(based on producing 50,000 units per annum)
Total cost	**60**	

Note

The first air conditioning unit took 1.5 hours to make and labour cost $8 per hour. A 95% learning curve exists, in relation to production of the unit, although the learning curve is expected to finish after making 100 units. Heat Co's management have said that any pricing decisions about the Energy Buster should be based on the time it takes to make the 100th unit of the product. You have been told that the learning co-efficient, $b = -0.0740005$.

All other costs are expected to remain the same up to the maximum demand levels.

Required:

(a) (i) Establish the demand function (equation) for air conditioning units

(3 marks)

(ii) Calculate the marginal cost for each air conditioning unit after adjusting the labour cost as required by the note above

(6 marks)

(iii) Equate marginal cost and marginal revenue in order to calculate the optimum price and quantity.

(3 marks)

(b) Explain why market skimming may be a suitable pricing strategy for Heat Co when launching the Energy Buster

(3 marks)

(Total: 15 marks)

215 TWO CO (JUNE 2011 EXAM)

Two Co specialises in the production of a range of air conditioning appliances for industrial premises. It is about to launch a new product, the 'Energy Buster', a unique air conditioning unit which is capable of providing unprecedented levels of air conditioning using a minimal amount of electricity. The technology used in the Energy Buster is unique so Two Co has patented it so that no competitors can enter the market for two years. The company's development costs have been high and it is expected that the product will only have a five-year life cycle.

Two Co is now trying to ascertain the best pricing policy that they should adopt for the Energy Buster's launch onto the market. Demand is very responsive to price changes.

Note

A 95% learning curve exists, in relation to production of the unit, although the learning curve is expected to finish after making 100 units.

All other costs are expected to remain the same up to the maximum demand levels.

Required:

Explain what is meant by a 'penetration pricing' strategy and a 'market skimming' strategy and discuss whether either strategy might be suitable for Two Co when launching the Energy Buster.

(Total: 10 marks)

216 CAM CO PRICING (JUNE 2013 EXAM)

Cam Co manufactures webcams, devices which can provide live video and audio streams via personal computers. It has recently been suffering from liquidity problems and hopes that these will be eased by the launch of its new webcam, which has revolutionary audio sound and visual quality. The webcam is expected to have a product life cycle of two years. Market research has already been carried out to establish a target selling price and projected lifetime sales volumes for the product. Cost estimates have also been prepared, based on the current proposed product specification. Cam Co uses life cycle costing to work out the target costs for its products, believing it to be more accurate to use an average cost across the whole lifetime of a product, rather than potentially different costs for different years. The average market price for a webcam is currently $150.

Required:

Explain the 'market skimming' (also known as 'price skimming') pricing strategy and discuss, as far as the information allows, whether this strategy may be more appropriate for Cam Co than charging one price throughout the webcam's entire life.

(Total: 10 marks)

217 PROCESS CO (DEC 2013 EXAM)

Process Co has two divisions, A and B. Division A produces three types of chemicals: products L, M and S, using a common process. Each of the products can either be sold by Division A to the external market at split-off point (after the common process is complete) or can be transferred to Division B for individual further processing into products LX, MX and SX.

In November 2013, which is a typical month, Division A's output was as follows:

Product	Kg
L	1,200
M	1,400
S	1,800

The market selling prices per kg for the products, both at split-off point and after further processing, are as follows:

	$		$
L	5.60	LX	6.70
M	6.50	MX	7.90
S	6.10	SX	6.80

The specific costs for each of the individual further processes are:

Variable cost of $0.50 per kg of LX

Variable cost of $0.70 per kg of MX

Variable cost of $0.80 per kg of SX

Further processing leads to a normal loss of 5% at the beginning of the process for each of the products being processed.

Required:

Calculate and conclude whether any of the products should be further processed in Division B in order to optimise the profit for the company as a whole.

(Total: 10 marks)

218 FURNIVAL

Furnival has a distillation plant that produces three joint products, P, Q and R, in the proportions 10:5:5. After the split-off point the products can be sold for industrial use or they can be taken to the mixing plant for blending and refining. The latter procedure is normally followed.

For a typical week, in which all the output is processed in the mixing plant, the following income statement can be prepared:

	Product P	Product Q	Product R
Sales volume (gallons)	1,000	500	500
Price per gallon ($)	12.50	20	10
Sales revenue ($)	12,500	10,000	5,000
	——	——	——
Joint process cost ($)			
(apportioned using output volume)	5,000	2,500	2,500
Mixing plant cost ($):			
Process costs	3,000	3,000	3,000
Other separable costs	2,000	500	500
	——	——	——
Total costs ($)	10,000	6,000	6,000
	——	——	——
Profit/(loss) ($)	2,500	4,000	(1,000)
	——	——	——

The joint process costs are 25% fixed and 75% variable, whereas the mixing plant costs are 10% fixed and 90% variable and all the 'other separable costs' are variable. If the products had been sold at the split-off point the selling price per gallon would have been:

	Product P	Product Q	Product R
	$5.00	$6.00	$1.50

There are only 45 hours available per week in the mixing plant. Typically 30 hours are taken up with the processing of Product P, Q and R (10 hours for each product line) and 15 hours are used for other work that generates (on average) a profit of $200 per hour after being charged with a proportionate share of the plant's costs (including fixed costs). The manager of the mixing plant considers that he could sell all the plant's processing time externally at a price that would provide this rate of profit. It has been suggested:

(i)   that, since Product R regularly makes a loss, it should be sold off at the split-off point

(ii)   that it might be possible advantageously to change the mix of products achieved in the distillation plant. It is possible to change the output proportions to 7:8:5 at a cost of $1 for each additional gallon of Q produced by the distillation plant.

Required:

Compare the costs and benefits for each of the above proposals. Recommend, for each proposal, whether it should or should not be implemented.

(i)   **Sell off R at the split-off point**   **(6 marks)**

(ii)   **Change the mix of products achieved in the distillation plant**   **(9 marks)**

(Total: 15 marks)

219   THEATRE

A theatre has a seating capacity of 500 people and is considering engaging MS and her orchestra for a concert for one night only. The fee that would be charged by MS would be $10,000. If the theatre engages MS, then this sum is payable regardless of the size of the theatre audience.

Based on past experience of events of this type, the price of the theatre ticket would be $25 per person. The size of the audience for this event is uncertain, but based on past experience it is expected to be as follows:

	Probability
300 people	50%
400 people	30%
500 people	20%

In addition to the sale of the theatre tickets, it can be expected that members of the audience will also purchase confectionery both prior to the performance and during the interval. The contribution that this would yield to the theatre is unclear, but has been estimated as follows:

Contribution from confectionery sales	*Probability*
Contribution of $3 per person	30%
Contribution of $5 per person	50%
Contribution of $10 per person	20%

Required:

(a)   **Using expected values as the basis of your decision, advise the theatre management whether it is financially worthwhile to engage MS for the concert.**

(5 marks)

(b)   **Prepare a two-way data table to show the profit values that could occur from deciding to engage MS for the concert.**   **(5 marks)**

(Total: 10 marks)

220 AMELIE

Amelie is setting up in business importing French cheeses. She could open up a small shop, a large outlet, or no shop at all if she decides to sell online only (which she won't be able to do for another few years at least.) There will be a 5 year lease on a few shops currently available in the centre of town, and Amelie wants to make the correct decision.

Amelie is also thinking about hiring a consultant to conduct a market research study. If the study is conducted, the results could indicate that the cheese market is either favourable or unfavourable.

Amelie believes there is a 50-50 chance that the market will be favourable, and expects her profits to be as follows if she opens her shop:

	Favourable market	Unfavourable market
Large shop	$60,000	($40,000) loss
Small shop	$30,000	($10,000) loss

The consultant has quoted a charge of $5,000 for the marketing research. He has also hinted that there is a 0.6 probability that the survey will indicate that the cheese market would be favourable.

There is a 0.9 probability that the cheese market will be favourable given a favourable outcome from the study. The consultant warned Amelie that there is only a probability of 0.12 of a favourable market if the marketing research results are not favourable. Amelie is confused.

Required:

(a)   Develop a decision tree for Amelie.   **(4 marks)**

(b)   Explain why Amelie should hire the market research consultant?   **(3 marks)**

(c)   After discussing the competence of the consultant with another business owner, Amelie now believes that she'd rather contact another market research company which guarantees perfect information concerning the cheese market profitability.

Calculate the value of this perfect information.   **(3 marks)**

                                                            (Total: 10 marks)

221 HI LIFE CO (DEC 2014 EXAM)

The Hi Life Co (HL Co) makes sofas. It has recently received a request from a customer to provide a one-off order of sofas, in excess of normal budgeted production. The order would need to be completed within two weeks. The following cost estimate has already been prepared:

Direct materials:		Note	$
Fabric	200 m^2 at $17 per m^2	1	3,400
Wood	50 m at $8.20 per m^2	2	410
Direct labour:			
Skilled	200 hours at $16 per hour	3	3,200
Semi-skilled	300 hours at $12 per hour	4	3,600
Factory overheads	500 hours at $3 per hour	5	1,500
Total production cost			12,110
Administration overheads at 10% of total production cost		6	1,211
Total cost			13,321

Notes

1   The fabric is regularly used by HL Co. There are currently 300 m^2 in inventory, which cost $17 per m^2. The current purchase price of the fabric is $17.50 per m^2.

2   This type of wood is regularly used by HL Co and usually costs $8.20 per m^2. However, the company's current supplier's earliest delivery time for the wood is in three weeks' time. An alternative supplier could deliver immediately but they would charge $8.50 per m^2. HL Co already has 500 m^2 in inventory but 480 m^2 of this is needed to complete other existing orders in the next two weeks. The remaining 20 m^2 is not going to be needed until four weeks' time.

3   The skilled labour force is employed under permanent contracts of employment under which they must be paid for 40 hours' per week's labour, even if their time is idle due to absence of orders. Their rate of pay is $16 per hour, although any overtime is paid at time and a half. In the next two weeks, there is spare capacity of 150 labour hours.

4   There is no spare capacity for semi-skilled workers. They are currently paid $12 per hour or time and a half for overtime. However, a local agency can provide additional semi-skilled workers for $14 per hour.

5   The $3 absorption rate is HL Co's standard factory overhead absorption rate; $1.50 per hour reflects the cost of the factory supervisor's salary and the other $1.50 per hour reflects general factory costs. The supervisor is paid an annual salary and is also paid $15 per hour for any overtime he works. He will need to work 20 hours' overtime if this order is accepted.

6   This is an apportionment of the general administration overheads incurred by HL Co.

Required:

Prepare, on a relevant cost basis, the lowest cost estimate which could be used as the basis for the quotation. Explain briefly your reasons for including or excluding each of the costs in your estimate.

(Total: 10 marks)

222   THE TELEPHONE COMPANY (DEC 2011 EXAM)

The Telephone Co (T Co) is a company specialising in the provision of telephone systems for commercial clients. There are two parts to the business:

- installing telephone systems in businesses, either first time installations or replacement installations

- supporting the telephone systems with annually renewable maintenance contracts.

T Co has been approached by a potential customer, Push Co, who wants to install a telephone system in new offices it is opening. Whilst the job is not a particularly large one, T Co is hopeful of future business in the form of replacement systems and support contracts for Push Co. T Co is therefore keen to quote a competitive price for the job. The following information should be considered:

(1)   One of the company's salesmen has already been to visit Push Co, to give them a demonstration of the new system, together with a complimentary lunch, the costs of which totalled $400.

(2)   The installation is expected to take one week to complete and would require three engineers, each of whom is paid a monthly salary of $4,000. The engineers have just had their annually renewable contract renewed with T Co. One of the three engineers has spare capacity to complete the work, but the other two would have to be moved from contract X in order to complete this one. Contract X generates a contribution of $5 per engineer hour. There are no other engineers available to continue with Contract X if these two engineers are taken off the job. It would mean that T Co would miss its contractual completion deadline on Contract X by one week. As a result, T Co would have to pay a one-off penalty of $500. Since there is no other work scheduled for their engineers in one week's time, it will not be a problem for them to complete Contract X at this point.

(3)   T Co's technical advisor would also need to dedicate eight hours of his time to the job. He is working at full capacity, so he would have to work overtime in order to do this. He is paid an hourly rate of $40 and is paid for all overtime at a premium of 50% above his usual hourly rate.

(4)   Two visits would need to be made by the site inspector to approve the completed work. He is an independent contractor who is not employed by T Co, and charges Push Co directly for the work. His cost is $200 for each visit made.

(5)   T Co's system trainer would need to spend one day at Push Co delivering training. He is paid a monthly salary of $1,500 but also receives commission of $125 for each day spent delivering training at a client's site.

(6)   120 telephone handsets would need to be supplied to Push Co. The current cost of these is $18.20 each, although T Co already has 80 handsets in inventory. These were bought at a price of $16.80 each. The handsets are the most popular model on the market and frequently requested by T Co's customers.

(7)   Push Co would also need a computerised control system called 'Swipe 2'. The current market price of Swipe 2 is $10,800, although T Co has an older version of the system, 'Swipe 1', in inventory, which could be modified at a cost of $4,600. T Co paid $5,400 for Swipe 1 when it ordered it in error two months ago and has no other use for it. The current market price of Swipe 1 is $5,450, although if T Co tried to sell the one they have, it would be deemed to be 'used' and therefore only worth $3,000.

(8)   1,000 metres of cable would be required to wire up the system. The cable is used frequently by T Co and it has 200 metres in inventory, which cost $1.20 per metre. The current market price for the cable is $1.30 per metre.

(9)   You should assume that there are four weeks in each month and that the standard working week is 40 hours long.

Required:

Prepare a cost statement, using relevant costing principles, showing the minimum cost that T Co should charge for the contract. Make DETAILED notes showing how each cost has been arrived at and EXPLAINING why each of the costs above has been included or excluded from your cost statement.

(Total: 15 marks)

223   CHOCOLATES ARE FOREVER (CAF)

CAF Ltd produces a single large item of confectionary, Product S, that is sold for $12 per unit.   You have been provided with the following information about the 'S' for the forthcoming year:

Sales: 6,000 units   Variable costs: $7 per unit

CAF's overheads are budgeted to amount to $20,000. CAF's Financial Director has asked you to prepare some documents for a presentation to the Board of Directors.

Required:

(a)   **Calculate, and briefly explain the significance of, CAF'S breakeven point and margin of safety, expressed as a percentage.**   **(3 marks)**

(b)   **Based on CAF's information above, construct and explain the purpose of the two following charts:**

   (1)   **A breakeven chart**

   (2)   **A profit – volume chart.**   **(12 marks)**

(Total: 15 marks)

224   FOTO FRAMES PLC

Foto Frames Plc. makes digital photo viewing frames which it sells to retailers for $25 per frame. Retailers typically sell the frames to consumers for $40 each.

Budgeted production for the forthcoming period is 200,000 frames. Budgeted fixed overheads are $2.4 million. Variable cost per frame is expected to be $6.50.

Retailers have started to use their buyer power over Foto Frames Plc. and have begun to demand a discount off the existing price charged to them. The directors of Foto Frames plc. are concerned that they may lose business if they do not offer some sort of discount to their customers and have asked for advice from a market research consultancy, firm.

The consultants have suggested that Foto Frames Plc. need to decrease the selling price charged to retailers by at least 10% if they are to retain their existing customers. However, they believe that Foto Frames Plc. can use some buyer power of their own over supplier of materials such that the variable cost per frame would fall by 5%.

Required:

(a)   Calculate the breakeven point in terms of units and sales revenue, and the margin of safety based upon the existing selling price and variable cost per frame.

(3 marks)

(b)   Draw the Profit/Volume chart based upon the existing selling price and variable cost per frame.

(3 marks)

(c)   Calculate the new breakeven point in terms of units and sales revenue, and the new margin of safety, assuming the company not only decreases the selling price by 10% but also uses its own buyer power over its suppliers and secure a 5% reduction in variable cost per frame.

(2 marks)

(d)   By how many units has the breakeven point changed?

(2 marks)

(Total: 10 marks)

225   HAIR CO (DEC 12 EXAM)

Hair Co manufactures three types of electrical goods for hair: curlers (C), straightening irons (S) and dryers (D.) The budgeted sales prices and volumes for the next year are as follows:

	C	S	D
Selling price	$110	$160	$120
Units	20,000	22,000	26,000

Each product is made using a different mix of the same materials and labour. Product S also uses new revolutionary technology for which the company obtained a ten-year patent two years ago. The budgeted sales volumes for all the products have been calculated by adding 10% to last year's sales.

The standard cost card for each product is shown below.

	C	S	D
	$	$	$
Material 1	12	28	16
Material 2	8	22	26
Skilled labour	16	34	22
Unskilled labour	14	20	28

Both skilled and unskilled labour costs are variable.

The general fixed overheads are expected to be $640,000 for the next year.

Required:

(a)   Calculate the weighted average contribution to sales ratio for Hair Co.

Note: round all workings to 2 decimal places.   (6 marks)

(b)   Using the graph paper provided, draw a multi-product profit-volume (PV) chart showing clearly the profit/loss lines assuming:

(i)   you are able to sell the products in order of the ones with the highest ranking contribution to sales ratios first; and

(ii)   you sell the products in a constant mix.

Note: only one graph is required.   (9 marks)

(Total: 15 marks)

226 MANGO LEATHER

Mango has been in the clothing market for the last 3 years and operates in an industry which is very competitive and volatile. Mango's management accountant has heard that break even analysis could be used to assess the risks of the business and helps decision making.

The following information on Mango and its product portfolio is also available – figures are per annum:

Products	Production/sales volume	Selling price (per unit)	Variable cost(excluding material cost) per unit	Material (leather) per unit
		$	$	(Meters)
Bags	1,000	400	150	1
Belts	2,000	125	50	0.25
Shoes	1,500	150	65	0.5
Jackets	3,500	300	125	1.5

Leather is regularly used in the production of all the products above. The company has recently discovered that there is likely to be a shortage of leather on the market for the coming year. Leather used in production is bought from a supplier on a JIT basis for $60 per meter. For now, enough material can be sourced from the supplier to satisfy the production requirement. Fixed cost per annum is $580,000.

Required:

(a) Calculate the break even sales revenue. **(2 marks)**

(b) Draw a profit volume chart by clearly showing all the workings to arrive at the graph. **(8 marks)**

(c) Explain how the unavailability of leather and the rise in its price affect the profitability and breakeven point of Mango. No calculation is required. **(5 marks)**

(Total: 15 marks)

227 B CHEMICALS *Online question assistance*

B Chemicals refines crude oil into petrol. The refining process uses two types of crude oil – heavy and light. A mixture of these oils is blended into either Super or Regular petrol.

In the refining process one gallon (g) of Super is made from 0.7 g of heavy crude and 0.5 g of light crude. One gallon of Regular is made from 0.5 g of heavy crude and 0.7 g of light crude oil. (There is a refining loss of 0.2 g in each case.)

At present, 5,000 g of heavy crude and 6,000 g of light crude oil are available for refining each day. Market conditions suggest that at least two-thirds of the petrol refined should be Super. The company makes contribution of $0.25 per gallon of Super and $0.10 per gallon of Regular.

Required:

(a) State the objective function and three constraints, one for heavy crude, one for light crude and one for market conditions. (4 marks)

(b) Graph the constraints and shade the feasible region. (6 marks)

(c) Deduce the optimal policy and the contribution generated, and comment briefly on your answer. (5 marks)

(Total: 15 marks)

 Online question assistance

228 TABLET CO (JUNE 2014, ADAPTED)

Tablet Co makes two types of tablet computer, the Xeno (X) and the Yong (Y). X currently generates a contribution of $30 per unit and Y generates a contribution of $40 per unit. There are three main stages of production: the build stage, the program stage and the test stage. Each of these stages requires the use of skilled labour which, due to a huge increase in demand for tablet computers over recent months, is now in short supply. The following information is available for the two products:

Stage	Xeno (X)	Yong (Y)
	Minutes per unit	Minutes per unit
Build ($10 per hour)	24	20
Program ($16 per hour)	16	14
Test ($12 per hour)	10	4

Tablet Co is now preparing its detailed production plans for the next quarter. During this period it expects that the skilled labour available will be 30,000 hours (1,800,000 minutes) for the build stage, 28,000 hours (1,680,000 minutes) for the program stage and 12,000 hours (720,000 minutes) for the test stage. The maximum demand for X and Y over the three-month period is expected to be 85,000 units and 66,000 units respectively. Fixed costs are $650,000 per month.

Due to rapid technological change, the company holds no inventory of finished goods.

Required:

On the graph paper provided, use linear programming to calculate the optimum number of each product which Tablet Co should make in the next quarter assuming it wishes to maximise contribution. Calculate the total profit for the quarter.

(Total: 15 marks)

229 COSMETICS CO (DEC 10 EXAM)

The Cosmetic Co is a company producing a variety of cosmetic creams and lotions. The creams and lotions are sold to a variety of retailers at a price of $23.20 for each jar of face cream and $16.80 for each bottle of body lotion. Each of the products has a variety of ingredients, with the key ones being silk powder, silk amino acids and aloe vera. Six months ago, silk worms were attacked by disease causing a huge reduction in the availability of silk powder and silk amino acids. The Cosmetic Co had to dramatically reduce production and make part of its workforce, which it had trained over a number of years, redundant.

The company now wants to increase production again by ensuring that it uses the limited ingredients available to maximise profits by selling the optimum mix of creams and lotions. Due to the redundancies made earlier in the year, supply of skilled labour is now limited in the short-term to 160 hours (9,600 minutes) per week, although unskilled labour is unlimited. The purchasing manager is confident that they can obtain 5,000 grams of silk powder and 1,600 grams of silk amino acids per week. All other ingredients are unlimited.

The following information is available for the two products:

	Cream	Lotion
Materials required: silk powder (at $2.20 per gram)	3 grams	2 grams
– silk amino acids (at $0.80 per gram)	1 gram	0.5 grams
– aloe vera (at $1.40 per gram)	4 grams	2 grams
Labour required: skilled ($12 per hour)	4 minutes	5 minutes
– unskilled (at $8 per hour)	3 minutes	1.5 minutes

Each jar of cream sold generates a contribution of $9 per unit, whilst each bottle of lotion generates a contribution of $8 per unit. The maximum demand for lotions is 2,000 bottles per week, although demand for creams is unlimited. Fixed costs total $1,800 per week. The company does not keep inventory although if a product is partially complete at the end of one week, its production will be completed in the following week.

Required:

Use linear programming to calculate the optimum number of each product that the Cosmetic Co should make per week, assuming that it wishes to maximise contribution.

Calculate the total contribution per week for the new production plan.

All workings MUST be rounded to 2 decimal places.

(15 marks)

230 STAY CLEAN (DEC 09 EXAM)

Stay Clean manufactures and sells a small range of kitchen equipment. Specifically the product range contains a dishwasher (DW), a washing machine (WM) and a tumble dryer (TD). The TD is of a rather old design and has for some time generated negative contribution. It is widely expected that in one year's time the market for this design of TD will cease, as people switch to a washing machine that can also dry clothes after the washing cycle has completed.

Stay Clean is trying to decide whether or not to cease the production of TD now *or* in 12 months' time when the new combined washing machine/drier will be ready. To help with this decision the following information has been provided.

(1)   The normal selling prices, annual sales volumes and total variable costs for the three products are as follows:

	DW	WM	TD
Selling price per unit	$200	$350	$80
Material cost per unit	$70	$100	$50
Labour cost per unit	$50	$80	$40
Contribution per unit	$80	$170	–$10
Annual sales	5,000 units	6,000 units	1,200 units

(2)   It is thought that some of the customers that buy a TD also buy a DW and a WM. It is estimated that 5% of the sales of WM and DW will be lost if the TD ceases to be produced.

(3)   All the direct labour force currently working on the TD will be made redundant immediately if TD is ceased now. This would cost $6,000 in redundancy payments. If Stay Clean waited for 12 months the existing labour force would be retained and retrained at a cost of $3,500 to enable them to produce the new washing/drying product. Recruitment and training costs of labour in 12 months' time would be $1,200 in the event that redundancy takes place now.

(4)   Stay Clean operates a just in time (JIT) policy and so all material cost would be saved on the TD for 12 months if TD production ceased now. Equally, the material costs relating to the lost sales on the WM and the DW would also be saved. However, the material supplier has a volume based discount scheme in place as follows:

Total annual expenditure ($)	Discount
0–600,000	0%
600,001–800,000	1%
800,001–900,000	2%
900,001–960,000	3%
960,001 and above	5%

Stay Clean uses this supplier for all its materials for all the products it manufactures. The figures given above in the cost per unit table for material cost per unit are net of any discount Stay Clean already qualifies for.

(5)   The space in the factory currently used for the TD will be sublet for 12 months on a short-term lease contract if production of TD stops now. The income from that contract will be $12,000.

(6)   The supervisor (currently classed as an overhead) supervises the production of all three products spending approximately 20% of his time on the TD production. He would continue to be fully employed if the TD ceases to be produced now.

Required:

(a)   **Calculate whether or not it is worthwhile ceasing to produce the TD now rather than waiting 12 months (ignore any adjustment to allow for the time value of money).**
                                                                                    (13 marks)

(b)   **Explain a pricing strategy that could be used to improve the financial position of the business in the next 12 months assuming that the TD continues to be made in that period.**
                                                                                    (2 marks)

                                                                                    (Total: 15 marks)

231 HS EQUATION

HS manufactures components for use in computers. The business operates in a highly competitive market where there are a large number of manufacturers of similar components. HS is considering its pricing strategy for the next 12 weeks for one of its components. The Managing Director seeks your advice to determine the selling price that will maximise the profit to be made during this period.

You have been given the following data:

Market demand

The current selling price of the component is $1,350 and at this price the average weekly demand over the last four weeks has been 8,000 components. An analysis of the market shows that, for every $50 increase in selling price, the demand reduces by 1,000 components per week. Equally, for every $50 reduction in selling price, the demand increases by 1,000 components per week.

Costs

The direct material cost of each component is $270. This price is part of a fixed price contract with the material suppliers and the contract does not expire for another year.

Production labour and conversion costs, together with other overhead costs and the corresponding output volumes, have been collected for the last four weeks and they are as follows:

Week	Output volume (units)	$000
1	9,400	7,000
2	7,600	5,688
3	8,500	6,334
4	7,300	5,446

No significant changes in cost behaviour are expected over the next 12 weeks.

Required:

(a) Calculate the optimum (profit-maximising) selling price of the component for the period. **(10 marks)**

(b) Identify and explain three reasons why it may be inappropriate for HS to use this theoretical pricing model in practice. **(5 marks)**

(Total: 15 marks)

232 MKL

Product 'M' is currently being tested by MKL and is to be launched in ten weeks' time. The 'M' is an innovative product which the company believes will change the entire market. The company has decided to use a market skimming approach to pricing this product during its introduction stage.

MKL continually reviews its product range and enhances its existing products by developing new models to satisfy the demands of its customers. The company intends to always have products at each stage of the product life cycle to ensure the company's continued presence in the market.

MKL is currently reviewing its two existing flagship products, Product K and Product L. You have been given the following information:

- Product K was introduced to the market some time ago and is now about to enter the maturity stage of its life cycle. The maturity stage is expected to last for ten weeks. Each unit has a variable cost of $38 and takes 1 standard hour to produce. The Managing Director is unsure which of four possible prices the company should charge during the next ten weeks. The following table shows the results of some market research into the level of weekly demand at alternative prices:

Selling price per unit	$100	$85	$80	$75
Weekly demand (units)	600	800	1,200	1,400

- Product L was introduced to the market two months ago using a penetration pricing policy and is now about to enter its growth stage. This stage is expected to last for 20 weeks. Each unit has a variable cost of $45 and takes 1.25 standard hours to produce. Market research has indicated that there is a linear relationship between its selling price and the number of units demanded, of the form $P = a - bx$. At a selling price of $100 per unit demand is expected to be 1,000 units per week. For every $10 increase in selling price the weekly demand will reduce by 200 units and for every $10 decrease in selling price the weekly demand will increase by 200 units.

The company currently has a production facility which has a capacity of 2,000 standard hours per week. This facility is being expanded but the extra capacity will not be available for ten weeks.

Required:

(a) **Calculate which of the four selling prices should be charged for product K, in order to maximise its contribution during its maturity stage** **(6 marks)**

(b) **Following on from your answer above in (a), calculate the selling price of product L during its growth stage.** **(9 marks)**

(Total: 15 marks)

233 GAM CO (JUNE 2014, ADAPTED)

Gam Co sells electronic equipment and is about to launch a new product onto the market. It needs to prepare its budget for the coming year and is trying to decide whether to launch the product at a price of $30 or $35 per unit.

The following information has been obtained from market research:

Price per unit $30		Price per unit $35	
Probability	Sales volume	Probability	Sales volume
0.4	120,000	0.3	108,000
0.5	110,000	0.3	100,000
0.1	140,000	0.4	94,000

Notes:

1   Variable production costs would be $12 per unit for production volumes up to and including 100,000 units each year. However, if production exceeds 100,000 units each year, the variable production cost per unit would fall to $11 for all units produced.

2   Advertising costs would be $900,000 per annum at a selling price of $30 and $970,000 per annum at a price of $35.

3   Fixed production costs would be $450,000 per annum.

Required:

(a)   **Calculate each of the six possible profit outcomes which could arise for Gam Co in the coming year.**   **(7 marks)**

(b)   **Calculate the expected value of profit for each of the two price options and recommend, on this basis, which option Gam Co would choose.**   **(3 marks)**

(Total: 10 marks)

234   GYM BUNNIES (JUNE 2013 EXAM)

Gym Bunnies (GB) is a health club. It currently has 6,000 members, with each member paying a subscription fee of $720 per annum. The club is comprised of a gym, a swimming pool and a small exercise studio.

A competitor company is opening a new gym in GB's local area, and this is expected to cause a fall in GB's membership numbers, unless GB can improve its own facilities. Consequently, GB is considering whether or not to expand its exercise studio in a hope to improve its membership numbers. Any improvements are expected to last for three years.

Option 1

No expansion. In this case, membership numbers would be expected to fall to 5,250 per annum for the next three years. Operational costs would stay at their current level of $80 per member per annum.

Option 2

Expand the exercise studio. The capital cost of this would be $360,000. The expected effect on membership numbers for the next three years is as follows:

Probability	Effect on membership numbers
0.4	Remain at their current level of 6,000 members per annum
0.6	Increase to 6,500 members per annum

The effect on operational costs for the next three years is expected to be:

Probability	Effect on operational costs
0.5	Increase to $120 per member per annum
0.5	Increase to $180 per member per annum

Required:

(a)   **Using the criterion of expected value, prepare and fully label a decision tree that shows the two options available to GB. Recommend the decision that GB should make.**

Note: Ignore time value of money.   **(12 marks)**

(b)   **Briefly discuss the problems of using expected values for decisions of this nature.**

(3 marks)

(Total: 15 marks)

235 RECYC

Recyc plc is a company which reprocesses factory waste in order to extract good quality aluminium. Information concerning its operations is as follows:

(1) Recyc plc places an advance order each year for chemical X for use in the aluminium extraction process. It will enter into an advance contract for the coming year for chemical X at one of three levels – high, medium or low, which correspond to the requirements of a high, medium or low level of waste available for reprocessing.

(2) The level of waste available will not be known when the advance order for chemical X is entered into. A set of probabilities have been estimated by management as to the likelihood of the quantity of waste being at a high, medium or low level.

(3) Where the advance order entered into for chemical X is lower than that required for the level of waste for processing actually received, a discount from the original demand price is allowed by the supplier for the total quantity of chemical X actually required.

(4) Where the advance order entered into for chemical X is in excess of that required to satisfy the actual level of waste for reprocessing, a penalty payment in excess of the original demand price is payable for the total quantity of chemical X actually required.

A summary of the information relating to the above points is as follows:

			Chemical X costs per kg		
Level of reprocessing	Waste available 000 kg	Probability	Advance order $	Conversion discount $	Conversion premium $
High	50,000	0.30	1.00		
Medium	38,000	0.50	1.20		
Low	30,000	0.20	1.40		
Chemical X: order conversion:					
Low to medium				0.10	
Medium to high				0.10	
Low to high				0.15	
Medium to low					0.25
High to medium					0.25
High to low					0.60

Aluminium is sold at $0.65 per kg. Variable costs (excluding chemical X costs) are 70% of sales revenue. Aluminium extracted from the waste is 15% of the waste input. Chemical X is added to the reprocessing at the rate of 1 kg per 100 kg of waste.

Required:

(a) **Prepare a summary which shows the budgeted contribution earned by Recyc plc for the coming year for each of nine possible outcomes.** **(10 marks)**

(b) **State the contribution for the coming year which corresponds to the use of (i) maximax, and (ii) maximin decision criteria, and comment on the risk preference of management which is indicated by each.** **(5 marks)**

(Total: 15 marks)

236 TICKET AGENT   *Walk in the footsteps of a top tutor*

A ticket agent has an arrangement with a concert hall that holds concerts on 60 nights a year whereby he receives discounts as follows per concert:

For purchase of:	He receives a discount of:
200 tickets	20%
300 tickets	25%
400 tickets	30%
500 tickets or more	40%

Purchases must be in full hundreds. The average price per ticket is $30.

He must decide in advance each year the number of tickets he will purchase. If he has any tickets unsold by the afternoon of the concert he must return them to the box office. If the box office sells any of these he receives 60% of their price.

His sales records over a few years show that for a concert with extremely popular artistes he can be confident of selling 500 tickets, for one with lesser known artistes 350 tickets, and for one with relatively unknown artistes 200 tickets.

His records show that 10% of the tickets he returns are sold by the box office. (**Note:** these are in addition to any sales made by the ticket agent).

His administration costs incurred in selling tickets are the same per concert irrespective of the popularity of the artistes.

Sales records show that the frequency of concerts will be:

With popular artistes	45%
With lesser known artistes	30%
With unknown artistes	25%
	————
	100%
	————

Required:

(a) Calculate:

- the expected demand for tickets per concert
- the level of his purchases of tickets per concert that will give him the largest profit over a long period of time and the profit per concert that this level of purchases of tickets will yield. **(10 marks)**

(b) Calculate the number of tickets the agent should buy, based on the following criteria:

- Maximin
- Maximax
- Minimax regret. **(5 marks)**

(Total: 15 marks)

237 SHIFTERS HAULAGE (DEC 08 EXAM)

Shifters Haulage (SH) is considering changing some of the vans it uses to transport crates for customers. The new vans come in three sizes; small, medium and large. SH is unsure about which type to buy. The capacity is 100 crates for the small van, 150 for the medium van and 200 for the large van. Demand for crates varies and can be either 120 or 190 crates per period, with the probability of the higher demand figure being 0.6.

The sale price per crate is $10 and the variable cost $4 per crate for all van sizes subject to the fact that if the capacity of the van is greater than the demand for crates in a period then the variable cost will be lower by 10% to allow for the fact that the vans will be partly empty when transporting crates.

SH is concerned that if the demand for crates exceeds the capacity of the vans then customers will have to be turned away. SH estimates that in this case goodwill of $100 would be charged against profits per period to allow for lost future sales regardless of the number of customers that are turned away.

Depreciation charged would be $200 per period for the small, $300 for the medium and $400 for the large van.

SH has in the past been very aggressive in its decision-making, pressing ahead with rapid growth strategies. However, its managers have recently grown more cautious as the business has become more competitive.

Required:

(a)   **Prepare a profits table showing the SIX possible profit figures per period.   (9 marks)**

(b)   **Using your profit table from (a) above discuss which type of van SH should buy taking into consideration the possible risk attitudes of the managers.   (6 marks)**

(Total: 15 marks)

238 COOL SYSTEMS

Cool Systems, a producer of air conditioning systems for customers in the building trade, is having some problems with the manufacturing process for a particular system, the Breeze. Under its current production process, 25% of the Breeze units are defective. The unit contribution of this system is $40 per unit. Under contract the company has with its customers, Cool systems refunds $60 for each 'Breeze' that the customer finds to be defective; the customers then repair the system to make it usable in their building work.

Before delivering the systems to customers, Cool Systems could spend an additional $30 per Breeze to rework any systems thought to be defective – regardless of whether the system really is defective. The reworked systems can be sold at the regular price and will definitely not be defective in the builders' projects. Unfortunately, Cool Systems cannot tell ahead of time which systems will fail to work in their builders' installations, but would not deliver a system where tests had revealed a problem.

The summary table that shows the budgeted contribution per unit earned by Cool Systems for each of the possible 4 outcomes has been correctly prepared as follows:

	Breeze system is not defective	Breeze system is defective
Cool Systems chooses to rework	$40 – $30 = $10	$40 – $30 = $10
Cool Systems chooses NOT to rework	$40	$40 – $60 = ($20)

A consultant engineer has developed a simple test device to evaluate the system before delivering. For each system, the test device registers positive (i.e. no problem), inconclusive or negative. The test is not perfect, but it is consistent for a particular system; this means the test yields the same result for a given system regardless of how many times it is tested.

To calibrate the test device, it was run on a sample batch of 100 systems. The results are presented in the table below:

	System in good condition: 75 systems in total	System in defective condition: 25 systems in total
Test result: Positive	52.5 systems	2.5 systems
Test result: Inconclusive	15 systems	7.5 systems
Test result: Negative	7.5 systems	15 systems

Required

Using a decision tree, establish the maximum price (per system) the company should be willing to pay for using the test device.

(Total: 10 marks)

239 ROBBER CO (JUNE 2012 EXAM)

Robber Co manufactures control panels for burglar alarms, a very profitable product. Every product comes with a one year warranty offering free repairs if any faults arise in this period.

It currently produces and sells 80,000 units per annum, with production of them being restricted by the short supply of labour. Each control panel includes two main components – one key pad and one display screen. At present, Robber Co manufactures both of these components in-house. However, the company is currently considering outsourcing the production of keypads and/or display screens. A newly established company based in Burgistan is keen to secure a place in the market, and has offered to supply the keypads for the equivalent of $4.10 per unit and the display screens for the equivalent of $4.30 per unit. This price has been guaranteed for two years.

The current total annual costs of producing the keypads and the display screens are:

	Keypads	Display screens
Production	80,000 units	80,000 units
	$000	$000
Direct materials	160	116
Direct labour	40	60
Heat and power costs	64	88
Machine costs	26	30
Depreciation and insurance costs	84	96
Total annual production costs	374	390

Notes:

(1) Materials costs for keypads are expected to increase by 5% in six months' time; materials costs for display screens are only expected to increase by 2%, but with immediate effect.

(2) Direct labour costs are purely variable and not expected to change over the next year.

(3) Heat and power costs include an apportionment of the general factory overhead for heat and power as well as the costs of heat and power directly used for the production of keypads and display screens. The general apportionment included is calculated using 50% of the direct labour cost for each component and would be incurred irrespective of whether the components are manufactured in-house or not.

(4) Machine costs are semi-variable; the variable element relates to set up costs, which are based upon the number of batches made. The keypads' machine has fixed costs of $4,000 per annum and the display screens' machine has fixed costs of $6,000 per annum. Whilst both components are currently made in batches of 500, this would need to change, with immediate effect, to batches of 400.

(5) 60% of depreciation and insurance costs relate to an apportionment of the general factory depreciation and insurance costs; the remaining 40% is specific to the manufacture of keypads and display screens.

Required:

(a) **Advise Robber Co whether it should continue to manufacture the keypads and display screens in-house or whether it should outsource their manufacture to the supplier in Burgistan, assuming it continues to adopt a policy to limit manufacture and sales to 80,000 control panels in the coming year.** **(8 marks)**

(b) **Robber Co takes 0.5 labour hours to produce a keypad and 0.75 labour hours to produce a display screen. Labour hours are restricted to 100,000 hours and labour is paid at $1 per hour. Robber Co wishes to increase its supply to 100,000 control panels (i.e. 100,000 each of keypads and display screens).**

Advise Robber Co as to how many units of keypads and display panels they should either manufacture and/or outsource in order to minimise their costs. **(7 marks)**

(c) **Discuss the non-financial factors that Robber Co should consider when making a decision about outsourcing the manufacture of keypads and display screens.**

(5 marks)

(Total: 20 marks)

BUDGETING AND CONTROL

240 PC CO PARTICIPATIVE BUDGETING (DEC 2011 EXAM)

You have recently been appointed as an assistant management accountant in a large company, PC Co. When you meet the production manager, you overhear him speaking to one of his staff, saying:

'Budgeting is a waste of time. I don't see the point of it. It tells us what we can't afford but it doesn't keep us from buying it. It simply makes us invent new ways of manipulating figures. If all levels of management aren't involved in the setting of the budget, they might as well not bother preparing one.'

Required:

Discuss the concept of a participative style of budgeting in terms of the objectives of a budgetary control system.

(Total: 10 marks)

241 SAUCE CO BUDGETING STYLE (JUNE 2012 EXAM)

Sauce Co manufactures and sells cartons of cooking sauces, which deteriorate over time and must be used within three months. Over the last two years, Sauce Co has experienced all kinds of problems. The financial and sales directors believe these to be a result of persistently unrealistic sales targets imposed by the managing director, who makes forecasts based on his own subjective and overly optimistic views about future sales. Whilst an incentive scheme is in place for employees, the company has not hit its targets for the last three years, so no bonuses have been paid out. Production volumes are currently based on anticipated sales rather than actual orders.

Required:

Discuss the likely impact that the budgeting style and inaccurate sales forecasts have had on the staff and business of Sauce Co.

(Total: 10 marks)

242 DESIGNIT (DEC 2012 EXAM)

Designit is a small company providing design consultancy to a limited number of large clients. The business is mature and fairly stable year on year. It has 30 employees and is privately owned by its founder. Designit prepares an annual fixed budget. The company's accounts department consists of one part-qualified accountant who has a heavy workload. He prepares the budget using spreadsheets. The company has a November year end.

Designit is now considering replacing the fixed budget with a monthly rolling budget, which Designit believes will make the budgeting process more relevant and timely and encourage managers to focus on the future rather than the past.

Required:

(a) **Explain what a monthly rolling budget is and how it would operate at Designit.**

(4 marks)

(b) **Discuss the problems that may be encountered if Designit decides to introduce monthly rolling budgets.**

(6 marks)

(Total: 10 marks)

243 NEWTOWN SCHOOL (JUNE 2013 EXAM)

Newtown School's head teacher has prepared the budget for the year ending 31 May 2014. The head teacher admits to being 'poor with numbers' and he makes several simplifying assumptions in his calculations of revenue. He uses incremental budgeting to budget for his expenditure, taking actual expenditure for the previous year as a starting point and simply adjusting it for inflation.

The school spent $30,000 during the year ended 31 May 2013 on standard maintenance checks and repairs that have to be carried out by the school every year in order to comply with government health and safety standards. These are expected to increase by 3% in the coming year. In the year ended 31 May 2013, $14,000 was also spent on redecorating some of the classrooms. No redecorating is planned for the coming year.

There were also improvements made to the school gym during the year costing $65,000 in total. This year, the canteen is going to be substantially improved, although the extent of the improvements and level of service to be offered to pupils is still under discussion.

The school's board of governors, who review the budget, are concerned that the budget surplus has been calculated incorrectly. They believe that it should have been calculated using expected income, based on the probabilities provided, and using expected expenditure, based on the information provided in notes 1 to 3. They believe that incremental budgeting is not proving a reliable tool for budget setting in the school since, for the last three years, there have been shortfalls of cash despite a budget surplus being predicted. Since the school has no other source of funding available to it, these shortfalls have had serious consequences, such as the closure of the school kitchen for a considerable period in the last school year, meaning that no hot meals were available to pupils. This is thought to have been the cause of the 10% fall in the number of pupils registered at the school on 1 June 2013.

Required:

(a) **Briefly outline the three main steps involved in preparing a zero-based budget.**

(3 marks)

(b) **Discuss the extent to which zero-based budgeting could be used by Newtown School to improve the budgeting process.** **(7 marks)**

(Total: 10 marks)

244 MIC AND LEARNING (DEC 2013 EXAM)

Mic Co produces microphones for mobile phones and operates a standard costing system. Before production commenced, the standard labour time per batch for its latest microphone was estimated to be 200 hours. The standard labour cost per hour is $12 and resource allocation and cost data were therefore initially prepared on this basis.

Production of the microphone started in July and the number of batches assembled and sold each month was as follows:

Month	No of batches assembled and sold
July	1
August	1
September	2
October	4
November	8

The first batch took 200 hours to make, as anticipated, but, during the first four months of production, a learning effect of 88% was observed, although this finished at the end of October. The learning formula is shown on the formula sheet and at the 88% learning rate the value of b is −0.1844245.

Mic Co uses 'cost plus' pricing to establish selling prices for all its products. Sales of its new microphone in the first five months have been disappointing. The sales manager has blamed the production department for getting the labour cost so wrong, as this, in turn, caused the price to be too high. The production manager has disclaimed all responsibility, saying that, 'as usual, the managing director prepared the budgets alone and didn't consult me and, had he bothered to do so, I would have told him that a learning curve was expected.'

Required:

(a)   Calculate the actual total monthly labour costs for producing the microphones for each of the five months from July to November.   (9 marks)

(b)   Discuss the implications of the learning effect coming to an end for Mic Co, with regard to costing, budgeting and production.   (4 marks)

(c)   Describe two advantages of involving senior staff at Mic Co in the budget setting process, rather than the managing director simply imposing the budgets on them.   (2 marks)

(Total: 15 marks)

245   NN

NN Ltd manufactures and markets a range of electronic office equipment. The company currently has a turnover of $40 million per annum. The company has a functional structure and currently operates an incremental budgeting system. The company has a budget committee that is comprised entirely of members of the senior management team. No other personnel are involved in the budget-setting process.

Each member of the senior management team has enjoyed an annual bonus of between 10% and 20% of their annual salary for each of the past five years. The annual bonuses are calculated by comparing the actual costs attributed to a particular function with budgeted costs for that function during the twelve month period ended 31 December in each year.

A new Finance Director, who previously held a senior management position in a 'not for profit' health organisation, has recently been appointed. Whilst employed by the health service organisation, the new Finance Director had been the manager responsible for the implementation of a highly successful zero-based budgeting system (ZBB).

Required:

(a)   Identify and discuss the factors to be considered when implementing a system of zero-based budgeting within NN Ltd.   (5 marks)

(b)   Identify and discuss the behavioural problems that the management of NN Ltd might encounter in implementing a system of ZBB, recommending how best to address such problems in order that they are overcome.   (10 marks)

(Total: 15 marks)

246 ZERO BASED BUDGETING I (DEC 10 EXAM)

Some commentators argue that: 'With continuing pressure to control costs and maintain efficiency, the time has come for all public sector organisations to embrace zero-based budgeting. There is no longer a place for incremental budgeting in any organisation, particularly public sector ones, where zero-based budgeting is far more suitable anyway.'

Required:

(a) Discuss the particular difficulties encountered when budgeting in public sector organisations compared with budgeting in private sector organisations, drawing comparisons between the two types of organisations. **(6 marks)**

(b) Explain the terms 'incremental budgeting' and 'zero-based budgeting'. **(4 marks)**

(Total: 10 marks)

247 ZERO BASED BUDGETING II (DEC 10 EXAM)

Some commentators argue that: 'With continuing pressure to control costs and maintain efficiency, the time has come for all public sector organisations to embrace zero-based budgeting. There is no longer a place for incremental budgeting in any organisation, particularly public sector ones, where zero-based budgeting is far more suitable anyway.'

Required:

(a) State the main stages involved in preparing zero-based budgets. **(3 marks)**

(b) Discuss the view that 'there is no longer a place for incremental budgeting in any organisation, particularly public sector ones,' highlighting any drawbacks of zero-based budgeting that need to be considered. **(7 marks)**

(Total: 10 marks)

248 STICKY WICKET (JUNE 10 EXAM)

Sticky Wicket (SW) manufactures cricket bats using high quality wood and skilled labour using mainly traditional manual techniques. The manufacturing department is a cost centre within the business and operates a standard costing system based on marginal costs.

At the beginning of April 2010 the production director attempted to reduce the cost of the bats by sourcing wood from a new supplier and de-skilling the process a little by using lower grade staff on parts of the production process. The standards were not adjusted to reflect these changes.

The variance report for April 2010 is shown below (extract).

Variances	Adverse $	Favourable $
Material price		5,100
Material usage	7,500	
Labour rate		43,600
Labour efficiency	48,800	
Labour idle time	5,400	

The production director pointed out in his April 2010 board report that the new grade of labour required significant training in April and this meant that productive time was lower than usual. He accepted that the workers were a little slow at the moment but expected that an improvement would be seen in May 2010. He also mentioned that the new wood being used was proving difficult to cut cleanly resulting in increased waste levels.

Sales for April 2010 were down 10% on budget and returns of faulty bats were up 20% on the previous month. The sales director resigned after the board meeting stating that SW had always produced quality products but the new strategy was bound to upset customers and damage the brand of the business.

Required:

Assess the performance of the production director using all the information above taking into account both the decision to use a new supplier and the decision to de-skill the process.

(Total: 10 marks)

249 PARTICIPATION IN MIC CO (DEC 2013 EXAM)

Mic Co produces microphones for mobile phones and operates a standard costing system.

The company uses 'cost plus' pricing to establish selling prices for all its products. Sales of its new microphone in the first five months have been disappointing. The sales manager has blamed the production department for getting the labour cost so wrong, as this, in turn, caused the price to be too high. The production manager has disclaimed all responsibility, saying that, 'as usual, the managing director prepared the budgets alone and didn't consult me and, had he bothered to do so, I would have told him that a learning curve was expected.'

Required:

Discuss the potential advantages and disadvantages of involving senior staff at Mic Co in the budget setting process, rather than the managing director simply imposing the budgets on them.

(Total: 10 marks)

250 LOCK CO (JUNE 2012 EXAM)

Lock Co makes a single product – a lock – and uses marginal costing. The production director at Lock Co believes that the way to persistently increase market share in the long term is to focus on quality, and is hoping to introduce a 'Total Quality Management' (TQM) approach. The finance director also shares this view and has said that 'standard costing will no longer have a place within the organisation if TQM is introduced.'

Required:

Discuss the view that there is no longer a place for standard costing if TQM is introduced at Lock Co.

(Total: 10 marks)

251   BIG CHEESE CHAIRS (DEC 09 EXAM)

Big Cheese Chairs (BCC) manufactures and sells executive leather chairs. They are considering a new design of massaging chair to launch into the competitive market in which they operate.

They have carried out an investigation in the market and using a target costing system have targeted a competitive selling price of $120 for the chair. BCC wants a margin on selling price of 20% (ignoring any overheads).

The frame and massage mechanism will be bought in for $51 per chair and BCC will upholster it in leather and assemble it ready for despatch.

Leather costs $10 per metre and two metres are needed for a complete chair although 20% of all leather is wasted in the upholstery process.

The upholstery and assembly process will be subject to a learning effect as the workers get used to the new design. BCC estimates that the first chair will take two hours to prepare but this will be subject to a learning rate (LR) of 95%. The learning improvement will stop once 128 chairs have been made and the time for the 128th chair will be the time for all subsequent chairs. The cost of labour is $15 per hour.

The learning formula is shown on the formula sheet and at the 95% learning rate the value of b is –0.074000581.

Required:

(a)   Calculate the average cost for the first 128 chairs made and identify any cost gap that may be present at that stage.   **(8 marks)**

(b)   The production manager denies any claims that a cost gap exists and has stated that the cost of the 128th chair will be low enough to yield the required margin.

Calculate the cost of the 128th chair made and state whether the target cost is being achieved on the 128th chair.   **(7 marks)**

(Total: 15 marks)

252   HENRY COMPANY (DEC 08 EXAM)

Henry Company (HC) provides skilled labour to the building trade. They have recently been asked by a builder to bid for a kitchen fitting contract for a new development of 600 identical apartments. HC has not worked for this builder before. Cost information for the new contract is as follows:

Labour for the contract is available. HC expects that the first kitchen will take 24 man-hours to fit but thereafter the time taken will be subject to a 95% learning rate. After 200 kitchens are fitted the learning rate will stop and the time taken for the 200th kitchen will be the time taken for all the remaining kitchens. Labour costs $15 per hour.

Overheads are absorbed on a labour hour basis. HC has collected overhead information for the last four months and this is shown below:

	Hours worked	Overhead cost $
Month 1	9,300	115,000
Month 2	9,200	113,600
Month 3	9,400	116,000
Month 4	9,600	116,800

HC normally works around 120,000 labour hours in a year.

HC uses the high low method to analyse overheads.

The learning curve equation is $y = ax^b$, where $b = \log r / \log 2 = -0.074$

Required:

(a) Calculate the total cost including all overheads for HC that it can use as a basis of the bid for the new apartment contract. **(13 marks)**

(b) If the second kitchen alone is expected to take 21.6 man-hours to fit demonstrate how the learning rate of 95% has been calculated. **(2 marks)**

(Total: 15 marks)

253 JUMP PERFORMANCE APPRAISAL (JUNE 10 EXAM)

Jump has a network of sports clubs which is managed by local managers reporting to the main board. The local managers have a lot of autonomy and are able to vary employment contracts with staff and offer discounts for membership fees and personal training sessions. They also control their own maintenance budget but do not have control over large amounts of capital expenditure.

A local manager's performance and bonus is assessed relative to three targets. For every one of these three targets that is reached in an individual quarter, $400 is added to the manager's bonus, which is paid at the end of the year. The maximum bonus per year is therefore based on 12 targets (three targets in each of the four quarters of the year). Accordingly the maximum bonus that could be earned is 12 × $400 = $4,800, which represents 40% of the basic salary of a local manager. Jump has a 31 March year end.

The performance data for one of the sports clubs for the last four quarters is as follows:

	Qtr to 30 June 2009	Qtr to 30 Sept 2009	Qtr to 31 Dec 2009	Qtr to 31 March 2010
Number of members	3,000	3,200	3,300	3,400
Member visits	20,000	24,000	26,000	24,000
Personal training sessions booked	310	325	310	339
Staff days	450	480	470	480
Staff lateness days	20	28	28	20
Days in quarter	90	90	90	90

Agreed targets are:

1 Staff must be on time over 95% of the time (no penalty is made when staff are absent from work)

2 On average 60% of members must use the clubs' facilities regularly by visiting at least 12 times per quarter 3. On average 10% of members must book a personal training session each quarter

Required:

(a) Calculate the amount of bonus that the manager should expect to be paid for the latest financial year. **(6 marks)**

(b) Discuss to what extent the targets set are controllable by the local manager (you are required to make a case for both sides of the argument). **(9 marks)**

(Total: 15 marks)

254 CRUMBLY CAKES (JUNE 09 EXAM)

 Timed question with Online tutor debrief

Crumbly Cakes make cakes, which are sold directly to the public. The new production manager (a celebrity chef) has argued that the business should use only organic ingredients in its cake production. Organic ingredients are more expensive but should produce a product with an improved flavour and give health benefits for the customers. It was hoped that this would stimulate demand and enable an immediate price increase for the cakes.

Crumbly Cakes operates a responsibility based standard costing system which allocates variances to specific individuals. The individual managers are paid a bonus only when net favourable variances are allocated to them. The new organic cake production approach was adopted at the start of March 2009, following a decision by the new production manager. No change was made at that time to the standard costs card. The variance reports for February and March are shown below:

Manager responsible	Allocated variances	February Variance $	March Variance $
Production manager			
	Material price (total for all ingredients)	25 Fav	2,100 Adv
	Material mix	0	600 Adv
	Material yield	20 Fav	400 Fav
Sales manager			
	Sales price	40 Adv	7,000 Fav
	Sales contribution volume	35 Adv	3,000 Fav

The production manager is upset that he seems to have lost all hope of a bonus under the new system. The sales manager thinks the new organic cakes are excellent and is very pleased with the progress made. Crumbly Cakes operate a JIT stock system and holds virtually no inventory.

Required:

(a)   Assess the performance of the production manager and the sales manager and indicate whether the current bonus scheme is fair to those concerned.   **(7 marks)**

In April 2009 the following standard data applied (not adjusted for the organic ingredients):*Ingredients (per cake)*	Kg	$
Flour	0.10	0.12 per kg
Eggs	0.10	0.70 per kg
Butter	0.10	1.70 per kg
Sugar	0.10	0.50 per kg
Total input	0.40	
Normal loss (10%)	(0.04)	
Standard weight of a cake	0.36	
Standard sales price of a cake		0.85
Standard contribution per cake after all variable costs		0.35

The budget for production and sales in April was 50,000 cakes. Actual production and sales was 60,000 cakes in the month, during which the following occurred:

Ingredients used	Kg	$
Flour	5,700	$741
Eggs	6,600	$5,610
Butter	6,600	$11,880
Sugar	4,578	$2,747
Total input	23,478	$20,978
Actual loss	(1,878)	
Actual output of cake mixture	21,600	
Actual sales price of a cake = $0.99		

All cakes produced must weigh 0.36 kg as this is what is advertised.

Required:

(b) Calculate the materials price and mix variances for April, and the sales price variance for April. You are not required to make any comment on the performance of the managers. **(8 marks)**

(Total: 15 marks)

 Calculate your allowed time, allocate the time to the separate parts...............

---

255 CARAT *Online question assistance*

Carat plc, a premium food manufacturer, is reviewing operations for a three-month period of 20X3. The company operates a standard marginal costing system and manufactures one product, ZP, for which the following standard revenue and cost data per unit of product is available:

Selling price	$12.00
Direct material A	2.5 kg at $1.70 per kg
Direct material B	1.5 kg at $1.20 per kg
Direct labour	0.45 hrs at $6.00 per hour

Fixed production overheads for the three-month period were expected to be $62,500.

Actual data for the three-month period was as follows:

Sales and production	48,000 units of ZP were produced and sold for $580,800.
Direct material A	121,951 kg were used at a cost of $200,000.
Direct material B	67,200 kg were used at a cost of $84,000.
Direct labour	Employees worked for 18,900 hours, but 19,200 hours were paid at a cost of $117,120.
Fixed production overheads	$64,000

Budgeted sales for the three-month period were 50,000 units of Product ZP.

Required:

(a) Calculate the materials mix and yield variances and suggest possible explanations for them.

(8 marks)

(b) Critically discuss the types of standard used in standard costing and their effect on employee motivation.

(7 marks)

(Total: 15 marks)

256 SAFE SOAP CO (DEC 2014)

The Safe Soap Co makes environmentally-friendly soap using three basic ingredients. The standard cost card for one batch of soap for the month of September was as follows:

Material	Kilograms	Price per kilogram ($)
Lye	0.25	10
Coconut oil	0.6	4
Shea butter	0.5	3

The budget for production and sales in September was 120,000 batches. Actual production and sales were 136,000 batches. The actual ingredients used were as follows:

Material	Kilograms
Lye	34,080
Coconut oil	83,232
Shea butter	64,200

Required:

(a) Calculate the total material mix variance and the total material yield variance for September.

(8 marks)

(b) In October the materials mix and yield variances were as follows:

Mix: $6,000 adverse

Yield: $10,000 favourable

The production manager is pleased with the results overall, stating:

'At the beginning of September I made some changes to the mix of ingredients used for the soaps. As I expected, the mix variance is adverse in both months because we haven't yet updated our standard cost card but, in both months, the favourable yield variance more than makes up for this. Overall, I think we can be satisfied that the changes made to the product mix are producing good results and now we are able to produce more batches and meet the growing demand for our product.'

The sales manager, however, holds a different view and says:

'I'm not happy with this change in the ingredients mix. I've had to explain to the board why the sales volume variance for October was $22,000 adverse. I've tried to explain that the quality of the soap has declined slightly and some of my customers have realised this and simply aren't happy but no-one seems to be listening. Some customers are even demanding that the price of the soap be reduced and threatening to go elsewhere if the problem isn't sorted out.'

Required:

(i) Briefly explain what the adverse materials mix and favourable materials yield variances indicate about production at Safe Soap Co in October.

Note: You are NOT required to discuss revision of standards or operational and planning variances. **(4 marks)**

(ii) Discuss whether the sales manager could be justified in claiming that the change in the materials mix has caused an adverse sales volume variance in October. **(3 marks)**

(Total: 15 marks)

257 SPIKE CO I (DEC 07 EXAM)

Spike Limited manufactures and sells good quality leather bound diaries. Each year it budgets for its profits, including detailed budgets for sales, materials and labour. If appropriate, the departmental managers are allowed to revise their budgets for planning errors.

In recent months, the managing director has become concerned about the frequency of budget revisions. At a recent board meeting he said 'There seems little point budgeting any more. Every time we have a problem the budgets are revised to leave me looking at a favourable operational variance report and, at the same time, less profit than promised.'

Two specific situations have recently arisen, for which budget revisions were sought:

Materials

A local material supplier was forced into liquidation. Spike Limited's buyer managed to find another supplier, 150 miles away at short notice. This second supplier charged more for the material and a supplementary delivery charge on top. The buyer agreed to both the price and the delivery charge without negotiation. 'I had no choice', the buyer said, 'the production manager was pushing me very hard to find any solution possible!' Two months later, another, more competitive, local supplier was found.

A budget revision is being sought for the two months where higher prices had to be paid.

Labour

During the early part of the year, problems had been experienced with the quality of work being produced by the support staff in the labour force. The departmental manager had complained in his board report that his team were 'unreliable, inflexible and just not up to the job'.

It was therefore decided, after discussion of the board report, that something had to be done. The company changed its policy so as to recruit only top graduates from good quality universities. This has had the effect of pushing up the costs involved but increasing productivity in relation to that element of the labour force.

The support staff departmental manager has requested a budget revision to cover the extra costs involved following the change of policy.

Required:

Discuss each request for a budget revision, putting what you see as both sides of the argument and reach a conclusion as to whether a budget revision should be allowed.

(Total: 10 marks)

258 SPIKE CO II (DEC 07 EXAM)

The market for leather bound diaries has been shrinking as the electronic versions become more widely available and easier to use. Spike Limited has produced the following data relating to leather bound diary sales for the year to date:

Budget

Sales volume	180,000 units
Sales price	$17.00 per unit
Standard contribution	$7.00 per unit

The total market for diaries in this period was estimated in the budget to be 1.8m units. In fact, the actual total market shrank to 1.6m units for the period under review.

Actual results for the same period

Sales volume	176,000 units
Sales price	$16.40 per unit

Required:

(a) Analyse the total sales volume variance into components for market size and market share. **(4 marks)**

(b) Comment on the sales performance of the business. **(6 marks)**

(Total: 10 marks)

259 BLOCK CO (JUNE 2013 EXAM)

Block Co operates an absorption costing system and sells three types of product – Commodity 1, Commodity 2 and Commodity 3. Like other competitors operating in the same market, Block Co is struggling to maintain revenues and profits in face of the economic recession which has engulfed the country over the last two years. Sales prices fluctuate in the market in which Block Co operates. Consequently, at the beginning of each quarter, a market specialist, who works on a consultancy basis for Block Co, sets a budgeted sales price for each product for the quarter, based on his expectations of the market. This then becomes the 'standard selling price' for the quarter. The sales department itself is run by the company's sales manager, who negotiates the actual sales prices with customers. The following budgeted figures are available for the quarter ended 31 May 2013.

Product	Budgeted production and sales units	Standard selling price per unit	Standard variable production costs per unit
Commodity 1	30,000	$30	$18
Commodity 2	28,000	$35	$28.40
Commodity 3	26,000	$41.60	$26.40

Block Co uses absorption costing. Fixed production overheads are absorbed on the basis of direct machine hours and the budgeted cost of these for the quarter ended 31 May 2013 was $174,400. Commodity 1, 2 and 3 use 0.2 hours, 0.6 hours and 0.8 hours of machine time respectively.

The following data shows the actual sales prices and volumes achieved for each product by Block Co for the quarter ended 31 May 2013 and the average market prices per unit.

Product	Actual production and sales units	Actual selling price per unit	Average market price per unit
Commodity 1	29,800	$31	$32.20
Commodity 2	30,400	$34	$33.15
Commodity 3	25,600	$40.40	$39.10

The following variances have already been correctly calculated for Commodities 1 and 2:

Sales price operational variances

Commodity 1: $35,760 Adverse

Commodity 2: $25,840 Favourable

Sales price planning variances

Commodity 1: $65,560 Favourable

Commodity 2: $56,240 Adverse

Required:

(a) Calculate, for Commodity 3 only, the sales price operational variance and the sales price planning variance. **(4 marks)**

(b) Using the data provided for Commodities 1, 2 and 3, calculate the total sales mix variance and the total sales quantity variance. **(11 marks)**

(Total: 15 marks)

260 VALET CO VARIANCES (JUNE 2014, ADAPTED)

Valet Co is a car valeting (cleaning) company. It operates in the country of Strappia, which has been badly affected by the global financial crisis. Petrol and food prices have increased substantially in the last year and the average disposable household income has decreased by 30%. Recent studies have shown that the average car owner keeps their car for five years before replacing it, rather than three years as was previously the case. Figures over recent years also show that car sales in Strappia are declining whilst business for car repairs is on the increase.

Valet Co offers two types of valet – a full valet and a mini valet. A full valet is an extensive clean of the vehicle, inside and out; a mini valet is a more basic clean of the vehicle. Until recently, four similar businesses operated in Valet Co's local area, but one of these closed down three months ago after a serious fire on its premises. Valet Co charges customers $50 for each full valet and $30 for each mini valet and this price never changes. Their budget and actual figures for the last year were as follows.

	Budget		Actual	
Number of valets:				
Full valets	3,600		4,000	
Mini valets	2,000		3,980	
	$	$	$	$
Revenue		240,000		319,400
Variable costs:				
Staff wages	(114,000)		(122,000)	
Cleaning materials	(6,200)		(12,400)	
Energy costs	(6,520)		(9,200)	
		(126,720)		(143,600)
Contribution		113,280		175,800
Fixed costs:				
Rent, rates and depreciation		(36,800)		(36,800)
Operating profit		76,480		139,000

The budgeted contribution to sales ratios for the two types of valet are 44.6% for full valets and 55% for mini valets.

Required:

(a)   **Using the data provided for full valets and mini valets, calculate:**

(i)   **The total sales mix contribution variance.**   **(4 marks)**

(ii)   **The total sales quantity contribution variance.**   **(4 marks)**

(b)   **Briefly describe the sales mix contribution variance and the sales quantity contribution variance.**   **(2 marks)**

(Total: 10 marks)

261   CHOC CO VARIANCES (DEC 2011 EXAM)

Choc Co is a company which manufactures and sells three types of biscuits in packets. One of them is called 'Ooze' and contains three types of sweeteners: honey, sugar and syrup. The standard materials usage and cost for one unit of 'Ooze' (one packet) is as follows:

		$
Honey	20 grams at $0.02 per gram	0.40
Sugar	15 grams at $0.03 per gram	0.45
Syrup	10 grams at $0.025 per gram	0.25
		1.10

In the three months ended 30 November 2011, Choc Co produced 101,000 units of 'Ooze' using 2,200 kg of honey, 1,400 kg of sugar and 1,050 kg of syrup. Note: there are 1,000 grams in a kilogram (kg).

Required:

(a) Calculate the following variances for materials in Ooze:

    (i)   Total materials usage variance   **(4 marks)**

    (ii)   Total materials mix variance   **(4 marks)**

    (iii)   Total materials quantity (yield) variance.   **(4 marks)**

(b) Briefly discuss whether the decision to change the mix was beneficial to Choc Co.

                                                    (3 marks)

                                                  (Total: 15 marks)

262 BED CO (DEC 2013 EXAM)

Bedco manufactures bed sheets and pillowcases which it supplies to a major hotel chain. It uses a just-in-time system and holds no inventories.

The standard cost for the cotton which is used to make the bed sheets and pillowcases is $5 per m^2. Each bed sheet uses 2 m^2 of cotton and each pillowcase uses 0.5 m^2. Production levels for bed sheets and pillowcases for November were as follows:

	Budgeted production levels (units)	Actual production levels (units)
Bed sheets	120,000	120,000
Pillowcases	190,000	180,000

The actual cost of the cotton in November was $5.80 per m^2. 248,000 m^2 of cotton was used to make the bed sheets and 95,000 m^2 was used to make the pillowcases.

The world commodity prices for cotton increased by 20% in the month of November. At the beginning of the month, the hotel chain made an unexpected request for an immediate design change to the pillowcases. The new design required 10% more cotton than previously. It also resulted in production delays and therefore a shortfall in production of 10,000 pillowcases in total that month.

The following variances have been correctly calculated:

Material price planning $343,000(A) (of which $248,000 relates to sheets)

Material price operational $68,600(F) (of which $49,600 relates to sheets)

The production manager at Bedco is responsible for all buying and any production issues which occur, although he is not responsible for the setting of standard costs.

Required:

(a) Calculate the following variances for the month of November, for both bed sheets and pillow cases, and in total:

    (i)   Material usage planning variance   **(3 marks)**

    (ii)   Material usage operational variance.   **(3 marks)**

(b) Assess the performance of the production manager for the month of November.

                                                    (9 marks)

                                                  (Total: 15 marks)

PERFORMANCE MEASUREMENT AND CONTROL

263 ROTECH GROUP PART 1: W CO (JUNE 2014)

The Rotech group comprises two companies, W Co and C Co.

W Co is a trading company with two divisions: The Design division, which designs wind turbines and supplies the designs to customers under licences and the Gearbox division, which manufactures gearboxes for the car industry.

C Co manufactures components for gearboxes. It sells the components globally and also supplies W Co with components for its Gearbox manufacturing division.

The financial results for the two companies for the year ended 31 May 2014 are as follows:

	W Co		C Co
	Design division	*Gearbox division*	
	$000	$000	$000
External sales	14,300	25,535	8,010
Sales to Gearbox division			7,550
			―――――
			15,560
			―――――
Cost of sales	(4,900)	(16,200)*	(5,280)
Administration costs	(3,400)	(4,200)	(2,600)
Distribution costs	–	(1,260)	(670)
	―――――	―――――	―――――
Operating profit	6,000	3,875	7,010
	―――――	―――――	―――――
Capital employed	23,540	32,320	82,975

* Includes cost of components purchased from C Co.

Required:

Discuss the performance of C Co and each division of W Co, calculating and using the following three performance measures:

(i)   Return on capital employed (ROCE).

(ii)   Asset turnover.

(iii)   Operating profit margin.

Note: There are 4.5 marks available for calculations and 5.5 marks available for discussion.

(Total: 10 marks)

264 PRINTING COMPANY

During 2013, a printing company designed and installed a Management Information System that met the business needs of a commercial environment which was characterised at that time by:

- a unitary structure with one profit centre
- central direction from senior managers
- 100% internal resourcing of ancillary services
- the employment exclusively of permanent full-time employees
- customers holding large stocks who accepted long delivery times
- most of the work concerned with long print runs for established large publishing houses.

A radical change in the business environment has resulted in the following outcomes:

- the development of a divisionalised structure with four profit centres that utilise each others services
- empowerment of team leaders and devolved decision making
- considerable outsourcing of activities
- a significant proportion of the employees work part-time and/or on temporary contracts
- customers now commonly operate JIT systems requiring immediate replenishment of stocks
- the typical customer requires specialist low volume but complex high value printing.

Required:

List the significant changes in the Management Information Systems that would probably be required to meet the needs of this new situation. Explain the reasons for your recommendations.

(Total: 10 marks)

Note: your answer does not require a consideration of technical matters.

265 CDE

CDE is a manufacturer of almost 100 hundred different automotive components that are sold in both large and small quantities on a just-in-time (JIT) basis to the major vehicle assemblers. Business is highly competitive and price sensitive. The company is listed on the stock exchange but CDE's share performance has not matched that of its main competitors.

CDE's management accounting system uses a manufacturing resource planning (MRP II) system to control production scheduling, inventory movements and inventory control, and labour and machine utilisation. The accounting department carries out a detailed annual budgeting exercise, determines standard costs for labour and materials, and allocates production overhead on the basis of machine utilisation. Strict accounting controls over labour and material costs are managed by the detailed recording of operator and machine timesheets and raw material movements, and by calculating and investigating all significant variances.

While the information from the MRP II system is useful to management, there is an absence of integrated data about customer requirements and suppliers. Some information is contained within spreadsheets and databases held by the Sales and Purchasing departments respectively. One result of this lack of integration is that inventories are higher than they should be in a JIT environment.

The managers of CDE (representing functional areas of sales, production, purchasing, finance and administration) believe that, while costs are strictly controlled, the cost of the accounting department is excessive and significant savings need to be made, even at the expense of data accuracy. Managers believe that there may not be optimum use of the production capacity to generate profits and cash flow and improve shareholder value. CDE's management wants to carry out sensitivity and other analyses of strategic alternatives, but this is difficult when the existing management accounting system is focused on control rather than on decision support.

Required:

(a) Outline the different types of information system available to manufacturing firms like CDE.

(5 marks)

(b) Recommend with reasons the information system that would be appropriate to CDE's needs.

(5 marks)

(Total: 10 marks)

266 THE MG ORGANISATION

The Information Systems strategy within the MG organisation has been developed over a number of years. However, the basic approach has always remained unchanged. An IT budget is agreed by the board each year. The budget is normally 5% to 10% higher than the previous year's to allow for increases in prices and upgrades to computer systems.

Systems are upgraded in accordance with user requirements. Most users see IT systems as tools for recording day-to-day transactions and providing access to accounting and other information as necessary. There is no Enterprise Resource Planning System (ERPS) or Executive Information System (EIS). The board tends to rely on reports from junior managers to control the business. While these reports generally provide the information requested by the board, they are focused at a tactical level and do not contribute to strategy formulation or implementation.

Required:

Advise the board on how an ERPS and EIS could provide benefits over and above those provided by transaction processing systems.

(Total: 10 marks)

267 OPEN AND CLOSED SYSTEMS

(a) Briefly explain the difference between open and closed loop control. (5 marks)

(b) Discuss whether an open or closed loop model would be appropriate for a manufacturing company.

(5 marks)

(Total: 10 marks)

268 BRACE CO (JUNE 2011 EXAM)

Brace Co is an electronics company specialising in the manufacture of home audio equipment. Historically, the company has used solely financial performance measures to assess the performance of the company as a whole. The company's Managing Director has recently heard of the 'balanced scorecard approach' and is keen to learn more.

Required:

Describe the balanced scorecard approach to performance measurement.

(Total: 10 marks)

269 NON-FINANCIAL MEASURES

Many firms still focus on profitability as their main measure of performance, despite increasing evidence that non-financial measures are often more important.

Required:

(a)   **Explain the problems of using a broad range of non-financial measures for the short- and long-term control of a business.**   **(6 marks)**

(b)   **An insurance company is considering introducing a balanced scorecard. State the four perspectives of the balanced scorecard and recommend, with explanations, ONE performance measure for each perspective.**   **(4 marks)**

(Total: 10 marks)

270 JAMAIR (DEC 2014)

Jamair was founded in September 2007 and is one of a growing number of low-cost airlines in the country of Shania. Jamair's strategy is to operate as a low-cost, high efficiency airline, and it does this by:

- Operating mostly in secondary cities to reduce landing costs.

- Using only one type of aircraft in order to reduce maintenance and operational costs. These planes are leased rather than bought outright.

- Having only one category of seat class.

- Having no pre-allocated seats or in-flight entertainment.

- Focusing on e-commerce with customers both booking tickets and checking in for flights online.

The airline was given an 'on time arrival' ranking of seventh best by the country's aviation authority, who rank all 50 of the country's airlines based on the number of flights which arrive on time at their destinations. 48 Jamair flights were cancelled in 2013 compared to 35 in 2012. This increase was due to an increase in the staff absentee rate at Jamair from 3 days per staff member per year to 4.5 days.

The average 'ground turnaround time' for airlines in Shania is 50 minutes, meaning that, on average, planes are on the ground for cleaning, refuelling, etc. for 50 minutes before departing again. Customer satisfaction surveys have shown that 85% of customers are happy with the standard of cleanliness on Jamair's planes.

The number of passengers carried by the airline has grown from 300,000 passengers on a total of 3,428 flights in 2007 to 920,000 passengers on 7,650 flights in 2013. The overall growth of the airline has been helped by the limited route licensing policy of the Shanian government, which has given Jamair almost monopoly status on some of its routes. However, the government is now set to change this policy with almost immediate effect, and it has become more important than ever to monitor performance effectively.

Required:

(a) Describe each of the four perspectives of the balanced scorecard. **(6 marks)**

(b) For each perspective of the balanced scorecard, identify one goal together with a corresponding performance measure which could be used by Jamair to measure the company's performance. The goals and measures should be specifically relevant to Jamair. For each pair of goals and measures, explain why you have chosen them. **(9 marks)**

(Total: 15 marks)

271 ROTECH GROUP PART 2: C CO (JUNE 2014)

C Co is currently working to full capacity. The Rotech group's policy is that group companies and divisions must always make internal sales first before selling outside the group. Similarly, purchases must be made from within the group wherever possible. However, the group divisions and companies are allowed to negotiate their own transfer prices without interference from Head Office.

C Co has always charged the same price to the Gearbox division as it does to its external customers. However, after being offered a 5% lower price for similar components from an external supplier, the manager of the Gearbox division feels strongly that the transfer price is too high and should be reduced. C Co currently satisfies 60% of the external demand for its components. Its variable costs represent 40% of revenue.

Required:

Advise, using suitable calculations, the total transfer price or prices at which the components should be supplied to the Gearbox division from C Co.

(Total: 10 marks)

272 SECOND PROCESS CO (DEC 2013 EXAM)

Process Co has two divisions, A and B. Division A produces three types of chemicals: products L, M and S, using a common process. Each of the products can either be sold by Division A to the external market at split-off point (after the common process is complete) or can be transferred to Division B for individual further processing into products LX, MX and SX.

It has been suggested that Division A should transfer products L and M to Division B for further processing, in order to optimise the profit of the company as a whole. Divisions A and B are both investment centres and all transfers from Division A to Division B would be made using the actual marginal cost. As a result, if Division A were to make the transfers as suggested, their divisional profits would be much lower than if it were to sell both products externally at split-off point. Division B's profits, however, would be much higher.

Required:

(a)   Discuss the issues arising from this suggested approach to transfer pricing.

(5 marks)

(b)   Process Co is becoming increasingly concerned that environmental costs may be increasing within the company. However, the company has not yet developed a structured way for accounting for these costs. It has heard of a number of different management accounting techniques which can be used to account for environmental costs, including 'input/output analysis', 'flow cost accounting', 'environmental activity-based costing' and 'life cycle costing'.

Briefly describe TWO of these techniques in the context of environmental management accounting.   (5 marks)

(Total: 10 marks)

273   DIVISION A

Division A, which is a part of the ACF Group, manufactures only one type of product, a Bit, which it sells to external customers and also to division C, another member of the group. ACF Group's policy is that divisions have the freedom to set transfer prices and choose their suppliers.

The ACF Group uses residual income (RI) to assess divisional performance and each year it sets each division a target RI. The group's cost of capital is 12% a year.

Division A

Budgeted information for the coming year is:

Maximum capacity	150,000 Bits
External sales	110,000 Bits
External selling price	$35 per Bit
Variable cost	$22 per Bit
Fixed costs	$1,080,000
Capital employed	$3,200,000
Target residual income	$180,000

Division C

Division C has found two other companies willing to supply Bits:

X could supply at $28 per Bit, but only for annual orders in excess of 50,000 Bits. Z could supply at $33 per Bit for any quantity ordered.

Division C provisionally requests a quotation for 60,000 Bits from division A for the coming year.

Required:

(a)   Calculate the transfer price per Bit that division A should quote in order to meet its residual income target.   (6 marks)

(b)   Calculate the two prices division A would have to quote to division C, if it became group policy to quote transfer prices based on opportunity costs.

(4 marks)

(Total: 10 marks)

274 B5 CARS EIS

B5 Cars manufactures motor vehicles for sale to the general public and companies. Several other motor vehicle manufacturers operate within the industry, which is highly competitive: there is a trade association which collects a wide range of information.

B5 Cars has five manufacturing plants and 53 sales outlets in the country in which it operates. Information for the company's executive information system (EIS) is obtained both from internal sources such as the production plants, and also external sources such as customers. Internally-generated information is sent to head office over a wide area network.

Due to the overall escalating cost of the company's EIS, the board has decided to collect only internally-produced information. This decision has been taken against the advice of the chief information officer.

Required:

(a) **Suggest and explain reasons why the company's EIS could be becoming expensive to operate.** **(5 marks)**

(b) **Evaluate the decision of the board to concentrate on internally-produced information. Clearly describe the information sources that will be lost and explain the effects on the company's information systems and its products.** **(10 marks)**

(Total: 15 marks)

275 PRECISION PARTS

You have recently been appointed to lead the management accounting department of W Ltd, which is a small engineering company engaged in the manufacture of precision parts. The market in which the company sells its products is small and W Ltd faces severe competition. Due to the production facilities available, the company is able to undertake only small-scale engineering work. Large-scale engineering jobs are turned away as the company does not possess the manufacturing facilities to undertake them. At best, it can act only as agent for another contractor to do the work.

The board of W Ltd is aware that the volume of work which is being turned away is increasing. This is particularly frustrating as the company is unable to utilise its capacity to the fullest extent all the time. W Ltd has achieved a steady increase in profit over the last few years. Nevertheless, the board of the company believes that it could increase profitability still further by expanding and thus being able to carry out the larger scale work which is currently being turned away.

Budgetary control and standard costing information has, for many years, been provided as the sole output of the management accounting department. The previous management accountant prided himself on the punctuality and comprehensiveness of the reports produced. Each job is priced by adding a percentage to its total cost calculated in accordance with the company's standard costing procedures. The annual cost budget is split into monthly parts and flexed to take account of a particular period's actual production. Monthly cost variances – comprising those for direct materials, direct labour, variable and fixed production overheads – are produced and provided to the relevant manager. In addition, sales price and volume variances are produced by the management accounting department each period.

Required:

(a) In consideration of the need for the board of W Ltd to be provided with information which assists its strategic decision making, comment critically on the management accounting reports currently provided. **(5 marks)**

(b) State and justify what changes you, as management accountant, would make in providing information which facilitates strategic planning in the company. Within your answer, describe what financial and non-financial information you would supply which is different from that already provided. **(10 marks)**

(Total: 15 marks)

276 MOTOR COMPONENT MANUFACTURER

You are responsible for managing the preparation of all revenue and cost budgets for a motor component manufacturer. You are aware that the external environment has a significant impact on the business activity and financial performance of your company and that the current information systems are underdeveloped and ineffective in this respect.

Required:

(a) Identify which aspects of the external environment you are likely to consider and give reasons for your choice. **(5 marks)**

(b) Identify where you might find the relevant sources of information. **(5 marks)**

(c) Suggest how an external environment information system could be introduced into your company. **(5 marks)**

(Total: 15 marks)

277 REES INVESTMENTS

Rees Investments invests money on behalf of its customers. The company guarantees its customers a favourable interest rate in return for long-term investments. Mark Rees started the company five years ago and he was originally the only investment analyst, making all the investment decisions.

The company was initially very successful, due to a combination of Rees' expertise and a favourable world economic climate. Specialising in investing in the emerging markets of Asia and Africa, Rees Investments achieved excellent returns on their investments; This allowed them to meet guarantees given to clients as well as funding the expansion of the company itself.

The company has grown and it currently employs 60 staff of whom 12 are investment analysts. However, investment returns have declined and the company is now having problems providing its guaranteed return to investors. Consequently, Mark Rees is reviewing investment procedures and exploring options for returning the company to the profitability it enjoyed in its early years.

(a)   One of the options Mark Rees is considering is the use of a decision support system to help his investment analysts make appropriate investment decisions.

Briefly describe what is meant by a decision support system and comment on its possible contribution to the investment decisions made by analysts at Rees Investments.   **(7 marks)**

(b)   Mark Rees is also considering the development of an expert system.

Required:

Briefly describe what is meant by an expert system and comment on its possible contribution to the investment decisions made by analysts at Rees Investments.   **(8 marks)**

(Total: 15 marks)

278   ACCOUNTANCY TEACHING CO (DEC 10 EXAM)

The Accountancy Teaching Co (AT Co) is a company specialising in the provision of accountancy tuition courses in the private sector. It makes up its accounts to 30 November each year. In the year ending 30 November 2009, it held 60% of market share. However, over the last twelve months, the accountancy tuition market in general has faced a 20% decline in demand for accountancy training leading to smaller class sizes on courses. In 2009 and before, AT Co suffered from an ongoing problem with staff retention, which had a knock-on effect on the quality of service provided to students. Following the completion of developments that have been ongoing for some time, in 2010 the company was able to offer a far-improved service to students. The developments included:

- A new dedicated 24 hour student helpline
- An interactive website providing instant support to students
- A new training programme for staff
- An electronic student enrolment system
- An electronic marking system for the marking of students' progress tests. The costs of marking electronically were expected to be $4 million less in 2010 than marking on paper. Marking expenditure is always included in cost of sales

Extracts from the management accounts for 2009 and 2010 are shown below:

	2009		2010	
	$000	$000	$000	$000
Turnover		72,025		66,028
Cost of sales		(52,078)		(42,056)
Gross profit		19,947		23,972
Indirect expenses:				
Marketing	3,291		4,678	
Property	6,702		6,690	
Staff training	1,287		3,396	
Interactive website running costs	–		3,270	
Student helpline running costs	–		2,872	
Enrolment costs	5,032		960	
Total indirect expenses		(16,312)		(21,866)
Net operating profit		3,635		2,106

On 1 December 2009 all employees were told that they would not receive a pay rise for at least one year. Total lecture staff costs (including freelance lecturers) were $41.663 million in 2009 and were included in cost of sales, as is always the case. No reduction was made to course prices in the year and the mix of trainees studying for the different qualifications remained the same. The same type and number of courses were run in both 2009 and 2010.

Due to the nature of the business, non-financial performance indicators are also used to assess performance, as detailed below.

	2009	2010
Percentage of students transferring to AT Co from another training provider	8%	20%
Number of late enrolments due to staff error	297	106
Percentage of students passing exams first time	48%	66%
Labour turnover	32%	10%
Number of student complaints	315	84
Average no. of employees	1,080	1,081

Required:

Assess the performance of the business in 2010 using both financial performance indicators calculated from the above information AND the non-financial performance indicators provided.

Note: **Clearly state any assumptions and show all workings clearly. Your answer should be structured around the following main headings: turnover; cost of sales; gross profit; indirect expenses; net operating profit. However, in discussing each of these areas you should also refer to the non-financial performance indicators, where relevant.**

(Total: 15 marks)

279 PROPOSALS FOR DIVISION X

Division X is in a stable market. The first draft of its plan for the next three years is regarded as unacceptable to group management because it shows a slow decline in profit and return on investment:

	Year 1 $m	Year 2 $m	Year 3 $m
Profit before interest and tax (PBIT)	3.0	2.7	2.4
Asset base (at beginning of year)	24.0	25.0	26.0

Proposals which may improve the situation in the next three years are being discussed; ONLY ONE can be accepted because of cash limitations. Projects are evaluated with a 10% required return on investment. These proposed projects are shown below.

(i)   Special-purpose machine

Capital expenditure in years 1 and 2, followed by operating cash flow in year 3:

Year 1 $m	Year 2 $m	Year 3 $m	NPV $m
−0.5	−0.5	2.0	0.634

(ii)   **R&D project**

Revenue expenditure in years 1 and 2, followed by operating cash flow in year 3:

Year 1	Year 2	Year 3	NPV
$m	$m	$m	$m
−1.0	−1.0	4.0	1.269

(iii) **Advertising**

This can be done in each year if required. Each annual campaign costs $1m, but produces additional contributions of $0.4m in the year of the campaign and $1.1m in the subsequent year. A decision has been made to run annual campaigns in years 1 and 2 only. The combined cash flows are:

Year 1	Year 2	Year 3	NPV
$m	$m	$m	$m
−0.6	+0.5	+1.1	0.694

Managers are currently evaluated on return on investment (ROI), and are paid bonuses when this reaches or exceeds 10%. At 10% ROI the manager of division X will receive 25% of his salary of $50,000 pa.

For each 1 % increase in ROI above 10%, and *pro rata*, he will receive an additional 2.5% of basic salary with an upper bonus limit of 50% of salary for that year.

Thus, for the first draft of the plan, the bonus based on the ROI has been correctly calculated as:

	Year 1	Year 2	Year 3
Bonus	$15,625	$13,500	$ Zero

Calculations ignore tax and depreciation. The asset base represents the assets employed in the division at the beginning of each year, and excludes cash balances which are transferred to the group, and is used for the calculation of residual income (RI) and ROI.

Required:

Calculate the ROI, and the manager's bonus each year for the three alternative proposals. Comment on the effects of the bonus system on the manager's choice of project.

(Total: 15 marks)

280 Y AND Z

Y and Z are two divisions of a large company that operate in similar markets. Division Y represents the original manufacturing trade of the business but Division Z is a relatively new service/maintenance business and has seen considerable growth in its first two years of operation. The divisions are treated as investment centres and every month they each prepare an operating statement to be submitted to the parent company. Operating statements for these two divisions for October are shown below:

Operating statements for October

	Y	Z
	$000	$000
Sales revenue	900	555
Less variable costs	345	312
Contribution	555	243
Less controllable fixed costs (includes depreciation on divisional assets)	98	42
Controllable income	460	201
Less apportioned central costs	338	180
Net income before tax	122	21
Total divisional net assets	$9.76m	$1.26m

The company currently has a target return on capital of 12% per annum. However, the company believes its cost of capital is likely to rise and is considering increasing the target return on capital. At present the performance of each division and the divisional management are assessed primarily on the basis of Return on Investment (ROI).

Required:

(a) Calculate the annualised Return on Investment (ROI) for divisions Y and Z, and discuss the relative performance of the two divisions using the ROI data and other information given above. **(9 marks)**

(b) Calculate the annualised Residual Income (RI) for divisions Y and Z, and explain the implications of this information for the evaluation of the divisions' performance.

(6 marks)

(Total: 15 marks)

281   OLIVER'S SALON (JUNE 09 EXAM)

 Timed question with Online tutor debrief

Oliver is the owner and manager of Oliver's Salon which is a quality hairdresser that experiences high levels of competition. The salon traditionally provided a range of hair services to female clients only, including cuts, colouring and straightening. A year ago, at the start of his 2009 financial year, Oliver decided to expand his operations to include the hairdressing needs of male clients. Male hairdressing prices are lower, the work simpler (mainly hair cuts only) and so the time taken per male client is much less.

The prices for the female clients were not increased during the whole of 2008 and 2009 and the mix of services provided for female clients in the two years was the same. The latest financial results are as follows:

	2008		2009	
	$	$	$	$
Sales		200,000		238,500
Less cost of sales:				
Hairdressing staff costs	65,000		91,000	
Hair products – female	29,000		27,000	
Hair products – male			8,000	
		94,000		126,000
Gross profit		106,000		112,500
Rent	10,000		10,000	
Administration salaries	9,000		9,500	
Electricity	7,000		8,000	
Advertising	2,000		5,000	
Total expenses		28,000		32,500
Profit		78,000		80,000

Oliver is disappointed with his financial results. He thinks the salon is much busier than a year ago and was expecting more profit. He has noted the following extra information:

1 Some female clients complained about the change in atmosphere following the introduction of male services, which created tension in the salon.

2 Two new staff were recruited at the start of 2009. The first was a junior hairdresser to support the specialist hairdressers for the female clients. She was appointed on a salary of $9,000 per annum. The second new staff member was a specialist hairdresser for the male clients. There were no increases in pay for existing staff at the start of 2009 after a big rise at the start of 2008 which was designed to cover two years' worth of increases.

Oliver introduced some non-financial measures of success two years ago.

	2008	2009
Number of complaints	12	46
Number of male client visits	0	3,425
Number of female client visits	8,000	6,800
Number of specialist hairdressers for female clients	4	5
Number of specialist hairdressers for male clients	0	1

Required:

(a)   **Assess the financial performance of the Salon using the data above.**   **(10 marks)**

(b)   **Analyse and briefly comment on the non-financial performance of Oliver's business, under the headings of quality and resource utilisation.**   **(5 marks)**

(Total: 15 marks)

 Calculate your allowed time, allocate the time to the separate parts.....................

282 SQUARIZE (JUNE 2013 EXAM)

Squarize is a large company which, for many years, operated solely as a pay-tv broadcaster. However, five years ago, it started product bundling, offering broadband and telephone services to its pay-tv customers. Customers taking up the offer were then known in the business as 'bundle customers' and they had to take up both the broadband and telephone services together with the pay-tv service. Other customers were still able to subscribe to pay-tv alone but not to broadband and telephone services without the pay-tv service.

All contracts to customers of Squarize are for a minimum three-month period. The pay-tv box is sold to the customer at the beginning of the contract; however, the broadband and telephone equipment is only rented to them.

In the first few years after product bundling was introduced, the company saw a steady increase in profits. Then, Squarize saw its revenues and operating profits fall. Consequently, staff bonuses were not paid, and staff became dissatisfied. Several reasons were identified for the deterioration of results:

(1)   In the economy as a whole, discretionary spending had been severely hit by rising unemployment and inflation. In a bid to save cash, many pay-tv customers were cancelling their contracts after the minimum three-month period as they were then able to still keep the pay-tv box. The box comes with a number of free channels, which the customer can still continue to receive free of charge, even after the cancellation of their contract.

(2)   The company's customer service call centre, which is situated in another country, had been the cause of lots of complaints from customers about poor service, and, in particular, the number of calls it sometimes took to resolve an issue.

(3)   Some bundle customers found that the broadband service that they had subscribed to did not work. As a result, they were immediately cancelling their contracts for all services within the 14 day cancellation period permitted under the contracts.

In a response to the above problems and in an attempt to increase revenues and profits, Squarize made the following changes to the business:

(1)   It made a strategic decision to withdraw the pay-tv–broadband–telephone package from the market and, instead, offer each service as a standalone product.

(2)   It guaranteed not to increase prices for a 12-month period for each of its three services.

(3)   It transferred its call centre back to its home country and increased the level of staff training given for call centre workers.

(4)   It investigated and resolved the problem with customers' broadband service.

It is now one year since the changes were made and the finance director wants to use a balanced scorecard to assess the extent to which the changes have been successful in improving the performance of the business.

Required:

For each perspective of the balanced scorecard, identify ONE goal (objective) together with a corresponding performance measure that could be used by the company to assess whether the changes have been successful.

Justify the use of each of the performance measures that you choose.

(Total: 10 marks)

283 BATH CO (DEC 2011 EXAM)

Bath Co is a company specialising in the manufacture and sale of baths. Each bath consists of a main unit plus a set of bath fittings. The company is split into two divisions, A and B. Division A manufactures the bath and Division B manufactures sets of bath fittings. Currently, all of Division A's sales are made externally. Division B, however, sells to Division A as well as to external customers. Both of the divisions are profit centres.

The following data is available for both divisions:

Division A

Current selling price for each bath	$450
Costs per bath:	
Fittings from Division B	$75
Other materials from external suppliers	$200
Labour costs	$45
Annual fixed overheads	$7,440,000
Annual production and sales of baths (units)	80,000
Maximum annual market demand for baths (units)	80,000

Division B

Current external selling price per set of fittings	$80
Current price for sales to Division A	$75
Costs per set of fittings:	
Materials	$5
Labour costs	$15
Annual fixed overheads	$4,400,000
Maximum annual production and sales of sets of fittings (units) (including internal and external sales)	200,000
Maximum annual external demand for sets of fittings (units)	180,000
Maximum annual internal demand for sets of fittings (units)	80,000

The transfer price charged by Division B to Division A was negotiated some years ago between the previous divisional managers, who have now both been replaced by new managers. Head Office only allows Division A to purchase its fittings from Division B, although the new manager of Division A believes that he could obtain fittings of the same quality and appearance for $65 per set, if he was given the autonomy to purchase from outside the company. Division B makes no cost savings from supplying internally to Division A rather than selling externally.

Required:

(a)   Under the current transfer pricing system, prepare a profit statement showing the profit for each of the divisions and for Bath Co as a whole. Your sales and costs figures should be split into external sales and inter-divisional transfers, where appropriate.

(6 marks)

(b)   Head Office is considering changing the transfer pricing policy to ensure maximisation of company profits without demotivating either of the divisional managers. Division A will be given autonomy to buy from external suppliers and Division B to supply external customers in priority to supplying to Division A.

Calculate the maximum profit that could be earned by Bath Co if transfer pricing is optimised and recommend a transfer pricing policy Bath Co should adopt.

(9 marks)

(Total: 15 marks)

284   FP

FP sells and repairs photocopiers. The company has operated for many years with two departments, the Sales Department and the Service Department, but the departments had no autonomy. The company is now thinking of restructuring so that the two departments will become profit centres.

The Sales Department

This department sells new photocopiers. The department sells 2,000 copiers per year. Included in the selling price is $60 for a one-year guarantee to ensure that customers do not need to pay for repairs in the first year. On average 500 photocopiers per year need to be repaired under the guarantee. It is estimated that on average the repairs will take 3 hours each.

The Service Department

This department has two sources of work – the work needed to satisfy the guarantees for the Sales Department and repair work for external customers. Customers are charged at full cost plus 40%. The details of the budget for the next year for the Service Department revealed standard costs of:

Parts	At cost
Labour	$15 per hour
Variable overheads	$10 per labour hour
Fixed overheads	$22 per labour hour

The calculation of these standards is based on the estimated maximum market demand and includes the expected 500 repairs for the Sales Department. The average cost of the parts needed for a repair is $54. This means that the charge to the Sales Department for the repair work, including the 40% mark-up, will be $136,500.

Proposed change

It has now been suggested that FP should be structured so that the two departments become profit centres and that the managers of the Departments are given autonomy. The individual salaries of the managers would be linked to the profits of their respective departments.

Budgets have been produced for each department on the assumption that the Service Department will repair 500 photocopiers for the Sales Department and that the transfer price for this work will be calculated in the same way as the price charged to external customers.

However the manager of the Sales Department has now stated that he intends to have the repairs done by another company, RS, because it has offered to carry out the work for a fixed fee of $180 per repair and this is less than the price that the Service Department would charge.

Required:

(a) Calculate the individual profits of the Sales Department and the Service Department, and of FP as a whole from the guarantee scheme if:

   (i) the repairs are carried out by the Service Department and are charged at full cost plus 40%

   (ii) the repairs are carried out by the Service Department and are charged at marginal cost

   (iii) the repairs are carried out by RS. **(9 marks)**

(b) (i) Explain, with reasons, why a 'full cost plus' transfer pricing model may *not* be appropriate for FP. **(3 marks)**

   (ii) Comment on THREE other issues that the managers of FP should consider if they decide to allow RS to carry out the repairs. **(3 marks)**

(Total: 15 marks)

285 CTD

CTD has two divisions — FD and TM. FD is an iron foundry division which produces mouldings that have a limited external market and are also transferred to TM division.

TM division uses the mouldings to produce a piece of agricultural equipment called the 'TX' which is sold externally. Each TX requires one moulding. Both divisions produce only one type of product.

The performance of each Divisional Manager is evaluated individually on the basis of the residual income (RI) of his or her division. The company's average annual 12% cost of capital is used to calculate the finance charges. If their own target residual income is achieved, each Divisional Manager is awarded a bonus equal to 5% of his or her residual income. All bonuses are paid out of Head Office profits.

The following budgeted information is available for the forthcoming year:

	TM division TX per unit	FD division Moulding per unit
External selling price ($)	500	80
Variable production cost ($)	*366	40
Fixed production overheads ($)	60	20
Gross profit ($)	74	20
Variable selling and distribution cost ($)	25	**4
Fixed administration overhead ($)	25	4
Net profit ($)	24	12
Normal capacity (units)	15,000	20,000
Maximum production capacity (units)	15,000	25,000
Sales to external customers (units)	15,000	5,000
Capital employed	$1,500,000	$750,000
Target RI	$105,000	$85,000

* The variable production cost of TX includes the cost of an FD moulding.

** External sales only of the mouldings incur a variable selling and distribution cost of $4 per unit.

FD division currently transfers 15,000 mouldings to TM division at a transfer price equal to the total production cost plus 10%.

Fixed costs are absorbed on the basis of normal capacity.

Required:

(a) Calculate the bonus each Divisional Manager would receive under the current transfer pricing policy and discuss any implications that the current performance evaluation system may have for each division and for the company as a whole.

(10 marks)

(b) Both Divisional Managers want to achieve their respective residual income targets. Based on the budgeted figures, calculate:

(i) the maximum transfer price per unit that the Divisional Manager of TM division would pay

(ii) the minimum transfer price per unit that the Divisional Manager of FD division would accept.

(5 marks)

(Total: 15 marks)

286   WASH CO (DEC 2012 EXAM)

Wash Co assembles and sells two types of washing machines – the Spin (S) and the Rinse (R). The company has two divisions: the assembly division, and the retail division.

The company's policy is to transfer the machines from the assembly division to the retail division at full cost plus 10%. This has resulted in internal transfer prices, when S and R are being transferred to the retail division, of $220.17 and $241.69 respectively.

The retail division currently sells S to the general public for $320 per machine and R for $260 per machine. Assume it incurs no other costs except for the transfer price.

Based on this the following profit was achieved:

	Product S	Product R	Total *
	$	$	$
Assembly's division profit	64,064	119,737	183,801
Retail division's profit	319,456	99,790	419,246
			603,047*

The retail division's manager is convinced that, if he could obtain R at a lower cost and therefore reduce the external selling price from $260 to $230 per unit, he could significantly increase sales of R, which would be beneficial to both divisions.

He has questioned the fact that the overhead costs are allocated to the products on the basis of labour hours; he thinks it should be done using activity based costing.

You have obtained the following information for the last month from the assembly division:

	Product S	Product R
Production and sales (units)	3,200	5,450
Materials cost	$117	$95
Labour cost (at $12 per hour)	$6	$9
Machine hours (per unit)	2	1
Total no. of production runs	30	12
Total no. of purchase orders	82	64
Total no. of deliveries to retail division	64	80

Overhead costs:	$
Machine set-up costs	306,435
Machine maintenance costs	415,105
Ordering costs	11,680
Delivery costs	144,400
Total	877,620

Required:

(a) Using activity based costing to allocate the overheads, recalculate the transfer prices for S and R.

Note: round all workings to 2 decimal places. **(8 marks)**

(b) (i) Calculate last month's profit for each division, showing it both for each product and in total, if activity based costing is used. **(3 marks)**

(ii) Discuss whether activity based costing should be implemented, considering the decision from the view of each of the divisional managers. **(4 marks)**

(Total: 15 marks)

287 BISCUITS AND CAKES (JUNE 2012 EXAM)

The Biscuits division (Division B) and the Cakes division (Division C) are two divisions of a large, manufacturing company. Whilst both divisions operate in almost identical markets, each division operates separately as an investment centre. Each month, operating statements must be prepared by each division and these are used as a basis for performance measurement for the divisions.

Last month, senior management decided to recharge head office costs to the divisions. Consequently, each division is now going to be required to deduct a share of head office costs in its operating statement before arriving at 'net profit', which is then used to calculate return on investment (ROI). Prior to this, ROI has been calculated using controllable profit only. The company's target ROI, however, remains unchanged at 20% per annum. For each of the last three months, Divisions B and C have maintained ROIs of 22% per annum and 23% per annum respectively, resulting in healthy bonuses being awarded to staff. The company has a cost of capital of 10%.

The budgeted operating statement for the month of July is shown below:

	B	C
	$000	$000
Sales revenue	1,300	1,500
Less variable costs	(700)	(800)
Contribution	600	700
Less controllable fixed costs	(134)	(228)
Controllable profit	466	472
Less apportionment of head office costs	(155)	(180)
Net profit	311	292
Divisional net assets	$23.2m	$22.6m

Required:

(a) Calculate the expected annualised Return on Investment (ROI) using the new method as preferred by senior management, based on the above budgeted operating statements, for each of the divisions. (2 marks)

(b) The divisional managing directors are unhappy about the results produced by your calculations in (a) and have heard that a performance measure called 'residual income' may provide more information.

Calculate the annualised residual income (RI) for each of the divisions, based on the net profit figures for the month of July. (3 marks)

(c) Discuss the expected performance of each of the two divisions, using both ROI and RI, and making any additional calculations deemed necessary. Conclude as to whether, in your opinion, the two divisions have performed well. (5 marks)

(d) Division B has now been offered an immediate opportunity to invest in new machinery at a cost of $2.12 million. The machinery is expected to have a useful economic life of four years, after which it could be sold for $200,000. Division B's policy is to depreciate all of its machinery on a straight-line basis over the life of the asset. The machinery would be expected to expand Division B's production capacity, resulting in an 8.5% increase in contribution per month.

Recalculate Division B's expected annualised ROI and annualised RI, based on July's budgeted operating statement after adjusting for the investment. State whether the managing director will be making a decision that is in the best interests of the company as a whole if ROI is used as the basis of the decision. (5 marks)

(Total: 15 marks)

288 PUBLIC SECTOR ORGANISATION

A public sector organisation is extending its budgetary control and responsibility accounting system to all departments. One such department concerned with public health and welfare is called 'Homecare'. The department consists of staff who visit elderly 'clients' in their homes to support them with their basic medical and welfare needs.

A monthly cost control report is to be sent to the department manager, a copy of which is also passed to a Director who controls a number of departments. In the system, which is still being refined, the budget was set by the Director and the manager had not been consulted over the budget or the use of the monthly control report.

Shown below is the first month's cost control report for the Homecare department:

Cost Control Report – Homecare Department

Month ending May 20X0

	Budget	Actual	(Overspend)/underspend
Visits	10,000	12,000	(2,000)
	$	$	$
Department expenses:			
Supervisory salary	2,000	2,125	(125)
Wages (Permanent staff)	2,700	2,400	300
Wages (Casual staff)	1,500	2,500	(1,000)

	Budget	Actual	(Overspend)/underspend
Office equipment depreciation	500	750	(250)
Repairs to equipment	200	20	180
Travel expenses	1,500	1,800	(300)
Consumables	4,000	6,000	(2,000)
Administration and telephone	1,000	1,200	(200)
Allocated administrative costs	2,000	3,000	(1,000)
	15,400	19,795	(4,395)

In addition to the manager and permanent members of staff, appropriately qualified casual staff are appointed on a week to week basis to cope with fluctuations in demand. Staff use their own transport, and travel expenses are reimbursed. There is a central administration overhead charge over all departments. Consumables consist of materials which are used by staff to care for clients. Administration and telephone are costs of keeping in touch with the staff who often operate from their own homes.

As a result of the report, the Director sent a memo to the manager of the Homecare department pointing out that the department must spend within its funding allocation and that any spending more than 5% above budget on any item would not be tolerated. The Director requested an immediate explanation for the serious overspend.

You work as the assistant to the Directorate Management Accountant. On seeing the way the budget system was developing, he made a note of points he would wish to discuss and develop further, but was called away before these could be completed.

Required:

Develop and explain the issues concerning the budgetary control and responsibility accounting system which are likely to be raised by the management accountant. You should refer to the way the budget was prepared, the implications of a 20% increase in the number of visits, the extent of controllability of costs, the implications of the funding allocation, social aspects and any other points you think appropriate. You may include numerical illustrations and comment on specific costs, but you are not required to reproduce the cost control report.

(Total: 15 marks)

289 WOODSIDE CHARITY (JUNE 07 EXAM)

Woodside is a local charity dedicated to helping homeless people in a large city. The charity owns and manages a shelter that provides free overnight accommodation for up to 30 people, offers free meals each and every night of the year to homeless people who are unable to buy food, and runs a free advice centre to help homeless people find suitable housing and gain financial aid. Woodside depends entirely on public donations to finance its activities and had a fundraising target for the last year of $700,000. The budget for the last year was based on the following forecast activity levels and expected costs.

Free meals provision:	18,250 meals at $5 per meal
Overnight shelter:	10,000 bed-nights at $30 per night
Advice centre:	3,000 sessions at $20 per session
Campaigning and advertising:	$150,000

The number of free meals provided and the number of beds occupied each night depends on both the weather and the season of the year. The Woodside charity has three full-time staff and a large number of voluntary helpers.

The actual amount of funds raised in the last year was $620,000.

An operating statement has been prepared as follows:

	$	$	$
Budgeted surplus			98,750
Funding shortfall			(80,000)
			18,750

	Favourable	*Adverse*	
Free meals			
Price variance		4,000	
Usage variance		8,750	
Overnight shelter			
Price variance		4,380	
Usage variance	31,000		
Advice centre			
Price variance		9,100	
Usage variance		7,500	
Campaigning and advertising			
Expenditure variance		15,000	
Fixed cost			
Expenditure variance		18,000	
	31,000	66,730	(35,730)
Actual shortfall			(16,980)

Required:

(a) Discuss the charity's performance over the last year. **(6 marks)**

(b) Discuss problems that may arise in the financial management and control of a not-for-profit organisation such as the Woodside charity. **(9 marks)**

(Total: 15 marks)

Section 3

ANSWERS TO OBJECTIVE TEST QUESTIONS

SPECIALIST COST AND MANAGEMENT ACCOUNTING TECHNIQUES

ACTIVITY BASED COSTING

1   D

A total figure is needed and assuming distance travelled increases the costs of handling, then the correct answer is D.

2   D

The overhead absorption rate per production run is calculated as

$$OAR = \frac{Production\ set\text{-}up\ costs, in\ \$}{Number\ of\ production\ runs}$$

$$OAR = \frac{\$2,150}{3\ production\ runs\ every\ week}$$

OAR = $716.67 per production run.

For the Palace Bugle, 2 set-up runs × $716.67 per run = $1,433.33. Spread over 25,000 copies, this amounts to $\frac{\$1,433.33}{25,000\ papers}$ = $0.057 per copy.

3   D

Statement (1) provides a definition of a cost driver. Cost drivers for long-term variable overhead costs will be the volume of a particular activity to which the cost driver relates, so Statement (2) is correct. Statement (3) is also correct. In traditional absorption costing, standard high-volume products receive a higher amount of overhead costs than with ABC. ABC allows for the unusually high costs of support activities for low-volume products (such as relatively higher set-up costs, order processing costs and so on).

4   A

5   C

Overhead absorption rate = $\dfrac{\text{Total overhead cost}}{\text{Total number of direct labour hours}}$

Overhead absorption rate = $\dfrac{\$420,000}{66,000 \text{ Direct labour hours}}$

Overhead absorption rate = $6.36 per labour hour. Alpha uses 5 direct labour hours per unit so will have an overhead cost per unit of 5 hours × $6.36 per hour = $31.82.

6   C

The overhead cost per unit for each unit of product Beta will be the same as product Alpha, as both products use the same number of labour hours (5 hours.)

7   C

	Volume related	Purchasing related	Set-up related
Costs	$100,000	$145,000	$ 175,000
Consumption of activities (cost drivers)	66,000 labour hours	160 purchase orders	100 set-ups
Cost per unit of cost driver	$1.5151 per labour hour	$906.25 per purchase order	$1,750 per set-up
Costs per product			
Product Alpha:	6,000 labour hours cost: $ 9,090.91	75 purchase orders cost: $ 67,968.75	40 set-ups cost: $70,000
Product Beta:	60,000 labour hours cost: $ 90,909.09	85 purchase orders cost: $ 77,031.25	60 set-up cost: $105,000

Total overhead cost for Alpha = $9,090.91 + $67,968.75 + $70,000 = $147,060. Spread over 1,200 units, this represents a cost per unit of $122.55 approx

8   B

Total overhead cost for Beta = $90,909.09 + $77,031.25 + $105,000 = $272,940.34. Spread over 12,000 units, this represents a cost per unit of $22.75 approx

9   B

Set-up costs per production run = $140,000/28 = $5,000

Cost per inspection = $80,000/8 = $10,000

Other overhead costs per labour hour = $96,000/48,000 = $2

Overheads costs of product D:

Set-up costs (15 × $5,000) $75,000

Inspection costs (3 × $10,000) $30,000

Other overheads (40,000 × $2) $80,000

So total overhead costs pf product D: $185,000 and overhead cost per unit = 185,000/ 4,000 = $46.25

10   A

Absorption costing

Since the time per unit is the same for each product, the overheads per unit will also be the same.

$156,000 ÷ 6,000 units = $26

Activity based costing

Number of deliveries for X (1,000/200)	5
Number of deliveries for Y (2,000/400)	5
Number of deliveries for Z (3,000/1,000)	3
Total	13

Cost per delivery = $156,000/13 = $12,000

Cost per unit of Z = ($12,000/3,000 units) × 3 deliveries = $12

Decrease = $26 – $12 = $14.

11   C

Cost driver = number of set-ups

Cost pool = $84,000

Total set-ups= 20 (for A) + 8 (for B) = 28

Rate =$84,000/28=5 $3,000 per set-up

Cost for B = $3,000 × 8 set-ups= $24,000

Per unit = $24,000/40,000 = $0.60.

12   B

Total set-ups = Budget production/batch size x set-ups per batch

D (100,000/100 × 3)	3,000
R (100,000/50 × 4)	8,000
P (50,000/25 × 6)	12,000
	23,000

Cost per set-up = $150,000/23,000 = $6.52

Therefore cost per unit of R = $6.52 × 8,000 set-ups/100,000 units = $0.52.

13   A

Cost driver = number of set-ups   Cost pool = $12,000

Total set-ups = 20 (for A) + 4 (for B) = 24   Rate = $12,000/24 = $500 per set-up

Cost for A = $500 × 20 set-ups = $10,000   Per unit=$10,000/20,000 = $0.50

TARGET COSTING

Tutorial note

A technical article 'Target Costing and Lifecycle Costing' has been published on the ACCA website – make sure you read it as part of your revision.

14   C

15   D

Answer A is not correct: increasing the selling price is not possible, the industry is competitive so product will not sell effectively at higher prices. Answer B ('Reduce the expectation gap by reducing the selling price') is not target costing. Answer C ('Reducing the desired margin on the product') is not possible either: shareholders are demanding and would expect a good return.

16   C

To reduce the acceptable margin would normally require agreement from the owners and altering selling prices in any direction is not valid as the start point of target costing is to find a competing product's price, this cannot be changed.

17   A

The maximum rate per hour is $12.40

	$
Selling price	56.00
Profit (56 × 25/125)	11.20
Target cost	**44.80**
Material cost (16 × 10/8)	20.00
Labour – 2 hours	24.80
Labour rate per hour = 24.80/2	$12.40

18   B

	$
Target cost	38.00
Actual cost (38.00 × 100/95)	40.00
Material	10.00
Labour cost (3.75 hrs × $8/hr)	30.00
Required labour cost (3.5 hrs × $8/hr)	28.00
% Reduction is therefore 0.25/3.75	6.67%

Key answer tip:

A simpler approach is to take 2/30 = 6.67%.

Answer C measures efficiency based on the 3.50 hours rather than the 3.75 hours figure.

Answer D incorrectly calculates actual cost as 38.00 × 95% = 36.10 and then proceeds correctly.

19   D

Sales revenue 500 units @ $250	$125,000
Return on investment required 15% × $250,000	$37,500
Total cost allowed	$87.500
Target cost per unit	$175

20   D

LIFECYCLE COSTING

21   D

22   C

$$\text{Lifecycle costing cost per console} = \frac{\$\text{Total costs incurred in years 2015 to 2018 inclusive}}{\text{Number of manufactured consoles}}$$

$$\text{Lifecycle costing cost per console} = \frac{\$16,438,000}{36,100\,\text{units}}$$

Lifecycle costing cost per console = $455.35

23   D

24 A

Shortening the length of a lifecycle is not desirable and decline (for most products) is inevitable.

25 A

(i) This is true, justifying the time and effort of life cycle costing.

(ii) As above.

(iii) This is not true: life cycle costing is not about setting selling prices, it is about linking total revenues to total costs. Even if it were about setting a selling price, the early sales may well be at a loss since it is TOTAL revenues and costs that are considered. Furthermore, the pre-launch costs are sunk at launch and are therefore irrelevant when setting a selling price.

(iv) This is true. The deliberate attempt to maximise profitability is the key to life cycle costing.

26 B

27 A

The original life cycle cost per unit = ($43,000 + (20,000 × $15) + $30,000)/20,000 = $18.65

THROUGHPUT ACCOUNTING

28 C

Overall the cost per unit should reduce, and so the measure for throughput should improve.

A is wrong as the TPAR measures return based on the slowest machine not the fastest. B is wrong since rent has increased so the TPAR will worsen from its current level. D is wrong since we cannot meet demand even at the moment so reducing prices will reduce throughput per unit without any extra sales level benefit.

29 B

$$\text{Return per factory hour} = \frac{\text{Throughput per unit}}{\text{Bottleneck hrs per unit}} = \frac{\$210 - \$26}{5 \, \text{hours}} = \$36.80$$

$$\text{Cost per factory hour} = \frac{\text{Total factory cost}}{\text{Total bottleneck hrs}} = \frac{(\$19 + \$15) \times 150 \, \text{units}}{4 \, \text{machines} \times 8 \, \text{hours a day} \times 5 \, \text{days a week}}$$

$$= \$31.875$$

$$\text{Throughput accounting ratio} = \frac{\text{Return per factory hr}}{\text{Cost per factory hr}} = \frac{\$36.80}{\$31.875} = 1.15$$

30   B

The first step is to identify the bottleneck.

Process P output is 6 × 8 × 0.9 = 43.2 per hour. Process Q output is 9 × 6 × 0.85 = 45.9 per hour. In the absence of other information, then process P is slower, and so is the bottleneck.

Cloud:

Throughput:	$
Selling price ($20 × 0.85)	17.00
Material cost	5.00
Throughput per unit	12.00
Time in process P (hrs)	2
TP per hour	6.00

31   C

Key answer tips

Although the formulae below have been expressed in the normal way, i.e. in hours, the calculations have been performed in minutes as this is easier.

			GL1	GL2	GL3
Return per factory hour	$= \dfrac{\text{Throughput per unit}}{\text{Bottleneck hrs per unit}} =$		$\dfrac{40-12}{2\,\text{min}}$	$\dfrac{50-8}{4\,\text{min}}$	$\dfrac{60-6}{5\,\text{min}}$
			= $14	= $10.5	= $10.8
Cost per factory hour	$= \dfrac{\text{Total factory cost}}{\text{Total bottleneck hrs}} =$			$\dfrac{£120,000}{200\,\text{hrs} \times 60\,\text{min}}$	
				= $10	
Throughput accounting ratio	$= \dfrac{\text{Return per factory hr}}{\text{Cost per factory hr}} =$		$\dfrac{£14}{£10}$	$\dfrac{£10.5}{£10}$	$\dfrac{£10.8}{£10}$
			= 1.4	= 1.05	1.08

32 D

All of these points are true, except D.

Throughput accounting was designed as a performance measurement tool, not a decision-making tool.

One of its advantages is that it will be used by managers to make decisions that have outcomes that are goal congruent with corporate aims. However, it was designed as a performance measurement tool.

33 C

Answer C is the same as total throughput/total conversion costs, which is an alternative, correct, definition (which gives the same value).

Answers B and D are the same: they are the correct ratio inverted.

Answer A is often referred to as the return per hour.

34 D

The throughput accounting ratio is defined as throughput/total factory costs (these can both be calculated per hour, but that is, more work for the same answer).

Throughput = sales – all material costs = $9,000 – $3,000 = $6,000

(Note that we use materials purchased instead of materials used.)

Total factory costs 5 all other production costs = $2,000 + $1,500 = $3,500

TA ratio = $6,000/$3,500 = 1.7.

35 C

The throughput accounting ratio is defined as throughput/total factory costs.

Throughput accounting aims to discourage inventory building, so the ratios do not take account of inventory movements.

Throughput = sales – all material costs = $35 × 800 – $13,000 = $15,000

(Note that we use materials purchased instead of materials used.)

Total factory costs= all other production costs= $6,900 + $4,650 = $11,550

TA ratio = $15,000/$11,550 = 1.3.

ENVIRONMENTAL ACCOUNTING

Tutorial note

A technical article 'Environmental Management Accounting' has been published on the ACCA website – make sure you read it as part of your revision.

36   A

37   D

38   A

Statements (iii) and (iv) are not true

39   D

(i) is an example of an environmental appraisal cost, and (ii) is an example of an environmental internal failure cost.

40   D

DECISION-MAKING TECHNIQUES

RELEVANT COST ANALYSIS

41   B

The book value is an historic cost and therefore not relevant. There is no intention to replace material X. There are two options for material X, scrap at a value of 50p per kg or use as a replacement for material Y, which would save $4 per kg ($6 – $2). The latter is the preferable option so the relevant cost is $4 per kg for 10 kgs = $40.

42   C

Labour is in short supply so there is an opportunity cost. The contribution from Contract Z will still be earned but will be delayed. The relevant cost is therefore the wages earned plus the penalty fee.

($15 × 100) + ($1,000) = $2,500

43   B

The material is in regular use by the organisation and so would be replaced if it is used on the special order. The material is readily available at a price of $3.24 per kg.

Therefore the relevant cost of the material is 1,250 kgs × $3.24 = $4,050.

44   D

Replacement material cost saved (4 kg @ $5.00)	$20.00
Less further processing cost ($0.75 × 5 kg)	$3.75
Value of M in current use, for each unit made	$16.25

Therefore opportunity cost of using M on the job being tendered for is $16.25/5 kg = $3.25 per kg.

45   C

Since material J is in regular use and is readily available in the market, its relevant cost is the replacement price of $8/kg.

So 2,000 kgs × $8/kg = $16,000

46   A

3,700 kg × $3.80 + 500 kg × $6.30 = $17,210

Tutorial note

The company needs 4,200 kg. It has 3,700 kg in inventory. It will therefore need to buy 500 kg and these can be bought for $6.30 per kg. The tricky bit is the value to the company of the 3,700 kg in inventory. The $4.50 original purchase price is of course a sunk cost and cannot be relevant. The inventory can be sold for $3.20 per kg, so this is its very minimum value.

The inventory is worth $3.20 per kg unless the company has an even better alternative - and there is a better alternative. The company can take the inventory and, by spending $3.70 per kg on it, can turn it into something worth $7.50 per kg. If something will be worth $7.50 if we spend $3.70 on it, then it is at present worth $3.80. This then is the value of the inventory to the company and to fulfil the contract the company will use 3,700 kg of inventory with a value of $3.80 per kg

47   C

The relevant cash flow is:

Lost disposal proceeds (net)	$10,300
Additional costs of set up	$1,300
Total	$11,600

48   A

The relevant cash flow is:

Extra variable overheads: 450 hours × $4/hr	$1,800
Rent	$1,200
Total	$3,000

Fixed costs are not incremental and idle time would normally mean that the machines are not in use are so are not an incurred cost.

49   D

The options are:

Agency 600 × $9/hr =	$5,400
Internal transfer 600 × (7 + 3) =	$6,000
Hire new $1,200 + (600 × $6/hr)	$4,800

Cleverclogs would select the lower of the costs and so this is the relevant cash flow.

50   D

It could be argued that it is also a sunk cost but the better and more exact description is that it is a committed cost as the cash has not yet been actually paid over.

51   C

52   B

The book value is not relevant as it is a sunk cost. The relevant cost of the paper in inventory is the resale value as that is its next best use. The remaining material required must be bought at the replacement cost of $26.

100 reams @ $10	$1,000
150 reams @ $26	$3,900
	————
	$4,900
	————

COST VOLUME PROFIT ANALYSIS

53   B

Current breakeven point is: $640,000/40 =	16,000 units
New breakeven point is: $400,000/35 =	11,429 units
Change in level of breakeven is 16,000 − 11,429 =	4,571 units
Current Contribution is: $60 − $20 =	$40
New contribution is $60 − $20 − $5 =	$35

Operating risk reduces with less fixed costs in a business.

54 C

Number of units required to make target profit = fixed costs + target profit/contribution per unit of P1.

Fixed costs = ($1.2 × 10,000) + ($1 × 12,500) − $2,500 = $22,000.

Contribution per unit of P = $3.20 + $1.20 = $4.40.

($22,000 + $60,000)/$4.40 = 18,636 units.

55 A

The breakeven revenue is FC/CS = $1,600,000/0.4 =	$4,000,000
Budget revenue is FC × 6 = $1,600,000 × 6 =	$9,600,000
Margin of safety is = (9,600,000 − 4,000,000)/9,600,000 =	58.3%

56 C

Contribution: $5,000,000 − ($1,400,000 + $400,000) =	$3,200,000
For 20,000 units, that is a contribution of	$160 per unit
Fixed costs amount to $1,600,000 + $1,200,000 =	$2,800,000
BEP units = FC/Unit contribution i.e. $2,800,000/$160 =	17,500

57 A

Selling price per unit ($36/0.75) =	$48
Contribution per unit $48 − $36 =	$42
Fixed costs	$18,000
Therefore, breakeven point (units) is $18,000/$12 =	1,500

58 A

Breakeven volume in units $79,104/$12 =	6,592
Margin of safety = (7,500 − 6,592)/7,500 =	12.1%

59   D

	Now $	Revised $
Selling price	20	21,600
Variable cost	8	8,416
	12	13,184

Breakeven volume $79,104/$12 = 6,592

$79,104/$13,184 = 6,000

Decrease in breakeven volume = 592/6,592 × 100% = 9%

60   D

The breakeven revenue (BER) = Fixed costs/average CS ratio

BER = $1,400,000/0.2375 (W1) = $5,894,737

(W1)

	Product F $	Product G $	Total $
Budget revenue	6,000,000	2,000,000	8,000,000
Contribution	1,500,000	400,000	1,900,000
C/S	0.25	0.2	
Average C/S			0.2375

61   C

Because the C/S ratio of product G is lower than F the change in mix would reduce the average C/S ratio. As a consequence the BER would increase by an amount but not by the amount of extra sales of product G. This is not relevant.

62   B

Statement (i) is correct. The line which passes through the origin indicates the sales revenue at various levels of activity. At an activity level of 10,000 units, the sales revenue is $100,000, therefore the selling price is $10 per unit.

Statement (ii) is incorrect. The sloping line which intercepts the vertical axis at $30,000 shows the total cost at various levels of activity. The total cost for 10,000 units is $80,000, from which we subtract the $30,000 fixed costs.

Statement (iii) is correct. The fixed cost is the cost incurred at zero activity, and is shown as a horizontal line at $30,000.

Statement (i) is incorrect. The profit for 10,000 units is the difference between the sales value $100,000 and the total cost of $80,000, which amounts to $20,000.

LIMITING FACTORS

63 A

Product	A	B	C	D
Selling price per unit	$160	$214	$100	$140
Raw material costs	$24	$56	$22	$40
Direct labour cost at $11 per hour	$66	$88	$33	$22
Variable overhead cost	$24	$18	$24	$18
Contribution per unit	$46	$52	$21	$60
Direct labour hours per unit	6	8	3	2
Contribution per labour hour	$7.67	$6.50	$7	$30
Rank	2	4	3	1
Normal monthly hours (total units × hours per unit)	1,800	1,000	720	800

If the strike goes ahead, only 2,160 labour hours will be available. Therefore make all of Product D, then 1,360 hours' worth of Product A (2,160 – 800 hrs).

64 A

Product cost per unit		E1		E2		E3		E4
		$		$		$		$
Conversion costs		40		65		65		55
Less general fixed costs absorbed	0.5 × $30	15	0.5 × $30	15	0.6 × $30	18	0.6 × $30	18
Variable conversion cost		25		50		47		37
Material cost		24		33		41		30
Total variable cost		49		83		88		67
Selling price		90		112		123		103
Contribution		41		29		35		36
Contribution for each $1 spent on material		1.71		0.88		0.85		1.20
Ranking		1st		3rd		4th		2nd

65 D

The company maximises contribution by producing Qutwo. Contribution per unit of material is:

$$\frac{\$8.50}{2.5\,kg} = \$3.40 \text{ and this is the shadow price.}$$

66   D

	$
Direct material	3.00
Direct labour (W1)	9.00
Variable overhead	1.00
Specific fixed cost	2.50
	15.50

(W1)   Relevant cost = Contribution Forgone + Direct labour = $10/2 + $4 = $9

67   D

	R	S	T
	$	$	$
Contribution per unit			
$(100 − 15 − 20 − 15)$	50		
$(150 − 30 − 35 − 20)$		65	
$(160 − 25 − 30 − 22)$			83
Direct labour cost per unit	20	35	30
Contribution per $1 of direct labour	2.50	1.85	2.77
Profitability ranking	2nd	3rd	1st

68   B

By definition, a shadow price is the amount by which contribution will increase if an extra kg of material becomes available. 20 × $2.80 = $56.

Tutorial note

In this question, the shadow price is $2.80 per unit, and therefore if 20 kgs of additional material Z becomes available, the increase in contribution would be $56 (20 × $2.80). The answer is therefore B. In the first distractor A, the cost of the material (20 kg × $2) has also been added to the $56. This is because a common mistake made is to add the cost of the material in too.

Similarly, in distractor C, the $40 has been deducted from the $56 leaving a figure of $16. This is because candidates often fail to realise that the shadow price is the amount over and above the normal cost that one would be prepared to pay for an extra unit of scarce material if it becomes available. Therefore, this would lead candidates to think that contribution would only increase by $0.80 ($2.80–$2) for each extra kg of material Z that becomes available resulting in a total increase in contribution of only $16.

69   C

A shadow price for a scarce resource is its opportunity cost. It is the amount of contribution that would be lost if one unit less of that resource were available. It is similarly the amount of additional contribution that would be earned if one unit more of that resource were available. (This is on the assumption that the scarce resource is available at its normal variable cost.)

PRICING DECISIONS

70 C

Not all discrimination is illegal (e.g. the cost of rail travel at peak times). Early adopters normally pay more and maximising sales volume normally means a lower profit.

71 C

72 A

If demand is inelastic or the product life cycle is short, a price skimming approach would be more appropriate.

73 D

74 B

75 B

76 C

Prime cost + 80% = 12 × (1.8) = $21.6

MC + 60% = 15 × (1.6) = $24.00

TAC + 20% = 21 × (1.2) = $25.20

Net margin would mean 21 × 100/86 = $24.40

77 D

$P = a + bQ$ and $b = -20/1000$ or -0.02

By substitution:

$400 = a - 0.02 (5000)$

$a = 500$

So demand equation is:

$P = 500 - 0.02Q$

$MR = 500 - 0.04Q$

78   C

MR = 500 – 0.04Q (as above)

MC = 200

Set MR = MC in order to profit maximise thus:

500 – 0.04Q = 200

–0.04 Q = – 300

Q = 7500

Substitute Q = 7500 in to the demand equation thus:

P = 500 – 0.02 (7500)

P = 350

79   B

The demand formula is P = a + bQ, with   b = change of price/change of demand quantity

b = –20/500 = –0.04

By substitution:

400 = a –0.04 (5,000)

400 = a – 200

a = 600

Hence: P = 600 – 0.04Q

80   B

P = 600 – 0.04Q

MR = 600 – 0.08Q

MC = 80

For profit maximisation MR = MC

600 – 0.08Q = 80

Q = –520/–0.08 = 6,500

Again by substitution:

P = 600 – 0.04 (6,500) so P = 340

81   C

Without brand loyalty or a long shelf life then a strategy of penetration is unlikely to work. Additionally the uniqueness of the product prevents low prices.

MAKE-OR-BUY AND OTHER SHORT-TERM DECISIONS

82   B

The correct items are:

- The variable costs of purchase from the new supplier
- The level of discount available from the new supplier
- The redundancy payments to the supervisor of the product in question
- The materials no longer bought to manufacture the product

83   C

Material A:

Stock – saved disposal costs =	($400)
Bought 300 kg @ $6.25/kg =	1,875
Net cost	$1,475

Material B
Regularly used so replacement cost needed

800 kg @ $3.75/kg	$3,000
Total	$4,475

84   C

The supervisor is a sunk cost.

85   B

The irrelevant items are:

- The diaries made a loss in the year just passed is a sunk event
- The diaries made a positive contribution in the year just passed is a sunk event
- The budget for next year shows a loss includes fixed costs and these are not relevant
- The business was founded to produce and sell diaries – things change!

86   A

	Before	After	Increment
	$	$	$
Revenue	375,000	625,000	250,000
Royalty		9,375	–9,375
Compound cost		78,125	–78,125
Production cost	150,000	187,500	–37,500
Improvement			125,000

Fixed costs will not change overall regardless of the allocation system. Revenue before = 25,000 × $15 = $375,000 and revenue after = 25,000 × 1.25 × $20 = $625,000.

Royalty = 25,000 × 1.25 × $2.50 = $78,125.

DEALING WITH RISK AND UNCERTAINTY IN DECISION-MAKING

87   C

A pessimistic buyer would seek to achieve the best results if the worst happens. He would adopt the maximin approach, which involves selecting the alternative that maximises the minimum payoff achievable. The minimum payoffs for each truck are as follows:

Truck A – Minimum $1,400

Truck B – Minimum $1,800

Truck C – Minimum $3,600

Therefore, the 'C' series truck would be chosen.

88   A

This maximises the average daily contribution if the growth rate is forty per cent.

89   C

Regret table		Type of truck		
		A Series	B Series	C Series
		$	$	$
Growth rate	15%	1,200	1,800	0
	30%	3,100	2,600	0
	40%	0	2,100	1,000
Max Regret		3,100	2,600	1,000

90   C

Expected value calculations:

A Series: ($2,400 × 0.4) + ($1,400 × 0.25) + ($4,900 × 0.35) = $3,025

B Series: ($1,800 × 0.4) + ($1,900 × 0.25) + ($2,800 × 0.35) = $2,175

C Series: ($3,600 × 0.4) + ($4,500 × 0.25) + ($3,900 × 0.35) = $3,930

91   C

92   B

Without information, the expected profits are:

Product X: $20,000 × 0.2 + $15,000 × 0.5 + $6,000 × 0.3	=	$13,300
Product Y: $17,000 × 0.2 + $16,000 × 0.5 + $7,000 × 0.3	=	$13,500

So without information, product Y would be selected.

With perfect information, product X would be selected if the market was good, and product Y in the other two cases. The expected value would then be:

$20,000 × 0.2 + $16,000 × 0.5 + $7,000 × 0.3	=	$14,100

The expected value of perfect information is therefore: $14,100 – $13,500 = $600

93   A

New profit figures before salary paid:

Good manager: $180,000 × 1.3 = $234,000 Average manager: $180,000 × 1.2 = $216,000 Poor: $180,000 x 1.1 = $198,000

EV of profits = (0.35 × $234,000) + (0.45 × $216,000) + (0.2 × $198,000) = $81,900 + $97,200 + $39,600 = $218,700

Deduct salary cost and EV with manager = $178,700

Therefore do not employ manager as profits will fall by $1,300.

94   A

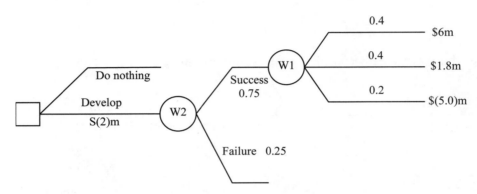

(W1) EV   =   ($6m × 0.4) + ($1.8m × 0.4) − ($5m × 0.2)

= $2.12m

(W2) EV   =   ($2.12m × 0.75) + ($Nil × 0.25)

= $1.59m

Net benefit: $1.59m − $2m = ($0.41m)

BUDGETING AND CONTROL

BUDGETARY SYSTEMS

95   A

(2) is wrong – activities drive costs and the aim is to control the causes (drivers) of costs, rather than the costs themselves. This, in turn, will ensure that the costs are better managed, and better understood.

96   B

(1) is wrong – it would fall under strategic planning.

97   A

TYPES OF BUDGET

98   A

99   C

(1) is wrong, it that would be feedback control. (2) is also wrong, feed-forward control occurs before the activity starts.

100 D

An incremental budget starts with the current period's budget and 'builds' on this to produce the budget for the next period.

101 B

102 B

	E	F	G	Total
Budgeted number of batches to be produced:		75,000/200	120,000/60	60,000/30
		= 375	= 2,000	= 2,000
Machine set-ups per batch:		5	3	9
Total machine set-ups		1,875	6,000	18,000	25,875

Budgeted cost per set-up: $180,000/25,875 = $6.96 per set-up

Therefore the budgeted machine set-up cost per unit of F produced is:

($6.96 × 3)/60 = $0.35 per unit or $6.96 × 6,000/120,000 = $0.35 per unit

103 D

104 D

A flexible budget controls operational efficiency by producing a realistic budget cost allowance for the actual level of activity achieved. This allows a more meaningful control comparison with the actual results. Statement (i) is therefore correct.

Incremental budgeting uses the current period's results as a base and adjusts this to allow for any known changes, including the cost increases caused by extra planned units of activity. Statement (ii) is therefore incorrect.

In a rolling budget system an extra quarter is added to the end of the budget when the most recent quarter has expired. The remaining budget might be updated at this point. Statement (iii) is therefore incorrect.

105 A

This is an example of feed-forward control, as the manager is using a forecast to assist in making a future decision

106 C

107 D

108 A

(2) is not correct. ABB can provide useful information for a total quality management programme (TQM) by relating the cost of an activity to the level of service provided and asking the user departments if they feel they are getting a cost-effective service.

QUANTITATIVE ANALYSIS IN BUDGETING

109 B

460 – 400 = 60 clients

$40,000 – $36,880 = $3,120

VC per unit = $3,120/60 = $52

Therefore FC = $40,000 – (460 × $52) = $16,080

Key answer tips

Workings for the following two questions:

One: $16,400 = (800 × VC) + FC

Multiply this by 1.5, we get $24,600 = (1,200 × VC) + 1.5 FC

Two: $23,600 = (1,200 × VC) + 1.4F

Subtracting the last two equations we get $1,000 = 0.1 FC so $10,000 = FC

At the 1,100 unit level the fixed cost would be $14,000

By substitution:

One: $16,400 = 800 ×VC + $10,000

6,400 = 800 × VC

6,400/800 = VC

VC = $8.

---

110 A

$23,600 = 1.4FC + 1,200VC   and $16,400 = FC + 800VC

($23,600 − 1,200VC) = 1.4FC + 1,200VC   and $16,400 − 800VC = FC

$$\frac{(\$23,600 - 1,200VC) = FC}{1.4}$$

By substitution:

$16,400 − 800VC	= ($23,600 − 1,200VC)/1.4
$22,960 − 1,120VC	= $23,600 − 1,200VC
$1,200VC − 1,120VC	= $23,600 − $22,960
80VC	= $640
VC per unit	= $8

111 D

This question uses the same data as Q96 − therefore, initially calculate variable cost per unit as above to be $8.00 per unit, then substitute this value into the equation for the higher level of activity as follows:

$23,600 = 1.4FC + (1,200 × $8VC)

$23,600 = 1.4FC + $9,600

$23,600 − $9,600 − 1.4FC

$14,000 = 1.4FC (i.e. after increasing fixed costs by 40% upon exceeding 900 units)

Note: therefore fixed costs at lower level of activity = $14,000/1.4 = $10,000 (not required)

112 $34,400

A high low method analysis will first of all split out the budgeted VC and FC:

	Units	$ Cost
High	1,400	31,600
Low	1,000	30,000
Increment	400	1,600

VC per unit is $1,600/400 = $4/u

Substitution in high:

TC = FC + VC

TC = FC + (1,400 × 4)

31,600 = FC + 5,600

FC = $26,000

For 2,100 units, Fixed costs	= $26,000
VC (2,100 × 4)	= $8,400
Total	= $34,400

113 A

Units	Total time	Average time/unit
1	100	100
2	190	95

Learning rate is based on the improvement in the average 95/100 = 95%

114 C

Batches	Total time	Average time/unit
1	500	500
2		500 × r
4		500 × r²
8		500 × r³
16	5,731	500 × r⁴

$5,731 = 16 \times 500\ r^4$

$5,731/(16 \times 500) = r^4$

r = 0.92 or 92%

115 C

Key answer tips

We must work in batches here, where 1 batch = 50 units

Time for the first order:

$Y = ax^b$

$Y = 400 \times 12^{-0.152}$

Y = 274.17285 hours

Total time = 3,290.07 hours

Time for first 1400 units (28 batches)

$Y = ax^b$

$Y = 400 \times 28^{-0.152}$

Y = 241.04158 hours

Total time = 6,749.16 hours

Time for second order = 6,749.16 – 3,290.07 = 3,459.09 hours

Cost of second order = 3,459.09 × $12/hr = $41,509.08

116 B

$100r^2 = (100 + 70 + 59 + 55)/4$, giving $r = 84.3\%$

Tutorial note

We could also explain this answer as follows: by the time we have produced two units, we have an average per unit of (100 minutes + 70 minutes)/2 units = 85%. If we were to stop there, the rate of learning would be 85%.

By the time we have got to 4 units, we have an average of (100 minutes + 70 minutes + 59 minutes + 55 minutes)/4 units = 71 minutes. These 71 minutes represent (71/85) = 83.53% of the previous average of 85 minutes.

The overall rate of learning is an average of these two rates of learning , so we have (85% + 83.53%)/2 = 84.265, say 84.3%.

117 D

Using the learning curve model $Y = ax^b$

$b = \log 0.8/\log 2 = -0.3219$

	Cumulative average minutes		Total minutes
For the 3rd unit	$Y = 22 \times 3^{-0.3219} = 15.45$	× 3	= 46.34
For the 4th unit	$Y = 22 \times 4^{-0.3219} = 14.08$	× 4	= 56.32

Therefore the time for the 4th unit is $56.32 - 46.34 = 9.98$ minutes.

STANDARD COSTING

118 A

Option B is an current standard, option C is an idea standard and option D is an attainable standard.

119 C

Statement (ii) is not correct. Standards can include allowances for inefficiencies in operations, through the use of attainable standards. Statement (iii) is not correct either, standards and budgets are both used for planning and control purposes.

120 C

121 A

Flexible budgeting is a reporting system wherein the planned level of activity is adjusted to the actual level of activity before the budget to actual comparison report is prepared. It may be appropriately employed for any item which is affected by the level of activity. In standard costing, product costs are predetermined and set up as a goal to be attained. Actual performance is compared to the standard. A primary objective of a standard costing system is to control costs.

122 D

123 C

The standard labour rate should be the expected rate/hour, but allowing for standard levels of idle time. For example, if the work force is paid $9 per hour but idle time of 10% is expected, the standard labour rate will be $10 per hour, not $9.

124 C

MATERIALS MIX AND YIELD VARIANCES

125 A

A favourable material mix variance is more likely to lead to an adverse material yield variance

126 B

127 C

	Material A kg	Material B kg	Material C kg	Total kg
Actual input	13,200	7,600	5,600	26,400
Actual input in std proportions				⇓
50:40:20	12,000	9,600	4,800	⇐ 26,400
Difference in quantity	1,200 A	2,000 F	800 A	
× Std price	× 10	× 5	× 9	
Mix variance	$12,000 A	$10,000 F	$7,200 A	$9,200 A

Key answer tips

An alternative calculation of the mix variance above can be done, using the standard average price per kilogram, as presented below.

Std weighted average price per kg $= \dfrac{(50 \times 10) + (40 \times 5) + (20 \times 9)}{50 + 40 + 20 \text{ kg}}$ = $8/kg

	Material A kg	Material B kg	Material C kg	Total kg
Actual input	13,200	7,600	5,600	26,400
Actual input in std proportions 50:40:20	12,000	9,600	4,800	⇐ 26,400
Difference in quantity	1,200	(2,000)	800	
× Difference in price (weighted average std price − Ind. material std price)				
× (8 − 10)	x − 2			
× (8 − 5) × 3				
× (8 − 9)			x − 1	
Mix variance	$2,400 A	$6,000 A	$800 A	$9,200 A

128 B

Yield variance

$$\text{Std cost per kg of output} = \frac{(50 \times 10) + (40 \times 5) + (20 \times 9)}{100\,\text{kg}} = \$8.80/\text{kg}$$

		kg
1	Std yield of actual input $26,400 \times \dfrac{100}{110}$	24,000
2	Actual yield	23,180
3		820 A
4	× Std cost per kg of output	× 8.80
	Yield variance	$7,216 A

129 C

	Actual mix	Std Mix	SP × Act mix	SP × Std mix
Lettuce	62,000	45,937.5	12.400	9.1875
Peppers	81,000	76,562.5	32.400	30.6250
Beetroot	102,000	122,500.0	81.600	98.0000
	245,000	245,000.0	126.400	137.78125
Difference				11.41250

130 B

Actual yield	1,500.00
Standard yield	1,531.25
Difference	31.25
Standard cost of a plate	0.09
Yield variance = 31.25 × 0.09 =	2.8125 F
Standard yield is 245,000 × 1/160 =	1,531.25

Standard cost of a plate is:

	Quantity (g)	Price ($)	Cost ($)
Lettuce	30	0.0002	0.006
Peppers	50	0.0004	0.020
Beetroot	80	0.0008	0.064
Standard cost:			0.09

131 A

	$
Actual usage in standard proportions	
D = 4,000 litres at $9 per litre	= 36,000
E = 3,500 litres at $5 per litre	= 17,500
F = 2,500 litres at $2 per litre	= 5,000
	———
10,000 litres	58,500
Actual usage in actual proportions	
D = 4,300 litres at $9 per litre	38,700
E = 3,600 litres at $5 per litre	18,000
F = 2,100 litres at $2 per litre	4,200
	———
	60,900

Mix variance is (58,500 – 60,900 = $2,400 Adverse

SALES MIX AND QUANTITY VARIANCES

132 D

	Actual mix	Standard mix	Standard contribution from actual mix $	Standard contribution from standard mix $
Type A	200,000	150,000	800,000	600,000
Type B	40,000	90,000	200,000	450,000
	240,000	240,000	1,000,000	1,050,000
Difference in contribution			50,000 Adv	

Since Yellow uses MC then the variance should be calculated at standard contribution

133 C

Total actual sales	240,000
Total budget sales	220,000
Difference	20,000
Average standard contribution	$4.375
$((5 \times 4) + (3 \times 5))/8 = 4.375$	
Favourable variance is	$87,500

134 D

Tutorial note

A sales mix variance indicates the effect on profit of changing the mix of actual sales from the standard mix. Looking a July's budgeted sales levels, we can see that the standard mix of sales is one 'X' for two 'Y's, It means that we expect that every time an 'X' is sold, two units of 'Y' will be sold at the same time. The least profitable unit, 'X', represents a third of the budgeted sales volume.

The actual sales mix is 1'X' for four 'Y's, and is different from the budgeted sales mix. The least profitable unit, 'X', represents a fifth of sales volume. To calculate Jones' sales mix variance, we can use the 'Toolbox' method detailed in your ACCA Complete Text.

	Actual Quantities, Actual Mix AQAM	Actual Quantities, Standard Mix AQSM	Difference	At standard profit	Variance
Product X	2,000 units	3333 units	−1,333	$4	($5,332) A
Product Y	8,000 units	6667 units	1,333	$6	$7,998 F
	10,000 units	**10,000 units**	**0**		**$2,667 F**

135 A

The sales quantity variance is the difference between the actual sales volume in the standard mix and budgeted sales, valued at the standard profit per unit:

	X	Y	Z	Total
Budgeted sales units, in standard mix	1,000 units (1/6 of total)	2,000 units (1/3 of total)	1,000 units (1/2 of total)	6,000 units
Actual sales volume, in standard mix 1/6; 1/3;1/2	991.67	1,983.33	2,975	5,950
Difference in units	8.33 ADV	16.67 ADV	25 ADV	
Standard profit per unit, as per question	$2	$5	$2	
Variance	$16.67 ADV	$83.34 ADV	$50 ADV	**$150 ADV**

PLANNING AND OPERATIONAL VARIANCES

136 C

Statement 1 is not true: the publication of material price planning variances should not always lead to automatic updates of standard costs. There must be a good reason for deciding that the original standard cost is unrealistic.

Statement 2 is not true either. Although planning variances are not usually the responsibility of operational managers, these variances do need to be investigated by senior management when they are substantial, so that lessons may be learned for the future.

137 D

	Budget units	Actual units	Change
Sales	504,000	532,000	Up 5.55%
Market share	18%	20%	Up 2%
Market size	2,800,000	2,660,000	Down 5%

138 C

	Budget units	Revised units	Actual units	Change
Sales	504,000	478,800	532,000	Up 5.55%
Market share	18%	18%	20%	Up 2%
Market size	2,800,000		2,660,000	Down 5%

Market size variance is (478,800 − 504,000) × $12 = $302,400 Adv

139 B

Market share variance is (532,000 − 478,800) × 12 = $638,400 Fav

140 D

Both statements are correct. Planning variances are usually assumed to be the responsibility of senior managers, as operational managers will rarely take responsibility for what is deemed uncontrollable. Also, planning variances reflect a difference between out-of-date standards and revised standards. The budget may need to be revised to enable actual performance to be compared with a standard that reflects changed conditions.

141 B

Operational variances are deemed to be within the control of the production manager, planning variances are usually the concern of senior management.

142 D

PERFORMANCE ANALYSIS AND BEHAVIOURAL ASPECTS

143 D

The production manager controls both the mix and the production process and must alone bear responsibility for this initial poor performance.

144 D

PERFORMANCE MEASUREMENT AND CONTROL

PERFORMANCE MANAGEMENT INFORMATION SYSTEMS

145 B

146 A

147 C

EIS systems are usually suited to Senior Executives and strategic planning.

148 A

(1) is correct: high processing speed is needed, due to the high volume of data. (2) is not correct, as TPS systems monitor and collect PAST data.

149 D

150 B

SOURCES OF MANAGEMENT INFORMATION

151 B

(i) is not correct: Internal information is produced by the company itself, so managers are aware of limitations in its quality or reliability.

152 D

153 C

154 D

155 D

156 B

MANAGEMENT REPORTS

157 C

158 C

159 B

(1) is an example of input control, and (3) is an example of output control.

160 C

Logical access control is concerned with preventing those who already have access to a computer from gaining access to data or software.

PERFORMANCE ANALYSIS IN PRIVATE SECTOR ORGANISATIONS

161 B

(i) and (ii) are financial indicators, and (iv) is a risk indicator.

162 B

163 D

Measuring the budgeted number of quotations actually issued would be monitoring the output and activity of the department but it would not be helpful in improving the department's performance in terms of the accuracy or speed of quotations in the scenario described.

164 C

Customer profitability analysis – Financial

New product requests from customers – Innovation or flexibility

Customer ordering processing times – Internal business process

165 D

166 D

'Number of returns in the month' is an absolute measure and not appropriate to measure 'quality'. 'Number of faulty goods returned as a percentage of number of orders received in the month' is not a bad measure, but orders may not have been delivered; 'Average customer satisfaction rating where customers were asked a range of questions including quality, delivery and customer service' seems to lack focus as a measure.

167 C

168 A

Co X (2,140/20,000) × 100 = 10.7%

Co Y (2,180/26,000) × 100 = 8.38%

169 C

Company B has a higher asset turnover and is therefore using its assets more efficiently than A. The two companies have the same ROCE and are therefore generating the same profit from every $1 of asset employed. The profit of the two companies is the same but company A has a higher profit margin and is therefore controlling its costs better than company B. The calculations are:

	Co A	Co B
ROCE	20% (10,000/50,000 × 100)	20% (10,000/50,000 × 100)
Profit margin	20% (10,000/50,000 × 100)	5% (10,000/200,000 × 100)
Asset turnover	1 (50,000/50,000)	4 (50,000/200,000)

170 A

20X1: (4,400/20,000) × 365 = 80 days

20X2: (6,740/26,000) × 365 = 95 days

171 C

Inventory days = 44,000/324,500 × 365 days = 49 days

Average inventories/COS × 365

Average inventories = (50,000 + 38,000)/2 = 44,000

Current ratio = 108,000/56,000 = 1.93:1

Current assets: Current liabilities

Current assets = Trade receivables 60,000 + Prepayments 4,000 + Cash in hand 6,000 + Closing inventories 38,000 = 108,000

Current liabilities = Bank overdraft 8,000 + Trade payables 40,000 + Accruals 3,000 + Declared dividends 5,000 = 56,000

DIVISIONAL PERFORMANCE AND TRANSFER PRICING

172 A

Division A: Profit = $14.4 m × 30% = $4.32 m

Imputed interest charge = $32.6 m × 10% = $3.26 m

Residual income = $1.06 m

Division B: Profit = $8.8 m × 24% = $2.112 m

Imputed interest charge = $22.2 m × 10% = $2.22 m

Residual income = $(0.108) m

173 B

Tutorial note

Division A can sell all of its output on the outside market at $12 per unit. Any internal transfer will be at the expense of external sales. However, the external sales also include a packaging cost of $1.50 per unit which is not incurred on an internal transfer and this saving can be passed on to the buying division. Therefore, the correct transfer price from a decision-making point of view is $12 (the market price) – $1.50 (the saving in packaging cost) = $10.50.

174 B

Increase in variable costs from buying in (2,200 units × $40 ($140 – $100)) = $88,000

Less the specific fixed costs saved if A is shut down = ($10,000)

Decrease in profit = $78,000

175 D

$$ROCE = \frac{\text{Profit before interest and tax}}{\text{Capital employed}} = \frac{500}{2,400} = 20.8\%$$

Capital employed is equity + long-term debt = 1,500 + 900 = 2,400

or

Total assets less current liabilities = 3,400 – 1,000 = 2,400

176 C

	$
Profit	500
Imputed interest 11% × 2,400	(264)
Residual income	236

177 B

Controllable profit is 1,200 + 90 + 30 + 50 =	$1,370m
Assets at start of year are	$4,500m
Notional interest charges at 12% (4,500 × 0.12)	$540m
Residual Income	$830m

178 D

ROI = 30%; ROI = 1,370/4,500 = 30.4%

179 C

The project is acceptable to the company as a whole, because the RI is positive and the ROI exceeds the target return of 10%.

The manager of division D will be willing to undertake the project, whichever performance measure is used, since both the ROI and the RI will increase. Therefore, both measures will motivate the divisional manager to act in the interest of the company as a whole.

180 A

181 B

182 B

We must set a price high enough for TM to cover its costs, but not so high that RM cannot make a profit.

For TM, an item sold externally has VC of 60% × $24.00 = $14.40. Of this, $1.50 will not be incurred on an internal transfer so it is not relevant here, VC on internal transfer = $14.40 – $1.50= $12.90. We do not know RM's cost structure, so we leave the price at $12.90; this will ensure that RM is not discouraged from taking an internal transfer when it is profitable to do so.

PERFORMANCE ANALYSIS IN NON-FOR-PROFIT ORGANISATIONS AND THE PUBLIC SECTOR

183 D

184 A

Reducing mortality rates is likely to be a stated objective of the hospital and as such is a measure of output, or effectiveness. Cost per patient is a measure of output related to input i.e. efficiency

185 B

186 A

Class sizes are the result of the number of pupils educated (output), the number of teachers employed (input) and how well the timetable is organised in using those teachers. Exam success considers the quality of the output (effectiveness)

187 B

(1) is not correct: Output does not usually have a market value, and it is therefore more difficult to measure efficiency

188 D

EXTERNAL CONSIDERATIONS AND BEHAVIOURAL ASPECTS

189 C

Delaying payments to payables affects cash, not profit. Shortening the useful economic life of a non-current asset would reduce profit, and overstatement of an accrual also reduces profit.

190 D

There is nothing to suggest that imposed standards are more likely to be achieved. Where managers are allowed to participate in the setting of standards, they are usually more motivated and this can lead to more acceptance of these standards.

Managers should be targeted on factors which they can control, and be set targets which are specific to their business area.

It is recognised that ideal standard do not generally motivate, therefore standards are generally set at an achievable level with some stretch built in.

191 C

It is important to take account of all stakeholders when setting performance targets.

192 A

Managers should also have targets which are based on the overall performance of the company and not solely based on their own responsibility centre to aid goal congruence.

Capital investment decisions may be reviewed centrally and judged on the basis of net present value (NPV).

Setting targets involving the overall performance of the company may not be motivating if poorly performing managers are rewarded in the same way as managers who are performing well.

193 C

It is important that performance measures are set to encourage the long term growth of the company. A focus on short term profit could result in risky and dysfunctional behaviour.

The government is also interested in many other aspects including price stability, economic growth and compliance with laws.

Companies have a range of stakeholders, all of which can affect the company and should be considered. Some of these stakeholders are external such as the government, the general public and pressure groups.

Section 4

ANSWERS TO PRACTICE QUESTIONS

SPECIALIST COST AND MANAGEMENT ACCOUNTING TECHNIQUES

194 ABKABER PLC *Online question assistance*

Key answer tips

Part (a) is a routine calculation of profit using ABC and traditional methods. Part (b) asks for a discussion of ABC for Abkaber. It is vital that you relate as many of your points as possible to the specific circumstances given.

(i) **Absorption costing using labour hour absorption rate**

Total overhead cost	=	$2,400,000 + $6,000,000 + $3,600,000
	=	$12,000,000
Total labour hours	=	200,000 + 220,000 + 80,000
	=	500,000
Overhead absorption rate/labour hour	=	$12,000,000/500,000 = $24

	Sunshine	Roadster	Fireball
Units of production and sale	2,000	1,600	400
Direct labour hours	200,000	220,000	80,000
	$	$	$
Direct labour ($5/hour)	1,000,000	1,100,000	400,000
Materials (at $400/600/900)	800,000	960,000	360,000
Overheads ($24/direct labour hour)	4,800,000	5,280,000	1,920,000
Total costs	6,600,000	7,340,000	2,680,000

	Sunshine	Roadster	Fireball
	$	$	$
Cost per unit	3,300	4,587.5	6,700
Selling price	4,000	6,000.0	8,000
Profit/(loss) per unit	700	1,412.5	1,300
Total profit/(loss) per product	1,400,000	2,260,000	520,000

Total profit = $4,180,000

(ii) **Activity Based Costing**

Number of deliveries to retailers	100 + 80 + 70	=	250
Charge rate for deliveries	$2,400,000/250	=	$9,600
Number of set-ups	35 + 40 + 25	=	100
Charge rate for set-ups	$6,000,000/100	=	$60,000
Number of purchase orders	400 + 300 + 100	=	800
Charge rate for purchase orders	$3,600,000/800	=	$4,500

	Sunshine	Roadster	Fireball
Units of production and sale	2,000	1,600	400
	$	$	$
Direct labour (as above)	1,000,000	1,100,000	400,000
Materials (as above)	800,000	960,000	360,000
Overheads:			
Deliveries at $9,600 (100:80:70)	960,000	768,000	672,000
Set-ups at $60,000 (35:40:25)	2,100,000	2,400,000	1,500,000
Purchase orders at $4,500 (400:300:100)	1,800,000	1,350,000	450,000
Total costs	6,660,000	6,578,000	3,382,000
	$	$	$
Cost per unit	3,330	4,111.25	8,455
Selling price	4,000	6,000.00	8,000
Profit/(loss) per unit	670	1,888.75	(455)
Total profit/(loss) per product	$1,340,000	$3,022,000	$(182,000)

Total profit = $4,180,000

195   FIT CO LIFESTYLE (DEC 2011 EXAM)

Tutorial note

A technical article on this lifecycle costing topic has been published on the ACCA website - make sure you read it as part of your revision.

(a)   **Life cycle cost per unit**

	$
R & D costs	160,000
Product design costs	800,000
Marketing costs	3,950,000
Fixed production costs	1,940,000
Fixed distribution costs	240,000
Fixed selling costs	360,000
Administration costs	2,600,000
Variable manufacturing costs	12,400,000
(100,000 × $40 + 200,000 × $42)	
Variable distribution costs	1,300,000
(100,000 × $4 + 200,000 × $4.50)	
Variable selling costs	940,000
(100,000 × $3 + 200,000 × $3.20)	
	–––––––––
Total costs	24,690,000
	–––––––––

Therefore cost per unit = $24,690,000/300,000 = $82.30

(b)   **Benefits of life cycle costing**

- The visibility of ALL costs is increased, rather than just costs relating to one period. This facilitates better decision-making.

- Individual profitability for products is more accurate because of this. This facilitates performance appraisal and decision-making, and means that prices can be determined with better knowledge of the true costs.

- More accurate feedback can take place when assessing whether new products are a success or a failure, since the costs of researching, developing and designing those products are also taken into account.

Note: Other valid benefits would also be awarded marks.

	ACCA marking scheme		
			Marks
(a)	Life cycle cost		
	R & D costs		0.5
	Product design costs		0.5
	Marketing costs		0.5
	Fixed production costs		0.5
	Fixed distribution costs		0.5
	Fixed selling costs		0.5
	Administration costs		0.5
	Variable manufacturing costs		0.5
	Variable distribution costs		0.5
	Variable selling costs		0.5
	Total costs		0.5
	Cost per unit (correct figure)		0.5
		Maximum	6
(b)	Benefits of life cycle costing		
	Per valid point made	up to	1.5
		Maximum	4
Total			**10**

196 ABC IS NOT THE SOLUTION

Generally a new accounting method has to be understandable, relatively easy to use and make a difference to the business.

Property costs

The problem here is all activities and functions of a business tend to take place in the businesses property making it very difficult to trace an individual cost (like rates) back to an individual activity. It is not uncommon that a business's cost base (services in particular) is dominated by property costs and so ABC cannot easily deal with this major cost.

If this is the case that means the impact ABC might have is greatly reduced and this reduces its benefit. Introducing new accounting systems is a costly and time-consuming affair and so management want to be reasonably certain that benefits (better information for example) will follow. As a result ABC might die in the boardroom as something that just is not worth doing.

Controllability

If a cost is fixed then changing the number of drivers (units, deliveries etc.) will not change the overall cost. It could be that the internal cost of a delivery is warehousing staff, space, lighting and so on and these costs may not change if less (or more) deliveries take place. The space might still be needed, the lights might still have to stay on and the warehouse employees are is busy doing other things if a delivery does not arrive.

Consequently this too reduces that benefits from introducing ABC. If introducing ABC cannot reduce cost or better control cost then what is the point in its introduction?

Conclusion

ABC can sometimes fail to deliver the level of benefits required to justify its introduction.

ACCA marking scheme	
	Marks
2 marks per point made and explained	10
Total	10

197 WEBCAMS (JUNE 2013 EXAM)

Revised target cost

	$	$
Manufacturing cost		
Direct material (W1)	21.60	
Direct labour (W2)	10.96	
Machine costs	21	
Quality control costs	10	
Rework costs (W3)	1.80	
		65.36
Product development cost	25	
Marketing cost	35	
Non-manufacturing costs		60
Total cost		125.36

Workings

(W1) Direct material cost

Parts to be replaced by standard parts = $40 × 0.8 = $32.

New cost of those at 45% (100% – 55%) = $14.40.

Unique irreplaceable parts: original cost = $40 × 20% = $8.

New cost $7.20

Revised direct material cost = $14.40 + $7.20 = $21.60

(W2) Direct labour

Direct labour – cost per unit for first one hundred units:

$Y = ax^b$

$45 \times 100^{-0.152} = 22.346654$ minutes

Total time for 100 units = 2,234.6654 minutes.

Time for the 100th unit:

Time for 99 units = $45 \times 99{-}0.152$

= 22.380818 minutes.

For 99 units = 2,215.701 minutes.

Therefore, time for 100th unit = 2,234.6654 – 2,215.701 = 18.9644 minutes.

Time for remaining 49,900 units = 946,323.56 minutes.

Total labour time for 50,000 units = 948,558.23 minutes.

Therefore total labour cost = 948,558.23/60 × $34.67 = $548,108.56.

Therefore average labour cost per unit = $548,108.56/50,000 = $10.96.

Note: Some rounding is acceptable and marks would still be given.

(W3) Rework cost

Total cost = 50,000 × 10% × $18 = $90,000.

Cost per average unit = $90,000/50,000 = $1.80.

ACCA marking scheme	
	Marks
Revised lifetime cost	
Direct material cost	2.5
Direct skilled labour cost:	
Cumulative average time per unit for 100 units	1
Cumulative total time for 100 units	0.5
Cumulative average time per unit for 99 units	1
Cumulative total time for 99 units	0.5
Incremental time for 100th unit	1
Total time for 49,900 units	0.5
Total time for 50,000 units	0.5
Total labour cost for 50,000 units	0.5
Average labour cost per unit	0.5
Machine costs	0.5
Quality control costs	0.5
Rework cost	1
Non-manufacturing cost	1
Total cost	0.5
Maximum	10
Total	**10**

198 ENVIRONMENTAL MANAGEMENT ACCOUNTING

Tutorial note

A technical article on this EMA topic has been published on the ACCA website - make sure you read it as part of your revision.

1   Waste disposal costs

FTX is likely to incur environmental costs associated with waste: for example, landfill taxes, or the costs of disposal of raw materials and chemicals not used in drug production, FTX may also be vulnerable to fines for compliance failures such as pollution.

Control measures could be implemented to identify how much material is wasted in production by using the 'mass balance' approach, whereby the weight of materials bought is compared to the product yield. From this process, potential cost savings may be identified. The cost of packaging lends itself particularly well to this analysis: by analysing how much packaging the drug uses and what percentage of that packaging is recyclable, FTX could also reduce its costs whilst being environmentally friendly.

2   Water consumption costs

Like any other business, FTX will pay for water twice: first to buy it, and, secondly, to dispose of it. If FTX looks to reduce its water bill, it is important for the business to identify where water is used in the drug production process and how consumption can be decreased.

3   Energy consumption costs

Like any other business or household, FTX should be able to reduce its energy costs significantly by switching production to night-time for example (when electricity is cheaper). Furthermore, environmental management accounts may help to identify inefficiencies and wasteful practices and therefore opportunities for cost savings.

4   Transport and travel costs

Environmental Management Accounting can often help to identify savings in terms of business travel and transport of goods and materials. An obvious control measure, in this case, would be the replacement of FTX's vehicles by more fuel-efficient vans or cars.

199   GADGET CO (DEC 10 EXAM)

Tutorial note

This was the best-answered question on the paper in December 2010. You should at least earn the full five marks available in section (a).

(a)   Cost per unit under full absorption costing

	$
Total annual overhead costs:	
Machine set up costs	26,550
Machine running costs	66,400
Procurement costs	48,000
Delivery costs	54,320
	6,900
	————
	195,270
	————

Overhead absorption rate:

	A	B	C	Total
Production volumes	15,000	12,000	18,000	
Labour hours per unit	0.1	0.15	0.2	
Total labour hours	1,500	1,800	3,600	6,900

Therefore, overhead absorption rate = $195,270/6,900 = $28.30 per hour

Cost per unit

	A	B	C
	$	$	$
Raw materials ($1.20 × 2/3/4 kg)	2.4	3.6	4.8
Direct labour ($14.80 × 0.1/0.15/0.2 hrs)	1.48	2.22	2.96
Overhead ($28.30 × 0.1/0.15/0.2 hrs)	2.83	4.25	5.66
	———	———	———
Full cost per unit	6.71	10.07	13.42
	———	———	———

(b)   Cost per unit using ABC

Tutorial note

Be careful not to mix up the driver for machine set-ups (which should have been the 36 machine setups) with the driver for machine running costs (which should have been 32,100 machine hours). However, don't worry: even with this mistake, you can complete the calculations correctly and earn follow-on marks.

Cost drivers:

Cost pools	$	Cost driver
Machine set up costs	26,550	36 production runs (16 + 12 + 8)
Machine running costs	66,400	32,100 machine hours (7,500 + 8,400 + 16,200)
Procurement costs	48,000	94 purchase orders (24 + 28 + 42)
Delivery costs	54,320	140 deliveries (48 + 30 + 62)
	195,270	

Cost per machine set up	$26,550/36 = $737.50
Cost per machine hour	$66,400/32,100 = $2.0685
Cost per order	$48,000/94 = $510.6383
Cost per delivery	$54,320/140 = $388

Allocation of overheads to each product:

	A	B	C	Total
	$	$	$	$
Machine set up costs	11,800	8,850	5,900	26,550
Machine running costs	15,514	17,375	33,510	66,400
Procurement costs	12,255	14,298	21,447	48,000
Delivery costs	18,624	11,640	24,056	54,320
	58,193	52,163	84,913	195,270
Number of units produced	15,000	12,000	18,000	
	$	$	$	
Overhead cost per unit	3.88	4.35	4.72	
Total cost per unit	A	B	C	
Materials	2.4	3.6	4.8	
Labour	1.48	2.22	2.96	
Overheads	3.88	4.35	4.72	
	7.76	10.17	12.48	

<table>
<tr><td colspan="3" align="center">ACCA marking scheme</td></tr>
<tr><td></td><td></td><td>Marks</td></tr>
<tr><td>(a)</td><td>Contribution per unit</td><td></td></tr>
<tr><td></td><td>Overhead absorption rate</td><td>2</td></tr>
<tr><td></td><td>Cost for A</td><td>1</td></tr>
<tr><td></td><td>Cost for B</td><td>1</td></tr>
<tr><td></td><td>Cost for C</td><td>1</td></tr>
<tr><td></td><td align="right">Maximum</td><td>5</td></tr>
<tr><td>(b)</td><td>Cost under ABC</td><td></td></tr>
<tr><td></td><td>Correct cost driver rates</td><td>5</td></tr>
<tr><td></td><td>Correct overhead unit cost for A</td><td>1</td></tr>
<tr><td></td><td>Correct overhead unit cost for B</td><td>1</td></tr>
<tr><td></td><td>Correct overhead unit cost for C</td><td>1</td></tr>
<tr><td></td><td>Correct cost per unit under ABC</td><td>2</td></tr>
<tr><td></td><td align="right">Maximum</td><td>10</td></tr>
<tr><td>Total</td><td></td><td>15</td></tr>
</table>

200 DUFF CO (JUNE 2014, ADAPTED)

(a) Full budgeted production cost per unit using absorption costing

Product	X	Y	Z	Total
Budgeted annual production (units)	20,000	16,000	22,000	
Labour hours per unit	2.5	3	2	
Total labour hours	50,000	48,000	44,000	142,000

Overhead absorption rate = $1,377,400/142,000 = $9.70 per hour.

Product	X	Y	Z
	$ per unit	$ per unit	$ per unit
Direct materials	25	28	22
Direct labour	30	36	24
Overhead ($9.70 × 2.5/3/2)	24.25	29.10	19.40
Full cost per unit	79.25	93.10	65.40

(b) Full budgeted production cost per unit using activity based costing

Product	X	Y	Z	Total
Budgeted annual production (units)	20,000	16,000	22,000	
Batch size	500	800	400	
Number of batches (i.e. set ups)	**40**	**20**	**55**	**115**
Number of purchase orders per batch	4	5	4	
Total number of orders	**160**	**100**	**220**	**480**
Machine hours per unit	1.5	1.25	1.4	
Total machine hours	**30,000**	**20,000**	**30,800**	**80,800**

Cost driver rates:

Cost per machine set up	$280,000/115 = $2,434.78
Cost per order	$316,000/480 = $658.33
Cost per machine hour	($420,000 + $361,400)/80,800 = $9.67

Allocation of overheads to each product:

Product	X	Y	Z	Total
	$	$	$	
Machine set up costs	97,391	48,696	133,913	280,000
Material ordering costs	105,333	65,833	144,834	316,000
Machine running and facility costs	290,100	193,400	297,836	781,336*
Total	492,824	307,929	576,583	1,377,336
Number of units produced	20,000	16,000	22,000	
Overhead cost per unit	$24.64	$19.25	$26.21	

Total cost per unit:	$ per unit	$ per unit	$ per unit
Direct materials	25	28	22
Direct labour	30	36	24
Overhead	24.64	19.25	26.21
ABC cost per unit	79.64	83.25	72.21

*A difference of $64 arises here as compared to the cost pool total of $781,400 because of rounding differences. This has been ignored.

Marking scheme			Marks
(a)	Full absorption cost		
	Overhead absorption rate		2
	Cost for X incl labour and materials		1
	Cost for Y incl labour and materials		0.5
	Cost for Z incl labour and materials		0.5
			4
(b)	Activity based cost		
	Correct cost driver rates		4.5
	Overhead unit cost for X		1
	Overhead unit cost for Y		1
	Overhead unit cost for Z		1
	Adding labour and materials costs		2
	Total cost for X		0.5
	Total cost for Y		0.5
	Total cost for Z		0.5
			11
Total			**15**

201 THE UNIVERSAL HEALTH SYSTEM (JUNE 2012 EXAM)

(a) **Deriving a target price and cost in a manufacturing company**

Step 1: A product is developed that is perceived to be needed by customers and therefore will attract adequate sales volumes.

Step 2: A target price is then set based on the customers' perceived value of the product. This will therefore be a market based price.

Step 3: The required target operating profit per unit is then calculated. This may be based on either return on sales or return on investment.

Step 4: The target cost is derived by subtracting the target profit from the target price.

Step 5: If there is a cost gap, attempts will be made to close the gap. Techniques such as value engineering may be performed, which looks at every aspect of the value chain business functions, with an objective of reducing costs while satisfying customer needs.

Step 6: Negotiation with customers may take place before deciding whether to go ahead with the project.

(b) **Deriving target costs**

(i) **For services under the 'payment by results' scheme**

The obvious target price is the pre-set tariff that is paid to the trust for each service. This is known with certainty and since the trust is a not for profit organisation, there will be no need to deduct any profit margin from the tariff. Problems may arise because of the fact that it is already known that costs sometimes exceed the pre-set tariff. These issues are discussed in (d).

(ii) **For transplant and heart operations**

For these operations, the trust is paid on the basis of its actual costs incurred. However, since the trust only has a restricted budget for such services, it is still important that it keeps costs under control. The target cost could be based on the average cost of these services when performed in the past, or the minimum cost that it has managed to provide such services on before, in order to encourage cost savings. It is important that quality is not affected, however.

(c) **Difficulties for the Sickham UHS Trust in using target costing**

The main difficulties for the trust are as follows:

It is difficult to find a precise definition for some of the services

In order for target costing to be useful, it is necessary to define the service being provided. Whilst the introduction of the pre-set tariff will make this more easy for some services, as this definition can be used, for other services not covered by the tariff, definition could be difficult.

It is difficult to decide on the correct target cost for services

For the pre-set tariff services, the obvious target cost would be the pre-set tariff. However, bearing in mind that the Trust knows that some services can be provided at less than this and some services cannot be provided at this price at all, one has to question whether it is right to use this as the target cost. A target cost which is unachievable could be demotivational for staff and one which is easily met will not provide an incentive to keep costs down.

As regards the other operations, the target can be set at a level which is both achievable but feasible, so this should result in less of an issue.

It would be difficult to use target costing for new services

The private sector initially developed the use of target costing in the service sector with the intention that it should only be used for new services rather than existing ones. Considering the work that a hospital performs particularly, it would be difficult to establish target costs when there is no comparative data available, unless other hospitals have already provided services and the information can be obtained from them.

The costing systems at the Sickham UHS Trust are poor

If costs are to be analysed in depth, the analysis must be based on accurate and timely costing systems, which do not appear to currently exist at the Sickham UHS Trust. A large part of the hospitals' costs for services are going to be overhead costs and these need to be allocated to services on a consistent basis. This is not currently happening.

Tutorial note

Only three difficulties were required.

		ACCA marking scheme		
				Marks
(a)	Steps			
	Develop product			1
	Set target price			1
	Set profit margin			1
	Set target cost			1
	Close gap			1
	Value engineering			1
	Negotiate			1
			Maximum	6
(b)	Deriving target costs			
	(i) Scheme target costs			2
	(ii) Other services' target costs			2
(c)	Difficulties			
	Each difficulty described		up to	2
			Maximum	5
Total				15

202 THIN CO (JUNE 2011 EXAM)

(a) Throughput accounting ratio (TAR)

TAR is traditionally defined as: return per factory hour/cost per factory hour. In this context, we are dealing with a hospital, so it will be: return per hospital hour/cost per hospital hour.

Since, in throughput accounting, all costs except material costs are treated as fixed costs, total hospital costs will be all the salaries plus the general overheads:

$45,000 + $38,000 + $75,000 + $90,000 + $50,000 + $250,000 = $548,000.

Total hours of bottleneck resource, the surgeon's time, = 40 hrs × 47 weeks = 1,880 hours.

Therefore cost per hospital hour = $548,000/1,880 = $291.49.

Return per hospital hour now needs to be calculated.

	$
Selling price per unit	4,250
Materials cost:	
– injection	(1,000)
– anaesthetic	(45)
– dressings	(5.6)
Throughput per unit	3,199.40
Time on BNR in hours	1.25
Return per hour ($)	2,559.52
TAR	$2,559.52/$291.49
	= 8.78

(b) **Optimum production plan**

Limiting factor analysis can be used to determine the optimum production plan. Each procedure first needs to be ranked according to its TAR, then as many of each procedure should be performed as possible, starting with the most profitable procedure first.

				A	B	C
				$	$	$
TAR				8.96	9.11	8.78
Ranking				2	1	3
Name	*Number*	*Hrs each*	*Total hours*	*T/P per hour*		*Total T/P*
B	800	1	800	2,654.40		2,123,520
A	600	0.75	450	2,612.53		1,175,638.5
C	504	1.25	630	2,559.52		1,612,497.6
			1,880			4,911,656.1

The optimum production plan is therefore to perform the maximum number of procedures A and B (600 and 800 respectively) and perform only 504 of procedure C.

Total profit will be:

	$
Throughput	4,911,656.1
Less total costs	(548,000)
Profit	4,363,656.1

(c) **Profitability increase**

At present, if the company adheres to the optimum production plan above, it will be satisfying customer demand for procedures A and B but not for procedure C.

The most obvious way to try and increase profit would be to try and exploit demand for procedure C.

There are two main factors that would need to be overcome in order for this demand to be exploited.

Firstly, another surgeon would need to be employed. Most other members of staff clearly have excess time available, because the surgeon's required time is at least double their required time.

Secondly, the other theatre would need to be equipped with the necessary equipment so that the second surgeon could operate in it.

ACCA marking scheme			
			Marks
(a)	TAR		
	Cost per hour		3
	Return per hour – C		2
	Ratio – C		1
			———
		Maximum	6
			———
(b)	Optimum production plan		
	Ranking		1
	Optimum number of A		1
	Optimum number of B		1
	Optimum number of C		1
	Total throughput		1
	Less cost		0.5
	Profit		0.5
			———
		Maximum	6
			———
(c)	Demand satisfied for A & B but not for C		1
	Would need another surgeon		1
	Each other valid point		1
			———
		Maximum	3
			———
Total			**15**
			———

203 JOLA PUBLISHING CO (JUNE 08 EXAM)

Tutorial note

Many candidates demonstrated an understanding of this area but failed to get enough depth to score a good mark. There are thirteen minutes available, which should be sufficient time to plan and write up a succinct and relevant answer. Rather than just discussing overheads in general, a good approach would be to review each of the three overhead costs in turn. It should be possible to get two marks for the discussion of each overhead. A general introduction and overall conclusion would gain another two marks.

(a)   Cost per unit calculation using machine hours for overhead absorption

	CB ($)		TJ ($)
Paper (400 g at $2/kg)	0.80	(100 g at $1/kg)	0.10
Printing (50 ml at $30/ltr)	1.50	(150 ml at $30/ltr)	4.50
Machine cost (6 mins at $12/hr)	1.20	(10 mins at $12/hr)	2.00
Overheads (6 mins at $24/hr) (W1)	2.40	(10 mins at $24/hr)	4.00
	———		———
Total cost	5.90		10.60
Sales price	9.30		14.00
	———		———
Margin	3.40		3.40
	———		———

(W1) Workings for overheads:

Total overhead $2,880,000

Total machine hours (1,000,000 × 6 mins) + (120,000 × 10 mins) = 7,200,000 mins

= 120,000 hours

Cost per hour   = $2,880,000 ÷120,000

= $24 per hour

	CB ($)		TJ ($)
Paper (400 g at $2/kg)	0.80	(100 g at $1/kg)	0.10
Printing (50 ml at $30/ltr)	1.50	(150 ml at $30/ltr)	4.50
Machine cost (6 mins at $12/hr)	1.20	(10 mins at $12/hr)	2.00
Overheads (W2)	2.41	(W2)	3.88
	―――		―――
Total cost	5.91		10.48
Sales price	9.30		14.00
	―――		―――
Margin	3.39		3.52
	―――		―――

(b) Cost per unit calculations under ABC

(W2) Working for ABC overheads   **alternative approach**

	Total $	CB $	TJ $	No of drivers	Cost/ driver	CB $	TJ $
Property costs	2,160,000	1,800,000	360,000	120,000	18/hr	1.80	3.00
Quality control	668,000	601,200	66,800	200	3340/ inspection	0.6012	0.56
Production set up	52,000	13,000	39,000	16	3250/ run	0.013	0.325
	―――	―――	―――			―――	―――
Total	2,880,000	2,414,200	465,800	Cost per unit		2.41	3.88
Production level		1,000,000	120,000			―――	―――
Cost per unit		2.41	3.88				

The above overheads have been split on the basis of the following activity levels:

	Driver	CB	TJ
Property costs	Machine hours	100,000	20,000
Quality control	Inspections	180	20
Production set up	Set ups	4	12

A cost per driver approach is also acceptable.

Tutorial note

Ensure your answer is well laid out, in a logical manner, so you get follow-through marks, even if you make a silly error earlier on.

ACCA marking scheme			
			Marks
(a)	Paper cost CB		½
	Paper cost TJ		½
	Printing ink cost CB		½
	Printing ink cost TJ		½
	Machine cost CB		½
	Machine cost TJ		½
	Overhead OAR		1
	Overhead cost CB		½
	Overhead cost TJ		½
	Margins		1
			———
		Maximum	6
			———
(b)	Split of rent and rates		1½
	Split of quality control		1½
	Split of production set up cost		1½
	Overhead cost per unit CB		1½
	Overhead cost per unit TJ		1½
	Direct cost as above		1½
			———
		Maximum	9
			———
Total			**15**
			———

204 LIFECYCLE COSTING

(a)   It is generally accepted that most products will have quite a distinct product life cycle, as illustrated below:

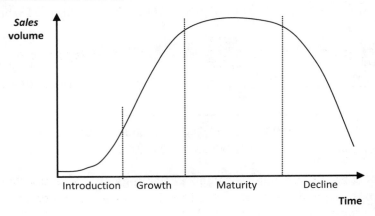

At the **introductory stage** the product is launched. If the product is accepted, it will move into the **growth stage,** where sales volume increases dramatically; unit costs fall as fixed costs are recovered over greater volumes. As market saturation is approached, with sales growth slowing, the product is entering its **maturity stage.** Initially profits will continue to increase, as initial set-up and fixed costs are recovered and marketing and distribution economies achieved. Eventually, in the **decline stage,** the product will move towards obsolescence as it is replaced by new and better alternatives.

(b) The commitment of a high proportion of a product's life cycle costs at the very early stages of the cycle has led to the need for accounting systems that compare the revenues from a product with all the costs incurred over the entire product life cycle.

Life cycle costing (LCC) is such a system, tracking and accumulating the actual costs and revenues attributable to each product from inception to abandonment. In this way, the final profitability of a given product is determined at the end of its life, whilst accumulated costs at any stage can be compared with life-cycle budgeted costs, product by product, for the purposes of planning and control.

Comparing this approach with the more traditional management accounting practices:

- Most accounting reporting systems are based upon periodic accounts, reporting product profitability in isolated calendar-based amounts, rather than focusing on the revenues and costs accumulated over the life cycle to date

- Recognition of the commitment needed over the entire life cycle of a product will generally lead to more effective resource allocation than the traditional annual budgeting system

- R&D, design, production set-up, marketing and customer service costs are traditionally reported on an aggregated basis for all products and recorded as a period expense. Life cycle costing traces these costs to individual products over their entire life cycles, to aid comparison with product revenues generated in later periods

- Relationships between early decisions re product design and production methods and ultimate costs can therefore be identified and used for subsequent planning.

205 EDWARD CO (DEC 07 EXAM) *Walk in the footsteps of a top tutor*

Key answer tips

This was an in-depth question on target costing that was done poorly by many students. The examiner has made it very clear that he will examine these themes again!

(a) **Target costing process**

Target costing begins by specifying a product an organisation wishes to sell. This will involve extensive customer analysis, considering which features customers value and which they do not. Ideally only those features valued by customers will be included in the product design.

The price at which the product can be sold at is then considered. This will take in to account the competitor products and the market conditions expected at the time that the product will be launched. Hence a heavy emphasis is placed on external analysis before any consideration is made of the internal cost of the product.

From the above price a desired margin is deducted. This can be a gross or a net margin. This leaves the cost target. An organisation will need to meet this target if their desired margin is to be met.

Costs for the product are then calculated and compared to the cost target mentioned above.

If it appears that this cost cannot be achieved then the difference (shortfall) is called a cost gap. This gap would have to be closed, by some form of cost reduction, if the desired margin is to be achieved.

Tutorial note

Easy marks were available here and a well prepared candidate should have been able to score full marks. Aim for at least three well explained points. Separate each point out using headings or a new paragraph. This will make it easier for the marker to review. The following headings could have been used:

1   *Estimate selling price*

2   *Deduct required profit*

3   *Calculate target cost*

4   *Close Gap*

(b)   **Cost per unit and cost gap calculation**

	$ per unit
Component 1	
$(4.10 + \dfrac{\$2,400}{4,000\,\text{units}})$	4.70
Component 2	
$(\dfrac{25}{100} \times 0.5 \times \dfrac{100}{98})$	0.128
Material – other	8.10
Assembly labour	
$(\dfrac{30}{60} \times \$12.60/\text{hr} \times \dfrac{100}{90})$	7.00
Variable production overhead (W1)	
$(\dfrac{30}{60} \times \$20/\text{hr})$	10.00
Fixed production overhead (W1)	
$(\dfrac{30}{60} \times \$12/\text{hr})$	6.00
	————
Total cost	35.928
Desired cost ($44 × 0.8)	35.20
	————
Cost gap	0.728
	————

Working: Production overhead cost. Using a high low method

Extra overhead cost between month 1 and 2	$80,000
Extra assembly hours	4,000
Variable cost per hour	$20/hr
Monthly fixed production overhead	
$700,000 – (23,000 × $20/hr)	$240,000
Annual fixed production overhead ($240,000 × 12)	$2,880,000

$$\text{FPO absorption rate } \frac{\$2,880,000}{240,000 \text{ hrs}} = \qquad \$12/hr$$

Tutorial note

There is plenty of time to do this calculation and so there is no need to panic or rush. Set out a cost card for the radio and then work through each of the costs mentioned in the question, including each cost as a separate line in the cost card. Clearly reference any workings back to the cost card. Remember to pick up the easy marks first -the more difficult hi-low and overhead absorption calculations were only worth four of the total marks. Even if these harder areas were ignored a good pass could still be obtained. Don't forget to identify the cost gap.

Note: The original question included a requirement to discuss closing the cost gap. The suggested solution to this requirement was as follows:

Steps to reduce a cost gap include:

Review radio features

Remove features from the radio that add to cost but do not significantly add value to the product when viewed by the customer. This should reduce cost but not the achievable selling price. This can be referred to as value engineering or value analysis.

Team approach

Cost reduction works best when a team approach is adopted. Edward Limited should bring together members of the marketing, design, assembly and distribution teams to allow discussion of methods to reduce costs. Open discussion and brainstorming are useful approaches here.

Review the whole supplier chain

Each step in the supply chain should be reviewed, possibly with the aid of staff questionnaires, to identify areas of likely cost savings. Areas which are identified by staff as being likely cost saving areas can then be focussed on by the team. For example, the questionnaire might ask 'are there more than five potential suppliers for this component?' Clearly a 'yes' response to this question will mean that there is the potential for tendering or price competition.

Components

Edward Limited should look at the significant costs involved in components. New suppliers could be sought or different materials could be used. Care would be needed not to damage the perceived value of the product. Efficiency improvements should also be possible by reducing waste or idle time that might exist. Avoid, where possible, non-standard parts in the design.

Assembly workers

Productivity gains may be possible by changing working practices or by de-skilling the process. Automation is increasingly common in assembly and manufacturing and Edward Limited should investigate what is possible here to reduce the costs. The learning curve may ultimately help to close the cost gap by reducing labour costs per unit.

Clearly reducing the percentage of idle time will reduce product costs. Better management, smoother work flow and staff incentives could all help here. Focusing on continuous improvement in production processes may help.

Overheads

Productivity increases would also help here by spreading fixed overheads over a greater number of units. Equally Edward Limited should consider an activity based costing approach to its overhead allocation, this may reveal more favourable cost allocations for the digital radio or ideas for reducing costs in the business.

ACCA marking scheme			Marks
(a)	Process description		1
	Product specification		1
	Selling price		1
	Cost calculation		1
			—
		maximum	3
			—
(b)	Cost calculation:		
	Component 1		2
	Component 2		2
	Material other		1
	Assembly labour		2
	Variable production overhead		1
	High low calculation		1
	Fixed production OAR calculation		1
	Fixed production overhead		1
	Cost gap identified		1
			—
			12
			—
Total			15

Walk in the footsteps of a top tutor

The following answer was written to time to show what is achievable in the allocated time and how the answer can be structured to maximise marks.

(a)   Target costing in Edward Co should be carried out as follows:

1   Product specification

Target costing begins by specifying the product that the organisation wishes to sell. For Edward Co, the product is the new digital radio. The radio's features should fulfil the customer's needs.

2   Price

The price of the radio should be set next. Competitor's prices and market conditions must be considered.

3   Margin

Edward Co's required margin should then be deducted from the price. This will result in a target cost.

(b)   **Cost gap**

Step 1: Calculate the target cost

Target selling price	=	$44.00
Target margin (20%)	=	($8.80)
Target cost	=	$35.20

Tutorial note

Work through each cost in turn and include as a separate line in a cost card. Set up separate, clearly referenced workings if necessary. Do not get stuck on the difficult areas but instead take a guess and move on. The key is to complete the cost card and to get most of it correct.

Step 2: Calculate the expected cost

	$
Component 1 – Board	4.10
– Delivery costs $2,000/4,000	0.60
Component 2 – 0.25m × $0.50/m × 100/98	0.128
Other material	8.10
Assembly labour	7.00
$12.60 per hour × 0.5 hours × 100/90	
Production overheads (W1) – variable	10.00
– fixed	6.00
Total expected cost	35.928

(W1) Production overheads

	Overheads ($)	Labour Hours
Hi	700,000	23,000
Low	620,000	19,000
Difference	80,000	4,000

Variable overhead per labour hour = $80,000/4,000 = $20 per hour
Variable overhead per unit = 0.5 hours × $20 per hour = $10

Total overhead of $700,000 = Fixed overhead + variable overhead of
($20 × 23,000 hours)

700,000 – $460,000 = Fixed overhead of $240,000 (This is the monthly amount)

Fixed OAR = Annual fixed overhead of ($240,000 × 12)/ 240,000 assembly hours
= $12 per labour hour

Fixed overhead per unit = $12 per hour × 0.5 hours = $6

Step 3: Calculate the Cost Gap

Target cost = $35.20

Expected cost = $35.928

Cost gap = **Difference of $0.728**

206 YAM CO (JUNE 09 EXAM)

Tutorial note:

Note that over half the marks in this question are for the written requirements. This is typical of the exam and therefore it is imperative to practice answering these written requirements.

(a) The output capacity for each process is as follows:

The total processing hours of the factory is given but can be proven as follows:

18 hours × 5 days × 50 weeks × 50 production lines = 225,000 hours.

Given this, the production capacity for pressing must be 225,000 hours/0.5 hours per metre = 450,000 metres. Using this method the production capacity for all processes is as follows:

	Product A	Product B	Product C
Pressing	450,000	450,000	562,500
Stretching	900,000	562,500	900,000
Rolling	562,500	900,000	900,000

The bottleneck is clearly the pressing process which has a lower capacity for each product. The other processes will probably be slowed to ensure smooth processing.

Tutorial note:

*Clearly an alternative approach is simply to look at the original table for processing speed and pick out the slowest process. This is pressing. (full marks available for that **explained** observation). This would have been a much more straightforward approach in the exam.*

(b) **TPAR for each product**

Tutorial note:

*Clearly an alternative approach is simply to look at the original table for processing speed and pick out the slowest process. This is pressing. (full marks available for that **explained** observation). This would have been a much more straightforward approach in the exam.*

	Product A	Product B	Product C
Selling price	70.0	60.0	27.0
Raw materials	3.0	2.5	1.8
Throughput	67.0	57.5	25.2
Throughput per bottleneck hour*	134.0	115.0	63.0
Fixed costs per hour (W1)	90.0	90.0	90.0
TPAR	1.49	1.28	0.7
Working*	67/0.5 = 134	57.5/0.5 = 115	25.2/0.4 = 63

(W1) The fixed cost per bottleneck hour can be calculated as follows:

Total fixed costs are $18,000,000 plus the labour cost. Labour costs $10 per hour for each of the 225,000 processing hours, a cost of $2,250,000.

Total fixed cost is therefore $18,000,000 + $2,250,000 = $20,250,000

Fixed cost per bottleneck hours is $20,250,000/225,000 = $90 per hour

Key answer tips

Calculate the TPAR in three stages: firstly, calculate the throughput per bottleneck hour. Secondly, calculate the fixed cost per hour. Finally, calculate the TPAR. Carry forward marks would be awarded if the incorrect bottleneck process was identified in requirement (a).

(c)

Tutorial note:

In the throughput calculations, do not labour in the calculation of contribution. Labour is properly treated as a fixed cost so you should include it in the overheads part of the calculations.

Yam could improve the TPAR of product C in various ways:

Speed up the bottleneck process. By increasing the speed of the bottleneck process the rate of throughput will also increase, generating a greater rate of income for Yam if the extra production can be sold. Automation might be used or a change in the detailed processes. Investment in new machinery can also help here but the cost of that would need to be taken into account.

Increase the selling prices. It can be difficult to increase selling prices in what we are told is a competitive market. Volume of sales could be lost leaving Yam with unsold stock or idle equipment. On the other hand, given the business appears to be selling all it can produce, then a price increase may be possible.

Reduce the material prices. Reducing material prices will increase the net throughput rate. Metal is available from many sources being far from a unique product. Given the industry is mature the suppliers of the raw material could be willing to negotiate on price; this could have volume or quality based conditions attached. Yam will have to be careful to protect its quality levels. Bulk buying increases stock levels and the cost of that would need to be considered.

Reduce the level of fixed costs. The fixed costs should be listed and targets for cost reduction be selected. ABC techniques can help to identify the cost drivers and with management these could be used to reduce activity levels and hence cost. Outsourcing, de-skilling or using alternative suppliers (for stationery for example) are all possible cost reduction methods.

				Marks
ACCA marking scheme				
(a)	Identification of bottleneck			1.0
	Explanation			2.0
			Maximum	3.0
(b)	Sales prices (per product)			0.5
	Raw material cost (per product)			0.5
	Throughput per bottleneck hour (per product)			0.5
	Fixed costs			1.5
	Fixed cost per hour			0.5
	TPAR (per product)			0.5
			Maximum	8.0
(c)	Increase speed of bottleneck			1.0
	Increase selling prices – difficult to do			1.0
	Reduce material prices			1.0
	Reduce level of fixed costs			1.0
			Maximum	4.0
Total				**15**

207 GLAM CO (DEC 2014)

(a) Bottleneck activity

The bottleneck may have been worked out as follows:

Total salon hours = 8 × 6 × 50 = 2,400 each year. The capacity for each senior stylist must be 2,400 hours, which equates to 2,400 cuts each year (2,400/1). Since there are three senior stylists, the total capacity is 7,200 hours or 7,200 cuts each year. Using this method, the capacity for each activity is as follows:

	Cut	Treatment
Assistants	48,000	16,000
Senior stylists	7,200	4,800
Junior stylists	9,600	9,600

The bottleneck activity is clearly the work performed by the senior stylists. The senior stylists' time is called a bottleneck activity because it is the activity which prevents the salon's throughput from being higher than it is. The total number of cuts or treatments which can be completed by the salon's senior stylists is less than the number which can be completed by other staff members, considering the number of each type of staff available and the time required by each type of staff for each client.

(b)   TPAR

	Cut	Treatment	
	$	$	
Selling price	60	110	
Materials	0.60	8	(7.40+0.6)
Throughput	59.40	102	
Throughput per bottleneck hour	59.40	68	
Total salon costs per BN hour (W)	42.56	42.56	
TPAR	1.4	1.6	

Working: Total salon costs

(3 × $40,000) + (2 × $28,000) + (2 × $12,000) + $106,400 = $306,400 Therefore cost for each bottleneck hour = $306,400/7,200 = $42.56

Note: Answers based on total salary costs were $80,000 were also equally acceptable since the wording of question was open to interpretation.

ACCA marking scheme			
			Marks
(a)	Calculation and justification of bottleneck		3
	Explanation of bottleneck		1
			—
		Maximum	4
			—
(b)	TPAR		
	Throughput		1
	Throughput per bottleneck hour		1
	Total salon costs		1
	Cost per hour		1
	TPAR		2
			—
		Maximum	6
			—
Total			**10**
			—

208 SOLAR SYSTEMS CO (DEC 2013 EXAM)

(a) Throughput accounting ratio = throughput return per factory hour/cost per factory hour.

Cost per factory hour

Total factory costs/total available hours on bottleneck resource

= $12,000,000/2,700 hours (12 × 5 × 50 × 90% hours)

= $4,444.44

Throughput return	Large panels	Small panels
	$	$
Selling price	12,600	3,800
Materials	(4,300)	(1,160)
	———	———
Throughput per unit	8,300	2,640
Hours per unit required on Machine M	1.4	0.6
Throughput return per hour	**$5,928.57**	**$4,400**

Throughput accounting ratio

Throughput return per factory hour/cost per factory hour:

	Large	Small
	5,928.57/4,444.44	4,400/4,444.44
	= 1.33	= 0.99

In any organisation, one would expect the throughput accounting ratio to be greater than 1. This means that the rate at which the organisation is generating cash from sales of this product is greater than the rate at which it is incurring costs.

It follows on, then, that if the ratio is less than 1, changes need to be made quickly. Whilst the ratio for large panels is more than 1, it is just under 1 for small panels. However, if changes are made as suggested in (c) below, this could soon be rectified.

(b) **Increasing throughput**

Generally speaking, throughput can be increased by increasing sales volumes or prices on the one hand, or by cutting costs on the other hand. In the case of S Co, it is not possible to increase sales prices as the company has guaranteed not to increase them for three years. In order to increase production volumes without making any additional capital expenditure, the company needs to focus on how it could increase the productivity of Machine M. We are told that there is plenty of spare capacity on Machines C and A. Some suggestions to increase Machine M's capacity are as follows:

- Machine M is currently only fully functional 90% of the time. This means that 300 hours of time are lost whilst the machine is being maintained or workers are not available to man it. If the maintenance work could be carried out outside the usual working day (i.e. either before 7 am or after 8 pm), some additional time could be freed up. This should be possible given that we are told that the maintenance contractors work around the clock.

- Workers could be trained to use more than one of the machines. This would then mean that, if some workers were absent, one of the other workers could step in and work on another machine in order to keep it running. Again, this would help to keep the lost 300 hours productive.

- The most obvious machine time which is being lost is the one hour per day at lunchtime. This amounts to 250 lost production hours per year. These additional 250 hours could be used to produce an extra 178 large panels (250/1.4 hours.) Large panels should be made first in preference to small panels since they generate a higher throughput per machine hour. If workers were trained to use all three machines then, if their lunchtimes were staggered, it may be possible to keep machine M running for the whole working day. However, even after doing this, there would still be 590 additional hours of time required on Machine M if the full market demand is going to be satisfied. Therefore, more time needs to be made available.

- Finally then, in order to increase productive hours on M, the working hours of the factory would need to be increased. Either the working day could be made longer, given that workers must already be working shifts, or maybe the factory could open for one extra day per week.

	ACCA marking scheme		
			Marks
(a)	Throughput accounting ratios		
	Cost per factory hour		2
	Throughput per unit for large/small panels – 1 mark for each		2
	Throughput per hour for large/small panels – 1 mark for each		2
	TAR for large/small panels – 1 mark for each		2
	Discussion of TAR		1
			—
		Maximum	9
			—
(b)	Increasing productivity		
	Max 2 per suggestion		6
			—
Total			**15**
			—

DECISION MAKING TECHNIQUES

209 ACCESS INC

(a) **Make v buy decision**

The 'Buy' alternative $

		$
The 'Buy' alternative		
Cost of bought-in seats:	10 × 610	6,100
		6,100
The 'Make' alternative		
Sales of power units forgone	20 × 376	7,520
Cost savings of making fewer batteries	20 × (4,140 + 9,450)/90	(3,020)
Increase in cost of making seats	10 × (9,300 + 12,600)/60	3,650
		8,150

Note: In either case, 10 external sales of power units will be lost as these are now used internally. You could have included the cost of these lost sales in both of the above calculations. It is quicker to recognise they are a common cash flow and hence not relevant to the decision.

On the basis of the information given the required seats should be bought in rather than made.

(b)   The following factors should also be considered before a final decision is made:

- The external supplier can produce seats of the same quality as Access Inc.
- Customers will not view bought in seats as inferior.
- Dependence on an external supplier of extra seating assemblies does not lead to difficulty in maintaining sales volume in the future.
- None of the apportioned overheads are incremental – see answer to part (b) below.
- The average variable costs of production calculated above are constant over the relevant range of output, i.e. no economies of scale or learning effects result from the increased production.
- No goodwill is lost by the reduction in sales of power units to the existing external clients.
- No additional transport costs are encountered.
- Demand will be maintained at the increased level.

210   ROBBER CO (JUNE 2012 EXAM)

(a)

	Keypads $	Display screens $
Variable costs		
Materials ($160k × 6/12) + ($160k × 1.05 × 6/12)	164,000	
($116k × 1.02)		118,320
Direct labour	40,000	60,000
Machine set-up costs		
($26k – $4k) × 500/400	27,500	
($30k – $6k) × 500/400		30,000
	―――――	―――――
	231,500	208,320
Attributable fixed costs		
Heat and power ($64k – $20k)/($88k – $30k)	44,000	58,000
Fixed machine costs	4,000	6,000
Depreciation and insurance ($84/$96k × 40%)	33,600	38,400
	―――――	―――――
	81,600	102,400
Total incremental costs of making in-house	313,100	310,720
	―――――	―――――
Cost of buying (80,000 × $4.10/$4.30)	328,000	344,000
	―――――	―――――
Total saving from making	14,900	33,280
	―――――	―――――

Robber Co should therefore make all of the keypads and display screens in-house

(**Note:** It has been assumed that the fixed set-up costs only arise if production takes place.)

(Alternative method)

Relevant costs

	Keypads $	Display screens $
Direct materials		
($160,000/2) + $160,000/2 × 1·05	164,000	
$116,000 × 1·02		118,320
Direct labour	40,000	60,000
Heat and power		
$64,000 – (50% × $40,000)	44,000	
$88,000 – (50% × $60,000)		58,000
Machine set up costs:		
Avoidable fixed costs	4,000	6,000
Activity related costs (W1)	27,500	30,000
Avoidable depreciation and insurance costs:		
40% × $84,000/$96,000	33,600	38,400
Total relevant manufacturing costs	313,100	310,720
Relevant cost per unit:	3.91375	3.884
Cost per unit of buying in	4.1	4.3
Incremental cost of buying in	0.18625	0.416

As each of the components is cheaper to make in-house than to buy in, the company should continue to manufacture keypads and display screens in-house.

Working 1

Current no. of batches produced = 80,000/500 = 160.

New no. of batches produced = 80,000/400 = 200.

Current cost per batch for keypads = ($26,000 – $4,000)/160 = $137.5.

Therefore new activity related batch cost = 200 × $137.5 = $27,500.

Current cost per batch for display screens = ($30,000 – $6,000)/160 = $150.

Therefore new activity related batch cost = 200 × $150 = $30,000.

(b)   The attributable fixed costs remain unaltered irrespective of the level of production of keypads and display screens, because as soon as one unit of either is made, the costs rise. We know that we will make at least one unit of each component as both are cheaper to make than buy. Therefore they are an irrelevant common cost.

	Keypads $	Display screens $
Buy	4.1	4.3
Variable cost of making ($231,500/80,000)	2.89	
($208,320/80,000)		2.6
Saving from making per unit	1.21	1.7
Labour hour per unit	0.5	0.75
Saving from making per unit of limiting factor	2.42	2.27
Priority of making	1	2

Total labour hours available = 100,000. Make maximum keypads i.e. 100,000, using 50,000 labour hours (100,000 × 0.5 hours) Make 50,000/0.75 display screens, i.e. 66,666 display screens. Therefore buy in 33,334 display screens (100,000 – 66,666).

ACCA marking scheme			
			Marks
(a)	Incremental cost of buying in		0.5
	Direct materials		0.5
	Direct labour		0.5
	Heat and light		3
	Set-up costs		1
	Depreciation and insurance		0.5
	Total cost of making		0.5
	Total cost of buying Saving		0.5
	Conclusion		1
		Maximum	8
	(Method 2)		
	Direct materials		0.5
	Direct labour		0.5
	Heat and power		0.5
	Avoidable fixed costs		0.5
	Activity related costs (W1)		3
	Avoidable depreciation and insurance		0.5
	Total relevant manufacturing costs		0.5
	Relevant cost per unit		0.5
	Incremental cost of buying in		0.5
	Conclusion		1
		Maximum	8

(b)	If 100,000 control panels made		1
	Variable cost of making per unit		1
	Saving from making		1
	Saving per labour hour		1
	Ranking		1
	Make 100,000 keypads		1
	Make 66,666 display screens		1
	Buy 33,334 display screens		1
		Maximum	7
Total			15

211 CUT AND STITCH (JUNE 10 EXAM)

(a) The optimal production mix can be found by solving the two equations given for F and T.

$7W + 5L = 3,500$ (1)

$2W + 2L = 1,200$ (2)

Multiplying the second equation by 2.5 produces:

$7W + 5L = 3,500$

$5W + 5L = 3,000$

$2W = 500$

$W = 250$

Substituting W = 250 in the fabric equation (2) produces:

$2 \times 250 + 2L = 1,200$

$2L = 700$, so $L = 350$

The optimal solution is when 250 work suits are produced and 350 lounge suits are produced. **The contribution gained is $26,000**:

$C = 48W + 40L$

$C = (48 \times 250) + (40 \times 350)$

$C = 26,000$

(b) The shadow prices can be found by adding one unit to each constraint in turn.

Shadow price of T

$7W + 5L = 3,501$

$2W + 2L = 1,200$

Again multiplying the second equation by 2.5 produces:

$7W + 5L = 3,501$

$5W + 5L = 3,000$

$2W = 501$

$= 250.5$

Substituting W = 250.5 in the fabric equation produces:

(2 × 250.5) + 2L = 1,200

2L = 1,200 − 501

L = 349.5

Contribution earned at this point would be = (48 × 250.5) + (40 × 349.5) = 26,004 which is an increase of $4.

Hence the shadow price of T is $4 per hour.

Shadow price of F

7W + 5L = 3,500

2W + 2L = 1,201

Again multiplying the second equation by 2.5 produces:

7W + 5L = 3,500.0

5W + 5L = 3,002.5

2W = 497.5

W = 248.75

Substituting W = 248.75 in the fabric equation produces:

(2 × 248.75) +2L = 1,201

2L = 1,201 − 497.5

L = 351.75

Contribution earned at this point would be = (48 × 248.75) + (40 × 351.75) = 26,010, which is an increase of $10. Hence the shadow price of F is $10 per metre.

ACCA marking scheme		
		Marks
(a)	Optimal point calculation	3
	Contribution	1
		–––
		4
(b)	3 for each shadow price	6
Total		–––
		10
		–––

212 HAMMER (JUNE 10 EXAM)

(a) **Price under existing policy**

	$
Steel (0.4/0.95 × $4.00)	1.68
Other materials ($3.00 × 0.9 × 0.1)	0.27
Labour (0.25 × $10)	2.50
Variable overhead (0.25 × $15)	3.75
Delivery	0.50
	–––
Total variable cost	8.70
Mark-up 30%	2.61
	–––
Transfer price	11.31
	–––

(b)   The only difference would be to add the fixed costs and adjust the mark-up %.

	$
Existing total variable cost	8.70
Extra fixed cost (0.25 × $15 × 0.8)	3.00
	———
Total cost	11.70
Mark-up 10%	1.17
	———
Transfer price	12.87
	———

The price difference is therefore 12.87 − 11.31 = $1.56 per unit

ACCA marking scheme		Marks
(a)	Steel	1
	Other material	1
	Labour	1
	Variable overhead	1
	Delivery	1
	Mark-up	1
		—
	Total	6
(b)	Fixed cost	2
	Mark-up	2
		—
	Total	4
Total		**10**

213 CHAIR CO (DEC 2014)

(a)   Learning curve formula = y = ax^b

Cumulative average time per unit for 8 units:

Y = 12 × 8−.415

= 5.0628948 hours.

Therefore cumulative total time for 8 units = 40.503158 hours.

Cumulative average time per unit for 7 units:

Y = 12 × 7^{-415}

= 5.3513771 hours.

Therefore cumulative total time for 7 units = 37.45964 hours.

Therefore incremental time for 8th unit = 40.503158 hours − 37.45964 hours = 3.043518 hours.

Total labour cost for 8th unit =3.043518 × $15 = $45.65277

Material and overheads cost per unit = $230

Therefore total cost per unit = $275.65277

Therefore price per unit = $413.47915

(b) **(i)** **Actual learning rate**

Cumulative number of seats produced	Cumulative total hours	Cumulative average hours per unit
1	12.5	12.5
2	?	$12.5 \times r$
4	?	$12.5 \times r2$
8	34.3	$12.5 \times r3$

Using algebra: $34.3 = 8 \times (12.5 \times r^3)$

$4.2875 = (12.5 \times r^3)$

$0.343 = r^3$

$r = 0.70$

The learning effect was 70% as compared to the forecast rate of 75%, meaning that the labour force learnt more quickly than anticipated.

(ii) **Adjusted price**

The adjusted price charged will be lower than the original price calculated in part (a). This is because the incremental cost of the 8th unit will be lower given the 70% learning rate, even though the first unit took 12.5 hours. We know this because we are told that the cumulative time for 8 units was actually 34.3 hours. This is lower than the estimated cumulative time in part (a) for 8 units of 40.503158 hours and therefore, logically, the actual incremental time for the 8th unit must be lower than the estimated 3.043518 hours calculated in part (a). Consequently, total cost will be lower and price will be lower, given that this is based on cost.

ACCA marking scheme			
			Marks
(a)	Price		
	Cumulative average time per unit for 8 units		1.0
	Total time for 8 units		0.5
	Cumulative average time per unit for 7 units		1.0
	Total time for 7 units		0.5
	Incremental time for 8th unit		0.5
	Cost for 8th unit		0.5
	Total cost		0.5
	Price		0.5
		Maximum	5.0
(b)	(i)	Learning rate	
		Calculating learning rate	2.5
		Saying whether better or worse	0.5
		Maximum	3.0
	(ii)	Effect on price	2.0
Total			**10.0**

214 HEAT ONE CO (JUNE 2011 EXAM)

(a)   **Profit**

In order to ascertain the optimum price, you must use the formula $P = a - bQ$

Where P = price; Q = quantity; a = intersection (price at which quantity demanded will be nil); b = gradient of the demand curve.

The approach is as follows:

(i)   Establish the demand function

b = change in price/change in quantity = $15/1,000 = 0.015.

We know that if price = $735, quantity = 1,000 units.

Establish 'a' by substituting these values for P, Q and b into our demand function:

$735 = a - 0.015Q$

$15 + 735 = a$

Therefore a = 750.

Demand function is therefore $P = 750 - 0.015Q$

(ii)   Establish marginal cost

Tutorial note

*Do not make the mistake of including the fixed cost in the cost of the air conditioning unit: it was the **marginal cost** that was being tested.*

The labour cost of the 100th unit needs to be calculated as follows:

Formula = $y = ax^b$, with a = 1.5

Therefore, if x = 100 and b = −.0740005, then $y = 1.5 \times 100^{-0.0740005} = 1.0668178$

Therefore cost per unit = $1.0668178 \times 8 = 8.5345$

Total cost for 100 units = $853.45.

If x = 99, $y = 1.5 \times 99^{-0.0740005} = 1.0676115$

Therefore cost per unit = $8.5408

Total cost for 99 = $845.55

Therefore cost of 100th unit = $853.45 − $845.55 = $7.90.

Therefore total marginal cost = $42 + $7.90 = $49.90.

Fixed overheads have been ignored as they are not part of the marginal cost.

(iii)   Find profit

(1)   Establish the marginal revenue function

$MR = a - 2bQ$

$MR = 750 - 0.03Q$

(2)   Equate MC and MR

$49.90 = 750 - 0.03Q$

$0.03Q = 700.1$

$Q = 23,337$

(3)   Find optimum price

$P = 750 - (0.015 \times 23,337) = \$399.95$

(b)   Market skimming

With market skimming, high prices would initially be charged for the Energy Buster rather than low prices. This would enable Heat Co to take advantage of the unique nature of the product, thus maximising sales from those customers who like to have the latest technology as early as possible. The most suitable conditions for this strategy are:

- the product is new and different. This is indeed the case with the Energy Buster

- the product has a short life cycle and high development costs that need to be recovered quickly. The life cycle is fairly short and high development costs have been incurred

- since high prices attract competitors, there needs to be barriers to entry in order to deter competitors. In Heat Co's case, there is a barrier, since it has obtained a patent for the Energy Buster.

		ACCA marking scheme		Marks
(a)		Profit using demand-based approach		
	(i)	Establish demand function:		
		Find b		1
		Find a		1
		Write out demand function		1
				___
			Maximum	3
				___
	(ii)	Find MC:		
		Average cost of 100		1
		Total cost of 100		1
		Average cost of 99		1
		Total cost of 99		1
		Difference		1
		Correct total MC excluding fixed cost		1
				___
			Maximum	6
				___
	(iii)	Establish MR function		
		Equate MC and MR to find Q		1
		Find optimum price		1
				1
				___
			Maximum	3
				___
(b)		Reasons for adopting market skimming – 1 each	Maximum	3
Total				___
				15
				___

215 TWO CO (JUNE 2011 EXAM)

Tutorial note

A logical approach to adopt could be suggested as follows: explain market skimming, explain penetration pricing and then explain which one would be most appropriate for the company.

Penetration pricing

With penetration pricing, a low price would initially be charged for the Energy Buster. The idea behind this is that the price will make the product accessible to a larger number of buyers and therefore the high sales volumes will compensate for the lower prices being charged. A large market share would be gained and possibly, the Energy Buster might become accepted as the only industrial air conditioning unit worth buying.

The circumstances that would favour a penetration pricing policy are:

- highly elastic demand for the Energy Buster i.e. the lower the price, the higher the demand. The preliminary research does suggest that demand is elastic

- if significant economies of scale could be achieved by Two Co, then higher sales volumes would result in sizeable reductions in costs. This is not the case here, since learning ceases at 100 units

- if Two Co was actively trying to discourage new entrants into the market. In this case, new entrants cannot enter the market anyway, because of the patent

- if Two Co wished to shorten the initial period of the Energy Buster's life cycle so as to enter the growth and maturity stages quickly. We have no evidence that this is the case for Two Co, although it could be.

From the above, it can be seen that this could be a suitable strategy in some respects but it is not necessarily the best one.

Market skimming

With market skimming, high prices would initially be charged for the Energy Buster rather than low prices. This would enable Two Co to take advantage of the unique nature of the product, thus maximising sales from those customers who like to have the latest technology as early as possible. The most suitable conditions for this strategy are:

- the product is new and different. This is indeed the case with the Energy Buster

- the product has a short life cycle and high development costs that need to be recovered quickly. The life cycle is fairly short and high development costs have been incurred

- since high prices attract competitors, there needs to be barriers to entry in order to deter competitors. In Two Co's case, there is a barrier, since it has obtained a patent for the Energy Buster

- the strength and sensitivity of demand are unknown. Again, this is not the case here.

Once again, the Energy Buster meets only some of the conditions which would suggest that although this strategy may be suitable the answer is not clear cut. The fact that high development costs have been incurred and the life cycle is fairly short are fairly good reasons to adopt this strategy. Whilst we have demand curve data, we do not really know just how reliable this data really is, in which case a skimming strategy may be a safer option.

ACCA marking scheme		
		Marks
Market based strategies		
Penetration pricing		
Each valid point		1
	Maximum	5
Market skimming		
Each valid point		1
	Maximum	5
Total		**10**

216 CAM CO PRICING (JUNE 2013 EXAM)

Market skimming

Market skimming is a strategy that attempts to exploit those areas of the market which are relatively insensitive to price changes. Initially, high prices for the webcam would be charged in order to take advantage of those buyers who want to buy it as soon as possible, and are prepared to pay high prices in order to do so.

The existence of certain conditions is likely to make the strategy a suitable one for Cam Co. These are as follows:

- Where a product is new and different, so that customers are prepared to pay high prices in order to gain the perceived status of owning the product early. The webcam has superior audio sound and visual quality, which does make it different from other webcams on the market.

- Where products have a short life cycle this strategy is more likely to be used, because of the need to recover development costs and make a profit quickly. The webcam does only have a two year life cycle, which does make it rather short.

- Where high prices in the early stages of a product's life cycle are expected to generate high initial cash inflows. If this were to be the case for the webcam, it would be particularly useful for Cam Co because of the current liquidity problems the company is suffering. Similarly, skimming is useful to cover high initial development costs, which have been incurred by Cam Co.

- Where barriers to entry exist, which deter other competitors from entering the market; as otherwise, they will be enticed by the high prices being charged. These might include prohibitively high investment costs, patent protection or unusually strong brand loyalty. It is not clear from the information whether this is the case for Cam Co.

- Where demand and sensitivity of demand to price are unknown. In Cam Co's case, market research has been carried out to establish a price based on the customers' perceived value of the product. The suggestion therefore is that some information is available about price and demand, although it is not clear how much information is available.

It is not possible to say for definite whether this pricing strategy would be suitable for Cam Co, because of the limited information available. However, it does seem unusual that a high-tech, cutting edge product like this should be sold at the same price over its entire, short life cycle. Therefore, price skimming should be investigated further, presuming that this has not already been done by Cam Co.

ACCA marking scheme	
	Marks
Market skimming	
Explanation – maximum	2
Discussion of each condition – maximum per point 2 marks up to	6
Conclusion	2
	——
Total	**10**
	——

217 PROCESS CO (DEC 2013 EXAM)

Tutorial note:

The following calculations could be done on a unit basis if preferred, still earning full marks.

	Incremental revenue	Less VC	Net profit/(loss)	Further process?
L	(1,200 × 0.95 × $6.70) − (1,200 × $5.60) = $918	(1,200 × $0.5) × 0.95 =$(570)	$348	Yes
M	(1,400 × 0.95 × $7.90) − (1,400 × $6.50) = $1,407	(1,400 × $0.70) × 0.95 = $(931)	$476	Yes
S	(1,800 × 0.95 × $6.80) − (1,800 × $6.10) = $648	(1,800 × $0.80) × 0.95 =$(1,368)	$(720)	No

Process Co should further process L and M, since incremental revenue from further processing will exceed incremental costs. However, it should not further process S as incremental costs exceed incremental revenue in S's case.

ACCA marking scheme	
	Marks
Further processing	
L	3
M	3
S	3
Conclusion	1
	——
Total	**10**
	——

218 FURNIVAL

Key answer tips

Approach the question one step at a time, applying fundamental decision-making principles

(a)   Identify incremental revenues and incremental costs including opportunity costs.

(b)   Ignore fixed costs.

(c)   Ignore costs incurred prior to the split off point.

(i)   Process R further if incremental revenues are greater than incremental costs.

Incremental revenues

	$
Selling price at split off point (per gallon)	1.50
Selling price after mixing	10.00
	——
Increase per gallon	8.50
∴ Total for 500 gallons $8.50 × 500	$4,250

Incremental costs

Variable costs + Opportunity costs

	$
90% of process costs 0.90 × $3,000	2,700
Other separable costs	500
	——
Total	3,200

Opportunity costs

Mixing hours are limited and scarce. If R is not produced, the 'other work' could earn a contribution – this is foregone by processing R further.

Contribution = Profit + Fixed costs

Product R requires 10 hours work.

	$
Therefore, total profit from other work = $200 × 10 hours =	2,000
Fixed cost element 10% of $3,000 ($30 per hour × 10 hours) =	300
Total contribution	2,300
∴ Total incremental costs $3,200 + $2,300	5,500

Therefore do not process further. R should be sold at the split off point.

Tutorial note:

The joint process costs are ignored, as they are incurred prior to the separation point.

(ii)

Tutorial note

R is sold at the split off point and production remains at 500 gallons. Therefore, R is not relevant to the decision at hand and it may be ignored.

Consider new output from the distillation plant.

P :	700 gallons
Q :	800 gallons
R :	500 gallons
Production of P falls by (1,000 – 700)	300 gallons
Production of Q increases by (800 – 500)	300 gallons

Joint process costs will not change as total production remains at 2,000 gallons. Relevant costs only arise in the mixing plant.

		Product P		Product Q
Revenue per gallon		$12.50		$20.00
Variable costs:				
Process costs	$\dfrac{\$2,700}{1,000g}$	($2.70)	$\dfrac{\$2,700}{500g}$	($5.40)
Other	$\dfrac{\$2,000}{1,000g}$	($2.00)	$\dfrac{\$500}{500g}$	($1.00)
Contribution per gallon		$7.80		$13.60

Loss in contribution from P = 300 × $7.80 =	($2,340)
Gain in contribution from Q = 300 × $13.60 =	$4,080
Net gain	$1,740
Extra cost of Q = 300 × $1 =	($300)
Total	$1,440

However, this change in output will require additional machine hours:

Production of P: Hours used falls by $\dfrac{10}{1,000} \times 300$ = 3 hours

Production of Q: Hours used rise by $\dfrac{10}{500} \times 300$ = 6 hours

Therefore, additional hours required 3 hours

Thus 3 hours' contribution from 'other work' is forgone.

Contribution per hour from other work = $230 (see earlier).

Lost contribution with new plan = $230 × 3 hours = $690

Overall effect of new plan = $1,440 – $690 = $750 gain

Recommendations – Produce P : Q : R ratio of 7 : 8 : 5 and sell R at the split off point.

219 THEATRE

(a)

Ticket sales ($)	Confectionary sales ($)	Total sales ($)	Joint × probability	Sales × probability ($)
7,500	900	8,400	.5 × .3 = .15	1,260
7,500	1,500	9,000	.5 × .5 = .25	2,250
7,500	3,000	10,500	.5 × .2 = .10	1,050
10,000	1,200	11,200	.3 × .3 = .09	1,008
10,000	2,000	12,000	.3 × .5 = .15	1,800
10,000	4,000	14,000	.3 × .2 = .06	840
12,500	1,500	14,000	.2 × .3 = .06	840
12,500	2,500	15,000	.2 × .5 = .10	1,500
12,500	5,000	17,500	.2 × .2 = .04	700
Total			1.00	11,248

The expected value is $11,248 − $10,000 = $1,248. Therefore it is worthwhile engaging MS for the concert.

(b) The data table shows profit values from each combination of ticket sales and contribution from confectionary sales. So, for example, for 300 people and $3 per person total sales are $8,400 (from (a)) − $10,000 fee = $1,600 loss.

Confectionary sales Ticket sales	$3 per person	$5 per person	$10 per person
300 people	(1,600)	(1,000)	500
400 people	1,200	2,000	4,000
500 people	4,000	5,000	7,500

220 AMELIE

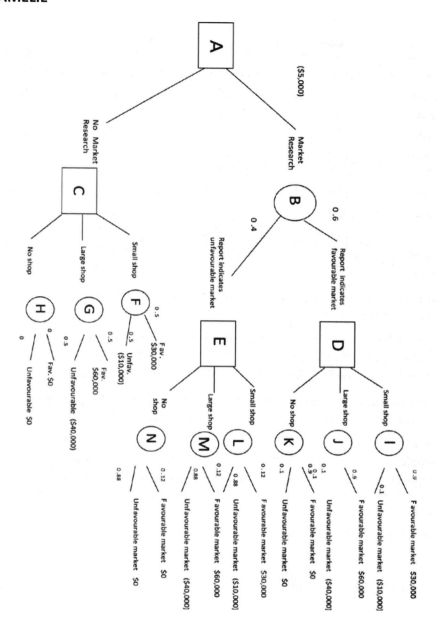

(b) In order to decide whether or not to hire the consultant, expected valued for decision alternatives are calculated, starting on the right hand side of the tree and moving leftwards (backtracking).

At node D :

EV(I) = (0 .9 * $30,000) – (0 .1 *$10,000) = $26,000

EV(J) = (0 .9 * $60,000) – (0 .1 *$40,000) = $50,000

EV(K) = (0 .9 * $0) – (0 .1 *$0) = $0

So, the decision at Node D should be to go for a large shop, as the EV of outcome J is the highest of the three possible decisions I, J and K.

At node E :

EV(L) = (0 .12 * $30,000) – (0 .88 *$10,000) = ($5,200)

EV(M) = (0 .12 * $60,000) – (0 .88 *$40,000) = ($28,000)

EV(N) = (0 .12 * $0) – (0 .88 *$0) = $0

So, the decision at Node E should be not to go for any shop at all, as the EV of outcome N is the only non-loss making option.

At node C :

EV(F) = (0 .5 * $30,000) – (0 .5 *$10,000) = $10,000

EV(G) = (0 .5 * $60,000) – (0 .5 *$40,000) = $10,000

EV(H) = (0 .5 * $0) – (0 .5 *$0) = $0

So, the decision at Node C should be to go for either a small or a large shop, as both offer the same positive EV of a profit.

To decide between hiring a consultant at $5,000 and not hiring a consultant, we need to calculate the EV of profits at node B :

EV (B) = (0.6 × $50,000) + (0 .4 × $0) = $30,000

Therefore, profits if a consultant is hired are expected to reach

$30,000 – cost of research $5,000 = $25,000

EV (C) = $10,000, if no market research is undertaken. The expected value of profits is higher if market research is undertaken, therefore Amelie should hire the consultant.

(c) We first need to calculate what the expected value of profits with perfect information would be. If the second consultant predicts a favourable cheese market (0.6 probability), we should opt for a large shop and obtain $60,000 profit. If the consultant predicts an unfavourable market, we should not go for no shop at all (and profits will be nil.)

Therefore EV of profits with perfect information	= 0.6 × $60,000 + (0 × $0)
	= $36,000

Expected profit with imperfect market research information from first consultant	
	= $25,000
Value of perfect information	**= $11,000**

221 HI LIFE CO (DEC 2014 EXAM)

Direct materials:		Note	$
Fabric	200 m² at $17.50 per m²	1	3,500
Wood	20 m at $8.20 per m	2	164
	30 m at $8.50 per m	2	255
Direct labour:			
Skilled	50 hours at $24 per hour	3	1,200
Semi-skilled	300 hours at $14 per hour	4	4,200
Factory overheads	20 hours at $15 per hour	5	300
Administration overheads		6	–
			———
Total cost			9,619
			———

1   Since the material is in regular use by HL Co, it is replacement cost which is the relevant cost for the contract.

2   30 m will have to be ordered from the alternative supplier for immediate delivery but the remaining 20 m can be used from inventory and replaced by an order from the usual supplier at a cost of $8.20 per m.

3   There is no cost for the first 150 hours of labour because there is spare capacity. The remaining 50 hours will be paid at time and a half, which is $16 × 1.5, i.e. $24 per hour.

4   HL Co will choose to use the agency workers, who will cost $14 per hour, since this is cheaper than paying existing semi-skilled workers at $18 per hour ($12 × 1.5) to work overtime.

5   None of the general factory costs are incremental, so they have all been excluded. However, the supervisor's overtime pay is incremental, so has been included. The supervisor's normal salary, on the other hand, has been excluded because it is not incremental.

6   These are general overheads and are not incremental, so no value should be included for them.

ACCA marking scheme	
	Marks
Fabric calculation	0.5
Fabric reason	0.5
Wood calculation	1.0
Wood reason	1.0
Skilled labour calculation	1.0
Skilled labour reason	1.0
Semi-skilled labour calculation	0.5
Semi-skilled labour reason	1.0
Factory overheads calculation	0.5
Factory overheads reason	1.5
Administration overheads reason	1.0
Total relevant cost (lowest cost estimate)	0.5
	———
Total	**10.0**
	———

222 THE TELEPHONE COMPANY (DEC 2011 EXAM)

Cost statement

	$	Note
Lunch	0	1
Engineers' costs	500	2
Technical advisor	480	3
Site visits	0	4
Training costs	125	5
Handsets	2,184	6
Control system	7,600	7
Cable	1,300	8
Total cost	12,189	

Notes

Note 1: Lunch

This past cost is a 'sunk cost' and should therefore be excluded from the cost statement. It has already arisen and is therefore not incremental.

Note 2: Engineers' costs

Since one of the engineers has spare capacity, the relevant cost of his hours is Nil. This is because relevant costs must arise as a future consequence of the decision, and since his wage will be paid regardless of whether he now works on the contract for Push Co, it is not an incremental cost.

The situation for the other two engineers is slightly different. Their time is currently fully utilised and earning a contribution of $5 per hour each. This is after deducting their hourly cost which, given a salary of $4,000 per month each, is $25 per hour ($4,000/4 × 40). However, in one week's time – when they would otherwise be idle – they can complete Contract X and earn the contribution anyway. Therefore, the only relevant cost is the penalty of $500 that will be payable for the delay on Contract X.

Note 3: Technical advisor

Since the advisor would have to work overtime on this contract, the relevant cost is the overtime rate of $60 ($40 × 1.5) per hour. This would total $480 for the whole job.

Note 4: Site visits

This is a cost paid directly by Push Co to a third party. Since it is not a relevant cost for T Co, it has been excluded.

Note 5: Training costs

Since the trainer is paid a monthly salary irrespective of what work he does, this element of his cost is not relevant to the contract, since it is not incremental. However, the commission of $125 will arise directly as a consequence of the decision and must therefore be included.

Note 6: Handsets

Although T Co has 80 of the 120 handsets required already in inventory, they are clearly in regular use in the business. Therefore, if the 80 are used on this contract, they will simply need to be replaced again. Consequently, the relevant cost for both the 40 that need to be bought and the 80 already in inventory is the current purchase price of $18.20 each. 120 × $18.20 = $2,184.

Note 7: Control system

The historic cost of Swipe 1, $5,400, is a 'sunk' cost and not relevant to this decision. However, since the company could sell it for $3,000 if it did not use it for this contract, the $3,000 is an opportunity cost here. The current market price for Swipe 1 of $5,450 is totally irrelevant to the decision as T Co has no intention of replacing Swipe 1, since it was bought in error. In addition to the $3,000, there is a modification cost of $4,600, bringing the total cost of converting Swipe 1 to $7,600. This is still a cheaper option than buying Swipe 2 for $10,800, therefore the company would choose to do the modification to Swipe 1. The cost of $10,800 of a new Swipe 2 system is therefore irrelevant now.

Note 8: Cable

The cable is in regular use by T Co, therefore all 1,000 metres should be valued at the current market price of $1.30 per metre. The $1.20 per metre is a sunk cost and not relevant.

ACCA marking scheme	
	Marks
Costing statement	
Lunch	1
Engineer costs	3
Technical advisor	1
Site visits	1
Training costs	2
Handsets	3
Control system	3
Cable	1
	—
Maximum	15
	—
Total	**15**
	—

223 CHOCOLATES ARE FOREVER (CAF)

(a) The Breakeven point is that number if units produced and sold at which CAF will make no profit or no loss:

$$\text{Breakeven point} = \frac{\text{Fixed costs}}{\text{Contribution per unit}}; \quad \text{Breakeven point} = \frac{\$20,000}{\$12 - \$7}$$

Breakeven point = 4,000 units.

The margin of safety expresses the gap between budgeted sales and breakeven sales. It measures by how much CAF needs to fall short of budgeted sales before it starts making a loss:

$$\text{Margin of Safety} = \frac{\text{Budgeted sales} - \text{Breakeven sales}}{\text{Budgeted sales}} \times 100\%$$

$$\text{Margin of Safety} = \frac{6,000 \text{ units} - 4,000 \text{ units}}{6,000 \text{ units}} \times 100\%; \quad \text{Margin of Safety} = 33.33\%$$

(b) A **breakeven chart** is a graphical representation of the data. It shows the breakeven point when the total cost line and the total revenue line intersect. The total cost line is a total variable cost line sitting on the fixed cost line. The Sales revenue line is also depicted and comes from the origin. (no sales, no revenue). The Margin of Safety can then be read off the chart on the horizontal axis — the difference between the budgeted output and the breakeven output.

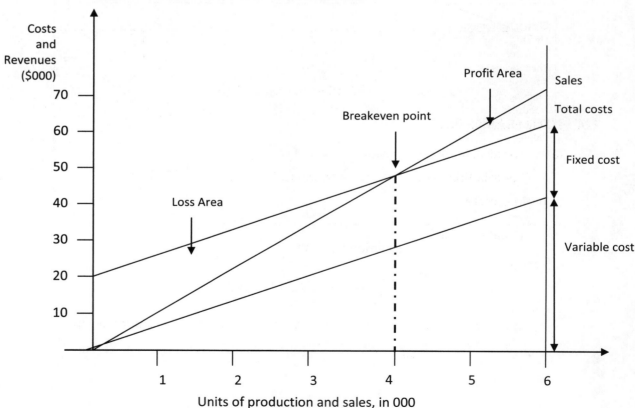

The Profit-Volume chart is an alternative chart, which is simpler, but gives a lot of the same information. By drawing a line between the fixed costs at zero output (where the amount of loss will equal the fixed costs) and the breakeven point – where the profit line crosses the x axis – the chart may be used to work out the expected profit at any level of output.

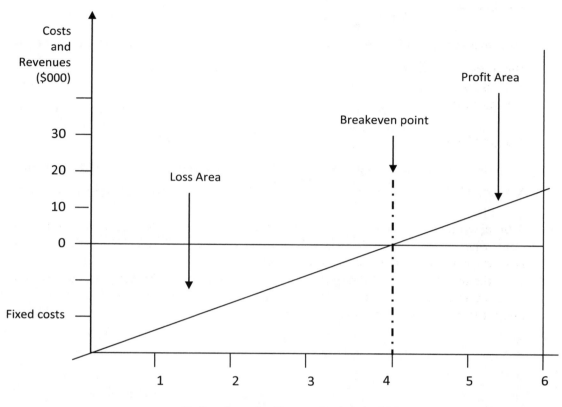

Units of production and sales, in 000

224 FOTO FRAMES PLC

(a) To calculate the breakeven sales volume:

Contribution per unit × volume of units = Fixed costs

Therefore,

$$\text{Volume} = \frac{\text{Fixed costs}}{\text{Contribution per unit}}$$

$$= \frac{2,400,000}{25-6.50} = 129,730 \text{ photo frames}$$

So, breakeven sales revenue = breakeven sales volume × selling price per frame

$$= 129,730 \times \$25 = \$3.24 \text{ m}$$

The margin of safety is

$$\frac{\text{Budgeted sales} - \text{Breakeven sales}}{\text{Budgeted sales}} \times 100\%$$

$$= \frac{200{,}000 \text{ units} - 129{,}730 \text{ units}}{200{,}000} \times 100\% = 35.1\%$$

That is, sales could fall below budget by 35% in volume terms before the company will begin to make a loss.

(b) Profit/Volume chart (P/V chart)

The Profit/Volume chart relates profit to be achieved with the volume of units to be made and sold. Two points are needed on the line in order to be able to draw the P/V chart.

If no units are made and sold, the loss will be equal to the fixed costs of $2.4 million.

If 129,730 units are made and sold, profit will be zero (129,730 units is the breakeven point from Part (a)).

Profit/Volume chart based on original selling price and variable cost per unit:

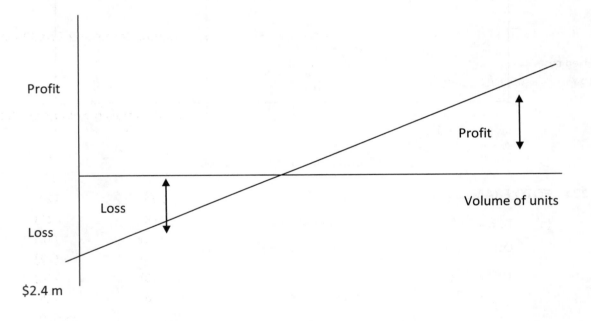

(c)

	$
New selling price per unit ($25 × 90%)	22.50
New variable cost per unit ($6.50 × 95%)	6.18
New contribution per unit	16.32

$$\text{New breakeven volume} = \frac{\text{Fixed costs}}{\text{Contribution per unit}}$$

$$= \frac{2,400,000}{16.32}$$

$$= 147,059 \text{ photo frames}$$

New breakeven sales revenue = 147,059 units × $22.50 = $3.31m

That is, the business needs to generate additional sales revenue of $70,000 in order to breakeven.

The new margin of safety is

$$\frac{\text{Budgeted sales} - \text{Breakeven sales}}{\text{Budgeted sales}} \times 100\%$$

$$= \frac{200,000 \text{ units} - 147,059 \text{ units}}{200,000 \text{ units}} \times 100\% = 26.5\%$$

That is, sales could now only fall by 26.5% in volume terms before the company will begin to make a loss.

(d) The breakeven point has increased by 17,329 units in volume terms and $70,000 in sales revenue terms.

225 HAIR CO (DEC 12 EXAM)

(a) Weighted average contribution to sales ratio (WA C/S ratio) = total contribution/total sales revenue.

Per unit:	C	S	D
	$	$	$
Selling price	110	160	120
Material 1	(12)	(28)	(16)
Material 2	(8)	(22)	(26)
Skilled labour	(16)	(34)	(22)
Unskilled labour	(14)	(20)	(28)
Contribution	60	56	28
Sales units	20,000	22,000	26,000
Total sales revenue	$2,200,000	$3,520,000	$3,120,000
Total contribution	$1,200,000	$1,232,000	$728,000

WA C/S ratio = $1,200,000 + $1,232,000 + $728,000/$2,200,000 + $3,520,000 + $3,120,000 = $3,160,000/$8,840,000 = 35.75%

Tutorial note

The pitfall to avoid here (and a very common mistake) is to add together the three unit contributions, then add the three unit selling prices, and divide the former by the latter, to give a C/S ratio of 36.9%. This is mathematically incorrect because it does not take into account the relative sales volume of each product, and it is not therefore a **weighted average** C/S ratio, but rather just an **average** C/S ratio.

(b)   PV chart

Tutorial note

There is a technical article on the ACCA website that describes all the different charts that could be examined: make sure you read it as part of your revision. You were asked for a multi-product profit-volume (PV) chart here - not a mere profit-volume chart, which is different. In order to plot the lines, you must do some preliminary calculations for cumulative profit and revenue, or you will not be able to plot the lines.

Calculate the individual C/S ratio for each product then rank them according to the highest one first.

Per unit:	C	S	D
	$	$	$
Contribution	60	56	28
Selling price	110	160	120
C/S ratio	0.55	0.35	0.23
Ranking	1	2	3

Product	Revenue	Cumulative revenue (x axis co-ordinate)	Profit	Cumulative profit (y axis co-ordinate)
	$	$	$	$
0	0	0	(640,000)	(640,000)
Make C	2,200,000	2,200,000	1,200,000	560,000
Make S	3,520,000	5,720,000	1,232,000	1,792,000
Make D	3,120,000	8,840,000	728,000	2,520,000

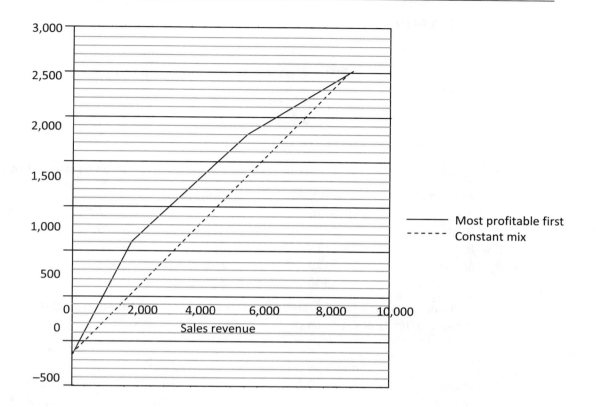

	ACCA marking scheme		
			Marks
(a)	Weighted average C/S ratio		
	Individual contributions		3
	Total sales revenue		1
	Total contribution		1
	Ratio		1
			——
		Maximum	6
			——
(b)	PV chart		
	Individual CS ratios		1.5
	Ranking		1
	Workings for chart		2
	Chart:		
	Labelling		1.5
	Plotting each of six points		3
			——
		Maximum	9
			——
Total			**15**
			——

226 MANGO LEATHER

(a) Breakeven sales revenue = $\dfrac{\text{Fixed costs}}{\text{Weighted Average Contribution to Sales Ratio}}$

Breakeven sales revenue = $\dfrac{\$580,000}{0.35844\,(\text{W1})}$

Breakeven sales revenue = $1,618,123.

(b) Products first need to be ranked according to their contribution to sales ratio:

Products	Selling price (per unit)	Contribution per unit	C/S ratio	Rank
Bags	$400	$190	0.475	2
Belts	$125	$60	0.480	1
Shoes	$150	$55	0.367	3
Jackets	$300	$85	0.283	4

Secondly, cumulative sales and profits need to be established in preparation for the multi-product breakeven chart:

Sales	Cumulative revenue	Contribution (W1)	Cumulative profit or loss
None	$0	$0	$(580,000)
Belts	$250,000	$120,000	$(460,000)
Bags	$650,000	$190,000	$(270,000)
Shoes	$875,000	$82,500	$(187,500)
Jackets	$1,925,000	$297,500	$110,000

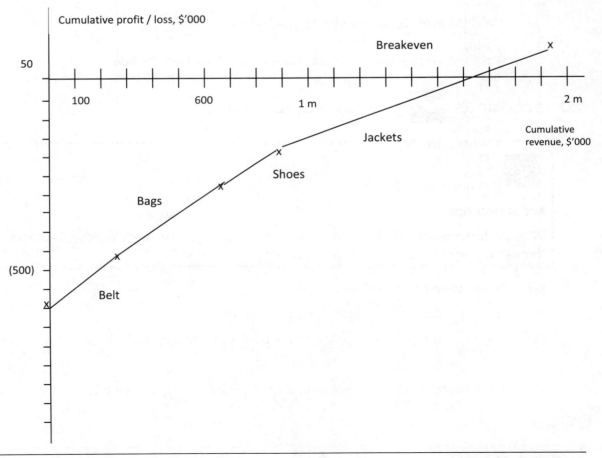

(c)   Mango's production process is very dependent on leather. Leather is the only material and represents a third of total variable costs.

An increase of the cost of leather will severely impact on Mango. Any increase will erode contribution margins significantly. A higher material cost will affect contribution by making it lower. This will impact on the breakeven point, as the weighted average C/S ratio calculated in (a) will be lower (assuming that the selling prices, fixed costs and demand remain constant.)

Graphically, the breakeven revenue point will move to the right along the x-axis and the breakeven revenue will increase.

The unavailability of leather will severely disrupt the production process and will affect customer confidence in Mango, although it may encourage the company to look for substitutes and manage its dependency on its unique material a bit better.

Working 1 – Weighted average contribution to sales ratio

Products	Sales units	Leather cost at @$60 per metre	Contribution per unit	Total sales	Total contribution
Bags	1,000	$60	$190	$400,000	$190,000
Belts	2,000	$15	$60	$250,000	$120,000
Shoes	1,500	$30	$55	$225,000	$82,500
Jackets	3,500	$90	$85	$1,050,000	$297,500
Total				**$1,925,000**	**$690,000**

$$\text{Weighted average contribution to sales ratio} = \frac{\text{Total contribution}}{\text{Total sales}}$$

$$\text{Weighted average contribution to sales ratio} = \frac{\$690,000}{\$1,925,000}$$

Weighted average contribution to sales ratio = 0.35844 or 35.84%

227 B CHEMICALS *Online question assistance*

Key answer tips

With any linear programming question the key is to use the Examiner's toolbox, i.e. to work through the different steps in a systematic manner.

(a)   **Formulation of LP problem**

Let x = the gallons of Super petrol produced

y = the gallons of Regular petrol produced each day; and

C = the total contribution

The company needs to maximise an objective function $C = 0.25x + 0.1y$

Subject to constraints:

supply of heavy crude	$0.7x + 0.5y \le 5{,}000$ (1)
supply of light crude	$0.5x + 0.7y \le 6{,}000$ (2)
market conditions	$x \ge 2/3\,(x + y)$
rearranging	$3x \ge 2x + 2y$
or x	$\ge 2y$ (3)
also x, y	≥ 0

(b)   Graph

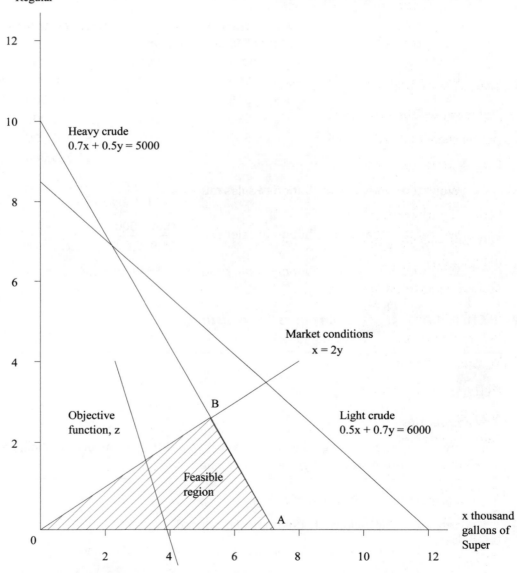

Note: the objective function is also shown.

(c)   **Optimal policy and comment**

From the graph, which also shows an objective function (z = 10,000 has been drawn), it is clear that the optimal solution lies at point A. This is the point where the line $0.7x + 0.5y$ = 5,000 cuts the horizontal axis, where y = 0 and x = 7,142.85.

The optimal production policy involves producing no Regular petrol and 7,142.85 gallons of Super petrol. The contribution that this generates is:

7,142.85 × \$0.25 = \$1,785.71 per day.

Comment

- Whilst the solution to the LP problem might involve no Regular petrol, a policy that abandons refining of one product may risk longer-term demand for that product

- The conclusion drawn is only as reliable as the underlying estimates whose accuracy should be checked

- It would only require a small change in estimates to move the optimal solution from A to B.

228   TABLET CO (JUNE 2014, ADAPTED)

Optimum production plan

Define the variables

Let x = number of units of Xeno to be produced.

Let y = number of units of Yong to be produced.

Let C = contribution.

State the objective function

C = 30x+ 40y

State the constraints

Build time: 24x + 20y ≤ 1,800,000

Program time: 16x + 14y ≤ 1,680,000

Test time: 10x + 4y ≤ 720,000

Non-negativity constraints

x, y ≥ 0

Sales constraints

x ≤ 85,000

y ≤ 66,000

Draw the graph

Build time

If x = 0, y = 1,800,000/20 = 90,000

If y = 0, x = 1,800,000/24 = 75,000

Program time

If x = 0, y = 1,680,000/14 = 120,000

If y = 0, x = 1,680,000/16 = 105,000

Test time

If x = 0, y = 720,000/4 = 180,000

If y = 0, x = 720,000/10 = 72,000

Solve using the iso-contribution line

If y = 40,000, C = 40,000 × $40 = $1,600,000

If C = $1,600,000 and y = 0, x = $1,600,000/$30 = 53,333.33

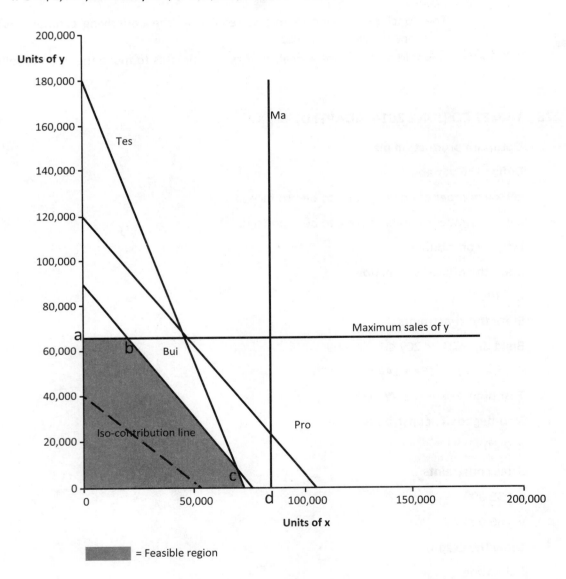

Moving the iso-contribution line out to the furthest point on the feasible region, the optimum production point is b. This is the intersection of the build time constraint and the sales constraint for y. Solving the simultaneous equations for these two constraints:

y = 66,000

24x + 20y = 1,800,000

24x + (20 × 66,000) = 1,800,000

24x + 1,320,000 = 1,800,000

24x = 480,000

x = 20,000

C = (20,000 × $30) + (66,000 × $40)

= $600,000 + $2,640,000 = $3,240,000

Fixed costs = 3 × $650,000 = $1,950,000.

Therefore profit = $1,290,000.

Marking scheme	
	Marks
Optimum production plan	
Stating the objective function	1
Defining constraint for built time	1
Defining constraint for program time	0.5
Defining constraint for test time	0.5
Non-negativity constraints	0.5
Sales constraint x	0.5
Sales constraint y	0.5
Iso-contribution line worked out	1
The graph:	
Labels	0.5
Build time line	0.5
Program time line	0.5
Test time line	0.5
Demand for x line	0.5
Demand for y line	0.5
Iso-contribution line	0.5
Feasible region identified and labelled/shaded	1
Optimum point identified	1
Equations solved at optimum point	3
Total contribution	0.5
Total profit	0.5
Total	**15**

229 COSMETICS CO (DEC 10 EXAM)

Tutorial note

In part (a), the numbers involved are not particularly complicated. It is important, when answering a linear programming question, to set out your workings clearly, with a logical progression in steps from defining the variables and constraints, through to drawing the graph and finding the solution. This makes it easier to mark. The recommended approach is to use the iso-contribution line to find the optimum solution; it is the quickest way to do it. You will not be penalised if you use the simultaneous equations method, but you will take longer to do it.

Define the variables

Let x = no. of jars of face cream to be produced

Let y = no. of bottles of body lotion to be produced

Let C = contribution

State the objective function

The objective is to maximise contribution, C

C = 9x + 8y

State the constraints

Silk powder	3x + 2y <- 5,000	Silk amino acids	1x + 0.5y <- 1,600
Skilled labour	4x + 5y <- 9,600		
Non-negativity constraints:	x, y ≥ 0	Sales constraint:	y ≤ 2,000

Draw the graph

Silk powder   3x + 2y = 5,000

If x = 0, then 2y = 5,000, therefore **y = 2,500**

If y = 0, then 3x = 5,000, therefore **x = 1,666.7**

Silk amino acids   1x +0.5y = 1,600

If x = 0, then 0.5y = 1,600, therefore **y = 3,200**

If y = 0, then **x = 1,600**

Skilled labour   4x + 5y = 9,600

If x = 0, then 5y = 9,600, therefore **y = 1,920 ;**   If y = 0, then 4x = 9,600, therefore **x = 2,400**

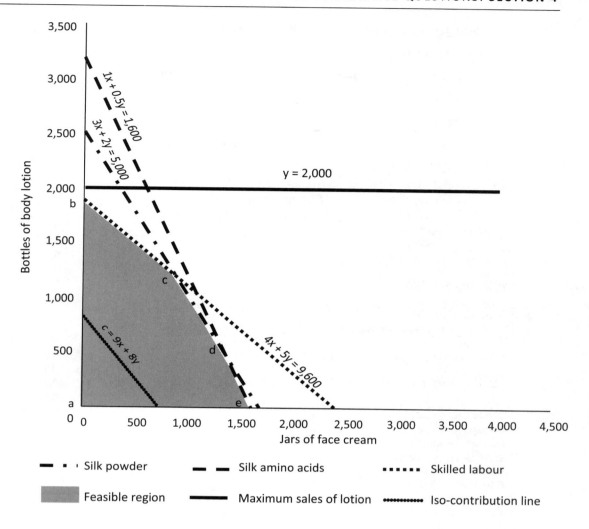

Solve using iso-contribution line

Tutorial note

It is essential to show all of your workings. For example, the iso-contribution line needs to be worked out and then drawn onto the graph. If you don't show how you worked it out, you may lose some marks.

If y =800 and x = 0, then if C = 9x + 8y

C = (8 × 800) = 6,400 Therefore, if y = 0, 9x = 6,400

Therefore x = 711.11

Using the iso-contribution line, the furthest vertex from the origin is point c, the intersection of the constraints for skilled labour and silk powder.

Solving the simultaneous equations for these constraints:

4x + 5y = 9,600 × 3

3x + 2y = 5,000 × 4

12x + 15y = 28,800   12x + 8y = 20,000

Subtract the second one from the first one 7y = 8,800, therefore y = **1,257.14**.

If y = 1,257.14 and:

4x + 5y = 9,600

Then 5 × 1,257.14 + 4x = 9,600

Therefore x = 828.58

If C = 9x + 8y

C = $7,457.22 + $10,057.12 = $17,514.34

ACCA marking scheme	
	Marks
Assigning letters for variables	0.5
Defining constraint for silk powder	0.5
Defining constraint for amino acids	0.5
Defining constraint for labour	0.5
Non-negativity constraint	0.5
Sales constraint: x	0.5
Sales constraint: y	0.5
Iso-contribution line worked out	1
The graph:	
Labels	0.5
Silk powder	0.5
Amino acids	0.5
Labour line	0.5
Demand for x line	0.5
Demand for y line	0.5
Iso-contribution line	1
Vertices a–e identified	0.5
Feasible region shaded	1
Optimum point identified	1
Equations solved at optimum point	3
Total contribution	1
Total	**15**

230 STAY CLEAN (DEC 09 EXAM)

(a)   The relevant costs of the decision to cease the manufacture of the TD are needed:

Cost or Revenue	Working reference	Amount ($)
Lost revenue	Note 1	(96,000)
Saved labour cost	Note 2	48,000
Lost contribution from other products	Note 3	(118,500)
Redundancy and recruitment costs	Note 4	(3,700)
Supplier payments saved	Note 5	88,500
Sublet income		12,000
Supervisor	Note 6	0
Net cash flow		(69,700)

Conclusion: It is not worthwhile ceasing to produce the TD now.

Note 1: All sales of the TD will be lost for the next 12 months, this will lose revenue of 1,200 units × $80 = $96,000

Note 2: All normal labour costs will be saved at 1,200 units × $40 = $48,000

Note 3: Related product sales will be lost.

This will cost the business 5% × ((5,000u × $150) + (6,000u × $270)) = $118,500 in contribution (material costs are dealt with separately below)

Note 4: If TD is ceased now, then:

Redundancy cost	($6,000)
Retraining saved	$3,500
Recruitment cost	($1,200)
Total cost	($3,700)

Note 5: Supplier payments:

	DW ($)	WM ($)	TD ($)	Net cost ($)	Discount level	Gross cost ($)
Current buying cost	350,000	600,000	60,000	1,010,000	5%	1,063,158
Loss of TD			(60,000)	(60,000)	5%	(63,158)
Loss of related sales at cost	(17,500)	(30,000)		(47,500)	5%	(50,000)
New buying cost				921,500	3%	950,000
Difference in net cost				88,500		

Note 6: There will be no saving or cost here as the supervisor will continue to be fully employed.

An alternative approach is possible to the above problem:

Cash flow	Ref	Amount ($)
Lost contribution – TD	Note 7	12,000
Lost contribution – other products	Note 8	(71,000)
Redundancy and recruitment	Note 4 above	(3,700)
Lost discount	Note 9	(19,000)
Sublet income		12,000
Supervisor	Note 6 above	0
Net cash flow		(69,700)

Note 7: There will be a saving on the contribution lost on the TD of 1,200 units × $10 per unit = –$12,000

Note 8: The loss of sales of other products will cost a lost contribution of 5% ((5,000 × $80) + (6,000 × $170)) = $71,000

Note 9 :

	DW	WM	TD	Total (net)	Discount	Total gross
Current buying cost	350,000	600,000	60,000	1,010,000	5%	1,063,158
Saved cost	(17,500)	(30,000)	(60,000)			
New buying cost	332,500	570,000	0	902,500	5%	950,000
				921,500	3%	950,000
Lost discount				(19,000)		

(b) Note: ONE strategy only needed

Complementary pricing

Since the washing machine and the tumble dryer are products that tend to be used together, Stay Clean could link their sales with a complementary price. For example they could offer customers a discount on the second product bought, so if they buy (say) a TD for $80 then they can get a WM for (say) $320. Overall then Stay Clean make a positive contribution of $130 (320 + 80 − 180 − 90).

Product line pricing

All the products tend to be related to each other and used in the utility room or kitchen. Some sales will involve all three products if customers are upgrading their utility room or kitchen for example. A package price could be offered and as long as Stay Clean make a contribution on the overall deal then they will be better off.

231 HS EQUATION

(a) $p = a − bq$ where p is price and q is demand for product

When price = $1,350, demand = 8,000 units

When price = $1,400, demand = 7,000 units

So:

(1) $1,350 = a − 8,000q$

and

(2) $1,400 = a − 7,000q$

so subtracting equation (1) from equation (2)

$50 = 1,000b$

$b = 0.05$

and substituting in equation (2):

$1,400 = a − 0.05 × 7,000$

$a = 1,750$

so Price = $1,750 − 0.05q$ and marginal revenue = $1,750 − 0.1q$

To find variable production cost per unit, we need to separate fixed and variable costs from the historic cost data:

Using the high-low method, dividing the difference in cost for the highest and lowest activity levels by the change in activity

Variable production cost per unit

$$= \$(7{,}000 - 5{,}446) \times 1{,}000 / (9{,}400 - 7{,}300)$$

$$= \$1{,}554 \times 1{,}000 / 2{,}100$$

$$= \$740$$

Direct material cost $= \$270$

Total variable cost $= \$(270 + 740)$

$$= \$1{,}010$$

Price is maximised where marginal cost (= variable cost) = marginal revenue

$1{,}010 = 1{,}750 - 0.1q$

$q = 7{,}400$ units

and price $= 1{,}750 - 0.05 \times 7{,}400$

$$= \$1{,}380$$

optimum price is $1,380

(b)

Tutorial note

Note that the question only asks for three reasons.

There are a number of reasons why it may be inappropriate for HS to use this model in practice:

- The model depends on the market structure being one in which there is:

  - Perfect competition (which is the closest situation to HS's market)

  - Monopolistic competition

  - Monopoly or

  - Oligopoly

  Whilst the market is highly competitive, it is unlikely that there is perfect competition (in which the action of one company cannot affect the market price).

- The model assumes that costs and demand follow a linear relationship and that there are no step changes in fixed costs. Again this may hold over a small range of volumes but is unlikely to be true for all possible volumes.

- This model can only be used if the company has detailed knowledge of demand and cost curves. It is unlikely that in practice HS would be able to derive accurate cost and demand curves.

232 MKL

(a) The selling price that should be charged for Product K is the one that maximises total contribution, i.e. a price of $75 for a demand of 1,400 units:

Selling price per unit	$100	$85	$80	$75
Variable cost	$38	$38	$38	$38
Unit contribution	$62	$47	$42	$37
Demand units	600 units	800 units	1200 units	1400 units
Total weekly contribution	**$37,200**	**$37,600**	**$50,400**	**$51,800**

(b) 1,400 units of Product K will use up 1,400 standard hours; in order to utilise all of the spare capacity, we now need to use 600 hours for Product L, for the first 10 weeks.

$$\frac{600 \text{ hours}}{1.25 \text{ hours}} = 480 \text{ units will use all the spare capacity.}$$

To maximise profits, the optimum price P will be expressed as $P = a - bQ$.

Here, $a = \$100 + (\frac{1,000}{200} \times \$10)$

So $a = \$150$ and $b = \frac{\$10}{200}$ 0.05

$P = \$150 - 0.05Q$

$P = \$150 - 0.05 \times 480 \text{ units}$

P = $126 for the first 10 weeks.

For the following 10 weeks when the extra capacity becomes available, the optimum price P will be expressed as $P = a - bQ$ and we need to equate MC = MR to maximise profits, with

$MR = a - 2bQ$.

Profit maximised when	MC = MR
When	$\$45 = a - 2bQ$
When	$\$45 = \$150 - 0.10Q$
When	$Q = 1,050$ units
And	$P = \$150 - 0.05 \times 1,050$
	P = $97.50

233   GAM CO (JUNE 2014, ADAPTED)

(a)   **Profit outcomes**

Unit contribution	Sales price per unit	
	$30	$35
Up to 100,000 units	$18	$23
Above 100,000 units	$19	$24

Sales price $30

Sales volume	Unit contribution	Total contribution	Fixed costs	Advertising costs	Profit
	$	$000	$000	$000	$000
120,000	19	2,280	450	900	930
110,000	19	2,090	450	900	740
140,000	19	2,660	450	900	1,310

Sales price $35

Sales volume	Unit contribution	Total contribution	Fixed costs	Advertising costs	Profit
	$	$000	$000	$000	$000
108,000	24	2,592	450	970	1,172
100,000	23	2,300	450	970	880
94,000	23	2,162	450	970	742

(b)   **Expected values**

Sales price $30

Sales volume	Profit	Probability	EV of profit
	$000		$000
120,000	930	0.4	372
110,000	740	0.5	370
140,000	1,310	0.1	131
			___
			873
			___

Sales price $35

Sales volume	Profit $000	Probability	EV of profit $000
108,000	1,172	0.3	351.6
100,000	880	0.3	264
94,000	742	0.4	296.8
			———
			912.4
			———

If the criterion of expected value is used to make a decision as to which price to charge, then the price charged should be $35 per unit since the expected value of this option is the greatest.

		Marking scheme	Marks
(a)		Profit outcomes	
		Unit contribution up to 100,000 units	0.5
		Unit contribution above 100,000 units	0.5
		Each line of table for price of $30 (3 in total)	1
		Each line of table for price of $35 (3 in total)	1
			—
			7
			—
(b)		Expected values	
		Expected value for $30	1
		Expected value for $35	1
		Recommendation	1
			—
			3
			—
Total			**10**
			—

234 GYM BUNNIES (JUNE 2013 EXAM)

(a)   **Decision tree**

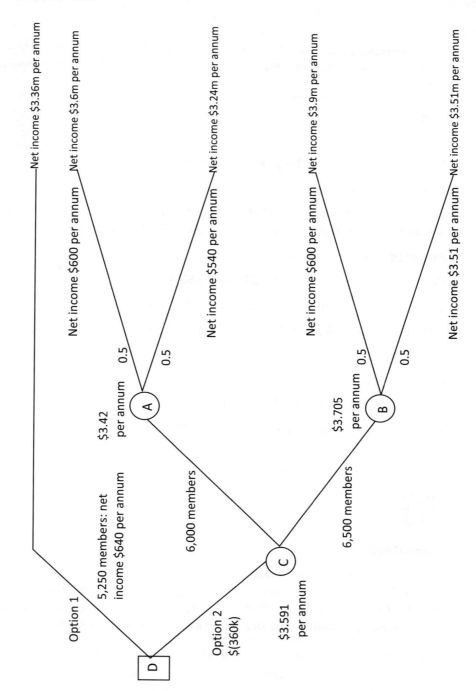

Tutorial note

A minor but notable point: you may lose half a mark for failing to multiply values up by three to reflect the three-year period, or for failing to deduct the expansion cost of $360,000.

Workings

Option 1

Net income = $720 – $80 = $640 per annum.

Option 2

If costs $120 per annum, net income = $720 – $120 = $600 per annum. If costs $180 per annum, net income = $720 – $180 = $540 per annum.

Expected value and decision:

EV at A = (0.5 × $3.6m) + (0.5 × $3.24m) = $3.42m

EV at B = (0.5 × $(3.9m) + (0.5 × $3.51m) = $3.705m

EV at C = (0.4 × $3.42m) + (0.6 × $3.705m) = $3.591m per annum

At D, compare EV of:

Option 1: (3 × $3.36m) = **$10.08m**

Option 2: ($3 × $3.591m) – $360k = **$10.413m**

Therefore choose option 2 – expand exercise studio.

(b)

Tutorial note

This requirement was only worth 3 marks, which is why the requirement asked for only a 'BRIEF' discussion. The marks available for a requirement are indicative of the length of answer expected. Writing a whole page of answer for this requirement is simply wasting valuable time that could have been spent elsewhere in the exam.

The expansion decision is a one-off decision, rather than a decision that will be repeated many times. Expected values, on the other hand, give us a long run average of the outcome that would be expected if a decision was to be repeated many times. The actual outcome may not be very close to the expected value calculated and the technique is therefore not really very useful here.

Also, estimating accurate probabilities is difficult because this exact situation has not arisen before.

The expected value criterion for decision-making is useful where the attitude of the investor is risk neutral. We do not know what the management of Gym Bunnies' attitude to risk is, which makes it difficult to say whether this criterion is a good one to use. In a decision such as this one, it would be useful to see what the worst case scenario and best case scenario results would be too, in order to assist decision-making.

ACCA marking scheme		Marks
(a)	Decision tree diagram	
	Start with decision point	0.5
	Option 1 format	0.5
	Option 2 format	5
	Expected value and decision	
	EV at A	1
	EV at B	1
	EV at C	2
	Compare EVs at D	1
	Recommendation that follows	1
		–––
	Maximum	12
(b)	Discussion	3
		–––
Total		**15**
		–––

235 RECYC

(a) **Payoff table**

		Level of waste		
		High	Medium	Low
Advance	High	962.5	636.5	397.5
order of	Medium	912.5	655.5	442.5
chemical	Low	837.5	617.5	457.5

Workings

(W1)

Advance order of chemical X	Level of waste	Prob.	Contrib. (excl. X) (W2) $000	Chemical X cost (W3) $000	Net contribution $000
High	High	0.30	1,462.5	500	962.5
	Medium	0.50	1,111.5	475	636.5
	Low	0.20	877.5	480	397.5
Medium	High	0.30	1,462.5	550	912.5
	Medium	0.50	1,111.5	456	655.5
	Low	0.20	877.5	435	442.5
Low	High	0.30	1,462.5	625	837.5
	Medium	0.50	1,111.5	494	617.5
	Low	0.20	877.5	420	457.5

(W2) Waste available

	High	Medium	Low
Aluminium extracted (000 kg)	7,500	5,700	4,500
	$000	$000	$000
Sales revenue (at $0.65 per kg)	4,875.0	3,705.0	2,925.0
Variable cost (at 70%)	3,412.5	2,593.5	2,047.5
Contribution	1,462.5	1,111.5	877.5

(W3) Examples of workings for chemical X cost

- High advance level of order for chemical X and low actual requirement: The price of $1.00 is subject to a penalty of $0.60 per kg. The cost of chemical X is, therefore, 300,000 kg × $1.60 = $480,000

- Low advance level of order for chemical X and medium actual requirement: The price is subject to a discount of $0.10 per kg. The cost of chemical X is, therefore, 380,000 × $1.30 = $494,000.

(b) Maximax suggests that the decision maker should look for the largest possible profit from all the outcomes. In this case this is a high advance order of chemical X where there is a possibility of a contribution of $962,500. This indicates a risk seeking preference by management. Although it offers the possibility of the highest contribution, there is also a 20% likelihood that the worst outcome of $397,500 will occur.

Maximin suggests that the decision maker should look for the strategy which maximises the minimum possible contribution. In this case this is a low advance order of chemical X where the lowest contribution is $457,500. This is better than the worst possible outcomes from high or medium advance orders of chemical X. This indicates a risk-averse management posture.

236 TICKET AGENT *Walk in the footsteps of a top tutor*

Key answer tips

It would be easy to get absorbed in the detail of this question and to spend too much time trying to perfect the calculations. However, to pass the exam, focus on the easy marks. If mistakes are made in earlier calculations, carry forward marks will be available.

(a) The question specifies that a long-run perspective is being taken so decisions can be made by reference to expected values.

Expected sales demand

An easy 3 marks are available here.

	Probability	Demand	EV
Popular artistes	0.45	500	225
Lesser known artistes	0.30	350	105
Unknown artistes	0.25	200	50
			380

Expected demand = 380 tickets per concert

This part is harder but there are 20 minutes available for this requirement and therefore enough time to understand the scenario and to set out clear workings.

Maximising profit

To determine the best decision, the expected profits for each possible order level need to be calculated.

- Payoff table showing profit (W1, W2)

There are 12 calculations to complete. Show the workings for at least one, so that the marker can follow the approach

		Actual sales demand		
		200	350	500
	200	1,200	1,200	1,200
Purchase	300	(570)	2,250	2,250
Level	400	(2,040)	2,190	3,600
	500	(2,460)	1,770	6,000

- Expected values

		EV
200 tickets	1,200 × 1	1,200
300 tickets	(570) × 0.25 + 2,250 × 0.75	1,545
400 tickets	(2,040) × 0.25 + 2,190 × 0.3 + 3,600 × 0.45	1,767
500 tickets	(2,460) × 0.25 + 1,770 × 0.3 + 6,000 × 0.45	2,616

Don't forget to conclude. Another easy mark available.

The optimum purchase level is 500 tickets per concert, which will give an expected profit of $2,616 per concert.

Workings

(W1) The gross profit made per ticket is the discount received on the selling price of $30.

Purchase level	Discount			Profit per ticket sold
200	20%	20% × $30	=	$6.00
300	25%	25% × $30	=	$7.50
400	30%	30% × $30	=	$9.00
500	40%	40% × $30	=	$12.00

(W2) Each net profit calculation consists of up to three elements:

1   the profit on the units sold;

2   the cost of the units which are unsold and returned;

3   the value of the returns

EV of returns = $30.00 × 60% × 10% = $1.80 per return.

Example calculation:

Buy 300 tickets but can only sell 200 ⇒ Sell 200 tickets and return 100 tickets

	$
Sales 200 tickets × 7.50 (W1)	1,500
EV of returns 100 tickets × $1.80	180
	1,680
Cost of returns 100 tickets × $22.50 (25% discount)	(2,250)
	(570)

> This part is relatively easy.

> This part is harder. Take a guess if unsure and move on.

(b) **Maximax**

> An easy 2 marks .

The agent should order 500 tickets as this gives a maximum possible gain of $6,000 per concert

Maximin

The agent should buy 200 tickets to maximise the minimum possible pay-off ($1,200).

Minimax regret

A regret table is found by comparing the actual profit with what could have been made given the level of demand that occurred:

> This is harder. Even if you can't do the calculation, explain what minimax regret is. This will gain 1 easy mark.

		Actual sales demand		
		200	350	500
	200	0	1,050	4,800
Purchase	300	1,770	0	3,750
Level	400	3,240	60	2,400
	500	3,660	480	0

The agent would thus order 400 tickets as this limits the maximum regret to $3,240.

This level of order would give an average profit of $1,767 per concert.

(c) The advice depends on the risk perspective of the agent

| More easy marks available. The advice should be linked back to parts (a) and (b). Points should be separate and succinct. |

- If he is willing to take a long term perspective and accept short-term uncertainty, then the expected value calculations in part (a) should be adopted, giving an order of 500 tickets

- If he is an optimist, then the maximax criteria would suggest ordering 500 tickets

- If he is a pessimist, then the maximin criteria would suggest ordering 200 tickets

- If he is a sore loser, then the minimax regret approach would suggest buying 400 tickets.

In reality the agent may be best advised to insist on knowing who the artists are before having to place an order.

237 SHIFTERS HAULAGE (DEC 08 EXAM)

(a) Maximax stands for maximising the maximum return an investor might expect. An investor that subscribes to the maximax philosophy would generally select the strategy that could give him the best possible return. He will ignore all other possible returns and only focus on the biggest, hence this type of investor is often accused of being an optimist or a risk-taker.

Maximin stands for maximising the minimum return an investor might expect. This type of investor will focus only on the potential minimum returns and seek to select the strategy that will give the best worst case result. This type of investor could be said to be being cautious or pessimistic in his outlook and a risk-avoider.

Expected value averages all possible returns in a weighted average calculation.

For example if an investor could expect $100 with a 0.3 probability and $300 with a 0.7 probability then on average the return would be:

$(0.3 \times \$100) + (0.7 \times \$300) = \$240$

This figure would then be used as a basis of the investment decision. The principle here is that if this decision was repeated again and again then the investor would get the EV as a return. Its use is more questionable for use on one-off decisions.

Key answer tips

Easy marks were available here. This is a core knowledge area and no application of knowledge was required. There will be easy marks for knowledge in each exam.

(b)   Profit calculations

	Small van	Medium van	Large van
Capacity	100	150	200
Low demand (120)	300 (W1)	468 (W3)	368 (W5)
High demand (190)	300 (W2)	500 (W4)	816 (W6)

Workings	(W1)	(W2)	(W3)	(W4)	(W5)	(W6)
Sales	1,000	1,000	1,200	1,500	1,200	1,900
VC	(400)	(400)	(480)	(600)	(480)	(760)
Goodwill	(100)	(100)		(100)		
VC adjustment			48		48	76
Depreciation	(200)	(200)	(300)	(300)	(400)	(400)
Profit	300	300	468	500	368	816

Tutorial note

Some candidates were confused about which level of demand should be used. The only levels of demand mentioned were 120 and 190 units and therefore these should have been used. Other candidates were confused about the appropriate adjustments that should have been made for variable costs, goodwill and depreciation.

Profit tables are a key part of risk and uncertainty. The approach to preparing them will always be similar and therefore candidates should practice a number of questions before sitting the exam.

ACCA marking scheme		
		Marks
(a)	Maximax explanation	3.0
	Maximin explanation	3.0
	Expected value explanation	3.0
	Maximum	9.0
(b)	Small van sales	1
	Small van VC	1
	Small van goodwill or VC adjustment	1.0
	Small van depreciation	1.0
	Medium van – as above for small van	1.0
	Large van as above for small van	1.0
		6.0
Total		15

238 COOL SYSTEMS

Decision Tree:

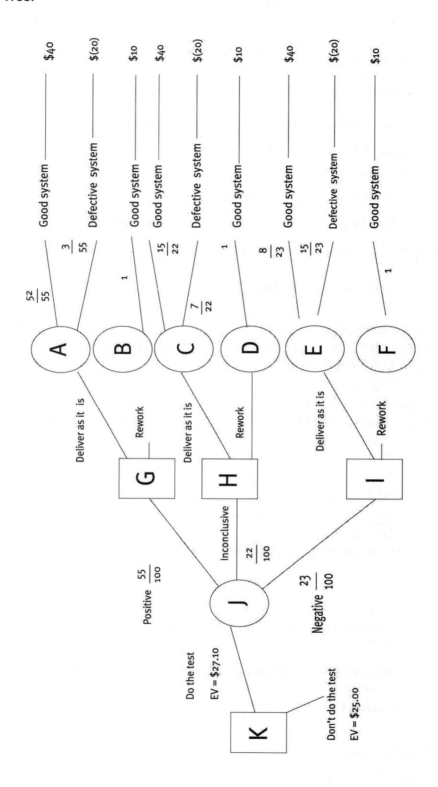

Evaluation

EV(A) = [(52/55) × $40)] − [(3/55)X $20)] = $36.73

EV(B) = $10

So our choice at 'G' will be to **deliver the system as it is**.

EV(C) = EV(E) = [(15/22) × $40)] − [(7/22)X $20)] = $20.91

EV(D) = $10

So our choice at 'H' will be to deliver the system as it is.

EV(E) = [(8/23) × $40)] − [(15/23)X $20)] = $0.87

EV(F) = $10

So our choice at 'I' will be to **rework the system**.

EV(J) = (0.55X $36.73) + (0.22X$20.91) + (0.23 × $10) = $27.10

Therefore EV of Imperfect Information: $27.10 − $25.00 = $2.10

239 ROBBER CO (JUNE 2012 EXAM)

(a)

	Keypads $	Display screens $
Variable costs		
Materials ($160k × 6/12) + ($160k × 1.05 × 6/12)	164,000	
($116k × 1.02)		118,320
Direct labour	40,000	60,000
Machine set-up costs		
($26k − $4k) × 500/400	27,500	
($30k − $6k) × 500/400		30,000
	231,500	208,320
Attributable fixed costs		
Heat and power ($64k − $20k)/($88k − $30k)	44,000	58,000
Fixed machine costs	4,000	6,000
Depreciation and insurance ($84/$96k × 40%)	33,600	38,400
	81,600	102,400
Total incremental costs of making in-house	313,100	310,720
Cost of buying (80,000 × $4.10/$4.30)	328,000	344,000
Total saving from making	14,900	33,280

Robber Co should therefore make all of the keypads and display screens in-house

(**Note:** It has been assumed that the fixed set-up costs only arise if production takes place.)

(Alternative method)

Relevant costs

	Keypads	Display screens
	$	$
Direct materials		
($160,000/2) + $160,000/2 × 1·05	164,000	
$116,000 × 1·02		118,320
Direct labour	40,000	60,000
Heat and power		
$64,000 – (50% × $40,000)	44,000	
$88,000 – (50% × $60,000)		58,000
Machine set up costs:		
Avoidable fixed costs	4,000	6,000
Activity related costs (W1)	27,500	30,000
Avoidable depreciation and insurance costs:		
40% × $84,000/$96,000	33,600	38,400
	———	———
Total relevant manufacturing costs	313,100	310,720
	———	———
Relevant cost per unit:	3.91375	3.884
Cost per unit of buying in	4.1	4.3
	———	———
Incremental cost of buying in	0.18625	0.416
	———	———

As each of the components is cheaper to make in-house than to buy in, the company should continue to manufacture keypads and display screens in-house.

Working 1

Current no. of batches produced = 80,000/500 = 160.

New no. of batches produced = 80,000/400 = 200.

Current cost per batch for keypads = ($26,000 – $4,000)/160 = $137.5.

Therefore new activity related batch cost = 200 × $137·5 = $27,500.

Current cost per batch for display screens = ($30,000 – $6,000)/160 = $150.

Therefore new activity related batch cost = 200 × $150 = $30,000.

(b)   The attributable fixed costs remain unaltered irrespective of the level of production of keypads and display screens, because as soon as one unit of either is made, the costs rise. We know that we will make at least one unit of each component as both are cheaper to make than buy. Therefore they are an irrelevant common cost.

	Keypads	Display screens
	$	$
Buy	4.1	4.3
Variable cost of making ($231,500/80,000)	2.89	
($208,320/80,000)		2.6
Saving from making per unit	1.21	1.7
Labour hour per unit	0.5	0.75
Saving from making per unit of limiting factor	2.42	2.27
Priority of making	1	2

Total labour hours available = 100,000. Make maximum keypads i.e. 100,000, using 50,000 labour hours (100,000 × 0.5 hours) Make 50,000/0.75 display screens, i.e. 66,666 display screens. Therefore buy in 33,334 display screens (100,000 – 66,666).

(c)   **Non-financial factors**

- The company offering to supply the keypads and display screens is a new company. This would make it extremely risky to rely on it for continuity of supplies. Many new businesses go out of business within the first year of being in business and, without these two crucial components, Robber Co would be unable to meet demand for sales of control panels. Robber Co would need to consider whether there are any other potential suppliers of the components. This would be useful as both a price comparison now and also to establish the level of dependency that would be committed to if this new supplier is used. If the supplier goes out of business, will any other company be able to step in? If so, at what cost?

- The supplier has only agreed to these prices for the first two years. After this, it could put up its prices dramatically. By this stage, Robber Co would probably be unable to begin easily making its components in house again, as it would probably have sold off its machinery and committed to larger sales of control panels.

- The quality of the components could not be guaranteed. If they turn out to be poor quality, this will give rise to problems in the control panels, leading to future loss of sales and high repair costs under warranties for Robber Co. The fact that the supplier is based overseas increases the risk of quality and continuity of supply, since it has even less control of these than it would if it was a UK supplier.

- Robber Co would need to establish how reliable the supplier is with meeting promises for delivery times. This kind of information may be difficult to establish because of the fact that the supplier is a new company. Late delivery could have a serious impact on Robber Co's production and delivery schedule.

ACCA marking scheme		
		Marks
(a)	Incremental cost of buying in	0.5
	Direct materials	0.5
	Direct labour	0.5
	Heat and light	3
	Set-up costs	1
	Depreciation and insurance	0.5
	Total cost of making	0.5
	Total cost of buying Saving	0.5
	Conclusion	1
		___
	Maximum	8
		___
	(Method 2)	
	Direct materials	0.5
	Direct labour	0.5
	Heat and power	0.5
	Avoidable fixed costs	0.5
	Activity related costs (W1)	3
	Avoidable depreciation and insurance	0.5
	Total relevant manufacturing costs	0.5
	Relevant cost per unit	0.5
	Incremental cost of buying in	0.5
	Conclusion	1
		___
	Maximum	8
		___
(b)	If 100,000 control panels made	
	Variable cost of making per unit	1
	Saving from making	1
	Saving per labour hour	1
	Ranking	1
	Make 100,000 keypads	1
	Make 66,666 display screens	1
	Buy 33,334 display screens	1
		___
	Maximum	7
		___
(c)	Non-financial factors	
	Per factor	1 or 2
		___
	Maximum	5
		___
Total		**20**
		___

BUDGETING AND CONTROL

240 PC CO PARTICIPATIVE BUDGETING (DEC 2011 EXAM)

Objectives of a budgetary control system

- **To compel planning**

  Budgeting makes sure that managers plan for the future, producing detailed plans in order to ensure the implementation of the company's long term plan. Budgeting makes managers look at the year ahead and consider the changes in conditions that might take place and how to respond to those changes in conditions.

- **To co-ordinate activities**

  Budgeting is a method of bringing together the activities of all the different departments into a common plan. If an advertising campaign is due to take place in a company in three months' time, for example, it is important that the production department know about the expected increase in sales so that they can scale up production accordingly. Each different department may have its own ideas about what is good for the organisation. For example, the purchasing department may want to order in bulk in order to obtain bulk quantity discounts, but the accounts department may want to order in smaller quantities so as to preserve cash flow.

- **To communicate activities**

  Through the budget, top management communicates its expectations to lower level management. Each department has a part to play in achieving the desired results of the company, and the annual budget is the means of formalising these expectations. The whole process of budget setting, whereby information is shared between departments, facilitates this communication process.

- **To motivate managers to perform well**

  The budget provides a basis for assessing how well managers and employees are performing. In this sense, it can be motivational. However, if the budget is imposed from the top, with little or no participation from lower level management and employees, it can have a seriously demotivational effect. This is discussed further in part (b).

- **To establish a system of control**

  Expenditure within any organisation needs to be controlled and the budget facilitates this. Actual results are compared to expected results, and the reasons for any significant, unexpected differences are investigated. Sometimes the reasons are within the control of the departmental manager and he/she must be held accountable; at other times, they are not.

(Other possible objectives include:

- **To evaluate performance**

  Often, managers and employees will be awarded bonuses based on achieving budgeted results. This makes more sense than evaluating performance by simply comparing the current year to the previous year. The future may be expected to be very different than the past as economic conditions change. Also, events happen that may not be expected to reoccur. For example, if weather conditions are particularly wet one year, a company making and selling umbrellas would be expected to make higher than usual sales. It would not be fair to assess managers against these historical sales levels in future years, where weather conditions are more normal.

- **To delegate authority to budget holders**

  A formal budget permits budget holders to make financial decisions within the specified limits agreed, i.e. to incur expenditure on behalf of the organisation.

- **To ensure achievement of the management's objectives**

  Objectives are set not only for the organisation as a whole but also for individual targets. The budget helps to work out how these objectives can be achieved.)

ACCA marking scheme		Marks
Objectives		
Each objective		2
	Maximum	10
Total		**10**

241 SAUCE CO BUDGETING STYLE (JUNE 2012 EXAM)

Tutorial note

The Examiner reports that this was rather well answered in the Exam. Many candidates scored full marks and some really good points were made, such as: Using inaccurate sales budgets means that the company could miss out on other lucrative opportunities as they fail to respond and act on them. Or : Inaccurate financial information being presented/reported and investors making incorrect financial decisions.

Staff

- Since the budgeting style has been an imposed one rather than a participative one, morale amongst staff is likely to be low, since they have not been involved in the process at all.

- Additionally, since sales targets appear to be unachievable and staff have not received performance related bonuses, staff are not motivated to try and achieve targets since they feel like they are impossible to achieve. Team spirit will be low and an atmosphere of 'doing the bare minimum' is likely to exist.

- Since budgets are imposed from the top down, the culture will not be one in which operational management generate ideas, as they will feel like they are not appreciated and that their views are not taken into account.

Business

- Since sales levels are overestimated, production volumes must also be too high. As well as this leading to high inventory costs because actual sales are then lower than expected, since the product is also perishable, waste levels have probably been high. These will be significant costs to the company.

- Also, when customers do receive their goods, it is likely that they will be close to their expiry date, since they will have been taken from inventory that has been held for some time. This will be frustrating for customers because products may then perish before the end customer gets to use them. Also, it is likely that a sauce that is two months old does not taste as good as a sauce that is only a few days old. Both of these factors may be causing damage to the company's reputation.

- Too many staff are probably being employed in the business, bearing in mind that the staffing levels will be related to forecast production volumes. One can only assume that whilst initially, production volumes relate to the forecast, as it becomes apparent that sales are not as high as anticipated and inventory levels increase, production slows down. Staff are probably sitting idle for some of the time, which is demotivating for them and costly to the company.

ACCA marking scheme		
		Marks
Likely impact		
Per point discussed		2
	Maximum	10
Total		**10**

242   DESIGNIT (DEC 2012 EXAM)

(a)   **Explanation**

The rolling budget outlined for Designit would be a budget covering a 12-month period and would be updated monthly. However, instead of the 12-month period remaining static, it would always roll forward by one month. This means that, as soon as one month has elapsed, a budget is prepared for the corresponding month one year later. For example, Designit would begin by preparing a budget for the 12 months from 1 December 2012 to 30 November 2013, to correspond with its year end. Then, at the end of December 2012, a budget would be prepared for the month December 2013, so that the unexpired period covered by the budget is always 12 months.

When the budget is initially prepared for the year ending 30 November 2013, the first month is prepared in detail, with much less detail being given to later months, where there is a greater uncertainty about the future. Then, when this first month has elapsed and the budget for the month of December 2013 is prepared, it is also necessary to revisit and revise the budget for January 2013, which will now be done in more detail.

Note: This answer gives more level of detail than would be required to gain full marks.

(b)   **Problems**

Designit only has one part-qualified accountant. He is already overworked and probably has neither the time nor the experience to prepare rolling budgets every month. One would only expect to see monthly rolling budgets of this nature in businesses which face rapid change. There is no evidence that this is the case for Designit. If it did decide to introduce rolling budgets, it would probably be sufficient if they were updated on a quarterly rather than a monthly basis. If this monthly rolling budget is going to be introduced, it is going to require a lot of input from many of the staff, meaning that they will have less time to dedicate to other things.

ACCA marking scheme		
		Marks
(a)	Explanation	
	Updated after one month elapsed	1
	Always 12 months	1
	Example given	1
	First month in detail	1
	Later month less detail	1
	Need to revisit earlier months	1
		―――
	Maximum	6
		―――
(b)	Problems	
	More time	1
	Lack of experience	1
	Too regular	2
		―――
	Maximum	4
		―――
Total		**10**
		―――

243   NEWTOWN SCHOOL (JUNE 2013 EXAM)

(a)   **Zero-based budgeting (ZBB)**

The three main steps involved in preparing a zero-based budget are as follows:

(1)   Activities are identified by managers. Managers are then forced to consider different ways of performing the activities. These activities are then described in what is called a 'decision package', which:

- analyses the cost of the activity
- states its purpose
- identifies alternative methods of achieving the same purpose
- establishes performance measures for the activity
- assesses the consequence of not performing the activity at all or of performing it at different levels.

As regards this last point, the decision package may be prepared at the base level, representing the minimum level of service or support needed to achieve the organisation's objectives. Further incremental packages may then be prepared to reflect a higher level of service or support.

(2)   Management will then rank all the packages in the order of decreasing benefits to the organisation. This will help management decide what to spend and where to spend it. This ranking of the decision packages happens at numerous levels of the organisation.

(3)   The resources are then allocated, based on order of priority up to the spending level.

(b)   Use of ZBB at Newtown School

There is definitely a place for ZBB at Newtown School. At the moment, incremental budgeting is responsible for recurring unexpected cash shortages, which is deterring new pupils from joining the school. Had a deficit been predicted for the year ended 31 May 2013, perhaps $65,000 would not have been spent on improving the school gym, and then it would not have been necessary to close the school kitchen. ZBB would be good to establish the way cash is spent on those activities that are, to a certain extent, discretionary.

For example, although there is a need for pupils to have somewhere to eat lunch, it is not essential for children to have a cooked meal every day. It is essential that children do have somewhere to eat though and, as a bare minimum, they would need an area where they could eat their sandwiches and have access to fresh water. ZBB could be used to put together decision packages which reflect the different levels of service available to the children. For example, the most basic level of service could be the provision of an area for the children to eat a lunch brought from home. The next level would be the provision of some cold and maybe hot food for the children, but on a self-service basis. Finally, the highest level of service would be a restaurant for the children where they get served hot meals at tables. At Newtown School the catering manager could prepare the decision packages and they would then be decided upon by the head teacher, who would rank them accordingly.

Similarly, although some level of sports education is needed, the extent of the different activities offered is discretionary. ZBB could be used to create decision packages for each of these services in order to prioritise them better than they are currently being prioritised.

ZBB takes a long time to implement and would not be appropriate to all categories of expenditure at the school. Much of the budgeting is very straight forward. Incremental budgeting could still be used as a starting point for essential expenditure such as salary costs, provided that changes in staff numbers are also taken into account. There is an element of essential, recurring expenditure in relation to repairs and maintenance too, since the costs of the checks and repairs needed to comply with health and safety standards seem to largely stay the same each year, with an inflationary increase.

	ACCA marking scheme		
			Marks
(a)	Zero-based budgeting		
	Step 1		1
	Step 2		1
	Step 3		1
			—
		Maximum	3
			—
(b)	Use of ZBB to Newtown School		1.5
	Each point made		
			—
		Maximum	7
			—
Total			**10**
			—

244 MIC AND LEARNING (DEC 2013 EXAM)

(a) Monthly costs

Month	Cumulative number of batches	Cumulative average hours per batch	Cumulative total hours	Incremental number of batches	Incremental total hours	Actual labour cost per month $
July	1	200	200	1	200	2,400
August (W1)	2	176	352	1	152	1,824
September	4	154.88	619.52	2	267.52	3,210.24
October	8	136.294	1,090.352	4	470.832	5,649.60
November (W2)	16	124.4	1,990.36	8	900.008	10,800.096

Workings

(W1) Calculations for August

Cumulative average hours per batch: 200 × 0.88 = 176 hours.

Cumulative total hours = 2 × 176 = 352 hours.

Incremental number of batches = cumulative no. of 2 batches for August less cumulative number of 1 batch for July = 1 batch.

Incremental total hours = cumulative total hours of 352 for August − 200 for July = 152 hours.

Actual labour cost = incremental total hours of 152 × $12 per hour = $1,824.

(W2)

Time for 7th batch:

$Y = ax^b = 200 × 7^{-0.1844245}$

= 139.693 hours.

Total time for 7 batches = 139.693 × 7 = 977.851 hours.

Total time for 8 batches = 1,090.352 hours.

Therefore 8th batch took 112.501 hours (1,090.352 – 977.851)

Time for batches 9–16 = 112.501 × 8 = 900.008 hours.

Therefore cumulative average time for batches 1–16 = 1,090.352 + 900.008 = 1,990.36 hours.

Cumulative average time for 16 batches = 1,990.36/16 = 124.4 hours per batch.

Note: The labour costs for November could be arrived at quickly simply by taking the 112.501 hours for the 8th batch, multiplying it by 8 batches and applying this number to the $12 per hour labour cost. This quick calculation is totally sufficient to earn full marks.

(b) **Implications of end of learning period**

The learning period ended at the end of October. This means that from November onwards the time taken to produce each batch of microphones is constant. Therefore, in future, when Mic Co makes decisions about allocating its resources and costing the microphones, it should base these decisions on the time taken to produce the 8th batch. The resource allocations and cost data prepared for the last six months will have been inaccurate since they were based on a standard time per batch of 200 hours.

Mic Co could try to improve its production process so that the learning period could be extended. It may be able to do this by increasing the level of staff training provided. Alternatively, it could try and motivate staff to work harder through payment of bonuses, although the quality of production needs to be maintained.

(c) Since they are based on information from staff who are most familiar with the department, they are more likely to improve the accuracy of the budget. In Mic Co's case, the selling price could have been set more accurately and sales may have been higher if the production manager had been consulted.

Staff are more likely to be motivated to achieve any targets as it is 'their' budget and they therefore have a sense of ownership and commitment. The production manager at Mic Co seems resigned to the fact that he is not consulted on budgetary matters.

ACCA marking scheme			
			Marks
(a)	Monthly costs		
	Per monthly cost: July–October		1.5
	November		3
			—
		Maximum	9
			—
(b)	End of learning period		
	1 mark per point discussed	Maximum	4
			—
(c)	1 mark per advantage described	Maximum	2
			—
Total			**15**
			—

245 NN

(a) **The adoption of zero-based budgeting within NN Ltd**

During recent years the management of NN Ltd has used the traditional approach to incremental budgeting. The approach entails the use of the previous year's budget being rolled forward into the next year's budget purely budget.

Zero-based budgeting was developed to overcome the shortcomings of the technique of incremental budgeting. The implementation of a zero-based budgeting would require each manager within NN Ltd to effectively start with a blank sheet of paper and a budget allowance of zero. The managers would be required to defend their budget levels at the beginning of each and every year.

The implementation of a system of zero-based budgeting will require a consideration of the following:

- The need for major input by management
- The fact that it will prove extremely time consuming
- The need for a very high level of data capture and processing
- The subjective judgement inherent in its application
- The fact that it might be perceived as a threat by staff
- Whether its adoption may encourage a greater focus upon the short-term to the detriment of longer-term planning.

(b) The implementation of zero-based budgeting will require a major planning effort by our personnel. It is through the planning process that important guidelines and directions are provided for the development and ranking of the decision packages. Also, the planning process will enable managers to prepare for the uncertainty of the future. Long-range planning allows managers to consider the potential consequences of current decisions over an extended timeframe.

Zero-based budgeting addresses and supports comprehensive planning, shared decision-making, the development and application of strategies and allocation of resources as a way of achieving established goals and objectives. In addition, zero-based budgeting supports the added processes of monitoring and evaluation.

Zero-based budgeting, when properly implemented, has the potential to assist the personnel of an organisation to plan and make decisions about the most efficient and effective ways to use their available resources to achieve their defined mission, goals and objectives.

There is no doubt that the process of zero-based budgeting will consume a great deal more management time than the current system of budgeting does. This will certainly be the case in implementation of the system because managers will need to learn what is required of them. Managers may object that it is too time-consuming to introduce zero-based budgeting, however, it could be introduced on a piece-meal basis. As regards the imposition upon management time, managers may object that they simply do not have the necessary time in order to undertake an in-depth examination of every activity each year. However, if this proves to be the case then we could consider the establishment of a review cycle aimed at ensuring that each activity is reviewed on at least one occasion during every two or three years.

A series of training seminars for management should be held to help in the transition to a system of zero-based budgeting and to tackle reluctance or resistance to change. It is also important to 'sell the benefits' that would arise from a successful implementation. A zero-based budgeting system would assist our managers to:

- Develop and/or modify the organisation's mission and goals
- Establish broad policies based on the mission and goals
- Efficiently identify the most desirable programs to be placed in operation
- Allocate the appropriate level of resources to each program
- Monitor and evaluate each program during and at the end of its operation and report the effectiveness of each program.

Thus, as a consequence of the adoption of zero-based budgeting our managers should be able to make decisions on the basis of an improved reporting system.

It is quite possible that zero-based budgeting would help identify and eliminate any budget bias or 'budget slack' that may be present. Budgetary slack is 'a universal behavioural problem' which involves deliberately overstating cost budgets and/or understating revenue budgets to allow some leeway in actual performance. We must acknowledge that in organisations such as ours where reward structures are based on comparisons of actual with budget results, bias can help to influence the amount paid to managers under incentive schemes. However, we should emphasise that if managers are to earn incentives as a consequence of incentive schemes that are based upon a comparison of actual outcomes with budgeted outcomes, then a zero-based budget would provide a fair yardstick for comparison.

It is important to provide reassurance to our managers that we do not intend to operate a system of zero-based budgeting against the backdrop of a blame-culture. This will help to gain their most positive acceptance of the change from a long established work practice that they may perceive afforded them a degree of 'insurance'.

246 ZERO BASED BUDGETING I (DEC 10 EXAM)

(a) Difficulties in the public sector

In the public sector, the objectives of the organisation are more difficult to define in a quantifiable way than the objectives of a private company. For example, a private company's objectives may be to maximise profit. The meeting of this objective can then be set out in the budget by aiming for a percentage increase in sales and perhaps the cutting of various costs. If, on the other hand, the public sector organisation is a hospital, for example, then the objectives may be largely qualitative, such as ensuring that all outpatients are given an appointment within eight weeks of being referred to the hospital. This is difficult to define in a quantifiable way, and how it is actually achieved is even more difficult to define.

This leads onto the next reason why budgeting is so difficult in public sector organisations. Just as objectives are difficult to define quantifiably, so too are the organisation's outputs. In a private company the output can be measured in terms of sales revenue. There is a direct relationship between the expenditure that needs to be incurred i.e. needs to be input in order to achieve the desired level of output. In a hospital, on the other hand, it is difficult to define a quantifiable relationship between inputs and outputs. What is more easy to compare is the relationship between how much cash is available for a particular area and how much cash is actually needed. Therefore, budgeting naturally focuses on inputs alone, rather than the relationship between inputs and outputs.

Finally, public sector organisations are always under pressure to show that they are offering good value for money, i.e. providing a service that is economical, efficient and effective. Therefore, they must achieve the desired results with the minimum use of resources. This, in itself, makes the budgeting process more difficult.

(b)   Incremental and zero-based budgeting

'Incremental budgeting' is the term used to describe the process whereby a budget is prepared using a previous period's budget or actual performance as a base, with incremental amounts then being added for the new budget period.

'Zero-based budgeting', on the other hand, refers to a budgeting process which starts from a base of zero, with no reference being made to the prior period's budget or performance. Every department function is reviewed comprehensively, with all expenditure requiring approval, rather than just the incremental expenditure requiring approval.

ACCA marking scheme			Marks
(a)	Explanation		
	Difficulty setting objectives quantifiably		2
	Difficulty in saying how to achieve them		1
	Outputs difficult to measure		2
	No relationship between inputs and outputs		2
	Value for money issue		2
		Maximum	6
(b)	Incremental and zero-based budgeting		
	Explaining 'incremental budgeting'		2
	Explaining 'zero-based budgeting'		2
	Any other valid comment re contrast between the two		1
		Maximum	4
Total			**10**

247   ZERO BASED BUDGETING II (DEC 10 EXAM)

(a)   Stages in zero-based budgeting

Zero-based budgeting involves three main stages:

1   Activities are identified by managers. These activities are then described in what is called a 'decision package'. This decision package is prepared at the base level, representing the minimum level of service or support needed to achieve the organisation's objectives. Further incremental packages may then be prepared to reflect a higher level of service or support.

2   Management will then rank all the packages in the order of decreasing benefits to the organisation. This will help management decide what to spend and where to spend it.

3   The resources are then allocated based on order of priority up to the spending level.

(b) **No longer a place for incremental budgeting**

The view that there is no longer a place for incremental budgeting in any organisation is a rather extreme view. It is known for encouraging slack and wasteful spending, hence the comment that it is particularly unsuitable for public sector organisations, where cash cutbacks are being made. However, to say that there is no place for it at all is to ignore the drawbacks of zero-based budgeting. These should not be ignored as they can make ZBB implausible in some organisations or departments. They are as follows:

- Departmental managers will not have the skills necessary to construct decision packages. They will need training for this and training takes time and money.

- In a large organisation, the number of activities will be so large that the amount of paperwork generated from ZBB will be unmanageable.

- Ranking the packages can be difficult, since many activities cannot be compared on the basis of purely quantitative measures. Qualitative factors need to be incorporated but this is difficult.

- The process of identifying decision packages, determining their purpose, costs and benefits is massively time consuming and therefore costly.

- Since decisions are made at budget time, managers may feel unable to react to changes that occur during the year. This could have a detrimental effect on the business if it fails to react to emerging opportunities and threats.

It could be argued that ZBB is more suitable for public sector than for private sector organisations. This is because, firstly, it is far easier to put activities into decision packages in organisations which undertake set definable activities. Local government, for example, have set activities including the provision of housing, schools and local transport. Secondly, it is far more suited to costs that are discretionary in nature or for support activities. Such costs can be found mostly in not for profit organisations or the public sector, or in the service department of commercial operations.

Since ZBB requires all costs to be justified, it would seem inappropriate to use it for the entire budgeting process in a commercial organisation. Why take so much time and resources justifying costs that must be incurred in order to meet basic production needs? It makes no sense to use such a long-winded process for costs where no discretion can be exercised anyway. Incremental budgeting is, by its nature, quick and easy to do and easily understood. These factors should not be ignored.

In conclusion, whilst ZBB is more suited to public sector organisations, and is more likely to make cost savings in hard times such as these, its drawbacks should not be overlooked.

ACCA marking scheme			
			Marks
(a)	Stages involved in zero-based budgeting		
	Each stage		1
		Maximum	3
(b)	Discussion		
	Any disadvantage of inc. that supports statement (max. 3)		1
	Incremental budgeting is quick and easy		1
	Any disadvantage of ZBB that refutes statement (max. 3)		1
	Easier to define decision packages in public sector		2
	more appropriate for discretionary costs		1
	Conclusion		1
		Maximum	7
Total			**10**

248 STICKY WICKET (JUNE 10 EXAM)

The performance of the production director could be looked at considering each decision in turn.

The new wood supplier: The wood was certainly cheaper than the standard saving $5,100 on the standard the concern though might be poor quality. The usage variance shows that the waste levels of wood are worse than standard. It is possible that the lower grade labour could have contributed to the waste level but since both decisions rest with the same person the performance consequences are the same. The overall effect of this is an adverse variance of $2,400, so taking the two variances together it looks like a poor decision. As the new labour is trained it could be that the wood usage improves and so we will have to wait to be sure.

The impact that the new wood might have had on sales cannot be ignored. No one department within a business can be viewed in isolation to another. Sales are down and returns are up. This could easily be due to poor quality wood inputs. If SW operates at the high quality end of the market then sourcing cheaper wood is risky if the quality reduces as a result.

The lower grade of labour used: SW uses traditional manual techniques and this would normally require skilled labour. The labour was certainly paid less, saving the company $43,600 in wages. However, with adverse efficiency and idle time of a total of $54,200 they actually cost the business money overall in the first month. The efficiency variance tells us that it took longer to produce the bats than expected. The new labour was being trained in April 2010 and so it is possible that the situation will improve next month. The learning curve principle would probably apply here and so we could expect the average time per batch to be less in May 2010 than it was in April 2010.

249 PARTICIPATION IN MIC CO (DEC 2013 EXAM)

Involving senior staff at Mic Co in the budget setting process

Advantages

- Since they are based on information from staff who are most familiar with the department, they are more likely to improve the accuracy of the budget. In Mic Co's case, the selling price could have been set more accurately and sales may have been higher if the production manager had been consulted.

- Staff are more likely to be motivated to achieve any targets as it is 'their' budget and they therefore have a sense of ownership and commitment. The production manager at Mic Co seems resigned to the fact that he is not consulted on budgetary matters.

- Morale amongst staff is likely to improve as they feel that their experience and opinions are valued.

- Knowledge from a spread of several levels of management is pooled.

- Co-ordination is improved due to the number of departments involved in the budget setting process.

Disadvantages

- The whole budgeting process is more time consuming and therefore costly.

- The budgeting process may have to be started earlier than a non-participative budget would need to start because of the length of time it takes to complete the process.

- Managers may try to introduce budgetary slack, i.e. making the budget easy to achieve so that they receive any budget-based incentives.

- Disagreements may occur between the staff involved, which may cause delays and dissatisfaction. In Mic Co's case, however, the fact that the production manager was not consulted has led to disagreement after the event.

- Can support 'empire building' by subordinates.

ACCA marking scheme		Marks
Each advantage		1
Each disadvantage		1
	Maximum	10
Total		**10**

250 LOCK CO (JUNE 2012 EXAM)

- TQM relies on a culture of continuous improvement within an organisation. For this to succeed, the focus must be on quality, not quantity. The cost of failing to achieve the desired level of quality must be measured in terms of internal and external failure costs.

- Traditional variance analysis focuses on quantity rather than quality. This could mean that, for example, lower grade labour is used in an attempt to reduce costs. This would be totally at odds with a TQM culture, which is the basis of the problem of the two systems running side by side.

- A traditional standard system allocates responsibility for variances to the different departmental managers. When a TQM system is adopted, all employees' roles in ensuring quality are highlighted and everyone is seen as equally important in the quality assurance process. This difference would make it difficult for the two systems to co-exist.

- Traditional standard costing systems usually make allowances for waste. This would be totally contrary to the TQM philosophy, which aims to eliminate all waste.

- Continuous improvement makes the standard cost system less relevant due to regular small changes to the process. It would seem to be the case that the two systems would struggle to co-exist at Lock Co.

ACCA marking scheme		
		Marks
TQM and standard costing		
Per valid discussion point		2
Conclusion		2
		———
	Maximum	10
		———
Total		**10**
		———

251 BIG CHEESE CHAIRS (DEC 09 EXAM)

(a) The average cost of the first 128 chairs is as follows:

		$
Frame and massage mechanism		51.00
Leather	2 metres × $10/mtr × 100/80	25.00
Labour	(W1)	20.95
		———
Total		96.95
		———

Target selling price is $120.

Target cost of the chair is therefore $120 × 80% = $96

The cost gap is $96.95 − $96.00 = $0.95 per chair

(W1) The cost of the labour can be calculated using learning curve principles. The formula can be used or a tabular approach would also give the average cost of 128 chairs. Both methods are acceptable and shown here.

Tabulation:

Cumulative output (units)	Average time per unit (hrs)	Total time (hrs)	Average cost per chair at $15 per hour
1	2		
2	1.9		
4	1.805		
8	1.71475		
16	1.6290125		
32	1.54756188		
64	1.47018378		
128	1.39667459	178.77	20.95

Formula:

$Y = ax^b$

$Y = 2 \times 128^{-0.074000581}$

$Y = 1.396674592$

The average cost per chair is $1.396674592 \times \$15 = \$20.95$

(b) The cost of the 128th chair will be:

		$
Frame and massage mechanism		51.00
Leather	2 metres × $10/mtr × 100/80	25.00
Labour	1.29 hours × $15 per hour (W2)	19.35
		———
Total		95.35
		———

Against a target cost of $96 the production manager is correct in his assertion that the required return is now being achieved.

(W2) Using the formula, we need to calculate the cost of the first 127 chairs and deduct that cost from the cost of the first 128 chairs.

$Y = ax^b$

$Y = 2 \times 127^{-0.074000581}$

$Y = 1.39748546$

Total time is $127 \times 1.39748546 = 177.48$ hours

Time for the 128th chair is $178.77 - 177.48 = 1.29$ hours

	ACCA marking scheme		
			Marks
(a)	Frame cost		1.0
	Leather cost		2.0
	Labour average time for 128 units		1.0
	Labour total time for 128 units		1.0
	Average cost per chair		1.0
	Target cost		1.0
	Cost gap		1.0
			———
		Maximum	8.0
(b)	Frame		1
	Leather		1
	Average time per unit		2.0
	Total time		1.0
	Time for 128th chair		1.0
	Conclusion		1.0
			———
		Maximum	7.0
Total			**15**
			———

252 HENRY COMPANY (DEC 08 EXAM)

(a)   Bid calculations for HC to use as a basis for the apartment contract.

Cost	Hours		Rate per hour		Total
					$
Labour	9,247	(W1)	$15		138,705
Variable overhead	9,247		$ 8	(W2)	73,976
Fixed overhead	9,247		$ 4	(W2)	36,988
					———
Total cost					249,669
					———

Workings

(W1) Need to calculate the time for the 200th kitchen by taking the total time for the 199 kitchens from the total time for 200 kitchens.

   For the 199 Kitchens

   Using

   $y = ax^b$ OR $y = ax^b$

   $y = 24 \times 199^{-0.074}$ $y = (24 \times 15) \times 199^{-0.074}$

   $y = 16.22169061$ hours $y = 243.32536$

   Total time $= 16.22169061 \times 199$ Total cost $= \$48,421.75$

   Total time $= 3,228.12$ hours

For the 200 Kitchens

$y = ax^b$ OR $y = ax^b$

$y = 24 \times 200^{-0.074}$ $y = (24 \times 15) \times 200^{-0.074}$

$y = 16.21567465$ hours   Total cost = $48,647.02

Total time = 16.21567465×200 200th cost = $225.27

Total time = 3,243.13 hours

The 200th Kitchen took 3,243.13 − 3,228.12 = 15.01 hours

Total time is therefore:

For first 200	3,243.13 hours
For next 400 (15.01 hours × 400)	6,004.00 hours
Total	9,247.13 hours (9,247 hours)

(W2) The overheads need to be analysed between variable and fixed cost elements.

Taking the highest and lowest figures from the information given:

	Hours	Cost $
Highest	9,600	116,800
Lowest	9,200	113,600
Difference	400	3,200

Variable cost per hours is $3,200/400 hours = $8 per hour

Total cost = variable cost + fixed cost

$116,800 = 9,600 \times 8 +$ fixed cost

Fixed cost = $40,000 per month

Annual fixed cost = $40,000 × 12 = $480,000

Fixed absorption rate is $480,000/120,000 hours = $4 per hour

---

Key answer tips

Requirements (b)and (c) involved learning curve calculations. This is a core knowledge area and candidates who had practised learning curve calculations scored well.

(b) A table is useful to show how the learning rate has been calculated.

Number of Kitchens	Time for Kitchen (hours)	Cumulative time (hours)	Average time (hours)
1	24.00	24.00	24.00
2	21.60	45.60	22.80

The learning rate is calculated by measuring the reduction in the average time per kitchen as cumulative production doubles (in this case from 1 to 2). The learning rate is therefore 22.80/24.00 or 95%

		Marks
(a)	Average time for the 199th kitchen	1.0
	Total time for 199 kitchens	1.0
	Average time for the 200th kitchen	1.0
	Total time for 200 kitchens	1.0
	200th kitchen time	1.0
	Cost for the first 200	1.0
	Cost for the next 400	1.0
	Variable cost per hour	2.0
	Fixed cost per month	1.0
	Fixed cost per hour	1.0
	Cost for variable overhead	1.0
	Cost for fixed overhead	1.0
		13
(b)	Average time per unit and explanation	2
Total		**15**

Table title: **ACCA marking scheme**

253 JUMP PERFORMANCE APPRAISAL (JUNE 10 EXAM)

(a) Bonus calculation:

	Qtr to 30 June 2009	Qtr to 30 September 2009	Qtr to 31 December 2009	Qtr to 31 March 2010	Bonus; hits'
Staff on time?					
On-time %	430/450 = 95.5%	452/480 = 94.2%	442/470 = 94.0%	460/480 = 95.8%	
Bonus earned?	Yes	No	No	Yes	2
Members visits					
Target visits	60% × 3,000 × 12 = 21,600	60% × 3,200 × 12 = 23,040	60% × 3,300 × 12 = 23,760	60% × 3,400 × 12 = 24,480	
Actual visits	20,000	24,000	26,000	24,000	
Bonus earned?	No	Yes	Yes	No	2
Personal training					
Target	10% × 3,000 = 300	10% × 3,200 = 320	10% × 3,300 = 330	10% × 3,400 = 340	
Actual sessions	310	325	310	339	
Bonus earned	Yes	Yes	No	No	2
Total					6

The bonus earned by the manager would be 6 × $400 = $2,400, which is 50% of the total bonus available.

(b)   An important principle of any target based bonus system is that the targets must be based on controllable aspects of the manager's role.

Staff on time

The way in which a manager manages staff can have a big bearing on whether or not an individual staff member is keen to work and arrive on time. We are told that the local manager has the power to vary employment contracts so he should be able to agree acceptable shift patterns with staff and reward them for compliance. In this respect the lateness of staff is controllable by the manager.

On the other hand an individual staff member may be subject to home pressures or problems with public or other transport meaning that even they cannot control the time of arrival at work on some days. The manager cannot control these events either. If this problem became regular for a member of staff then the local manager could vary the contract of employment accordingly.

Overall, lateness to work is controllable by the local manager.

Member use of facilities

The local manager controls the staff and hence the level of customer service. Good quality customer services would probably encourage members to use the facilities more often. Equally, by maintaining the club to a high standard then the local manager can remove another potential reason for a member not to use the facilities regularly.

On the other hand customers are influenced by many factors outside of the club. Their state of health or their own work pressures can prevent members being able to come to the club.

Overall, the local manager can only partly control the number of member visits.

Personal training sessions

Again, the local manager controls the level of customer service and the standard of maintenance in the personal training department. He also has control over prices so, if the bookings fall, he is able to reduce price or make special offers to encourage use of the facilities.

On the other hand, personal training sessions may be seen as a luxury by customers and in times of financial difficulty they are expendable by them. Personal training sessions are often available from other sources and competition can force down the sales of the club. The manager can respond to that by improving services. He cannot, however, make significant investment in improving the facilities without board approval.

Overall, the local manager can only partly control the number of personal training sessions booked.

(c)   There are a variety of methods that the performance data can be manipulated:

Cut off

The unethical manager could record visits in a different period than was actually the case. For example in quarter three the target for personal training sessions was not met by 20 sessions. This was probably obvious to the manager in the last few days of that quarter. He could have therefore recorded some sessions as having taken place in the next quarter. Indeed, only one session would have to be moved in this way in order for the manager to meet the target in the final quarter and gain another $400 of bonus.

Reduce prices to below economic levels to encourage use

The targets that the manager is subject to are mainly volume driven. A reduction in prices would harm profitability but would not damage the manager's bonus potential. More sessions are bound to follow if the price is set low enough.

(Other ideas would be acceptable including advising staff to take the day off if they were going to be late. This would damage service levels admittedly, but would potentially gain a bonus for lateness.)

ACCA marking scheme		Marks
(a)	Per target	2
	Total	6
(b)	For each target – supporting controllability	1.5
	For each target – denying controllability	1.5
	Target	9
(c)	For each idea of manipulation up to	2.5
		5
Total		**20**

254 CRUMBLY CAKES (JUNE 09 EXAM)

Tutorial note

The concept of 'controllability' is important for the exam. A common theme in exam questions is that a manager's bonus is linked to a number of variances. However, on analysis it often becomes apparent that the manager is not being assessed on the variances which they control, i.e. their assessment is unfair.

(a)   Production manager

Assessing the performance of the two managers is difficult in this situation. In a traditional sense the production manager has seriously over spent in March following the move to organic ingredients. He has a net adverse variance against his department of $2,300 in one month. No adjustment to the standards has been made to allow for the change to organic.

The manager has not only bought organically he has also changed the mix, increasing the input proportion of the more expensive ingredients. This may have contributed to the increased sales of cakes.

However, the decision to go organic has seen the sales of the business improve. We are told that the taste of the cakes should be better and that customers could perceive a health benefit. However, the production manager is allocated none of the favourable sales variances that result. If we assume that the improved sales are entirely as a result of the production manager's decision to change the ingredients then the overall net favourable variance is $7,700.

The production manager did appear to be operating within the original standard in February, indicating a well performing department. Indeed he will have earned a small bonus in that month.

Sales manager

A change to organic idea would need to be 'sold' to customers. It would presumably require a change of marketing and proper communication to customers. The sales manager would probably feel he has done a good job in March. It is debatable, however, whether he is entirely responsible for all of the favourable variances.

The move to organic certainly helped the sales manager as in February he seems to have failed to meet his targets.

Bonus scheme

The problem here is that the variances have to be allocated to one individual. The good sales variances have been allocated to the sales manager when in truth the production manager's decision to go organic appears to have been a good one and the driver of the business success. Responsibility accounting systems struggle to cope with 'joint' success stories, refuting in general a collective responsibility.

Under the current standards the production manager has seemingly no chance to make a bonus. The main problems appear to be the out-of-date standards and the fact that all sales variances are allocated to the sales manager, despite the root cause of the improved performance being at least in part the production manager's decision to go organic. The system does not appear fair.

General comments

It would appear that some sharing of the total variances is appropriate. This would be an inexact science and some negotiation would be needed.

One problem seems to be that the original standards were not changed following the decision to go organic. In this sense the variances reported are not really 'fair'. Standards should reflect achievable current targets and this is not the case here.

Key answer tips

The normal loss of 10% will only impact the material yield variance. The standard ingredients to make a cake must be adjusted from 0.36 kg to 0.4 kg. However, even if the normal loss had been ignored a good mark could still have been obtained in this exam question.

(b) **Materials price variances**

Ingredient	Act price/kg	Std price/kg	Actual quantity kg	(AP – SP) × AQ MPV
Flour	0.13	0.12	5,700	57 (A)
Eggs	0.85	0.70	6,600	990 (A)
Butter	1.80	1.70	6,600	660 (A)
Sugar	0.60	0.50	4,578	458 (A)
				———
Total				2,165 (A)
				———

Materials mix variances

	Flour kg	Eggs kg	Butter kg	Sugar kg	Total kg
(1) AQAM	5,700	6,600	6,600	4,578	23,478
(2) AQSM (W1)	5,869.5	5,869.5	5,869.5	5,869.5	23,478
(3) SQapSM (W1)	6,000	6,000	6,000	6,000	24,000
					(W2)
Mix variance:					
(2) – (1)	169.5	–730.5	–730.5	1,291.5	
× SP	× 0.12	× 0.7	× 1.7	× 0.5	
	———	———	———	———	
	20F	511A	1,242A	646F	1,087A
	———	———	———	———	———

(W1)

From Std cost card:	litres			
Flour	0.1	25.0%	23,478	5,869.5
Eggs	0.1	"		
Butter	0.1	"		
Sugar	0.1	"		
	———			
	0.4			
	———			
		25.0%	24,000	6,000

(W2)

$$\text{SQap} = \frac{21,600}{0.36} \quad 0.4$$

$$= 24,000$$

Material mix variance – alternative calculation

Ingredient	Act mix	Std mix	Std price	Variance
Flour	5,700	5,870	0.12	20 (F)
Eggs	6,600	5,870	0.70	511 (A)
Butter	6,600	5,870	1.70	1,241 (A)
Sugar	4,578	5,870	0.50	646 (F)
Totals	23,478	23,478		1,086 (A)

Sales price variance

	Act price	Std price	Act volume	(AP – SP) * Act Vol variable	Adv or Fav
Cake	0.99	0.85	60,000	8,400	Fav

ACCA marking scheme		
		Marks
(a)	Production manager assessment	2.0
	Sales manager assessment	2.0
	Bonus scheme comment	3.0
	Maximum	7.0
(b)	Price variance	3.0
	Mix variance	3.0
	Sales price variance	2.0
	Maximum	8
Total		**15**

255 CARAT *Online question assistance*

Key answer tips

This question is largely a straightforward test of your ability to calculate variances, including material mix and yield variances, and labour variances when idle time is recorded. However, do not overlook part (c) of the question: there are 7 marks available for a description of the different types of standard cost. The answer here describes a basic, current, attainable and ideal standard. It would also be relevant to answer the question by discussing 'ex post' and 'ex ante' standards, as a means of separating planning and operational variances.

(a) **Standard cost and standard contribution**

	$	$
Standard sales price		12.00
Material A: (2.5 × $1.70)	4.25	
Material B: (1.5 × $1.20)	1.80	
Labour: (0.45 × $6.00)	2.70	
		8.75
Contribution per unit		3.25

Calculation of variances

(i) **Sales variances**

	$
48,000 units should sell for (× $12)	576,000
They did sell for	580,800
Sales price variance	**4,800** (F)

	Units
Budgeted sales volume	50,000
Actual sales volume	48,000
Sales volume variance	2,000 (A)

Standard contribution/unit	$3.25
Sales volume contribution variance	**$6,500** (A)

(ii) **Materials variances**

Material A price variance	$
121,951 kg should cost (× $1.70)	207,317
They did cost	200,000
Material A price variance	**7,317** (F)

Material B price variance	$
67,200 kg should cost (× $1.20)	80,640
They did cost	84,000
Material A price variance	**3,360** (A)

Mix variance

The standard mix is 2.5 kg of A for each 1.5 kg of B, i.e. 62.5% Material A and 37.5% Material B.

	Actual quantities used		Actual quantities in standard mix	Mix variance	Std price	Mix variance
	kg		kg	kg	$	$
Material A	121,951	(62.5%)	118,219	3,732 (A)	1.70	6,344 (A)
Material B	67,200	(37.5%)	70,932	3,732 (F)	1.20	4,478 (F)
	189,151		189,151			**1,866 (A)**

Yield variance

The standard cost per kg of material for A and B together is:

($4.25 + $1.80)/(2.5 kg + 1.5 kg) = $6.05/4 kg = $1.5125 per kg.

	kg	
48,000 units of ZP should use (× 4 kg)	192,000	
They did use	189,151	
Total yield variance	2,849	(F)
Standard cost per kg	$1.5125	
Material yield variance	$4,309	**(F)**

(iii)   Labour variances

	$	
19,200 hours should cost (× $6.00)	115,200	
They did cost	117,120	
Labour rate variance	1,920	**(A)**

Idle time variance = (19,200 – 18,900) hours = 300 hours (A).

At the standard rate per hour, the idle time variance =

300 hours (A) × $6.00 = **$1,800 (A).**

Labour efficiency variance	Hours	
48,000 units of ZP should take (× 0.45 hours)	21,600	
They did use	18,900	
Total yield variance	2,700	(F)
Standard rate/hour	$6	
Labour efficiency variance	$16,200	**(F)**

The **adverse materials mix variance** indicates that more of the more expensive material A was used in the actual input than indicated by the standard mix. The favourable material A price variance suggests this may be due to the use of poorer quality material (hence more was needed than in the standard mix), or it might be that more material A was used because it was cheaper than expected. It could also be due to deciding to use less material B due to its increase in price (adverse price variance).

The **favourable material yield variance** indicates that more output was produced from the quantity of material used than expected by the standard. This increase in yield is unlikely to be due to the use of poorer quality material A but could be due to better quality material B. It is more likely, however, to be the result of employing more skilled labour, or introducing more efficient working practices.

It is only appropriate to calculate and interpret material mix and yield variances if quantities in the standard mix can be varied.

(b)　The **theory of motivation** suggests that having a clearly defined target results in better performance than having no target at all, that targets need to be accepted by the staff involved, and that more demanding targets increase motivation provided they remain accepted. It is against this background that basic, ideal, current and attainable standards can be discussed.

A **basic standard** is one that remains unchanged for several years and is used to show trends over time. Basic standards may become increasingly easy to achieve as time passes and hence, being undemanding, may have a negative impact on motivation. Standards that are easy to achieve will give employees little to aim at.

Ideal standards represent the outcome that can be achieved under perfect operating conditions, with no wastage, inefficiency or machine breakdowns. Since perfect operating conditions are unlikely to occur for any significant period, ideal standards will be very demanding and are unlikely to be accepted as targets by the staff involved as they are unlikely to be achieved. Using ideal standards as targets is therefore likely to have a negative effect on employee motivation.

Current standards are based on current operating conditions and incorporate current levels of wastage, inefficiency and machine breakdown. If used as targets, current standards will not improve performance beyond its current level and their impact on motivation will be a neutral one or a negative one since employees may feel unmotivated due to the lack of challenge.

Attainable standards are those that can be achieved if operating conditions conform to the best that can be practically achieved in terms of material use, efficiency and machine performance. Attainable standards are likely to be more demanding than current standards and so will have a positive effect on employee motivation, provided that employees accept them as achievable.

256 SAFE SOAP CO (DEC 2014)

(a) Variance calculations

Mix variance

Total kg of materials per standard batch = 0.25 + 0.6 + 0.5 = 1.35 kg

Therefore standard quantity to produce 136,000 batches = 136,000 × 1.35 kg = 183,600 kg

Actual total kg of materials used to produce 136,000 batches = 34,080 + 83,232 + 64,200 = 181,512 kg

Material	Actual quantity Standard mix		Actual quantity Actual mix	Variance	Standard cost per kg	Variance
	kgs		kgs	kgs	$	$
Lye	181,512 × 0.25/1.35 =	33,613.33	34,080	(466.67)	10	(4,666.70)
Coconut oil	181,512 × 0.6/1.35 =	80,672	83,232	(2,560)	4	(10,240)
Shea butter	181,512 × 0.5/1.35 =	67,226.67	64,200	3,026.67	3	9,080.01
		181,512	181,512			(5,826.69)A

Yield variance

Material	Standard quantity Standard mix		Actual quantity Standard mix	Variance	Standard cost per kg	Variance
			kgs	kgs	$	$
Lye	0.25 × 136,000 =	34,000	33,613.33	386.67	10	3,866.70
Coconut oil	0.6 × 136,000 =	81,600	80,672	928	4	3,712
Shea butter	0.5 × 136,000 =	68,000	67,226.67	773.33	3	2,319.99
		183,600	181,512			9,898.69F

(b) (i) A materials mix variance will occur when the actual mix of materials used in production is different from the standard mix. So, it is inputs which are being considered. Since the total mix variance is adverse for the Safe Soap Co, this means that the actual mix used in September and October was more expensive than the standard mix.

A material yield variance arises because the output which was achieved is different from the output which would have been expected from the inputs. So, whereas the mix variance focuses on inputs, the yield variance focuses on outputs. In both September and October, the yield variance was favourable, meaning that the inputs produced a higher level of output than one would have expected.

(ii)   Whilst the mix and yield variances provide Safe Soap Co with a certain level of information, they do not necessarily explain any quality issues which arise because of the change in mix. The consequences of the change may well have an impact on sales volumes. In Safe Soap Co's case, the sales volume variance is adverse, meaning that sales volumes have fallen in October. It is not known whether they also fell in September but it would be usual for the effects on sales of the change in mix to be slightly delayed, in this case by one month, given that it is only once the customers start receiving the slightly altered soap that they may start expressing their dissatisfaction with the product.

There may also be other reasons for the adverse sales volume variance but given the customer complaints which have been received, the sales manager's views should be taken on board.

ACCA marking scheme				*Marks*
(a)		Variance calculations		
		Mix variance		4
		Quantity variance		4
				—
			Maximum	8
(b)	(i)	Variances		
		Marks per variance explained		2
				—
			Maximum	4
	(ii)	Discussion		
		Per valid point		1
				—
			Maximum	3
Total				**15**

257   SPIKE CO I (DEC 07 EXAM)

Key answer tips

Ten marks may seem overwhelming at first but a good plan should make this more manageable. There are two separate areas to discuss, namely labour and materials. The ten marks can therefore be split into five marks for each area. Within each four mark section it should be possible to discuss three arguments for/against budget revision (3 marks) and to conclude (2 marks). Breaking the question down like this makes it much more manageable and increases the chance of success.

Materials

Arguments in favour of allowing a revision:

*   The nature of the problem is outside the control of the organisation. The supplier went in to liquidation; it is doubtful that Spike Limited could have expected this or prevented it from happening.

*   The buyer, knowing that budget revisions are common, is likely to see the liquidation as outside his control and hence expect a revision to be allowed. He may see it as unjust if this is not the case and this can be demoralising.

Arguments against allowing a budget revision:

- There is evidence that the buyer panicked a little in response to the liquidation. He may have accepted the first offer that became available (without negotiation) and therefore incurred more cost than was necessary.

- A cheaper, more local supplier may well have been available, so it could be argued that the extra delivery cost need not have been incurred. This could be said to have been an operational error.

Conclusion:

The cause of this problem (liquidation) is outside the control of the organisation and this is the prime cause of the overspend. Urgent problems need urgent solutions and a buyer should not be penalised in this case. A budget revision should be allowed.

Labour

Arguments in favour of allowing a revision:

- The board made this decision, not the departmental manager. It could be argued that the extra cost on the department's budget is outside their control.

Arguments against allowing a budget revision:

- This decision is entirely within the control of the organisation as a whole. As such, it would fall under the definition of an operational decision. It is not usual to allow a revision in these circumstances.

- It is stated in the question that the departmental manager complained in his board report that the staff level needed improving. It appears that he got his wish and the board could be said to have merely approved the change.

- The department will have benefited from the productivity increases that may have resulted in the change of policy. If the department takes the benefit then perhaps they should take the increased costs as well.

Conclusion:

This is primarily an operational decision that the departmental manager agreed with and indeed suggested in his board report. No budget revision should be allowed.

An alternative view is that the board made the final decision and as such the policy change was outside the direct control of the departmental manager. In this case a budget revision would be allowed.

ACCA marking scheme	
	Marks
Materials discussion	3
Conclusion	2
Labour discussion	3
Conclusion	2
	—
Total	**10**
	—

258 SPIKE CO II (DEC 07 EXAM)

Key answer tips

Part (a) is trickier but candidates will not fail if they can't answer this requirement. However, the examiner will continue to test some of the more advanced variances and so practice these before the exam.

In part (b) four marks will be available for discussing each variance in terms of business performance. Four variances were calculated in parts (b) and (c) and so there will be one mark for discussing each variance.

(a) **Market size and share variances**

Market size variance	= (Revised sales volume – budget sales volume) × Std contribution
	= (160,000 – 180,000) × 7
	= $140,000 (Adverse)
Market share variance	= (Actual sales volume – revised sales volume) × Std contribution
	= (176,000 – 160,000) × 7
	= $112,000 (Favourable)

(b) **Comment on sales performance**

Sales price

The biggest issue seems to be the decision to reduce the sales price from $17.00 down to $16.40. This 'lost' $105,600 of revenue on sales made compared to the standard price.

It seems likely that the business is under pressure on sales due to the increased popularity of electronic diaries. As such, they may have felt that they had to reduce prices to sustain sales at even the level they achieved.

Volume

The analysis of sales volume into market size and share shows the usefulness of planning and operational variances. Overall, the sales level of the business is down by 4,000 units, losing the business $28,000 of contribution or profit. This calculation does not in itself explain how the sales department of the business has performed.

In the face of a shrinking market they seem to have performed well. The revised level of sales (allowing for the shrinking market) is 160,000 units and the business managed to beat this level comfortably by selling 176,000 units in the period.

As mentioned above, the reducing price could have contributed to the maintenance of the sales level. Additionally, the improved quality of support staff may have helped maintain the sales level. Equally the actions of competitors are relevant to how the business has performed. If competitors have been active then merely maintaining sales could be seen as an achievement.

Spike should be concerned that its market is shrinking.

ACCA marking scheme		Marks
(a)	Market size variance	2
	Market share variance	2
		4
(b)	Comment on sales price	2
	Comment on sales volume	2
	Any valid comment 1 mark, maximum 2.	2
		6
Total		10

259 BLOCK CO (JUNE 2013 EXAM)

(a) **Sales price operational variance:** (actual price – market price) × actual quantity

Commodity 3: ($40.40 – $39.10) × 25,600 = $33,280F

Sales price planning variance: (standard price – market price) × actual quantity

Commodity 3: ($41.60 – $39.10) × 25,600 = $(64,000)A

An alternative approach to the variance calculations for Commodity 3 would be as follows:

Sales price operational variance

	Commodity 3
Should now	$39.10
Did	$40.40
Difference	$1.30F
Actual sales quantity	25,600
Variance	$33,280F

Sales price planning variance

	Commodity 3
Should now	$39.10
Should	$41.60
Difference	$2.50A
Actual sales quantity	25,600
Variance	$64,000A

(b) **Sales mix variance:**

(Actual sales quantity in actual mix at standard margin) – (actual sales quantity in standard mix at standard margin) = $768,640 (W1) and (W2) – $782,006 (W3) = $13,366 adverse.

Workings

(W1) **Standard margins per unit:**

Budgeted machine hours = (30,000 × 0.2) + (28,000 × 0.6) + (26,000 × 0.8) = 43,600. Overhead absorption rate = $174,400/43,600 = $4 per hour.

Product	Commodity 1	Commodity 2	Commodity 3
	$	$	$
Standard selling price	30	35	41.60
Variable production costs	(18)	(28.40)	(26.40)
Fixed production overheads	(0.8)	(2.4)	(3.2)
Standard profit margin	11.20	4.20	12

(W2) **Actual sales quantity in actual mix at standard profit margin:**

Product	Actual quantity in actual mix	Standard profit	$
Commodity 1	29,800	$11.20	333,760
Commodity 2	30,400	$4.20	127,680
Commodity 3	25,600	$12	307,200
	85,800		768,640

(W3) **Actual sales quantity in standard mix at standard profit margin:**

Product	Actual quantity in standard mix	Standard profit	$
Commodity 1	85,800 × 30/84 = 30,643	$11.20	343,202
Commodity 2	85,800 × 28/84 = 28,600	$4.20	120,120
Commodity 3	85,800 × 26/84 = 26,557	$12	318,684
	85,800		782,006

The sales quantity variance = (actual sales quantity in standard mix at standard margin) – (budgeted sales quantity in standard mix at standard profit margin) = $782,006 (W3 above) – $765,600 (W4) = $16,406 favourable.

(W4) Budgeted sales quantity in standard mix at standard profit margin:

Product	Quantity	Standard profit	$
Commodity 1	30,000	$11.20	336,000
Commodity 2	28,000	$4.20	117,600
Commodity 3	26,000	$12	312,000
	84,000		765,600

ACCA marking scheme		
		Marks
(a)	Planning and operational variances	
	Operational variance	2
	Planning variance	2
	Maximum	4
(b)	Mix and quantity variances	4
	Standard profit per unit	4
	Mix variance	1.5
	Quantity variance	1.5
	Maximum	11
Total		**15**

260 VALET CO VARIANCES (JUNE 2014, ADAPTED)

(a) Variances

(i) The sales mix contribution variance

Calculated as (actual sales quantity − actual sales quantity in budgeted proportions) × standard contribution per unit.

Standard contributions per valet:

Full = $50 × 44.6% = $22.30 per valet

Mini = $30 × 55% = $16.50 per valet

Actual sales quantity in budgeted proportions (ASQBP):

Full: 7,980 × (3,600/5,600) = 5,130

Mini: 7,980 × (2,000/5,600) = 2,850

Valet type	AQAM	AQBM	Difference	Standard contribution	Variance
				$	$
Full	4,000	5,130	(1,130)	22.30	25,199 A
Mini	3,980	2,850	1,130	16.50	18,645 F
					6,554 A

(ii) **The sales quantity contribution variance**

Calculated as (actual sales quantity in budgeted proportions – budgeted sales quantity) × standard contribution per unit.

Valet type	AQBM	BQBM	Difference	Standard contribution $	Variance $
Full	5,130	3,600	1,530	22.30	34,119 F
Mini	2,850	2,000	850	16.50	14,025 F
					_____
					48,144 F

(b) **Description**

The sales mix contribution variance: This variance measures the effect on profit of changing the mix of actual sales from the standard mix.

The sales quantity contribution variance: This variance measures the effect on profit of selling a different total quantity from the budgeted total quantity.

Marking scheme		Marks
(a) Calculations		
Sales mix contribution variance		4
Sales quantity contribution variance		4
		___
		8
		___
(b) Description		
One mark per description		2
		___
Total		**10**
		___

261 CHOC CO VARIANCES (DEC 2011 EXAM)

Tutorial note

It is not acceptable to calculate the variances in kg and not convert them into a monetary value using the standard costs for each ingredient. Variances need to be given a value in order to be used properly within a business. It's not sufficient to simply stop at a quantity. The most common mistake when values were calculated was to use the costs of $0.40 for honey, $0.45 for sugar and $0.25 for syrup given in the question. This was probably down to poor reading, since these costs were the total cost for 20 grams of honey, 15 grams of sugar and 10 grams of syrup. They needed to be converted into costs per kg.

(a) **(i)** **Usage variance**

	Std usage for actual output	Actual usage	Variance	Std cost per kg	Variance
	kgs	kgs	kgs	$	$
Honey	2,020	2,200	(180)	20	(3,600)
Sugar	1,515	1,400	115	30	3,450
Syrup	1,010	1,050	(40)	25	(1,000)
					(1,150) A

(ii) **Mix variance**

	Actual qty std mid	Actual qty actual mix	Variance	Std cost per kg	Variance
	kgs	kgs	kgs	$	$
Honey	2,066.67	2,200	(133.33)	20	(2,666.60)
Sugar	1,550	1,400	150	30	4,500
Syrup	1,033.33	1,050	(16.67)	25	(416.75)
					1,416.65 F

(iii) **Yield variance**

	Std quantity std mix	Actual qty actual mix	Variance	Std cost per kg	Variance
	kgs	kgs	kgs	$	$
Honey	2,020	2,066.67	(46.67)	20	(933.40)
Sugar	1,515	1,550	(35)	30	(1,050)
Syrup	1,010	1,033.33	(23.33)	25	(583.25)
					(2,566.65) A

The method used above is a more simple method for calculating the mix and yield variances than the one shown below. However, in the method shown below, the individual variances for each material are also meaningful, whereas they are not in the method shown above. Since the question only asks for the total variances, students will be given credit for either method.

(ii) Mix variance

	Actual qty std mix kgs	Actual qty actual mix kgs	Variance kgs	Budgeted WAC per kg $	Std cost per kg $	Difference	Variance $
Honey	2,066.67	2,200	(133.33)	24.44	20	(4.44)	592.59
Sugar	1,550	1,400	150	24.44	30	5.56	833.33
Syrup	1,033.33	1,050	(16.67)	24.44	25	0.56	(9.26)
							1,416.66 F

(iii) Yield variance

	Std usage for actual output kgs	Actual qty actual mid kgs	Variance kgs		Variance $
Honey	2,020	2,200	(180)	24.44	(4,400.00)
Sugar	1,515	1,400	115	24.44	2,811.11
Syrup	1,010	1,050	(40)	24.44	(977.78)
					(2,566.67) A

Budgeted weighted average cost

Honey	2,066.67	20	41,333.4
Sugar	1,550	30	46,500
Syrup	1,033.33	25	25,833.25
	4,650	113,666.65	24.44

WAC = $113,666.65/4,650 kg = $24.44

(b) Changing the mix appears to have saved Choc Co just over $1,400. This means that the new mix was cheaper. This might not mean however that this was beneficial. Changing the mix of ingredients in food products can also change taste, consistency or appearance. If these changes are preferred by the customers then fine. However, if customers dislike the changes then sales could suffer or the Choc Co brand might be damaged. Sales are not measured in this question and we have no information on how the customers have reacted.

The other effect of changing the mix could be to alter the yield or output. In this situation Choc Co has seen a reduction in cost terms of output or yield. The yield variance is nearly $2,600 adverse which means less output. This is not beneficial to Choc Co.

Overall usage therefore is up by $1,150 (mix plus yield) and so subject to the customer reaction Choc Co has not benefitted from the change in mix.

<table>
<tr><td colspan="3" align="center">**ACCA marking scheme**</td><td></td></tr>
<tr><td></td><td></td><td></td><td>*Marks*</td></tr>
</table>

			Marks
(a)	Material variances		
	(i)	Usage variance	4
	(ii)	Mix variance	4
	(iii)	Yield variance	4
		Maximum	12
(b)	I mark per point made		3
		Maximum	3
Total			**15**

262 BED CO (DEC 2013 EXAM)

(a) Planning and operational variances

(i) Material Usage Planning Variance (MUPV)

(Standard quantity for actual production – revised quantity for actual production) × standard price

RQ for each pillow case = 0.5 m × 1.1 = 0.55 m

Sheets   (240,000 – 240,000) × $5 = 0

Pillow cases   (90,000 – 99,000) × $5 = $45,000 (A)

Tutorial note

Simply calculating total variances is not enough; you need to calculate individual variances, for bed sheets and pillowcases.

(ii) Material Usage Operational Variance (MUOV)

(Actual quantity – revised quantity for actual production) × standard price

Sheets   (248,000 – 240,000) × $5 = $40,000 (A)

Pillow cases   (95,000 – 99,000) × $5 = $20,000 (F)

Total $20,000 Adverse

Tutorial note

Make sure the signage 'A' or 'F' is not missing next to the variance calculated. It is not sufficient to simply show an adverse variance in brackets.

(b) **Performance of the production manager**

In total, there has been an overspend of $339,400, which looks poor. However, when the reasons for this are examined, together with the variances calculated in (a), it is apparent that the production manager cannot be held solely responsible for the overspend. In fact, he has had little control over the situation.

Increase in cotton price

Since cotton is used to make bed sheets and the price of this rose in the world market by 20%, the production manager's performance has to be looked at in light of this. Because of the increased market price, the adverse material price planning variance is very high, since the budgeted cost of $5 per m2 was far below the actual market price of $6 per m2. The production manager cannot be held responsible for this since he does not set the standard costs. He can only be held responsible for any difference in price between the $6 market price and the $5.80 actual price paid. Since the $5.80 paid per m2 is less than the market price of $6 per m2, the manager performed well, as shown by the favourable material price operating variance of $68,600.

Increase in amount of cotton used

Since more cotton was used for actual production than budgeted, a total adverse material usage variance of $65,000 ($45,000 + $20,000) arose. However, of this, $45,000 (material usage planning variance) arose because of the request for a change in the design of the pillowcases by Bedco's customer. This was not within the control of the production manager and his performance should not therefore be assessed on it. However, an adverse material usage operational variance of $20,000 also arose; the performance of the production manager is weak here. Most of the adverse operational variance actually related to the production of bed sheets rather than pillowcases. It is not clear why this arose but it is definitely poor.

Bedco was also unable to produce all the pillowcases ordered by its customer in November as the order fell short by 10,000 units. If this was genuinely because of the late design change, however, it seems unfair to judge the production manager on this.

ACCA marking scheme			
			Marks
(a)	Variance calculations		
	MUPV		3
	MUOV		3
			——
		Maximum	6
			——
(b)	Discussion		
	Up to 2 marks per discussed point	Maximum	9
			——
Total			**15**
			——

PERFORMANCE MEASUREMENT AND CONTROL

263   ROTECH GROUP PART 1: W CO (JUNE 2014)

Ratios

(i)   ROCE = operating profit/capital employed × 100%

		$000	ROCE
W Co	Design division	6,000/23,540	25.49%
	Gearbox division	3,875/32,320	11.99%
C Co		7,010/82,975	8.45%

(ii)   Asset turnover = sales/capital employed × 100%

		$000	Asset turnover
W Co	Design division	14,300/23,540	0.61
	Gearbox division	25,535/32,320	0.79
C Co		15,560/82,975	0.19

(iii)   Operating profit margin = operating profit/sales × 100%

		$000	Operating profit
W Co	Design division	6,000/14,300	41.96%
	Gearbox division	3,875/25,535	15.18%
C Co		7,010/15,560	45.05%

Both companies and both divisions within W Co are clearly profitable. In terms of what the different ratios tell us, ROCE tells us the return which a company is making from its capital. The Design division of W Co is making the highest return at over 25%, more than twice that of the Gearbox division and nearly three times that of C Co. This is because the nature of a design business is such that profits are largely derived from the people making the designs rather than from the assets. Certain assets will obviously be necessary in order to produce the designs but it is the employees who are mostly responsible for generating profit.

The Gearbox division and C Co's ROCE are fairly similar compared to the Design division, although when comparing the two in isolation, the Gearbox division's ROCE is actually over three percentage points higher than C Co's (11.99% compared to 8.45%). This is because C Co has a substantially larger asset base than the Gearbox division.

From the asset turnover ratio, it can be seen that the Gearbox division's assets generate a very high proportion of sales per $ of assets (79%) compared to C Co (19%). This is partly because the Gearbox division buys its components in from C Co and therefore does not need to have the large asset base which C Co has in order to make the components. When the unit profitability of those sales is considered by looking at the operating profit margin, C Co's unit profitability is much higher than the Gearbox division (45% operating profit margin as compared to 15%). The Design division, like the Gearbox division, is also using its assets well to generate sales (asset turnover of 61%) but then, like C Co, its unit profitability is high too (42% operating profit margin.) This is why, when the two ratios (operating profit margin and asset turnover) are combined to make ROCE, the Design division comes out top overall – because it has both high unit profitability and generates sales at a high level compared to its asset base.

It should be noted that any comparisons between such different types of business are of limited use. It would be more useful to have prior year figures for comparison and/or industry averages for similar businesses. This would make performance review much more meaningful.

Marking scheme		
		Marks
Ratios		
Calculating ROCE		1.5
Calculating asset turnover		1.5
Calculating operating profit margin		1.5
Per valid comment		
	maximum	10
		───
Total		**10**
		───

264 PRINTING COMPANY

Tutorial note

This is really an examination of your knowledge of the requirements of a divisionalised company, and the answer below is more developed than you need. Use this question as a brainstorming exercise at the start of your revision programme.

Unitary to divisionalised structure

- Each division will now require its own accounts

- There is now a need to assess the financial and non-financial performance of every division

- Internal and external income will have to be identified – a cross charging/transfer pricing system will have to be devised that ensures corporate goal congruence

- Information concerning the various external markets is required to permit the performance of a manager to be distinguished from the performance of the business unit managed

Central direction to empowerment

- There may be a need to separate the transmission of strategic and operational information. The empowered team leaders will not require strategic information, but principally, data concerned with the day-to-day management of the business. Whereas the senior management may now be able to dispense with information concerned with operational details

- This may also require the development of new reporting formats that are understandable to the team leaders. They may need even more detailed information at more frequent intervals than was available previously

- New control systems will be required to meet the needs of the newly empowered team leaders and the senior management. The shift from a few to many decision makers will necessitate control systems to ensure standardisation and consistency throughout the company

The shift to outsourcing

- New information systems will be needed to facilitate access to the external providers of services e.g. approved contractor lists

- Authorisation/approval systems need to be developed to ensure procedures are being adhered to

- Systems to monitor the price and quality of work undertaken by contractors will be needed

- Financial appraisal systems may be installed to compare the 'life' costs of alternative suppliers in comparison with internal resourcing. If internal suppliers are permitted to bid for work and compete against contractors, then there is a need for the costing systems to clearly identify the activities driving costs

Expansion in part-time and temporary employees

- The traditional personnel systems will need to adapt to the new situation

- The employment of part-time staff to replace full timers will result in greater numbers of employees, perhaps by a factor of two or three times. Can the existing system cope? Is there sufficient storage and memory capacity?

- Part-timers and temporary staff tend to stay in jobs for shorter periods and hence creating more activity within the personnel department. Once again can the system cope with the additional workload?

- Long serving full-time employees will have more opportunity, and perhaps more incentive to understand and use effectively a complex MIS. On the other hand, part-timers and temporary staff will have less opportunity to 'come to grips' with a complex system, therefore it may be necessary to modify/simplify the systems to suit the new staffing situation.

Customers adopting JIT systems

- The company could previously operate with low or zero stocks, and therefore a small/simple stock holding system might suffice. The advent of JIT for customers puts the onus on the company to replenish stocks immediately. This will necessitate the installation of a larger, accurate and responsive inventory system. The system adopted will need to provide information concerning minimum stock levels, re-order cycles and Economic Order Quantities. None of this information may have been required previously because stock levels were not so business critical.

Long print runs to high value low volume

- The new customers will have more complex, individualistic and diverse requirements. The established ordering and printing systems will need to be modified to manage the heterogeneous business activity.

- High value business normally permits lower margins of error and deficiencies in quality standards. This may entail close monitoring and low tolerance control systems being installed.

  Note: This list of issues is not exhaustive and therefore other considerations mentioned by the candidates should be credited. The crucial requirement is to assess whether the examinees are thinking coherently about the consequences on the organisation of the change in the business environment.

265 CDE

Key answer tips

There are many types of information system that are available to firms like CDE. It is worth thinking about both (a) and (b) together, since you will obviously need to ensure that your recommended system for part (b) is one that you outline in (a). Note that there are only 10 marks available overall, so this is not an opportunity to write all you know about every system!

In making your recommendation in (b), it is critical that you recommend a system that meets the needs of CDE, so your answer should refer to points made in the scenario when justifying your recommendation.

(a)   The following types of information system are available to manufacturing firms like CDE:

A **transaction processing system** (TPS) serves the operational level of the organisation. The system records all of the daily routine transactions that take place within the organisation, relating to each particular aspect of operational activities.

Data from the TPS is fed into a **management information system** (MIS). An MIS takes the bulk of data from the TPS and develops it into something useful to management in support of its decision-making responsibility. The MIS is usually computer-based, making use of spreadsheets where 'what if?' analysis can be carried out.

An **enterprise resource planning** (ERP) system is a sophisticated MIS system that covers the whole range of the organisation's activities. It promises the 'seamless integration of all the information flowing through the company'. ERP can be thought of as a development of the MRP II system used currently by CDE. A data warehouse is maintained of inputs from the TPS and MIS systems, from which any required customised report can be produced.

A **strategic enterprise management** (SEM) system assists management in making high-level strategic decisions. Tools such as activity-based management (ABM) and the balanced scorecard are applied to the data in the data warehouse to enable the strategic goals of the organisation to be worked towards.

An **executive information system** (EIS) or **executive support system** (ESS) gives management access to both internal and external data. Managers can access information to monitor the operations of the organisation and to scan general business conditions. The data for an EIS is online and updated in real time to ensure its integrity for decision making at a senior management level.

(b)   CDE is a substantially sized company, listed on the stock exchange, and operating in a highly competitive and fast-moving business. It currently uses an MRP II system to control production scheduling and labour and machine utilisation. This is satisfactory as far as controlling day-to-day operational requirements, but there is an absence of information being collected and presented to management for strategic and decision support purposes.

I recommend that CDE moves towards establishing an EIS system. This will enable managers to integrate the data from the current MRP II system with the known data about customer requirements and available suppliers. Then managers will be able to see an overview of the business as a whole, and can drill down if they wish to see more detail on the contents of any particular figure.

Tutorial note

Other systems could be recommended here and marks would be awarded if reasons are provided. An ERP system would be highly effective at meeting the need for integrated information, the lack of which was mentioned a couple of times in the scenario. Or a SEM system would suit a business such as this in a fast moving, competitive, modern manufacturing environment.

266   THE MG ORGANISATION

Key answer tips

This requires you to look at the benefits of two system types over a TPS. Try to include reference to the situation of MG where possible in your answer.

Explanations of system types

A transaction processing system is designed primarily for processing transactions, often within a stand-alone system for a job-specific application. Management reports are produced from such systems, but these are essentially a summary of the transactions that have been processed or provide an analysis of data on the computer master files. The information produced by transaction processing systems is therefore of operational or tactical value, but not strategic value, and it is used to prepare reports for the line management responsible for the particular area of operations.

An ERPS is a commercial software package that integrates information from a variety of sources, both internal and external. The information is both financial and non-financial. An ERP system might capture transaction data from a number of different transaction systems, as well as information from external sources (such as suppliers). This information can then be used to prepare specially-designed reports for management covering a range of different activities, and of strategic as well as tactical value.

Benefits of an ERP system

ERP systems can be used to provide performance data for multi-functional activities, rather than specific transactions, and so can be valuable for activity-based costing, balanced scorecard performance analysis and supply chain management.

ERP systems can provide benefits in excess of transaction processing systems because they provide better-quality strategic management information for senior management. The actual value of any particular ERPS obviously depends on the circumstances of each case, but as a general rule, an information system is beneficial if the expected improvements in management decision-making exceed the cost of providing the system.

Benefits of an EIS

Executive information systems (EIS) as their name suggests, provide information to senior executives within an organisation, from information sources both inside and outside the organisation. They allow executives to monitor the performance of the organisation and scan general business conditions at any time and in 'real time'. They allow executives to obtain summary performance information, and 'drill down' into further detail if required. They can also be used to make 'one-off' file interrogations to obtain information. Crucially, they are easy to use, and an executive does not have to be an IT expert or systems expert to benefit from using an EIS.

An EIS allows senior management to obtain performance information in 'real time' and should therefore help management to improve their control over the organisation. This is a benefit that transaction processing systems are unable to provide.

267 OPEN AND CLOSED SYSTEMS

(a) An **open loop control system** is one which records and responds to its system's external environment as well as to its internal results. An example of this is the maintenance of a departmental budget. It must measure whether expenditure is being kept within the forecast limits, but it must also be able to respond to external influences. An economic recession may lead to a reduction in the amount of money that the department has to spend.

How an open loop control system works can be seen in the diagram below:

Figure 1: An open loop control system

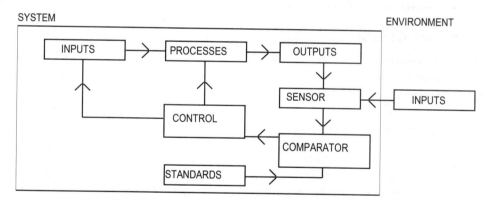

The system receives inputs, processes them, and produces outputs. The sensor is a device built in to the system that collects necessary information. The comparator is the means by which the actual results are compared with the pre-determined systems objectives. The control mechanism (also known as the activator or the effector), will take action when the system fails to meet its targets. There may also need to be action taken if the system's environment changes. In the budget example above, actual expenditure would be measured (by the sensor), compared with the forecast (by the comparator) and action taken by the departmental manager (the activator) to reduce costs if actual costs exceed forecast. The departmental manager may also need to take action by reducing expenditure if company sales are not as high as expected.

A **closed loop control system** is one where there is no direct link with the environment. Most closed loop systems are mechanistic in nature, and their only reactions to the outside world are indirect. An example of a closed loop control system is a water heating system. This sort of control system is illustrated by the diagram overleaf:

Figure 2: A closed loop control system

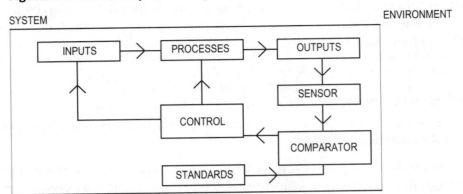

A heating system can continue to operate without any reference to its external environment, with the thermostat containing both the comparator and the activator. The only way that the heating system responds to the environment is when it is set up by a human setting the required temperature.

(b)   The total company must be operated according to an open loop system. A manufacturing company (or any other organisation) exists to satisfy the needs of its customers, and so there must be mechanisms to ensure that customers are satisfied and that the company is meeting its sales and other targets. The company must also be sufficiently flexible to be able to respond to the actions of its competitors, suppliers and distributors. It must be capable of assessing the changing needs of its market by using research and by listening to its customers. It must also react to government action and to advances in technology.

268   BRACE CO (JUNE 2011 EXAM)

The balanced scorecard is a strategic management technique for communicating and evaluating the achievement of the strategy and mission of an organisation. It comprises an integrated framework of financial and non-financial performance measures that aim to clarify, communicate and manage strategy implementation. It translates an organisation's strategy into objectives and performance measurements for the following four perspectives:

Financial perspective

The financial perspective considers how the organisation appears to shareholders. How can it create value for its shareholders? Kaplan and Norton, who developed the balanced scorecard, identified three core financial themes that will drive the business strategy: revenue growth and mix, cost reduction and asset utilisation.

Customer perspective

The customer perspective considers how the organisation appears to customers. The organisation should ask itself: 'to achieve our vision, how should we appear to our customers?'.

The customer perspective should identify the customer and market segments in which the business units will compete. There is a strong link between the customer perspective and the revenue objectives in the financial perspective. If customer objectives are achieved, revenue objectives should be too.

Internal perspective

The internal perspective requires the organisation to ask itself the question – 'what must we excel at to achieve our financial and customer objectives?'. It must identify the internal business processes that are critical to the implementation of the organisation's strategy. Kaplan and Norton identify a generic process value chain consisting of three processes: the innovation process, the operations process and the post-sales process.

Learning and growth perspective

The learning and growth perspective requires the organisation to ask itself whether it can continue to improve and create value.

If an organisation is to continue having loyal, satisfied customers and make good use of its resources, it must keep learning and developing. It is critical that an organisation continues to invest in its infrastructure – i.e. people, systems and organisational procedures – in order to provide the capabilities that will help the other three perspectives to be accomplished.

ACCA marking scheme	
	Marks
Balanced scorecard approach	
Stating what it is	2
Financial perspective	2
Customer perspective	2
Internal perspective	2
Learning and growth perspective	2
Total	**10**

269   NON-FINANCIAL MEASURES

(a)   Many businesses recognise the imperfections of financial measures oriented on the profit measure and may wish to devise NFMs for performance evaluation. NFMs fall into two categories, qualitative and quantitative. For example, it would be relatively easy to define quantitative measures in certain areas of management. Schemes of total quality management often define measures for such issues as customer care by accumulating data on:

- Complaints
- Rejections
- Disputes
- Errors in charging.

However, developing qualitative measures is difficult and often subjective. What is a satisfactory measure of customer care? What constitutes an effective service to the public in a non profit making entity such as a local authority? For example, a well known grocery chain has publicised its intention to concentrate on performance measures that provide competitive advantage and to spend less time on pure 'number crunching' of accounting data. They perceive that identifying problems at operating unit level (where the customer is served) is far more significant for strategic (long term) aims as well as for short term control.

Most systems involving the use of NFMs fail because staff are insufficiently educated about the aims of the organisation or are not sufficiently aware of the purpose of the measures.

In conclusion, the success or failure of NFMs is attributable to top management's ability to define the aims or mission of the organisation and direct the employees towards the achievement of that essential mission.

(b)

Tutorial note

In this question, only one measure is required for each perspective, and the answer below is more developed than what you would need to produce in the exam.

Financial perspective

- Meeting a key financial target such as ROCE.
- Sales growth. Insurance companies are concerned with market share and would like to see strong sales growth.

Customer perspective

- Customer retention. This is the proportion of customers who renew their policies from one year to the next. If the proportion is high, then it would imply that the insurance company is keeping its customers happy; if low, it would seem that the company is doing something wrong.
- Number of complaints. This measure could be used for just about any organisation. A high level of complaints would indicate where the company's customers are not pleased with the service that they are receiving.

Learning and growth perspective or innovation and learning perspective

- Labour turnover. Labour measures come within this perspective. A high labour turnover would indicate that the workforce is not happy, which may then lead to problems with their performance. It also means that those workers who leave will have to be replaced and that their replacements will need training, leading to extra cost and possibly initially poor performance.
- The number of new types of policies issued each year. This would be a good indication of innovation.

Internal business process perspective

- The percentage of policies issued or claims processed with the target time. This is an indication of how well the company performs its core functions.
- Unit cost. The cost per policy issued, or per claim processed, would be an indication of how well the business is performing its internal functions. Care must be taken that if the cost is reducing so then the service to the customer is not getting worse.

Note: Only ONE measure is required for each perspective.

270   JAMAIR (DEC 2014)

(a)   The four perspectives

Financial perspective – this perspective is concerned with how a company looks to its shareholders. How can it create value for them? Kaplan and Norton identified three core financial themes which will drive the business strategy: revenue growth and mix, cost reduction and asset utilisation.

Customer perspective – this considers how the organisation appears to customers. The organisation should ask itself: 'to achieve our vision, how should we appear to our customers?' The customer perspective should identify the customer and market segments in which the business will compete. There is a strong link between the customer perspective and the revenue objectives in the financial perspective. If customer objectives are achieved, revenue objectives should be too.

Internal perspective – this requires the organisation to ask itself: 'what must we excel at to achieve our financial and customer objectives?' It must identify the internal business processes which are critical to the implementation of the organisation's strategy. These will include the innovation process, the operations process and the post-sales process.

Learning and growth perspective – this requires the organisation to ask itself whether it can continue to improve and create value. The organisation must continue to invest in its infrastructure – i.e. people, systems and organisational procedures – in order to improve the capabilities which will help the other three perspectives to be achieved.

(b)   Goals and measures

Financial perspective

Goal	Performance measure
To use fewer planes to transport customers	Lease costs of plane per customer

Explanation – operating efficiency will be driven by getting more customers on fewer planes. This goal and measure cover the cost side of this.

Goal	Performance measure
To increase seat revenue per plane	Revenue per available passenger mile

Explanation – this covers the first part of achieving operating efficiency – by having fewer empty seats on planes.

Customer perspective

Goal	Performance measure
To ensure that flights are on time	'On time arrival' ranking from the aviation authority

Explanation – Jamair is currently number 7 in the rankings. If it becomes known as a particularly reliable airline, customers are more likely to use it, which will ultimately increase revenue.

Goal	**Performance measure**
To reduce the number of flights cancelled	The number of flights cancelled

Explanation – again, if flights are seen to be cancelled frequently by Jamair, customers will not want to use it. It needs to be perceived as reliable by its customers.

Internal perspective

Goal	**Performance measure**
To improve turnaround time on the ground	'On the ground' time

Explanation – less time spent on the ground means fewer planes are needed, which will reduce plane leasing costs. However, it is important not to compromise the quality of cleaning or make errors in refuelling as a consequence of reducing on the ground time.

Goal	**Performance measure**
To improve the cleanliness of Jamair's planes as reported in the customer satisfaction surveys.	The percentage of customers happy with the standard of the planes,

Explanation – at present, only 85% of customers are happy with the standard of cleanliness on Jamair's planes. This could be causing loss of revenue.

Goal	**Performance measure**
To develop the online booking system	Percentage downtime.

Explanation – since the company relies entirely on the booking system for customer booking of flights and check-in, it is critical that it can deal with the growing number of customers.

Learning perspective

Goal	**Performance measure**
To reduce the employee absentee rate	The number of days absent per employee

Explanation – it is critical to Jamair that its workforce is reliable as, at worse, absent staff lead to cancelled flights.

Goal

To increase ground crew training on cleaning and

refuelling procedures

Performance measure

Number of days' training per ground crew member

Explanation – if ground crew are better trained, they can reduce the number of minutes that the plane stays on the ground, which will result in fewer planes being required and therefore lower costs. Also, if their cleaning is better, customer satisfaction and retention will increase.

Note: Only one goal and measure were required for each perspective. In order to gain full marks, answers had to be specific to Jamair as stated in the requirements.

ACCA marking scheme			Marks
(a)	Perspectives		
	Explanation for each perspective		1.5
		Maximum	6.0
(b)	Goals and measures		
	Each goal/measure/explanation		2.0
	Presentation and structure		1.0
		Maximum	9.0
Total			**15.0**

271 ROTECH GROUP PART 2: C CO (JUNE 2014)

Transfer prices

From C Co's perspective

C Co transfers components to the Gearbox division at the same price as it sells components to the external market. However, if C Co were not making internal sales then, given that it already satisfies 60% of external demand, it would not be able to sell all of its current production to the external market. External sales are $8,010,000, therefore unsatisfied external demand is ([$8,010,000/0.6] – $8,010,000) = $5,340,000.

From C Co's perspective, of the current internal sales of $7,550,000, $5,340,000 could be sold externally if they were not sold to the Gearbox division. Therefore, in order for C Co not to be any worse off from selling internally, these sales should be made at the current price of $5,340,000, less any reduction in costs which C Co saves from not having to sell outside the group (perhaps lower administrative and distribution costs).

As regards the remaining internal sales of $2,210,000 ($7,550,000 – $5,340,000), C Co effectively has spare capacity to meet these sales. Therefore, the minimum transfer price should be the marginal cost of producing these goods. Given that variable costs represent 40% of revenue, this means that the marginal cost for these sales is $884,000. This is therefore the minimum price which C Co should charge for these sales.

In total, therefore, C Co will want to charge at least $6,224,000 for its sales to the Gearbox division.

From the Gearbox division's perspective

The Gearbox division will not want to pay more for the components than it could purchase them for externally. Given that it can purchase them all for 95% of the current price, this means a maximum purchase price of $7,172,500.

Overall

Taking into account all of the above, the transfer price for the sales should be somewhere between $6,224,000 and $7,172,500.

Marking scheme	
	Marks
Transfer pricing	
Each valid comment/calculation	1 or 2
	—
Total	**10**
	—

272 SECOND PROCESS CO (DEC 2013 EXAM)

(a) The suggested transfer price being used is actual marginal cost.

This means that whilst Division A would recover its variable costs of producing products L and M, there is no profit margin built in and, therefore, unless Head Office intervenes and forces Division A to transfer L and M to Division B, Division A will not want to transfer these products.

Also, Division A will not have the opportunity to recover any apportioned fixed costs since marginal cost does not include these. Not only would Division A not make any profit or recovery of apportioned fixed costs from the transfers using the suggested system, it would actually lower its overall profits if it were forced to transfer L and M for further processing rather than being allowed to sell them externally after the split-off point. Division A's manager would feel extremely demotivated if he/she were to be made to transfer L and M for further processing, as it would make performance look poorer for the Division.

All of the profit from both producing L and M and further processing them into LX and MX would be gained by Division B under the suggested system. If the criteria of return on investment (ROI) or residual income (RI) were then to be used to assess performance, as is usual for divisional performance assessment, Division B's ROI/RI would be seen to have increased as a result of the further processing. Division B would then effectively be taking the credit for a large part of the work carried out by Division A. The manager of Division B would be unlikely to complain about this as it works in favour of his Division.

Another point worth mentioning is that because actual cost would be used rather than standard cost, Division A would have little incentive to keep its variable costs down because it would pass all of its costs on to Division B. However, given that the suggested transfer price incorporates no profit for Division A, this point would hardly be arguable by Division B.

If Division A were told to make the transfers to Division B, their autonomy would be taken away from them. This would be likely to have a detrimental effect on the motivation of managers since one of the primary purposes of creating a divisional structure is to grant autonomy.

Tutorial note

Other points could be made, too. A candidate would not be expected to make all of the above points in order to earn full marks.

(b)   Environmental management accounting

Input/outflow analysis

This technique records material inflows and balances this with outflows on the basis that what comes in, must go out. So, if 100 kg of materials have been bought and only 80 kg of materials have been produced, for example, then the 20 kg difference must be accounted for in some way. It may be, for example, that 10% of it has been sold as scrap and 10% of it is waste. By accounting for outputs in this way, both in terms of physical quantities and, at the end of the process, in monetary terms too, businesses are forced to focus on environmental costs.

Flow cost accounting

This technique uses not only material flows but also the organisational structure. It makes material flows transparent by looking at the physical quantities involved, their costs and their value. It divides the material flows into three categories: material, system and delivery, and disposal. The values and costs of each of these three flows are then calculated. The aim of flow cost accounting is to reduce the quantity of materials which, as well as having a positive effect on the environment, should have a positive effect on a business's total costs in the long run.

Activity-based costing

ABC allocates internal costs to cost centres and cost drivers on the basis of the activities which give rise to the costs. In an environmental accounting context, it distinguishes between environment-related costs, which can be attributed to joint cost centres, and environment-driven costs, which tend to be hidden in general overheads.

Life cycle costing

Within the context of environmental accounting, life cycle costing is a technique which requires the full environmental consequences, and therefore costs, arising from production of a product to be taken account of across its whole life cycle, 'from cradle to grave'.

Tutorial note

Only two techniques are required here. A candidate would not be expected to make all of the above points in order to earn full marks.

ACCA marking scheme			Marks
(a)	Issues		
	Per valid point – maximum		2
		Maximum	5
(b)	Environmental accounting		
	Each description – maximum		3
		Maximum	5
Total			**10**

273   DIVISION A

(a)   Profit required by division A to meet RI target:

	$
Cost of capital $3.2m @ 12%	384,000
Target RI	180,000
Target profit	564,000
Add fixed costs	1,080,000
Target contribution	1,644,000
Contribution earned from external sales 90,000 @ ($35 – $22)	1,170,000
Contribution required from internal sales	474,000
Contribution per bit on internal sales ($474,000/60,000)	$7.90
Transfer price to division C $22.00 + $7.90	$29.90

(b)   The two transfer prices based on opportunity costs:

40,000 units (150,000 – 110,000) at the marginal cost of $22.00

20,000 units (110,000 – 90,000) at the external selling price of $35.00

274   B5 CARS EIS

Key answer tips

This question tests your knowledge of sources of information and the operation of an executive information system (EIS).

In answering the question you need to recognise the costs and benefits associated with information with particular reference to the distinction between internally produced information and that gathered from external sources.

(a)   One of the main reasons why B5 Cars' EIS is becoming expensive to operate is the amount of data which has been, and is being, accumulated. For an EIS to be effective there is a requirement for large amounts of information to be easily accessible - the data should be on-line and as up-to-date as possible. This has disc storage implications which increase over time as the volume of information increases.

The increased costs do not end with disk storage, however. As the system is required to handle larger volumes of data, there are numerous knock-on costs. The larger the database the more processing power required to conduct straightforward operations. Therefore, another increased expense may be a requirement to invest in hardware as the original processor proves inadequate to handle the volume of information within acceptable response times.

Data is obtained from various different external sources; this may be causing a requirement for extra disk storage in excess of the amount required as a result of the normal growth of the databank.

The information requirements of the executives using an EIS may change over time. This means that, however carefully the system was set up originally, there will be costs involved in making changes to the way in which the system is set up. The degree with which maintenance and support costs increase will be dependent to some extent on the original design of the programs and database and to what extent the information requirements alter.

Another area where costs may increase is the network service. As the volume of data increases, particularly if appropriate hardware investment is not made, it is likely that it will take longer to extract the required information. This will result in greater costs of actually using the line. The rental of the line may also have increased.

The EIS uses data collated from various sources. There are potential costs associated with the capture of this data; large amounts of data may need to be manually keyed in which has implications on staffing costs or the cost of hiring an agency to do the work.

(b) Management's decision to concentrate on internally-produced information will have serious implications.

Market information

It is important for companies to be aware of the activities of their competitors. By collecting only internally-produced information the management are getting a restricted picture of what is really taking place. Management need to know how their products measure up to those of their competitors in terms of quality, design etc.

Without external information the information system can hardly be described as an EIS, but would be providing information at an operational level. It is important for organisations to establish their own indicators as a means of measuring their performance, but it is at least as important to set these in context. For example, if a production unit is performing well against its own measures but is failing to perform well in relation to its competitors, management needs to be aware of this and take action to recover the situation.

Without competitor information B5 Cars may find that they are out of line with the rest of the industry. They may find that their competitors are offering free finance, as an example, whereas B5 Cars are offering 'cheap' finance at 7% APR; their main competitors may offer free finance for the first year after purchase. This information is invaluable to B5 Cars to ensure that they remain competitive.

Customer information

One of the sources of information which will be lost will be that relating to customers. This loss will have a damaging impact on the firm; any organisation needs to know about its market, both existing and potential, to survive and grow. Even if an organisation currently enjoys a strong position in its sector of the market it would be short-sighted to assume that this situation would remain without consideration of the ever-changing market. Predicting market behaviour is challenging enough with access to wide-ranging information from external sources; without these tools the task becomes virtually impossible.

The industry

There are many sources of information on specific industries, in this case the motor vehicle industry, which will be lost. Societies established for manufacturers in a particular industry can provide useful information and comparisons about all manufacturers within an industry.

The effect on the company's information system

An EIS needs to afford access to information which is up-to-date and relevant for managers to manage the organisation. The loss of access as described above will, in a very short time, produce the effect that the information available via the EIS is inadequate for effective decision-making. The decisions taken will be short-term and reactive.

The system will cease to be an EIS but will, instead, provide a control mechanism. The kind of information the system will provide will be at an operational level (how many man hours was taken to produce a particular car; how many hours of overtime etc.) rather than providing information to support management decisions.

The effect on the company's products

Without access to external information, B5 Cars will be unaware of technological innovations; as a result their products will lag behind the rest of the industry and their own innovations may not take full advantage of new technological breakthroughs. There is the danger of 'reinventing the wheel' which will leave them behind in terms of technological advances and incur unnecessary research and development costs.

External market information would assist B5 Cars to identify trends in the motor industry, from which they could attempt to create marketing opportunities. Without this information marketing opportunities will be forgone.

The dearth of market information will mean that the organisation cannot accurately position their products in terms of pricing which in turn will affect their profitability. With accurate market information a producer is in a better position to optimise profits by pricing their product at a price low enough to sell, but high enough to ensure maximum profits. The effects on the products identified above will adversely affect the customer's perception thereof.

The Board's decision appears to be misguided which, in the longer-term, may affect the organisation's profitability and future market share.

275 PRECISION PARTS

Key answer tips

This question which focuses upon position appraisal, requires you to assess the validity of management accounting data for strategic planning purposes. Ensure you relate your answer to the scenario.

(a)   The management accounting reports which are currently provided to the management of W Ltd comprise monthly cost variance reports covering direct materials, direct labour, variable and fixed production overheads, and regular sales price and volume variance reports. These will help management in its control of the company's operations, by focusing on areas where results actually achieved are materially different from those expected.

But **controlling activities is only one aspect of management accounting**. Other important responsibilities are the formulation of strategy and optimising the use of resources. The inward-looking reports currently produced focus only on what is happening within the company by reporting internally generated numbers to internal managers who are expected to adjust their internal actions.

A successful business must react to changes in its external environment and be outward looking. The current reports are inward-looking and appear to have no strategic content. However punctually and comprehensively they are produced, they are still inadequate as information to assist the board's strategic decision making.

(b)   Effective strategic planning starts with the **setting of objectives** and a **position audit** of the company. W Ltd appears to want to increase its profits, but it is unclear whether objectives exist in terms of earnings per share, products/markets, productivity, etc.

A position audit examines the current situation of the company in terms of resources, products, markets, operating systems, internal organisation, current results and returns to stockholders. The audit should be carried out now as a matter of urgency and repeated regularly to keep the information up to date. Planning is not an activity that can be carried out once a year and then forgotten about during the rest of the year; to be valuable it must be a regular ongoing process.

Environmental analysis considers the environmental conditions within which the company will be operating, looking at product demand, production technology, competition, etc. This analysis is particularly lacking from the management information that the management accounting department has previously provided.

Specific reports are recommended to be prepared as follows:

(i)   Statement of objectives

(ii)   Position audit

- Resources (people, fixed assets, finance)
- Products and markets
- Operating systems (including use of technology)
- Organisation
- Results (segmental analysis of profits, returns to shareholders).

(iii)   Environmental analysis

- Product demand: what market share is currently achieved and forecast for the future?
- Customers: why do the existing customers buy from W Ltd? Perhaps the company possesses specific skills or technology, or prices its products keenly. Whatever it is, the source of competitive advantage must be identified and built upon.
- Workforce: numbers and skill levels of existing employees. Why is so much work being turned away? If there is a shortage of skilled employees, new people must be trained or recruited.
- Technology: if it is a shortage of machines that is leading to so much work being turned away, then the cost of new machines should be compared with the forgone profits.

The **segmental analysis of results** recommended in the position audit should show the profits currently achieved on each of the company's existing products. Often profits can quite easily be improved by stripping out loss-making lines and shifting resources to the highest-profit products. Similar segmentation can be carried out by customer and by market. Without this information managers cannot make correct decisions about the products that the company should choose to make.

The **current budgetary control system could be improved** by calculating planning and operational variances rather than the traditional variances now reported. Line managers could then concentrate on improving operational matters for which they are genuinely responsible. The disadvantage of planning and operational variances is that too often all adverse variances are explained away as being planning errors.

The **standard costing system could be improved** by setting standards on the basis of activity-based costing (ABC) rather than any other method. This will identify the cost drivers for each process and is particularly important if the standard cost plus pricing basis is to be persevered with. A market-based pricing method would be preferable since it offers the prospect of maximising profits.

Finally, **information on current and future cash flows** must be reported regularly to managers. Companies fail because they run out of cash, not because they are unprofitable, and cash control will become important if any expansion plan is implemented. A monthly statement of current and forecast cash flows would be a valuable source of information to managers.

276 MOTOR COMPONENT MANUFACTURER

Key answer tips

The main theme of the question is 'external sources of information' for the purposes of planning and controlling business operations. Requirement (a) invites discussion of information needs, (b) invites discussion of information sources and (c) invites discussion of information systems.

(a)   Information areas

Customers – What are their needs and expectations? Are the needs changing? What is the potential for products and markets?

Competitors – Who are they? What are they doing? Can their ideas/products be copied? Size? Pricing policy? Profitability? Market share?

Legal Framework – compliance requirements to meet statutory standards e.g. safety, labelling and working conditions.

Suppliers – Information is required concerning:

- quality of supplier
- prices
- potential of new suppliers
- financial viability of suppliers

Political and environmental framework

The motor vehicle industry business will be influenced by government transport policy, vehicle emission standards and the health and safety laws concerned with production methods.

Financial and economic environment

Business activity is influenced by general level of economic activity. Inflation rates, interest rates, foreign exchange rates and the levels of imports and exports all impact upon business. All of the above issues are likely to have consequences for the company in terms of future

- business activity levels
- financial performance
- production method
- costs
- business viability
- market trends

and therefore need to be considered in the preparation of budgets – they will influence the future revenues, costs and growth of the company.

(b) **Sources**

Market research – commissioned or generally available from secondary sources.

Trade reports – magazines and conferences

Suppliers – price lists and brochures

Government reports – general reports and the occasional specific report on industrial sectors

Government statistics – economic indicators, industrial output, consumer spending, inflation rates.

Newspaper and other media reports – a great deal of this information is now available on the Internet – more accessible.

(c) **Implementation**

- data capture systems need to be developed with assigned responsibility for obtaining the information
- monitoring systems are required to ensure that new information and new information sources are identified and utilised
- ensure that the appropriate people receive the information that they require – avoid sending everyone all the data – may result in it being dismissed
- dissemination of the information via:

  company magazine

  e-mail/Internet

  occasional meetings to discuss the impact of significant issues

- may need to categorise the information as being relevant for strategic or operational decisions – that this categorisation may influence the frequency and detail required
- do the people preparing the budgets have the competence to interpret and incorporate the information provided into their estimates?
- is the information distributed in its raw form or is it modified to meet the internal users specific needs?

277 REES INVESTMENTS

Tutorial note:

Where possible points should be illustrated using examples relevant to the organisation described in the question.

(a) Decision support systems are software solutions designed to support managers making semi-structured or unstructured decisions. Such systems are best suited to situations where part of the problem is well understood, and hence can be automated, but part is not well understood and the manager will have to use judgement to come to a final decision. Many managers develop simple decision support systems using spreadsheets to provide them with an understanding of the data relevant data.

Decision support systems will usually consist of:

- A large database of information usually drawn from both internal and external sources.

- Problem exploration facilities which allow users to explore different scenarios using what-if and sensitivity analysis.

- Goal seeking and optimisation functions to allow users to determine the values of variables required to achieve a pre-determined or optimal solution.

- Graphical tools to display statistical data.

- In-built statistical, simulation and financial functions to allow users to develop relevant models quickly.

A decision support system could be useful at Rees Investments because the investment decisions are essentially semi-structured or unstructured. Hence a significant part of the problem can be understood from an analysis of data. However, Mark Rees will still be reliant upon his analysts correctly interpreting the information and making appropriate judgements. The decision support system is more likely to be successful if the current investment problems are caused by poor analysis of data rather than by poor judgement or by difficulties due to the worsening economic climate.

(b) An expert system is a software model of the knowledge, facts and reasoning of an acknowledged human expert. The expert system software usually represents knowledge as a set of inter-connected rules. These rules have usually been derived from discussions with experts as well as from observing and recording their decision making behaviour. Experts systems are usually perceived as a specialised form of a decision support system where reasoning is more important than computation. Such systems are particularly appropriate for handling situations where decisions have to be taken on incomplete information.

An expert system usually consists of:

- a knowledge base where the rules and facts are stored

- an inference engine which stores problem solving procedures to perform the reasoning

- a knowledge acquisition facility to allow the expert to enter knowledge and facts

- a knowledge presentation and explanation function to allow users to interrogate the expert system and to have the expert system's decision explained to them.

In the Rees Investments example, it would be possible to use expert system software to build an expert system of the knowledge and expertise of Mark Rees. In this way, less accomplished analysts could use his expertise to help them make their own investment decisions.

This may be particularly attractive to Mark Rees because:

- the company was successful when he used his approach

- he would be reasonably confident that analysts would be using a standard proven approach.

However, it has to be hoped that his approach is still valid in the changed economic environment and that the early success of the company was largely due to his expertise and not the favourable economic climate prevailing at that time.

278 ACCOUNTANCY TEACHING CO (DEC 2010 EXAM)

Turnover has decreased from $72.025 million in 2009 to $66.028 million in 2010, a fall of 8.3%. However, this must be assessed by taking into account the change in market conditions, since there has been a 20% decline in demand for accountancy training. Given this 20% decline in the market place, AT Co's turnover would have been expected to fall to $57.62m if it had kept in line with market conditions. Comparing AT Co's actual turnover to this, its actual turnover is 14.6% higher than expected. As such, AT Co has performed fairly well, given market conditions.

It can also be seen from the non-financial performance indicators that 20% of students in 2010 are students who have transferred over from alternative training providers. It is likely that they have transferred over because they have heard about the improved service that AT Co is providing. Hence, they are most likely the reason for the increased market share that AT Co has managed to secure in 2010.

Cost of sales

Cost of sales has decreased by 19.2% in 2010. This must be considered in relation to the decrease in turnover as well. In 2009, cost of sales represented 72.3% of turnover and in 2010 this figure was 63.7%. This is quite a substantial decrease. The reasons for it can be ascertained by, firstly, looking at the freelance staff costs.

The expected cost of sales for 2010 before any cost cuts was $47.738m assuming a consistent ratio of cost of sales to turnover. The actual cost of sales was only $42.056m, $5.682m lower. Staff costs are a substantial amount of this balance but since there was a pay freeze and the average number of employees hardly changed from year to year, the decreased costs are unlikely to be related to staff costs. The decrease is therefore most probably largely attributable to the introduction of online marking. AT Co expected the online marking system to cut costs by $4m, but it is possible that the online marking did not save as much as possible. Alternatively, the saved marking costs may have been partially counteracted by an increase in some other cost included in cost of sales.

Gross profit

As a result of the above, the gross profit margin has increased in 2010 from 27.7% to 36.3%. This is a big increase and reflects very well on management.

Indirect expenses

- Marketing costs: These have increased by 42.1% in 2010. Although this is quite significant, given all the improvements that AT Co has made to the service it is providing, it is very important that potential students are made aware of exactly what the company now offers. The increase in marketing costs has been rewarded with higher student numbers relative to the competition in 2010 and these will hopefully continue increasing next year, since many of the benefits of marketing won't be felt until the next year anyway. The increase should therefore be viewed as essential expenditure rather than a cost that needs to be reduced.

- Property costs: These have largely stayed the same in both years.

- Staff training: These costs have increased dramatically by over $2 million, a 163.9% increase. However, AT Co had identified that it had a problem with staff retention, which was leading to a lower quality service being provided to students. Also, due to the introduction of the interactive website, the electronic enrolment system and the online marking system, staff would have needed training on these areas. If AT Co had not spent this money on essential training, the quality of service would have deteriorated further and more staff would have left as they became increasingly dissatisfied with their jobs. Again, therefore, this should be seen as essential expenditure.

- Given that the number of student complaints has fallen dramatically in 2010 to 84 from 315, the staff training appears to have improved the quality of service being provided to students.

- Interactive website and the student helpline: These costs are all new this year and result from an attempt to improve the quality of service being provided and, presumably, improve pass rates. Therefore, given the increase in the pass rate for first time passes from 48% to 66% it can be said that these developments have probably contributed to this. Also, they have probably played a part in attracting new students, hence improving turnover.

- Enrolment costs have fallen dramatically by 80.9%. This huge reduction is a result of the new electronic system being introduced. This system can certainly be seen as a success, as not only has it dramatically reduced costs but it has also reduced the number of late enrolments from 297 to 106.

Net operating profit

This has fallen from $3.635m to $2.106m. On the face of it, this looks disappointing but it has to be remembered that AT Co has been operating in a difficult market in 2010. It could easily have been looking at a large loss. Going forward, staff training costs will hopefully decrease. Also, market share may increase further as word of mouth spreads about improved results and service at AT Co. This may, in turn, lead to a need for less advertising and therefore lower marketing costs.

It is also apparent that AT Co has provided the student website free of charge when really, it should have been charging a fee for this. The costs of running it are too high for the service to be provided free of charge and this has had a negative impact on net operating profit.

Note: Students would not have been expected to write all this in the time available.

Workings (Note: All workings are in $000)

(W1) **Turnover**

Decrease in turnover = $72,025 – $66,028/$72,025 = 8.3%

Expected 2010 turnover given 20% decline in market = $72,025 × 80% = $57,620
Actual 2010 turnover CF expected = $66,028 – $57,620/$57,620 = 14.6% higher

(W2) **Cost of sales**

Decrease in cost of sales = $42,056 – $52,078/$52,078 = 19.2%

Cost of sales as percentage of turnover: 2009 = $52,078/$72,025 = 72.3% 2010 = $42,056/$66,028 = 63.7%

Expected cost of sales for 2010, before costs cuts, = $66,028 × 72.3% = $47,738.

Actual cost of sales = $42,056.

Difference = $5,6823

Gross profit margin

2009: $19,947/$72,025 = 27.7%

2010: $23,972/$66,028 = 36.3%

(W3) Increase in marketing costs = $4,678 – $3,291/$3,291 = 42.1%

(W4) Increase in staff training costs = $3,396 – $1,287/$1,287 = 163.9%

(W5) Decrease in enrolment costs = $960 – 5,032/5,032 = 80.9%

(W6) Net operating profit

Decreased from $3,635 to $2,106. This is fall of 1,529/3,635 = 42.1%

ACCA marking scheme		
		Marks
Turnover		
8.3% decrease		0.5
Actual t/o 14.6% higher		0.5
Performed well CF market conditions		1
Transfer of students		1
		———
	Max. turnover	3
		———
Cost of sales		
19.2% decrease		0.5
63.7% of turnover		0.5
Online marking did not save as much as planned		1
		———
	Max. COS	2
		———
Gross profit – numbers and comment		1
Indirect expenses:		
Marketing costs		
42.1% increase		0.5
Increase necessary to reap benefits of developments		1
Benefits may take more than one year to be felt		0.5
Property costs – stayed the same		0.5
Staff training		
163.9% increase		0.5
Necessary for staff retention		1
Necessary to train staff on new website etc		1
Without training, staff would have left		1
Fewer student complaints		1
Interactive website and student helpline		
Attracted new students		1
Increase in pass rate		1
Enrolment costs		
Fall of 80.9%		0.5
Result of electronic system being introduced		1
Reduced number of late enrolments		1
		———
	Max. Indirect expenses	7
		———
Net operating profit		
Fallen to $2.106		0.5
Difficult market		1
Staff training costs should decrease in future		1
Future increase in market share		1
Lower advertising cost in future		1
Charge for website		1
		———
Max. net operating profit		3
		———
Total		**15**
		———

279 PROPOSALS FOR DIVISION X

The calculations of manager's bonus are shown in the following table.

	Year 1	Year 2	Year 3	Total
Original draft	$15,625	$13,500	Nil	$29,125
Project (i) – (W1)	$15,625	$13,250	$20,375	$49,250
Project (ii) – (W2)	Nil	Nil	$25,000	$25,000
Project (iii) – (W3)	$12,500	$16,000	$16,875	$45,375

Workings

For each 1% by which ROI exceeds 10%, the bonus is increased by 2.5% of $50,000, i.e. by $1,250.

(W1) Project (i)

	Year 1	Year 2	Year 3
PBIT	$3.0m	$2.7m	$4.4m
Asset base	$24m	$25.5m	$27m
ROI	12.5%	10.6%	16.3%
	$	$	$
Basic bonus @ 25% of salary	12,500	12,500	12,500
Additional bonus	3,125	750	7,875
Total bonus	15,625	13,250	20,375

Note:

Additional bonus Year 1 = 2.5 × $1,250 = $3,125

Additional bonus Year 2 = 0.6 × $1,250 = $750

Additional bonus Year 3 = 6.3 × $1,250 = $7,875

(W2) Project (ii)

	Year 1	Year 2	Year 3
PBIT	$2.0m	$1.7m	$6.4m
Asset base	$24m	$25m	$26m
ROI	8.3%	6.8%	24.6%
	$	$	$
Basic bonus @ 25% of salary	0	0	12,500
Additional bonus	0	0	12,500
Total bonus	0	0	25,000

Note: Additional bonus Year 3 = (ignoring the bonus cap) 14.6 × $1,250 = $18,250, but total bonus capped at 50% of $50,000 = $25,000.

(W3) Project (iii)

	Year 1	Year 2	Year 3
PBIT	$2.4m	$3.2m	$3.5m
Asset base	$24m	$25m	$26m
ROI	10.0%	12.8%	13.5%
Basic bonus @ 25% of salary	12,500	12,500	12,500
Additional bonus	0	3,500	4,375
Total bonus	12,500	16,000	16,875

Note:

Additional bonus Year 2 = 2.8 × $1,250 = $3,500

Additional bonus Year 3 = 3.5 × $1,250 = $4,375

The manager is likely to be influenced in his choice of projects by the personal rewards he can expect from them. In this case, he would favour Project (i) with total bonuses of $49,250, and Project (iii) with total bonuses of $45,375 over the three-year period. Both the first draft plan and adoption of Project (ii) are less attractive from this perspective. Moreover, this view is reinforced by the fact that most weight is likely to be given to bonuses achievable in the short term: on this basis Project (ii) is easily the least attractive, since no bonuses will arise until Year 3.

These considerations illustrate a common problem of bonus systems, namely that they may not achieve goal congruence. In the present case, Project (ii) is the most attractive from the organisation's point of view because its NPV is higher than the alternatives. However, because of its impact on the manager's own bonus Project (ii) is unlikely to be favoured. Indeed, from the manager's point of view it is the project with the lowest NPV that appears most attractive.

280 Y AND Z

(a) Return on Investment (ROI) = $\dfrac{\text{Profit}}{\text{Investment}}$

Unfortunately, both the top and the bottom of the equation can be calculated in different ways. There is no ambiguity, here. For the value of the investment, we shall use the $9.76m and the $1.26m. The profit figure, here, involves a choice – should we use the controllable income of $460,000 and $201,000 or should we use the $122,000 and $21,000 that are the net income before tax figures? If you think a question is ambiguous, you must state your assumption and choose whichever figures you think are appropriate.

One trick, here, is that whichever profit figure you choose it is expressed per month and has to be annualised as made clear in the requirement.

	Division Y	Division Z
Net income before tax ($000)		
(122 × 12 and 21 × 12)	1,464	252
Investment ($000)	÷ 9,760	÷ 1,260
ROI	15%	20%

On the basis of ROI, division Z is performing better than division Y.

Division Y's net income before tax is almost six times as much as division Z's, and its ROI does exceed the target, so division Y does increase the wealth of the shareholders to a greater extent than division Z. This is not reflected in the ROI, and indeed is a well-known flaw of the method, in that it is only a measure of relative profitability, not absolute profitability.

If the target return on capital of 12% is raised, then division Z has the greater margin of safety, whereas division Y's performance with its ROI of 15% would quickly become less and less attractive.

The net income before tax figures are very much affected by the apportioned central costs. It would be nice to know on what basis the apportionment has been made. Indeed a very convincing argument could be made that, if we are trying to judge performance in the two divisions, then we should only be looking at controllable profit as it would be unfair to judge managers on factors over which they have no control.

Division Z is relatively new compared to division Y and may still be investing heavily in growth. This may mean that there is still a lag between the investment in assets and generation of profits and this division could produce even higher returns on investment in future years. This would be expected for a service/maintenance business which is likely to require less machinery than the manufacturing operation in Division Y.

If there are unlimited funds available for investment, then both divisions earn above the target return and, provided they can find projects with similar returns to their existing projects, then they should seek additional funds. If there are limited funds available and division Z can find new projects with returns similar to its existing projects, then division Z will be the more attractive destination for funds.

	Division Y	Division Z
Controllable income ($000)		
(460 × 12 and 201 × 12	5,520	2,412
Investment ($000)	÷ 9,760	÷ 1,260
	56.6%	191.4%

The controllable income return on net assets is very much higher for Z than for Y and, compared to the ROIs calculated on the basis of net income before tax, show Z to be performing better than Y to a much greater extent. This is an indication than Z is earning its income with much less use of divisional net assets.

(b)

	Division Y $000	Division Z $000
Net income before tax	1,464.0	252.0
Imputed interest		
12% × $9.76m	1,171.2	
12% × $1.26m		151.2
	————	————
Residual income	292.8	100.8
	————	————

Division Y has a better performance on the basis of residual income, but residual income is not a useful comparator when comparing divisions of different sizes. Division Y has a bigger residual income, but so it should, as it is a much bigger division.

All in all, division Y does increase the wealth of the shareholders to a greater extent than division Z, but division Z does earn its income at a better rate than division Y.

281 OLIVER'S SALON (JUNE 09 EXAM)

(a)

Tutorial note

The safest way to harvest exam marks with financial indicators is this: calculate a ratio (0.5 marks), make a qualitative statement (1 mark) and suggest a cause or some other comment (1 mark).

Part (a) is a pure performance management question and the core of the paper. Mathematical descriptions are not performance assessments, and simply stating the % increases in numbers is not enough. Be careful to consider as wide a range of figures as possible : virtually all the numbers in the question carry marks.

Financial performance assessment

Hairdressing sales growth: Oliver's Salon has grown significantly during the two years, with an increase of 19.25% (W1). This is impressive in a mature industry like hairdressing.

The increase has come from the launch of the new male hairdressing with a significant contraction in the core female business – down 15% (W1).

Hairdressing gross margin: Oliver's hairdressing overall gross margin has reduced significantly, down from 53% to 47.2% in 2009 (W2).

There has been an increase in staff numbers for the female part of the business and this, combined with the fall in the volume of sales from female clients, has significantly damaged margins from that customer type, with a fall from 53% to 40.5% (W2).

The margins from male clients in 2009 are 63.5% which is better than that achieved in 2008 from the female clients. This is probably mainly due to faster throughput, so that despite the lower average prices charged the overall margin was still quite good.

Staff costs: The staffing levels have had to increase to accommodate the new male market and the extra levels of business. The new hairdresser for the male clients is being paid slightly more than the previously employed staff (W3). This might encourage dissatisfaction. The addition of a junior will clearly reduce the overall average wage bill but increases costs overall whilst the volume of female clients is shrinking.

Advertising spend: This has increased by 150% in the year (W4). This is probably nothing to worry about as it is likely that the launching of the new product range (males!) will have required advertising. Indeed, given the increase in sales of male hair services it is fair to say that the money was well spent.

Rent is clearly a fixed cost and administrative expenses have gone up a mere 5.5%; these costs appear under control given the overall volume of clients is well up on 2008.

Electricity costs have jumped 14.3% which seems a lot but is probably a cost which Oliver would find hard to control. Energy companies are often very large organisations where competition is rarely significant. Small businesses have little choice but to pay the going rate for energy.

Net profit: Overall net profit has worsened to 33.5% from 39% (W8). This is primarily due to the weakening gross margin and extra costs incurred for advertising. The advertising cost may not recur and so the net margin might improve next year.

Overall it is understandable that Oliver is disappointed with the financial results. With a 19.25% increase in overall sales he might have expected more net profit.

(b)

Tutorial note

The non-financial indicators candidates were asked to consider were surrounding quality and resource utilisation. The Examiner has reported that answers on quality dealt with the complaints issue well, but very few talked about the new members of staff and how their performance might be suspect. The lack of a pay rise can be de-motivating and so quality might suffer, this also needs to be picked up.

More thought is needed on resource utilisation. The male throughput per specialist was very high but this was perhaps due to the fact that male hair tends to be easier (quicker) to cut. The female situation was different, with fewer clients for more staff.

Non-financial performance

Quality: The number of complaints is up by 283% (W5) and is proportionately more frequent. This seems to be due to two main reasons. Firstly the switch away from a single gender salon has upset the existing customer base. It is possible that by trying to appeal to more customer types Oliver is failing to meet the needs of at least one group. It may be that the quality of hair services has not worsened but that the complaints are regarding the change towards a multi-gender business.

Secondly the wage rates paid to the new junior staff seem to be well below the wage rates of the existing staff (W3). This implies that they are in training and could be of poorer quality. It is stated that they are in a supporting role but if not properly supervised then mistakes could occur. This can easily lead to customer complaints.

Resource utilisation: The main resources that Oliver has are the staff and the rented property. As far as the property is concerned the asset is being used to a much higher degree with 27.8% more clients being serviced in the year (W6). However, as the overall margins are lower one might argue that just focusing solely on volume misses the point on asset utilisation.

As far as the staff usage is concerned it is a mixed scene. The female specialists are producing less per member of staff than in 2008 after the recruitment of one more staff member and a fall in volume of female clients. Each specialist served 2,000 female clients in 2008 and only 1,360 in 2009 (W9). Oliver may have been concerned with the complaints coming in and decided to do something about service levels by increasing resources for the female clients.

The specialist dealing with male clients has produced far more treatments than those serving the females. This is probably not unusual; we are told that the male customer requires only a simple service. Without comparative data we cannot say whether 3,425 customers per year is good. We also cannot say that this specialist is doing 'better' than the others. Cutting men's hair is quicker, so more output is inevitable.

Workings:

(W1) Sales growth overall is $238,500/$200,000 or +19.25%. The female hairdressing sales has though fallen by 15% ($200,000 − $170,000)/$200,000. This is entirely reflected in volume as there was no price increase in 2009 for female clients.

(W2) Gross margin overall is $106,000/$200,000 or 53% in 2008 and $112,500/238,500 or 47.2% in 2009. This can be analysed between the female and male clients:

	2008		2009	
	Female	$	Female	Male
	$		$	$
Sales	200,000		170,000	68,500
Less cost of sales:				
Hairdressing staff costs (W3)	(65,000)		(74,000)	(17,000)
Hair products – female	(29,000)		(27,000)	
Hair products – male				(8,000)
Gross profit	106,000		69,000	43,500
GP%	53%		40.5%	63.5%

(W3) Staff cost growth is $91,000/$65,000 or +40%. In absolute terms average staff costs were $65,000/4 = $16,250 in 2008.

Additional staff cost $26,000 ($91,000 − $65,000) in total for two people. The junior was paid $9,000 and so the new specialist for the male customers must have been paid $17,000

(W4) Advertising increased by $5,000/$2,000 or 150%

(W5) Number of complaints up by 46/12 or 283%. Complaints per customer visit up from 12/8,000 or 0.15% to 46/10,225 or 0.44%

(W6) Client growth is 10,225/8,000 or 27.8%

(W7) Number of female clients per specialist is 8,000/4 or 2,000 in 2008 and 6,800/5 or 1,360 in 2009. Number of male clients per specialist is 3,425 in 2009.

(W8) Net profit is $78,000/200,000 or 39% in 2008 and $80,000/238,500 or 33.5% in 2009.

ACCA marking scheme		
		Marks
(a)	Sales growth	2
	Gross margin	2
	Rent	1
	Advertising spend	1
	Staff costs	2
	Electricity	1
	Overall comment	1
		10
(b)	Quality – single gender	1
	Quality – wage levels	1
	Quality – other	1
	Resource utilisation – property	1
	Resource utilisation – staff	1
	Resource utilisation – other	1
	Maximum	5
Total		**15**

282 SQUARIZE (JUNE 2013 EXAM)

Goals and measures

Goals	Performance measures	Reason
Financial perspective		
Increase revenue	Percentage increase in total revenue	The changes have been implemented partly in an attempt to increase revenues, so it is sensible to measure the extent to which revenues have actually increased.
Increase operating profit margin	Percentage increase in operating profit	The changes have been implemented partly in an attempt to increase operating profit, so it is sensible to measure the extent to which operating profit has actually increased.
Customer perspective		
Increase customer acquisition	Total sales to new customers	The fourth change (to standalone products) was made in an attempt to attract new customers. This measure will help to assess whether the change has been successful.
Reduce loss of customers	Customer churn rate	The first three of the four changes made were made in an attempt to retain customers. This performance measure will help to assess whether the changes have been successful.

Internal business perspective

Reduce number of broadband contracts cancelled	Number of broadband contracts cancelled	This performance measure will enable Squarize to assess whether the improved broadband service has resulted in a reduction of the number of contracts cancelled.
Increase after sales service quality	Percentage of customer requests that are handled with a single call	Squarize transferred its call centre back to its home country. This measure will assess whether that has improved the service quality to customers as a result.

Learning and growth perspective

Increase call centre workers' skill levels	Number of training hours per employee	This measure will improve the likelihood of customers receiving an improved service. A better public image should result, leading to increased revenues as new customers are attracted to the business.
Increase employees' satisfaction	Percentage decrease in staff turnover	This measure will also help to improve customer service, thereby improving company image, attracting new customers and increasing revenues in the long term.

Tutorial note

Other reasonable suggestions will be equally acceptable.

ACCA marking scheme	
	Marks
Balanced scorecard	
Identifying the four perspectives	2
Each goal 0.5 marks, × 4 perspectives	2
Each performance measure, × 4 perspectives	2
Each reason 1 mark, × 4 perspectives	4
	——
Total	**10**
	——

283 BATH CO (DEC 2011 EXAM)

Tutorial note

Part (a) was not difficult and contained the easy marks, with a simple requirement to prepare a profit statement under the current transfer pricing system. Do not just produce some workings showing total profit for the company.

(a) **Profit statement**

	Division A $000	Division B $000	Company $000
Sales revenue:			
External (W1)	36,000	9,600	45,600
Inter-divisional transfers	0	6,000	
Total	36,000	15,600	45,600
Variable costs:			
External material costs (W2)	(16,000)	(1,000)	(17,000)
Inter-divisional transfers (W3)	(6,000)	0	
Labour costs (W4)	(3,600)	(3,000)	(6,600)
Total	(25,600)	(4,000)	(23,600)
Fixed costs	(7,440)	(4,400)	(11,840)
Profit	2,960	7,200	10,160

Workings ($000)

(W1) External sales

Div A: 80,000 × $450 = $36,000

Div B: 120,000 × $80 = $9,600

Div B: 80,000 × $75 = $6,000

(W2) External material costs

Div A: 80,000 × $200 = $16,000

Div B: 200,000 × $5 = $1,000

(W3) Inter-divisional transfers

Div A: 80,000 × $75 = $6,000

(W4) Labour costs

Div A: 80,000 × $45 = $3,600

Div B: 200,000 × $15 = $3,000

(b)

Tutorial note

'Optimised' means a transfer price set at a level that would make the total company profit as high as possible. In order for this to be the case, the transfer price needs to be set somewhere between Division B's marginal cost of $20 and the current market price of the fittings of $65 per set. Any price between this range would make sure that Division A bought the fittings from Division B, provided that Division A was told that it could only buy the fittings from outside the group if the price was lower than the price being charged by Division B. If Division B was allowed to sell to the external market too, then the profit could be maximised at $11,060.

Even if that escaped you, you could get to the maximum profit by having Division B selling 180,000 sets of fittings outside the group and then selling the remaining 20,000 sets of fittings to B at $75. This was a half decent attempt at the question but the reality would be, of course, that, in the real world, Division A would not want to pay $75 for the fittings if it could buy them from an external supplier for only $65. This is not, therefore, optimisation of transfer pricing, because this would require the company to have a policy of making Division A buy from B, EVEN if fittings were cheaper elsewhere and this would cause behavioural issues, with Division A's manager becoming de-motivated.

Bath Co's profit if transfer pricing is optimised

	Division A	Division B	Company
	$000	$000	$000
Sales revenue:			
External (W1)	36,000	14,400	50,400
Internal sales (W2)		1,300	
Total	36,000	15,700	50,400
Variable costs:			
External material costs (W3)	(19,900)	(1,000)	(20,900)
Inter-divisional transfers (W2)	(1,300)		
Labour costs	(3,600)	(3,000)	(6,600)
Total	(24,800)	(4,000)	(27,500)
Fixed costs	(7,440)	(4,400)	(11,840)
Profit	3,760	7,300	11,060

Note: A transfer price of $65 has been used on the assumption that the company will introduce the policy discussed in (c). Provided that the transfer price is set between the minimum of $20 (Division B's marginal cost) and $65 (the cost to Division A of buying from outside the group), the actual transfer price is irrelevant in this calculation. The overall profit of the company will be the same.

Workings ($000)

(W1) External sales

Div A: 80,000 × $450 = $36,000

Div B: 180,000 × $80 = $14,400

(W2) Internal sales/inter-divisional transfers

20,000 × $65 = $1,300

(W3) Material costs

Div A: 60,000 × $265 + (20,000 × $200) = $19,900

Div B: 200,000 × $5 = $1,000

Recommendation

Since it is in Division B's best interest to work to full capacity and the manager of Division B knows that Division A can obtain fittings for $65 per set, it should not be difficult for B to agree to sell to A at this price. A policy of negotiated transfer prices would achieve this fairly quickly.

However, the company also needs to have a policy that divisions buy internally first, where this would be in the best interests of the overall profitability of the company.

ACCA marking scheme		Marks
(a) Profit statement		
Sales revenue:		
External		1
Inter-divisional transfers		0.5
External material costs		1
Inter-divisional transfers		0.5
Labour costs		1
Fixed costs		1
Profit		1
	Maximum	6
(b) Revised profit		
External sales		1
Inter-divisional transfers		1
Material costs		2
Internal transfers (materials)		1
Labour costs		1
Fixed costs		1
Profit		1
Recommendation		1
	Maximum	9
Total		15

284 FP

Key answer tips

A tricky question on transfer pricing. In part (a) you need to ensure that all costs have been included, especially the impact of the transfer price.

(a)

	Per repair	Total cost for 500 repairs
	$	$
Parts	54	
Labour 3 hours @ $15 each	45	
Variable overhead 3 hours at $10 per hour	30	
	―――	
Marginal cost	129	64,500
Fixed overhead 3 hours at $22 per hour	66	33,000
	―――	―――
Total cost	195	97,500
Mark-up	78	39,000
	―――	―――
Selling price	273	136,500
	―――	―――

Transfers at 40% mark-up

	Sales	Service	FP
	$	$	$
	120,000	136,500	120,000
	136,500	97,500	97,500
	―――	―――	―――
Profit	(16,500)	39,000	22,500
	―――	―――	―――

Transfers at marginal cost

	Sales	Service	FP
	$	$	$
	120,000	64,500	120,000
	64,500	97,500	97,500
	―――	―――	―――
Profit	55,500	(33,000)	22,500
	―――	―――	―――

Repairs carried out by RS

	Sales	Service	FP
	$	$	$
	120,000	0	120,000
	90,000	33,000	123,000
	————	————	————
Profit	30,000	(33,000)	(3,000)
	————	————	————

(b)   (i)   Transfers at full cost plus may not be appropriate for FP because, at this price, the Sales Department can buy more cheaply from external suppliers and will not wish to purchase from the Service Department. This decision would be dysfunctional for the company as a whole as an overall loss is made.

It would also lead to any inefficiencies of the Service Department being passed on to the Sales Department which would give no incentive to control costs.

(ii)   Issues to consider include:

- Can RS guarantee the quality and reliability of the repairs?

- Is the offer by RS a short-term offer? Would the price rise in the longer term?

- Can the Service Department find other work to take up the capacity released if RS does the guarantee repairs?

- Can the Service Department find cost savings to reduce costs?

(c)   Operating the two departments as profit centres may have the following advantages:

- If managers are given autonomy to take decisions, this may lead to improved profitability owing to specialist knowledge and the ability to make decisions quickly

- If realistic targets are set which are within managers' control, then managers may be motivated to improve performance

- Head office time may be freed up to focus on strategic issues

- Profit centres may provide a training ground for senior management positions.

There could also be disadvantages as follows:

- Loss of control by head office

- Dysfunctional decision making

- Duplication of functions such as personnel and administration.

285 CTD

(a)   The current transfer price is ($40 + $20)) × 1.1 = $66.

		FD	FD	TM	TM
		$000	$000	$000	$000
Internal sales	15,000 × $66		990		
External sales	5,000 × $80		400		
	15,000 × $500				7,500
			———		———
			1,390		7,500
Production – variable costs	20,000 × $40	(800)			
	15,000 × $366			(5,490)	
Selling/distribution – variable costs	5,000 × $4	(20)			
	15,000 × $25			(375)	
		———		———	
		(820)		(5,865)	
			———		———
			570		1,635
Production overheads	20,000 × $20	(400)			
	15,000 × $60				(900)
Administration overheads	20,000 × $4	(80)			
	15,000 × $25				(375)
		———		———	
Net profit			90		360
Interest charge	$750,000\$1,500,000 × 12%		(90)		(180)
			———		———
Residual income (RI)			0		180
			———		———
Target RI			85		105
Bonus	$180,000 × 5%		0		9

Implications of the current reward system

While the TM manager has received a bonus and presumably will be pleased about it, the FD manager has received nothing. This will not be very motivating and may lead to problems within the division as a whole, such as inefficiency, staff turnover and unreliability. Since the TM division relies so completely on the FD division, this situation is clearly unacceptable.

Key answer tips

The calculations involved in this question are very straightforward, but don't be deceived – the real thrust of this question is to make sure that you both understand the principles of different transfer pricing methods, and can apply them to a situation.

(b) (i) In order to achieve a 5% bonus, the manager of TM division will be willing to accept a decrease in residual income of $(180,000 – 105,000) = $75,000. This is an increase in transfer price of the 15,000 units transferred of $75,000/15,000 = $5. Thus the transfer price would rise to $66 + $5 = $71.

(ii) In order to achieve a 5% bonus, the manager of FD division will want an increase in residual income of $85,000. This is an increase in transfer price of the 15,000 units transferred of $85,000/15,000 = $5.67. Thus the transfer price would have to rise to $66 + $5.67 = $71.67.

286 WASH CO (DEC 2012 EXAM)

(a) **Transfer price using ABC**

Machine set up costs: driver = number of production runs.

30 + 12 = 42.

Therefore cost per set up = $306,435/42 = $7,296.07

Machine maintenance costs: driver = machine hours: 11,850 (S= 6,400; R=5,450) $415,105/11,850 = $35.03

Ordering costs: driver = number of purchase orders

82 + 64 = 146.

Therefore cost per order = $11,680/146 = $80

Delivery costs: driver = number of deliveries.

64 + 80 = 144.

Therefore cost per delivery = $144,400/144 = $1,002.78

Allocation of overheads to each product:

	Product S	Product R	Total
	$	$	$
Machine set-up costs	218,882	87,553	306,435
Machine maintenance costs	224,192	190,913	415,106
Ordering costs	6,560	5,120	11,680
Delivery costs	64,178	80,222	144,400
Total overheads allocated	513,812	363,808	877,620
Number of units produced	3,200	5,450	8,650

	$	$
Overhead cost per unit	160.57	66.75
Transfer price per unit:		
Materials cost	117	95
Labour cost	6	9
Overhead costs	160.57	66.75
Total cost	283.57	170.75
Add 10% mark up	28.36	17.08
Transfer price under ABC	311.93	187.83

(b) **(i)** **ABC monthly profit**

Using ABC transfer price from part (b):

Assembly division	Product S	Product R	Total
Production and sales	3,200	5,450	
	$	$	
10% mark up	28.36	17.08	
Profit	90,752	93,086	183,838

Retail division	Product S	Product R	Total
Production and sales	3,200	5,450	
	$	$	
Selling price	320	260	
Cost price	(311.93)	(187.83)	
Profit per unit	8.07	72.17	
Total profit	25,824	393,327	419,151

(ii) **Discussion**

From the various profit figures for the two bases of allocating overheads, various observations can be made.

- There is obviously very little difference between the TOTAL profits of each division whichever method is used. It is the reallocation of profits from R to S or S to R that is the important factor in this situation, given that the retail division wants to reduce prices but increase sales volumes for R.

- As regards the assembly division, when labour hours are used to allocate overheads, there is a big difference between the profits that each of the two products makes. When ABC is used, this difference becomes much smaller.

- As regards the retail division, when labour hours are used, product S generates 76% of the profit. When this method of allocation is then changed so that ABC is used, the main share of the profit then moves to product R. In the case of ABC, the profit moves so much to R that S only generates a profit per unit of $8.07 for the retail division, which is very low for a selling price of $320.

- From the assembly division manager's point of view, any change that results in increased sales of either R or S to the retail division would be a good thing for the assembly division, given that both products are profitable. However, the assembly division's manager would probably oppose the implementation of ABC to achieve this end result because firstly, it is complex and secondly, it is unnecessary here. The aim of this exercise is to set more accurate transfer prices for R and S, which should mean a reduction in R's transfer price and an increase in S's, according to the information given. This would then have the effect of enabling the retail division to lower its price for R and increase sales volumes. This goal is achieved simply by changing the basis of overhead absorption from labour hours to machine hours, without the need for activity based costing.

- The retail manager's view is likely to be exactly the same. If the basis of absorption is changed so that a lower transfer price is charged, the retail division could potentially reduce their selling price for R, provided that the increased sales volumes more than make up for the reduced margin. There is no need to get into the complexities of ABC when the results it produces are not that different.

ACCA marking scheme		Marks
(a) Transfer price using ABC		
Identify cost drivers		1
Cost driver rates		2
Total overheads allocated		2
Overhead cost per unit		1
Total cost per unit		1
Transfer price per unit		1
		───
	Maximum	8
		───
(b) ABC profit calculation and discussion		
(i) Profit		3
(ii) 1 mark per valid comment		Max 4
		───
	Maximum	7
		───
Total		15
		───

287   BISCUITS AND CAKES (JUNE 2012 EXAM)

(a)

Tutorial note

*Big trap to avoid here: the question requires the calculation of an **annualised** return on investment and residual income for two divisions. In order to annualise the ROI and RI, you must multiply the monthly net profit figure by 12.*

Return on investment = net profit/net assets

Division B: $311,000 × 12/$23,200,000 = 16.09%;

Division C: $292,000 × 12/$22,600,000 = 15.5%

(b)   **Residual income**

	B	C
	$000	$000
Net profit	3,732	3,504
Less: imputed interest charge		
$22.6 × 10%		(2,260)
$23.2m × 10%	(2,320)	
	———	———
Residual income	1,412	1,244
	———	———

(c)

Tutorial note

In order to discuss the performance of the divisions well, you must recalculate the ROI and/or RI using controllable profit. Weaker answers would perform other calculations on the two divisions and give some general commentary, even though the question asked for a discussion 'using both ROI and RI'.

ROI

Divisions B and C have ROIs of 16.09% and 15.5% respectively, compared to the target of 20%. This suggests that the divisions have not performed well, but the reason for this is that now, uncontrollable head office costs are being taken into effect before calculating the ROI. The target ROI has not been reduced to reflect the change in the method being used to calculate it. Using the old method, ROI would have been as follows:

B: ($311,000 + $155,000) × 12/$23.2m = 24.1%

C: ($292,000 + $180,000) × 12/$22.6m = 25.06%

From this it can be seen that both divisions have actually improved their performance, rather than it having become worse.

RI

From the residual income figures, it can clearly be seen that both Division B and C have performed well, with healthy RI figures of $1.4m and $1.2m respectively, even when using net profit rather than controllable profit as bases for the calculations. The cost of capital of the company is significantly lower than the target return on investment that the company seeks, making the residual income figure show a more positive position.

(d)   Division B's ROI with investment

Depreciation = 2,120,000 – 200,000/48 months = $40,000 per month.

Net profit for July = 311k + ($600k × 8.5%) – $40k = $322k

Annualised net profit: $322k × 12 = $3,864k.

Opening net assets after investment = $23,200k + $2,120 = $25,320k.

ROI = $3,864k/25,320k = 15.26%

Therefore, Division B will not proceed with the investment, since it will cause a decrease in its ROI.

If RI is calculated with the investment, the result is as follows:

	B
	$000
	3,864
Less: imputed interest charge $25.32m at 10%	(2,532)
Residual income	1,332

This calculation shows that, if the investment is undertaken, RI is actually higher than without the investment. The suggestion is, therefore, that the investment should have been proceeded with. So, use of ROI has resulted in behaviour by Division B's manager that is not good for the company as a whole.

ACCA marking scheme		Marks
(a)	ROI/RI calculations	
	ROI for B	1
	ROI for C	1
	Maximum	2
(b)	ROI/RI discussion	
	RI for B	1.5
	RI for C	1.5
	Maximum	3

(c)	Discussion		
	ROI discussion		2
	RI discussion		2
	Extra ROI calculation under old method		1
	Valid conclusion drawn		1
		Maximum	5
(d)	ROI/RI after investment		
	ROI calculation		2
	RI calculation		1
	Comments and conclusion		2
		Maximum	5
Total			**15**

288 PUBLIC SECTOR ORGANISATION

Budget preparation

It would be in line with the principles of modern management if the department manager was encouraged to participate more in setting the budget. In this way, he would be more likely to show commitment to the organisational goals in general and the budget in particular. He is closer to the activity for which the budget is prepared, and so the relevance and accuracy of the budget should be improved. This involvement should extend also to discussion of the form and frequency of the reporting which is to take place for his/her department.

Activity volume

The volume of visits undertaken is 20% greater than that budgeted. It is inappropriate to compare the actual costs of visiting 12,000 clients with a budget for 10,000 clients. Costs such as wages, travel expenses and consumables would be expected to be higher than the fixed budget in these circumstances.

One way to deal with this is to adjust, or flex, the budget to acknowledge the cost implications of the higher number of visits, or to be aware of it when making any comparison. If a factor of 1.20 is applied to the overall wages budget for permanent and casual staff (i.e. on the assumption that it is a variable cost), the flexed budget $5,040 ($4,200 × 1.2) is greater than the actual cost of $4,900. Taking a similar approach to travel expenses and consumables expenses:

- actual travel expenses are exactly in line with the flexed budget (1,500 × 1.20), but

- the consumables costs seem to be highly overspent compared to the flexed budget (4,000 × 1.2).

To circulate a report as originally constructed seems to highlight and publicise some invalid comparisons from which inappropriate conclusions may be drawn. It is recommended that for cost control purposes, a report is prepared which compares actual spending with a flexed budget based on the actual activity. This would require an estimate of the variable, fixed and semi-variable nature of the cost items.

Controllability

It is possible to question whether all the costs shown need to feature in the report. For example, the allocated administrative costs and equipment depreciation are book entries that do not directly affect the department and are not likely to be controllable by employees of the department. There are, therefore, adverse variances on the report contributing to the overall overspend that are not the responsibility of the departmental manager. The difference between actual and budgeted cost of administration serves no useful purpose in this report, because the manager can take no action to influence this directly. The only justification to include this is if the manager can bring about some pressure to reduce this spending by someone else.

It may be unwise to adopt the guide of a 5% deviation to judge variances. The key is whether a cost is out of control and can be corrected by managerial action. Also, 5% of some values can be significant whilst on others 5% of the total cost might be of little consequence.

Funding allocation

The Director is correct in pointing out that 'the department must live within its funding allocation'. However, it is not like a commercial organisation where more output can result in more revenue and hence more money to spend. Increased funding will only be achieved if this organisation and the department is allocated more funds as a result of national or local government decisions to support an increase in services.

It would be appropriate for the funding allocation to be compared with the flexible budget (based on actual activity) to encourage the managers to be aware of and live within the budget allocation. Ways can always be found to spend more money, and so authority structures must be in place to ensure that requests to spend have been budgeted and appropriately funded. Hence the organisational arrangements which authorised the increased visits would be examined.

The nature of the activity for which the budget is being developed should not be lost sight of. It is more complex to deal with budget decisions related to the welfare needs of society than those for a typical manufacturing firm. There are no clear input-output relationships in the former, and hence it is difficult to judge what is justifiable spending for the department compared with other departments and public sector organisations.

Other aspects

One possible outcome from discussion over the appropriate form of report would be the use of non-financial measures. The total staff hours worked, client satisfaction and size of the potential client population are all examples of extensions to the reporting procedure which would help to place the results in context.

The style of the approach adopted by the Director may show some lack of behavioural insight. The despatch of a memo to deal with a prototype report may result in lower staff morale and increased tension in the Homecare department. This may lead to inappropriate future decisions on spending and budget 'game playing' within the department. It may, of course, be a conscious decision of the Director to place the manager in the position of having to reduce spending to the allocated level.

Although this is the first month's report, in the future it may be helpful to use an additional column of the report to show the year-to-date figures. This would help to identify trends and assist discussion of whether costs are being controlled over the longer term. To show future results for only one month may be insufficient; for example, the repairs to equipment may not follow a regular pattern and this would be revealed if cumulative data existed.

289 WOODSIDE CHARITY (JUNE 07 EXAM)

(a) Discussion of performance of Woodside Charity

In a year which saw fundraising fall $80,000 short of the target level, costs were over budget in all areas of activity except overnight shelter provision. The budget provided for a surplus of $98,750, but the actual figures for the year show a shortfall of $16,980.

Free meals provision cost $12,750 (14%) more than budgeted. Most of the variance (69%) was due to providing more meals than budgeted, although $4,000 of it was due to an increase in the average cost per meal.

Variable cost of overnight shelter provision was $26,620 (11%) less than budgeted. $31,000 was saved because usage of the service was below budget, but an adverse variance of $4,380 arose because of an increase in the average unit cost of provision.

Variable advice centre costs were $16,600 (37%) above budget. This was due to increased usage of the service, which was 17% up on budget from 3,000 to 3,500 sessions, and to an increase in the average cost of provision, which rose by 17% from $15 to $17.60 per session.

Fixed costs of administration and centre maintenance were $18,000 (28%) above budget and the costs of campaigning and advertising were $15,000 (10%) above budget.

While investigation of some of the variances in the reconciliation statement below may be useful in controlling further cost increases, the Woodside charity appears to have more than achieved its objectives in terms of providing free meals and advice. The lower usage of overnight shelter could lead to transfer of resources from this area in the next budget to the services that are more in demand. The reasons for the lower usage of overnight shelter are not known, but the relationship between the provision of effective advice and the usage of overnight shelter could be investigated.

(b)

Financial management and control in a not-for-profit organisation (NFPO) such as the Woodside charity must recognise that the primary objectives of these organisations are essentially non-financial. Here, these objectives relate to helping the homeless and because the charity has no profit-related objective, financial management and control must focus on providing value for money. This means that resources must be found economically in order to keep input costs as low as possible; that these resources must be used as efficiently as possible in providing the services offered by the charity; and that the charity must devise and use effective methods to meet its objectives. Financial objectives could relate to the need to obtain funding for offered services and to the need to control costs in providing these services.

Preparing budgets

The nature of the activities of a NFPO can make it difficult to forecast levels of activity. In the case of the Woodside charity, homeless people seeking free meals would be given them, and more food would be prepared if necessary, regardless of the budgeted provision for a given week or month. The level of activity is driven here by the needs of the homeless, and although financial planning may produce weekly or monthly budgets that consider seasonal trends, a high degree of flexibility may be needed to respond to unpredictable demand. This was recognised by the charity by budgeting for a fundraising surplus for unexpected costs.

It is likely that forecasting cost per unit of service in a NFPO can be done with more precision if the unit of service is small and the service is repetitive or routine, and this is true for the Woodside charity. It is unlikely, though, that a detailed analysis of costs has been carried out along these lines, and more likely that an incremental budget approach has been used on a total basis for each service provided. It depends on the financial skills and knowledge available to the charity from its three full-time staff and team of volunteers.

Controlling costs

Because of the need for economy and efficiency, this is a key area of financial management and control for a NFPO. The costs of some inputs can be minimised at the point of buying, for example the Woodside charity can be economical when buying food, drink, crockery, blankets, cleaning materials and so on. The costs of other inputs can be minimised at the point of use, for example the Woodside charity can encourage economy in the use of heating, lighting, water consumption, telephone usage and postage. In an organisation staffed mainly by volunteers with an unpredictable clientele, cost control is going to depend to a large extent on the way in which responsibility and authority are delegated.

Collecting information

Cost control is not possible without collecting regularly information on costs incurred, as well as storing and processing this information. In the Woodside charity, provision has been made in the budget for fixed administration costs and the administration duties must hopefully relate in part to this collecting of costing information. Without it, budgeting and financial reporting would not be possible. Annual accounts would be needed in order to retain charitable status and to show providers of funds that their donations were being used to their best effect.

Meeting objectives

A NFPO organisation must be able to determine and demonstrate whether it is meeting its declared objectives and so needs to develop measures to do this. This can be far from easy. The analysis of the performance of the Woodside charity over the last year shows that it may be possible to measure objective attainment quantitatively, i.e. in terms of number of free meals served, number of bed-nights used and number of advice sessions given. Presumably, objectives are being met to a greater extent if more units of service are being provided, and so the adverse usage variances for free meals and advice sessions can in fact be used to show that the charity is meeting a growing need.

The meaning of quantitative measures of service provision may not be clear, however. For example, the lower usage of bed-nights could be attributed to the effective provision of advice to the homeless on finding housing and financial aid, and so may also be seen as a success. It could also be due to dissatisfaction amongst the homeless with the accommodation offered by the shelter. In a similar vein, the higher than budget number of advice sessions may be due to repeat visits by homeless people who were not given adequate advice on their first visit, rather than to an increase in the number of people needing advice. Qualitative measures of objective attainment will therefore be needed in addition to, or to supplement, quantitative ones.

Fundamentals Level – Skills Module

Performance Management

Specimen Exam applicable from
December 2014

Time allowed

Reading and planning: 15 minutes
Writing: 3 hours

This paper is divided into two sections:

Section A – ALL TWENTY questions are compulsory and MUST be
attempted

Section B – ALL FIVE questions are compulsory and MUST be
attempted

Formulae Sheet is on page 12.

Do NOT open this paper until instructed by the supervisor.

**During reading and planning time only the question paper may
be annotated. You must NOT write in your answer booklet until
instructed by the supervisor.**

This question paper must not be removed from the examination hall.

The Association of Chartered Certified Accountants

Section A – ALL TWENTY questions are compulsory and MUST be attempted

Please use the space provided on the inside cover of the Candidate Answer Booklet to indicate your chosen answer to each multiple choice question.
Each question is worth 2 marks.

1 The following statements have been made about different types of standards in standard costing systems:

(1) Basic standards provide the best basis for budgeting because they represent an achievable level of productivity.
(2) Ideal standards are short-term targets and useful for day-to-day control purposes.

Which of the above statements is/are true?

A 1 only
B 2 only
C Neither 1 nor 2
D Both 1 and 2

2 The following statements have been made about management information systems:

(1) They are designed to report on existing operations
(2) They have an external focus

Which of the above statements is/are true?

A 1 only
B 2 only
C Neither 1 nor 2
D Both 1 and 2

3 The following statements have been made about zero based budgeting:

(1) Employees will focus on eliminating wasteful expenditure
(2) Short-term benefits could be emphasised over long-term benefits

Which of the above statements is/are true?

A 1 only
B 2 only
C Neither 1 nor 2
D Both 1 and 2

4 The following statements have been made about changing budgetary systems:

(1) The costs of implementation may outweigh the benefits
(2) Employees will always welcome any new system which improves planning and control within the organisation

Which of the above statements is/are true?

A 1 only
B 2 only
C Neither 1 nor 2
D Both 1 and 2

5 Tech World is a company which manufactures mobile phone handsets. From its past experiences, Tech World has realised that whenever a new design engineer is employed, there is a learning curve with a 75% learning rate which exists for the first 15 jobs.

A new design engineer has just completed his first job in five hours.

Note: At the learning rate of 75%, the learning factor (b) is equal to –0·415.

How long would it take the design engineer to complete the sixth job?

A 2·377 hours
B 1·442 hours
C 2·564 hours
D 5 hours

6 The following are types of management accounting techniques:

(i)   Flow cost accounting
(ii) Input/output analysis
(iii) Life-cycle costing
(iv) Activity based costing

Which of the above techniques could be used by a company to account for its environmental costs?

A (i) only
B (i) and (ii) only
C (i), (ii) and (iii) only
D All of the above

7 A company makes a single product which it sells for $2 per unit.

Fixed costs are $13,000 per month.

The contribution/sales ratio is 40%.

Sales revenue is $62,500.

What is the margin of safety (in units)?

A 15,000
B 16,250
C 30,000
D 31,250

8 The following statements have been made about the balanced scorecard:

(1) It focuses solely on non-financial performance measures
(2) It looks at both internal and external matters concerning the organisation

Which of the above statements is/are true?

A 1 only
B 2 only
C Neither 1 nor 2
D Both 1 and 2

9   A company manufactures a product which requires four hours per unit of machine time. Machine time is a bottleneck resource as there are only ten machines which are available for 12 hours per day, five days per week. The product has a selling price of $130 per unit, direct material costs of $50 per unit, labour costs of $40 per unit and factory overhead costs of $20 per unit. These costs are based on weekly production and sales of 150 units.

What is the throughput accounting ratio (to 2 decimal places)?

A   1·33
B   2·00
C   0·75
D   0·31

10 S Company is a manufacturer of multiple products and uses target costing. It has been noted that Product P currently has a target cost gap and the company wishes to close this gap.

Which of the following may be used to close the target cost gap for product P?

A   Use overtime to complete work ahead of schedule
B   Substitute current raw materials with cheaper versions
C   Raise the selling price of P
D   Negotiate cheaper rent for S Company's premises

11 The following are all types of costs associated with management information.

(i)   Use of bar coding and scanners
(ii) Payroll department's processing of personnel costs
(iii) Completion of timesheets by employees

Which of the above are examples of direct data capture costs?

A   (i) only
B   (i) and (ii) only
C   (i) and (iii) only
D   All of the above

12 A company has entered two different new markets.

In market A, it is initially charging low prices so as to gain rapid market share while demand is relatively elastic.

In market B, it is initially charging high prices so as to earn maximum profits while demand is relatively inelastic.

Which price strategy is the company using in each market?

A   Penetration pricing in market A and price skimming in market B
B   Price discrimination in market A and penetration pricing in market B
C   Price skimming in market A and penetration pricing in market B
D   Price skimming in market A and price discrimination in market B

13 Highfly Co manufactures two products, X and Y, and any quantities produced can be sold for $60 per unit and $25 per unit respectively.

Variable costs per unit of the two products are as follows:

	Product X	Product Y
	$	$
Materials (at $5 per kg)	15	5
Labour (at $6 per hour)	24	3
Other variable costs	6	5
Total	45	13

Next month, only 4,200 kg of material and 3,000 labour hours will be available. The company aims to maximise its profits each month.

The company wants to use the linear programming model to establish an optimum production plan. The model considers 'x' to be number of units of product X and 'y' to be the number of units of product Y.

Which of the following objective functions and constraint statements (relating to material and labour respectively) is correct?

	Objective function	Material constraint	Labour constraint
A	60x + 25y	3x + y ≤ 4,200	4x + 0·5y ≤ 3,000
B	15x + 12y	3x + y ≥ 4,200	4x + 0·5y ≥ 3,000
C	15x + 12y	3x + y ≤ 4,200	4x + 0·5y ≤ 3,000
D	60x + 25y	3x + y ≥ 4,200	4x + 0·5y ≥ 3,000

14 The following are some of the areas which require control within a division:

(i) Generation of revenues
(ii) Investment in non-current assets
(iii) Investment in working capital
(iv) Apportioned head office costs

Which of the above does the manager have control over in an investment centre?

A (i), (ii) and (iii) only
B (ii), (iii) and (iv) only
C (i), (ii) and (iv) only
D All of the above

15 A company has received a special order for which it is considering the use of material B which it has held in its inventory for some time. This inventory of 945 kg was bought at $4·50 per kg. The special order requires 1,500 kg of material B. If the inventory is not used for this order, it would be sold for $2·75 per kg. The current price of material B is $4·25 per kg.

What is the total relevant cost of material B for the special order?

A $4,957·50
B $6,375
C $4,125
D $6,611·25

16 To produce 19 litres of product X, a standard input mix of 8 litres of chemical A and 12 litres of chemical B is required.

Chemical A has a standard cost of $20 per litre and chemical B has a standard cost of $25 per litre.

During September, the actual results showed that 1,850 litres of product X were produced, using a total input of 900 litres of chemical A and 1,100 litres of chemical B (2,000 litres in total).

The actual costs of chemicals A and B were at the standard cost of $20 and $25 per litre respectively.

It was expected that an actual input of 2,000 litres would yield an output of 1,900 litres (95%). The actual yield for September was only 1,850 litres, which was 50 litres less than expected.

For the total materials mix variance and total materials yield variance, was there a favourable or adverse result in September?

A The total mix variance was adverse and the total yield variance was favourable
B The total mix variance was favourable and the total yield variance was adverse
C Both variances were adverse
D Both variances were favourable

17 The following are all types of control within an organisation:

(i) Logical access controls
(ii) Database controls
(iii) Hierarchical passwords
(iv) Range checks

Which of the above controls help to ensure the security of highly confidential information?

A (i) and (ii) only
B (i) and (iii) only
C (i), (ii) and (iii) only
D All of the above

18 A business makes two components which it uses to produce one of its products. Details are:

Per unit information:	Component A $	Component B $
Buy in price	14	17
Material	2	5
Labour	4	6
Variable overheads	6	7
General fixed overheads	4	3
Total absorption cost	16	21

The business wishes to maximise contribution and is considering whether to continue making the components internally or buy in from outside.

Which components should the company buy in from outside in order to maximise its contribution?

A A only
B B only
C Both A and B
D Neither A nor B

19 The following costs arise in relation to production of a new product:

(i) Research and development costs
(ii) Design costs
(iii) Testing costs
(iv) Advertising costs
(v) Production costs

In calculating the lifetime costs of the product, which of the above items would be EXCLUDED?

A (i), (ii), and (iii) only
B (ii) and (iii) only
C (iv) and (v) only
D None of the above

20 The selling price of Product X is set at $550 for each unit and sales for the coming year are expected to be 800 units. A return of 30% on the investment of $500,000 in Product X will be required in the coming year.

What is the target cost for each unit of Product X?

A $385
B $165
C $187·50
D $362·50

(40 marks)

1   Brace Co is split into two divisions, A and B, each with their own cost and revenue streams. Each of them is managed by a divisional manager who has the power to make all investment decisions within the division. The cost of capital for both divisions is 12%. Historically, investment decisions have been made by calculating the return on investment (ROI) of any opportunities and at present, the return on investment of each division is 16%.

A new manager who has recently been appointed in division A has argued that using residual income to make investment decisions would result in 'better goal congruence' throughout the company.

Each division is currently considering the following separate investments:

	Division A	Division B
Capital required for investment	$82·8 million	$40·6 million
Sales generated by investment	$44·6 million	$21·8 million
Net profit margin	28%	33%

Required:

(a) **Calculate the return on investment for each of the two divisions.**   (2 marks)

(b) **Calculate the residual income for each of the two divisions.**   (4 marks)

(c) **Comment on the results, taking into consideration the manager's views about residual income.**   (4 marks)

(10 marks)

2   Cement Co is a company specialising in the manufacture of cement, a product used in the building industry. The company has found that when weather conditions are good, the demand for cement increases since more building work is able to take place. Cement Co is now trying to work out the level of cement production for the coming year in order to maximise profits. The company has received the following estimates about the probable weather conditions and corresponding demand levels for the coming year:

Weather	Probability	Demand
Good	25%	350,000 bags
Average	45%	280,000 bags
Poor	30%	200,000 bags

Each bag of cement sells for $9 and costs $4 to make. If cement is unsold at the end of the year, it has to be disposed of at a cost of $0·50 per bag. Cement Co has decided to produce at one of the three levels of production to match forecast demand. It now has to decide which level of cement production to select.

Required:

(a) **Construct a pay-off table to show all the possible profit outcomes.**   (8 marks)

(b) **Determine the level of cement production the company should choose, based on the decision rule of maximin. Show your calculations clearly and justify your decision.**   (2 marks)

(10 marks)

3 Brick by Brick (BBB) is a business which provides a range of building services to the public. Recently they have been asked to quote for garage conversions (GC) and extensions to properties (EX) and have found that they are winning fewer GC contracts than expected.

BBB has a policy to price all jobs at budgeted total cost plus 50%. Overheads are currently absorbed on a labour hour basis, resulting in a budgeted total cost of $11,000 for each GC and $20,500 for each EX. Consequently, the products are priced at $16,500 and $30,750 respectively.

The company is considering moving to an activity based cost approach. You are provided with the following data:

Overhead category	Annual overheads $	Activity driver	Total number of activities per year
Supervisors	90,000	Site visits	500
Planners	70,000	Planning documents	250
Property related	240,000	Labour hours	40,000
Total	400,000		

A typical GC costs $3,500 in materials and takes 300 labour hours to complete. A GC requires only one site visit by a supervisor and needs only one planning document to be raised. The typical EX costs $8,000 in materials and takes 500 hours to complete. An EX requires six site visits and five planning documents. In all cases, labour is paid $15 per hour.

Required:

(a) Calculate the cost and the quoted price of a GC and an EX using activity based costing (ABC).   (5 marks)

(b) Assume that the cost of a GC falls by approximately 7% and the cost of an EX rises by approximately 2% as a result of a change to ABC.

Required:

Suggest possible pricing strategies for the two products which BBB sells and suggest one reason other than high prices for the current poor sales of the GC.   (5 marks)

(10 marks)

4 Thatcher International Park (TIP) is a theme park and has for many years been a successful business, which has traded profitably. About three years ago, the directors decided to capitalise on their success and as a result they reduced the expenditure made on new thrill rides, reduced routine maintenance where possible (deciding instead to repair equipment when it broke down) and made a commitment to regularly increase admission prices. Once an admission price is paid, customers can use any of the facilities and rides for free. These steps increased profits considerably, enabling good dividends to be paid to the owners and bonuses to the directors.

The last two years of financial results are as follows:

	2011 $'000	2012 $'000
Sales	5,250	5,320
Less expenses:		
Wages	2,500	2,200
Maintenance – routine	80	70
Repairs	260	320
Directors' salaries	150	160
Directors' bonuses	15	18
Other costs (including depreciation)	1,200	1,180
Net profit	1,045	1,372

Other information

	2011	2012
Book value of assets at start of year ($'000)	13,000	12,000
Dividend paid ($'000)	500	650
Number of visitors	150,000	140,000

TIP operates in a country where the average rate of inflation is around 1% per annum.

Required:

Assess the financial performance of TIP using the information given above.

Note: There are 5 marks available for calculations and 10 marks available for discussion.

(15 marks)

5 Truffle Co makes high quality, hand-made chocolate truffles which it sells to a local retailer. All chocolates are made in batches of 16, to fit the standard boxes supplied by the retailer. The standard cost of labour for each batch is $6·00 and the standard labour time for each batch is half an hour. In November, Truffle Co had budgeted production of 24,000 batches; actual production was only 20,500 batches. 12,000 labour hours were used to complete the work and there was no idle time. All workers were paid for their actual hours worked. The actual total labour cost for November was $136,800. The production manager at Truffle Co has no input into the budgeting process.

At the end of October, the managing director decided to hold a meeting and offer staff the choice of either accepting a 5% pay cut or facing a certain number of redundancies. All staff subsequently agreed to accept the 5% pay cut with immediate effect. At the same time, the retailer requested that the truffles be made slightly softer. This change was implemented immediately and made the chocolates more difficult to shape. When recipe changes such as these are made, it takes time before the workers become used to working with the new ingredient mix, making the process 20% slower for at least the first month of the new operation.

The standard costing system is only updated once a year in June and no changes are ever made to the system outside of this.

Required:

(a) Calculate the following variances for Truffle Co:

(i)   Labour rate planning variance
(ii) Labour rate operational variance
(iii) Labour efficiency planning variance
(iv) Labour efficiency operational variance   (8 marks)

(b) Assess the performance of the production manager for the month of November.   (7 marks)

(15 marks)

Formulae Sheet

Learning curve

$$Y = ax^b$$

Where Y = cumulative average time per unit to produce x units

a = the time taken for the first unit of output

x = the cumulative number of units produced

b = the index of learning (log LR/log2)

LR = the learning rate as a decimal

Demand curve

$$P = a - bQ$$

$$b = \frac{\text{change in price}}{\text{change in quantity}}$$

a = price when $Q = 0$

$$MR = a - 2bQ$$

End of Question Paper

Answers

Section A

1   C

2   A

3   D

4   A

5   B

$Y = ax^b$
Average time for six jobs: $5 \times 6^{-0.415} = 2.377$ hours
Total time required for six jobs = 6×2.377 hours = 14.262 hours
Average time for five jobs: $5 \times 5^{-0.415} = 2.564$ hours
Total time required for five jobs = 5×2.564 hours = 12.820 hours
Time required to perform the 6th job = Total time required for six jobs – total time required for five jobs.
Therefore, time required to perform the 6th job = 14.262 hours – 12.820 hours = 1.442 hours

6   D

7   A

Sales = $62,500
Break even sales = $13,000/0.4 = $32,500
Margin of safety (sales revenue) = $30,000
Margin of safety (units) $30,000/$2 = 15,000 units.

8   B

9   A

Return per factory hour = ($130 – $50)/4 hours = $20
Factory costs per hour = $20 + $40/4 = $15
TAR = $20/$15 = 1.33

10 B

11 C

12 A

13 C

Contribution for X = $15 ($60 – $45)
Contribution for Y = $12 ($25 – $13)
Objective function = 15x + 12y
Constraints:
Material = 3x + y ≤ 4,200 (as X uses 3 kgs of material (15/5), Y uses 1 kg (5/5))
Labour = 4x + 0.5y ≤ 3,000 (as X uses 4 labour hrs (24/6), Y uses 0.5 hrs (3/6))

14 A

15 A

Cost of the quantity to be bought = (1,500 − 945) x $4·25 = $2,358·75
Opportunity cost of quantity in hand = 945 x $2·75 = $2,598·75
Total relevant cost = $4,957·50

16 B

Materials	AM		(w1) SM		(w2) SM	
	AQ	SP	AQ	SP	SQ	SP
A	900	18,000	800	16,000	779	15,580
B	1,100	27,500	1,200	30,000	1,168	29,200
Total		T1 = 45,500		T2 = 46,000		T3 = 44,780

SM: A = 0·4 and B = 0·6

(w1) AQSM: A = 0·4 x 2,000 = 800 litres; B = 0·6 x 2,000 = 1,200 litres

(w2) SQSM: A = 0·4 x 1,947 = 779 litres; B = 0·6 x 1,947 = 1,168 litres

Actual production of 1,850 litres requires an input of 1,947 litres (1,850 x 0·95) in total of A and B. Therefore the SQ = 1,947 litres.

The Mix Variance is given by: T2 − T1 = $500 Favourable
The Yield Variance is given by: T3 − T2 = $1,220 Adverse

17 C

18 B

The marginal cost of making A is $12 per unit and of making B is $18 per unit. It is the marginal cost which is the relevant cost for the make or buy decision since the fixed costs will be incurred anyway. Therefore, it is cheaper to make A ($12 marginal cost CF $14 buy in cost) but it is cheaper to buy in B ($17 buy in cost CF $18 make cost).

19 D

20 D

Return: $500,000 x 30% = $150,000
Total sales revenue: $550 x 800 = $440,000
Therefore total cost = $440,000 − $150,000 = $290,000
Unit cost = $290,000/800 = $362·50

Section B

1   Brace Co

(a) Return on investment

Division A
Net profit = $44·6m x 28% = $12·488m
ROI = $12·488m/$82·8m = 15·08%

Division B
Net profit = $21·8m x 33% = $7·194m
ROI = $7·194m/$40·6m = $17·72%

(b) Residual income

Division A
Divisional profit = $12·488m
Capital employed = $82·8m
Imputed interest charge = $82·8m x 12% = $9·936m
Residual income = $12·488m − $9·936m = $2·552m

Division B

Divisional profit = $7·194m
Capital employed = $40·6m
Imputed interest charge = $40·6m x 12% = $4·872m
Residual income = $7·194 − $4·872 = $2·322m

(c) Comments

If a decision about whether to proceed with the investments is made based on ROI, it is possible that the manager of Division A will reject the proposal whereas the manager of Division B will accept the proposal. This is because each division currently has a ROI of 16% and since the Division A investment only has a ROI of 15·08%, it would bring the division's overall ROI down to less than its current level. On the other hand, since the Division B investment is higher than its current 16%, the investment would bring the division's overall ROI up.

When you consider what would actually be best for the company as a whole, you come to the conclusion that, since both investments have a healthy return, they should both be accepted. Hence, the fact that ROI had been used as a decision-making tool has led to a lack of goal congruence between Division A and the company as whole. This backs up what the new manager of Division A is saying. If they used residual income in order to aid the decision-making process, both proposals would be accepted by the divisions since both have a healthy RI. In this case, RI helps the divisions to make decisions which are in line with the best interests of the company. Once again, this backs up the new manager's viewpoint.

It is important to note, however, that each of the methods has numerous advantages and disadvantages which have not been considered here.

2 Cement Co

(a) Pay off table

			SUPPLY (no. of bags)		
			350,000 $'000	280,000 $'000	200,000 $'000
	Weather				
DEMAND	Good	$'000	1,750 (1)	1,400	1,000
	Average	$'000	1,085 (2)	1,400	1,000
	Poor	$'000	325	640	1,000

Profit per bag sold in coming year = $9 − $4 = $5
Loss per bag disposed of = $4 + $0·50 = $4·50

(1) 350,000 x $5 = $1,750,000
(2) [280,000 x $5] − [70,000 x $(4·50)] = $1,085,000 etc

(b) Maximin − identify the worst outcome for each level of supply and choose the highest of these worst outcomes.

	SUPPLY (no. of bags)		
	350,000 $'000	280,000 $'000	200,000 $'000
Worst	325	640	1,000

The highest of these is $1,000,000 therefore choose to supply only 200,000 bags to meet poor conditions.

3 Brick by Brick

(a) Costs and quoted prices for the GC and the EX using ABC to absorb overheads

	GC $	EX $
Materials	3,500	8,000
Labour 300 hrs x $15/hr	4,500	
500 hrs x $15/hr		7,500
Overheads		
− Supervisor (W2)/(W3)	180	1,080
− Planners (W2)/(W3)	280	1,400
− Property (W2)/(W3)	1,800	3,000
Total cost	10,260	20,980
Quoted price	15,390	31,470

(W2)	Costs	Number of drivers	Cost per driver
Supervisor	90,000	500	180
Planners	70,000	250	280
Property	240,000	40,000	6

(W3)	Supervisor	Planner	Property
Cost per driver (W2)	$180	$280	$6
GC	80 x 1 = 180	280 x 1 = 280	6 x 300 = 1,800
EX	180 x 6 = 1,080	280 x 5 = 1,400	6 x 500 = 3,000

(b) The pricing policy is a matter for BBB to decide. They could elect to maintain the current 50% mark-up on cost and if they did, the price of the GC would fall by around 7% in line with the costs. This should make them more competitive in the market. They could also reduce the prices by a little less than 7% (say 5%) in order to increase internal margins a little.

It is possible that the issue lies elsewhere. If the quality of the work or the reputation and reliability of the builder is questionable, then reducing prices is unlikely to improve sales. It is conceivable that BBB has a good reputation for EX but not for GC, but more likely that a poor reputation would affect all products. Equally, poor service levels or lack of flexibility in meeting customer needs may be causing the poor sales performance. These too will not be 'corrected' by merely reducing prices.

It is also possible that the way salesmen discuss or sell their products for the GC is not adequate, so that in some way customers are being put off placing the work with BBB. BBB is in competition and it perhaps needs to reflect this in its pricing more (by 'going rate pricing') and not seek to merely add a mark-up to its costs. BBB could try to penetrate the market by pricing some jobs cheaply to gain a foothold. Once this has been done, the completed EX or GC could be used to market the business to new customers.

The price of the EX would also need consideration. There is no indication of problems in the selling of the EX and so BBB could consider pushing up their prices by around 2% in line with the cost increase. The answer in part (a) above shows that the price goes up for a typical extension to $31,470 from $30,750 a rise of $720. This does not seem that significant and so might not lose a significant number of sales.

The reliability and reputation of a builder is probably more important than the price which they charge for a job and so it is possible that the success rate on job quotes may not be that price sensitive.

4 Thatcher International Park

TIP's financial performance can be assessed in a number of ways:

Sales growth
Sales are up about 1·3% (W1) which is a little above the rate of inflation and therefore a move in the right direction. However, with average admission prices jumping about 8·6% (W2) and numbers of visitors falling, there are clearly problems. Large increases in admission prices reduce the value proposition for the customer; it is unlikely that the rate of increase is sustainable or even justifiable. Indeed with volumes falling (down by 6·7% (W6)), it appears that some customers are being put off and price could be one of the reasons.

Maintenance and repairs
There appears to be a continuing drift away from routine maintenance with management preferring to repair equipment as required. This does not appear to be saving any money as the combined cost of maintenance and repair is higher in 2012 than in 2011. It also gives rise to health and safety risks which could result in injury or even death to the customer. This could lead to claims against the company, seriously damaging the park's reputation and, ultimately, the park being closed down.

Directors' pay
Absolute salary levels are up 6·7% (W3), well above the modest inflation rate. It appears that the shareholders are happy with the financial performance of the business and are prepared to reward the directors accordingly. Bonus levels are also well up. It may be that the directors have some form of profit related pay scheme and are being rewarded for the improved profit performance. The directors are likely to be very pleased with the increases to pay.

Wages
Wages are down by 12% (W5). This may partly reflect the loss of customers (down by 6·7% (W6)) if we assume that at least part of the wages cost is variable. It could also be that the directors are reducing staff levels beyond the fall in the level of customers to enhance short-term profit and personal bonus. Customer service and indeed safety could be compromised here.

Net profit
Net profit is up a huge 31·3% (W7) and most shareholders would be pleased with that. Net profit is a very traditional measure of performance and most would say this was a sign of good performance.

Return on assets
The profitability can be measured relative to the asset base which is being used to generate it. This is sometimes referred to as ROI or return on investment. The return on assets is up considerably to 11·4% from 8% (W8). This is partly due to the significant rise in profit and partly due to the fall in asset value. We are told that TIP has cut back on new development so the fall in asset value is probably due to depreciation being charged with little being spent during the year on assets. In this regard, it is inevitable

that return on assets is up but it is more questionable whether this is a good performance. A theme park (and thrill rides in particular) must be updated to keep customers coming back. The directors of TIP are risking the future of the park.

Workings:

(W1) Sales growth is $5,320,000/$5,250,000 = 1·01333 or 1·3%

(W2) Average admission prices were:

2011: $5,250,000/150,000 = $35 per person
2012: $5,320,000/140,000 = $38 per person
An increase of $38/$35 = 1·0857 or 8·57%

(W3) Directors' pay up by $160,000/$150,000 = 1·0667 or 6·7%

(W4) Directors' bonuses levels up from $15,000/$150,000 or 10% to $18,000/$160,000 or 12·5% of turnover. This is an increase of 3/15 or 20%.

(W5) Wages are down by (1 – $2,200,000/$2,500,000) or 12%

(W6) Loss of customers is (1 – 140,000/150,000) or 6·7%

(W7) Profits up by $1,372,000/$1,045,000 = 1·3129 or 31·3%

(W8) Return on assets:

2011: $1,045,000/$13,000,000 = 1·0803 or 8·03%
2012: $1,372,000/$12,000,000 = 1·114 or 11·4%

5   Truffle Co

(a)   Planning and operational variances

Labour rate planning variance
(Revised rate – standard rate) x actual hours paid = [$12 – ($12 x 0·95)] x 12,000 = $7,200 F.

Labour rate operational variance
(Revised rate – actual rate) x actual hours paid = $11·40 – $11·40 x 12,000 = 0

Labour efficiency planning variance
(Standard hours for actual production – revised hours for actual production) x standard rate
[10,250 – (20,500 x 0·5 x 1·2)] x $12 = $24,600 A.

Labour efficiency operational variance
(Revised hours for actual production – actual hours for actual production) x standard rate
(12,300 – 12,000) x $12 = $3,600 F.

(b)   Performance of production manager

In order to assess the production manager's performance fairly, only the operational variances should be taken into account. This is because planning variances reflect differences which arise because of factors which are outside the control of the production manager. The operational variance for the labour rate was $0, which means that the labour force were paid exactly what was agreed at the end of October: their reduced rate of $11·40 per hour. The manager clearly did not have to pay anyone for overtime, for example, which would have been expected to push this rate up. The rate reduction was secured by the company and was not within the control of the production manager, so he cannot take credit for the favourable rate planning variance of $7,200. The company is the source of this improvement.

As regards labour efficiency, the planning variance is $24,600 adverse. This is because the standard labour time per batch was not updated in November to reflect the fact that it would take longer to produce the truffles. The manager cannot be held responsible for this.

The operational variance, on the other hand, is once again something which the manager does have control of and should be held accountable for. In November, it is $3,600 favourable, which reflects positively on him. When the recipe is changed, as it has been in November, the chocolates usually take 20% longer to make in the first month whilst the workers are getting used to handling the new ingredient mix. Actual results show that the workers took less than the 20% extra time which they were expected to take, hence the positive operational variance.

Overall, then, the manager has performed well, given the change in the recipe.

Marks

Section A

Each question	2
Total marks	**40**

Section B

1 (a) Return on investment

ROI of A	1
ROI of B	1
	2

(b) Residual income

RI of A	2
RI of B	2
	4

(c) Comments

A rejects, B accepts under ROI	1
Both accept under RI	1
ROI produces wrong decision for company and RI produces right decision	1
Manager right	1
	4
Total marks	**10**

2 (a) Pay off table

Calculation of profit	1
Calculation of loss	1
'Demand' label	0·5
'Supply' label	0·5
Weather column	0·5
Supply column – 350,000	1·5
Supply column – 280,000	1·5
Supply column – 200,000	1·5
	8

(b) Decision criterion

Maximin	
Calculation	1
Justification	1
	2
Total marks	**10**

20

3 **(a)** Price under ABC

Materials

Labour   0·5

Supervisor overheads   0·5

Planner overheads   1

Property overheads   1

Price   1

                              1

                              5

(b) Pricing discussion

GC – Reduce price by 7%   1

GC – Reduce price by <7%   1

Quality, reputation, reliability, sales documentation   2

EX increases price by 2%   1

EX hold price   1

Maximum   5

Total marks   **10**

4 Sales growth   3

Maintenance   3

Directors pay   2

Wages   2

Net profit   2

Return on assets   3

Total marks   **15**

5 **(a)** Calculations

Labour rate planning variance   2

Labour rate operational variance   2

Labour rate planning variance   2

Labour rate operational variance   2

                              8

(b) Discussion

Only operational variances controllable   1

No labour rate operating variance   1

Planning variance down to company, not manager   2

Labour efficiency total variance looks bad   2

Manager has performed well as regards efficiency   2

Standard for labour time was to blame   2

Conclusion   2

Maximum   7

Total marks   **15**